She Is Everywhere!
Volume 3

Other titles available in the *She Is Everywhere!* anthology series:
She Is Everywhere!
She Is Everywhere! Volume 2

She Is Everywhere!
Volume 3

An Anthology of Writings in Womanist/Feminist Spirituality

GATHERED BY MARY SARACINO AND MARY BETH MOSER

Laura Amazzone, Michele Arista, Gael Belden, Lucia Chiavola Birnbaum, Nancy Caronia, Giana Cicchelli, Randy P. Conner, Ph.D., Lori Coon, Nancy Cosgriff, Elizabeth Cunningham, Max Dashu, Leslene della-Madre, Chickie Farella, Catlyn Fendler, Jean Feraca, Annie Finch, Mischa Geracoulis, Tricia Grame, Ph.D., Donna Henes, Sheila Marie Hennessy, Theresa Gale Henson, Joanna Clapps-Herman, Helen Hye-Sook Hwang, Nané Ariadne Jordan, Anne Key, Ph.D., Lê Pham Lê, Glenys Livingstone, Yvonne M. Lucia, Lindy Lyman, MamaCoAtl, Nicole Margiasso-Tran, Kathy Martone, Judy Millyard-Maselli, Etoyle McKee, Harita Meenee, Mary Beth Moser, Andrea Nicki, Malgorzata Oleszkiewicz-Peralba, Ph.D., Luciana Percovich, Shelley R. Reed, M.A.A.T., Sandy Miranda Robinett, Lydia Ruyle, Bridget Saracino, Mary Saracino, Lisa Sarasohn, Kirsten Schilling, Elisabeth P. Sikie, David Hatfield Sparks, Claudia von Werlhof, and Solace Wales

iUniverse, Inc.
Bloomington

She Is Everywhere! Volume 3
An Anthology of Writings in Womanist/Feminist Spirituality

The gatherers/editors of this anthology do not wish to define an author or define an author's work by trying to make the text of this anthology consistent in style, grammar, punctuation, etc.

iUniverse books may be ordered through booksellers or by contacting:

iUniverse
1663 Liberty Drive
Bloomington, IN 47403
www.iuniverse.com
1-800-Authors (1-800-288-4677)

Other titles available in the She Is Everywhere! anthology series:

She Is Everywhere! © 2005 Gathered by Lucia Chiavola Birnbaum, Ph.D., Josephine MacMillan, Kalli Halvorson, and Laura Amazzone

She Is Everywhere! Volume 2 © 2008 Gathered by Annette Lyn Williams, M.A., Karen Nelson Villanueva, M.A., and Lucia Chiavola Birnbaum, Ph.D.

ISBN: 978-1-4620-6433-5 (sc)
ISBN: 978-1-4620-6435-9 (hc)
ISBN: 978-1-4620-6434-2 (ebk)

Printed in the United States of America

iUniverse rev. date: 02/07/2012

Cover & interior design by Mary Saracino and Mary Beth Moser

Permissions

Grateful acknowledgment is made to the following for permission to reprint excerpts from the copyrighted written material and artwork and the photographs of artwork and images, listed below. Special thanks to Richard Rotruck for his graphic support in converting the images into the required format.

"Hail Mary," Michele Arista, first published in *The Journal of Feminist Studies in Religion*, Vol. 23, No 2, (Fall 2007): 87. Used by permission from the publisher.

"Hymn to Ma of Ephesus" and "Ave Matres" by Elizabeth Cunningham, first appeared in *Bright Dark Madonna*, a novel by Elizabeth Cunningham. Both poems used by permission from the author.

"Tarantata," by Mary Saracino, excerpt from *The Singing of Swans* (Pearlsong Press 2006) Copyright © 2006. Used by permission from the publisher

"The Interconnectedness of All Being: A New Spirituality for a New Civilization," by Claudia von Werlhof, originally appeared in Kumar, Corinne (Ed.): Asking, we walk: The south as new political imaginary, Bangalore (Streelekha), 2007, 2. Vol. pp. 379-386. Used by permission from the author and the publisher.

Artwork, Illustrations, and Photo Credits

The following images, artwork, illustrations and photos were used by permission of the artist and/or photographer.

Front cover painting, *Black Madonna Cradles the Earth*, Yvonne M. Lucia © 2010. Used by permission from the artist.

Front cover photo, *Black Madonna Cradles the Earth*, Van Zandbergen Photography (www.VZPhoto.com) © 2010. Used by permission from the photographer.

Back cover photo, *Contemplate Creation,* an original sculpture by Sheila Marie Hennessy © 2006. Used by permission from the artist.

Beyond The Symbol, VIII, 50" x 38", acrylic, mixed media on paper, © 2009 Tricia Grame; photo by Tricia Grame, http://tgrame.com/. Used by permission from the artist.

Isis, 54" x 54", acrylic on canvas, © 2010 Tricia Grame; photo by Tricia Grame, http://tgrame.com/. Used by permission from the artist.

Brigit's Wayside Well, Imbloc 2007, Kildare, Ireland © 2007 Nicole Margiasso. Used by permission.

Le Comari Laboratorio, Photo © 2011 Mary Beth Moser. Used by permission.

Crow Mother © 1998 Lydia Ruyle; photo © 2007 Pat Alles. Used by permission from the artist.

Isis © 1996 Lydia Ruyle; photo © 2007 Pat Alles. Used by permission from the artist.

Palden Lhamo © 2000 Lydia Ruyle; photo © 2000 Pat Alles. Used by permission from the artist.

Earth Mother © 1995 Lori Coon. Used by permission.

Full of Life © 1997 Chris Cordoni. Used by permission.

Placenta: Baby side © 2004 Nané Ariadne Jordan. Used by permission.

Womb Labyrinth: Birthing the Story Within © 2003 Nané Ariadne Jordan; original artwork: photo transfer to cloth with red thread and copper wire stitching. Used by permission from the artist.

To Her

Royalties generated from the sales of *She Is Everywhere! Volume 3* will be donated to help fund future editions of the *She Is Everywhere!* anthology series.

"Leading the way with whispers."
—Giana Cicchelli

"Most spiritual feminists conceive of Goddess as a continuum, encompassing living beings, ancestors, spirits, essences, qualities, and vast governing principles like Maat, Tao, and Wyrd—all names for divine Law. We see parallels in the pagan Gothic Halioruna ("Holy Mystery") and the Great Mystery of Native North America."
—Max Dashu

"The crypt represents the sacred womb of the earth, where all life comes from, and to this day some of the most important Virgin Mary sanctuaries are located in or next to a cave, a mountain, or a holy spring, water being the life-giving element."
—Malgorzata Oleszkiewicz-Peralba

"When you are gone, will I find your face in my own?"
—Elizabeth Cunningham

"We are Her daughter-selves—female and male alike. The Mother hands us *all* the wheat, the sacred knowledge of Life, as in Eleusis of Old. We all may be Her *Daughters*, entitled just so: to the seamless Original Heritage in Her core, our Core."
—Glenys Livingstone

"You are a burning blue flame, a mother tongue and sacred fire; a love, a kindred rainbow—you are the answer, the love, the completed sentence."
—Theresa Gale Henson

"A spiritual invocation to make the warrior teeth come back, back to the ancient sheath."
—Andrea Nicki

"If Mary is missing, put her back, and if she has been whitened, make her black."
—Michele Arista

"I learned of placenta as mother's friend and helpmate, a meta-mother-being herself, an ancient grandmother, who is capable of gifting healing beyond the womb."
—Nané Ariadne Jordan

"By researching spiritual practices in different contexts and searching for the common threads and the uncommon threads, we are able to see more clearly the self-imposed paradigms of our modern spiritual practice, and when the paradigms of our modern religions are found to be less than 'historic' or 'natural', the gravitas they have accumulated dissipates and fertile ground for new growth opens to the sun."
—Anne Key

"The vulva, representing as it does the passageway through which we enter life, and metaphorically, through which we leave it, was probably the first religious symbol of humankind."
—Donna Henes

"Everlasting is the fascination proceeding from divine feminine beings, wonderfully skilled in magic and medicine arts, who alone know the virtues of certain herbs, of certain flowers they arrange in filters and beverages, giving death and life, disease and health in the vast reign of Nature."
—Luciana Percovich

"We wanted to be like boys, like her younger brother Eddie, who didn't have to wear a shirt on hot summer days."
—Kirsten Schilling

"The Orphic Hymn to Nature brings to light the age-old Mother Goddess of many names, the supreme Creatress, 'dancing with whirling noiseless feet' her eternal dance of life and growth."
—Harita Meenee

"Female images have deep roots in time and blackness is associated with Mother Earth and fertility as the source of life and death around the world."
—Lydia Ruyle

Contents

List of Illustrations

Front cover: *Black Madonna Cradles the Earth*, original painting by Yvonne M. Lucia © 2010, Yvonne M. Lucia; photo © 2010 Van Zandbergen Photography

Le Comari Laboratorio; photo by Mary Beth Moser © 2011

Brigit's Wayside Well, Imbolc 2007, Kildare, Ireland; photo by Nicole Marigiasso-Tran © 2007 Nicole Margiasso

Beyond The Symbol, VIII, original artwork by Tricia Grame, 50" x 38", acrylic, mixed media on paper, © 2009 Tricia Grame; photo by Tricia Grame, http://tgrame.com/

Isis, original artwork by Tricia Grame, 54" x 54", acrylic on canvas, © 2010 Tricia Grame; photo by Tricia Grame, http://tgrame.com/

Earth Mother; original sculpture by Lori Coon ©1995 Lori Coon

Crow Mother, original artwork by Lydia Ruyle ©1998 Lydia Ruyle; photo © 2007 Pat Alles

Isis; original artwork by Lydia Ruyle © 1996 Lydia Ruyle; photo © 2007 Pat Alles

Palden Lhamo; original artwork ©2000 Lydia Ruyle; photo © 2000 Pat Alles

Saint Sara-La-Kali; photo © 2008 Malgorzata Oleszkiewicz-Peralba

Ex-votos at Saint Sara-La-Kali's statue; photo © 2008 Malgorzata Oleszkiewicz-Peralba

Mary Salomé's and Mary Jacobé's relics; photo © 2008 Malgorzata Oleszkiewicz-Peralba

Rebirth; original artwork by Kathy Martone © 2008 Kathy Martone; photo © 2008 Paul Gillis, www.artworkphotography.net

Gathering Forces; original artwork by Kathy Martone © 2009 Kathy Martone; photo © 2009 Paul Gillis, www.artworkphotography.net

Ixchel; photo © 2009 Theresa Gale Henson

Red Mother; photo © 2005, Shelley R. Reed

Sardegnan Nuraghe; photo © 2004 Sandy Miranda Robinett

Tanit Clothesline; photo © 2006 Mary Beth Moser

Sacred Well at Santa Cristina, Sardegna, Italy; photo © 2004 Mary Beth Moser

Full of Life; photo ©1997 Chris Cordoni

Placenta: Baby side; photo © 2004 Nané Ariadne Jordan

Womb Labyrinth: Birthing the Story Within, original artwork by Nané Ariadne Jordan, photo transfer to cloth, with red thread and copper wire stitching © 2003 Nané Ariadne Jordan

Mother and Daughter/The Forest; original sculpture, branch, paperclay, acrylic; 58" x 22" by Lindy Lyman © 2005 Lindy Lyman; photo by Marcia Ward, The Image Maker, Denver, CO

Lilith; original sculpture by Sheila Marie Hennessy © 2007 Sheila Marie Hennessy

Shaman's Dream/Shanti; original sculpture by Sheila Marie Hennessy © 2008 Sheila Marie Hennessy

Neolithic marble figurine from Sparta, Southern Greece. National Archaeological Museum of Athens, Greece; photo © 2008 Harita Meenee.

Back cover: *Contemplate Creation*, original sculpture by Sheila Marie Hennessy © 2006 Sheila Marie Hennessy. Used by permission

Note on Style for
She Is Everywhere! Volume 3

Like volumes one and two of *She Is Everywhere!,* this third edition of the anthology offers visions, values, tones, and images of women across the ages from the beginning of time. This is suggested in the many writing styles and the kaleidoscope of illustrations and artwork contained within its pages. Contributions to this anthology are "unedited" in the sense that no editor(s) modified anyone's vision—and this approach also extends to style. An example of this is Lucia Chiavola Birnbaum's preference of downcasing, a reflection of her dislike for capitalization, which, as an historian, she views as a custom that perpetuates the hierarchy of nation states and dominant cultures in the modern era. In other parts of this anthology, all pronoun references to Goddess, and all the many other names used to refer to the Divine She, are written in upper case: Her and/or She.

Prefaces

As I write this, it is a cold, wintry afternoon, at the midpoint between winter and spring. This magical day between the seasons is a perfect time to celebrate the work presented in *She Is Everywhere! Volume 3*. The authors whose scholarship and creative work appears between the covers of this anthology embody the courage to dance on the liminal lip of time and soar beyond the limits imposed by patriarchy.

While the scholarship in these scholarly articles is academically sound, the methodology is innovative and the message is revolutionary. So, too, the creative work—the poems, creative nonfiction, fiction, and artwork—in these pages vibrantly proclaims a clarion call for a much-needed paradigm shift.

This edition of *She Is Everywhere!* reaches beyond the boundaries of state and nation to include the voices of visionary womanist and feminist scholars, writers, and artists from around the world. Its intention is to contribute to a deeper telling of the story of the world, as seen through the lens of those working to reclaim the primacy of the Divine Female. As *She Is Everywhere!* founder, Lucia Chiavola Birnbaum notes in her path-breaking work, humankind's first mother is/was the Dark Mother of Africa. Our earliest ancestors carried Her values of justice with compassion, equality among all peoples, and transformation out of Africa as long ago as 100,000 BCE, perhaps even earlier.

For too long, and with dire consequences, we humans have forgotten our connection to this Source and to our origins in sub-Saharan Africa. This volume is a portal to a broader vision—an invitation to remember, reclaim, honor, and celebrate SHE in all of Her many manifestations. The work in this volume calls for us to right the imbalance and create a world in which all women, men, and children from every nation, of every hue, ethnicity, spiritual sensibility, and economic and social status can thrive and live together in peace.

As we enter the second decade of the twentieth century, wars rage across the planet, human-induced climate change wreaks havoc on the environment, corporate greed ravages the lives of humans, animals, and plants, and patriarchy—with all its attendant oppressions, some of which include sexism, racism, and classism—seeks to silence dissent.

Even so, She *is* everywhere—and so, too, are the scholars, writers, and visual artists who refuse to remain silent. In this volume, they offer their work to help us remember our connectedness to one another and to the Great Cosmic Creatrix, from whose womb all human DNA flows.

Yvonne M. Lucia's powerful painting, *The Black Madonna Cradles the World*, graces the front cover of this third volume of *She Is Everywhere!* The image serves to remind us that the world belongs to all of us and that each of us belongs to one another. Sheila Marie Hennessy's sculpture, *Contemplating Creation*, anchors the back cover of this volume, reminding us that the womb of creation is a labyrinth that we all walk in our journey to wholeness and to reclaiming Her.

The contributors to this volume offer keen insights into the vibrant and ever-expanding field of womanist/feminist spiritualities. From Helen Hye-Sook Hwang's study of the Mago tradition of Korea to Harita Meenee's translations of the Orphic Hymns of Greece; from Lucia Chiavola Birnbaum's reminder that the future has an ancient heart, to Claudia von Werlhof's ground-breaking article on deep feminism and spirituality in relation to Mother Earth; from the powerful artwork of Yvonne Lucia, Lydia Ruyle, Sheila Marie Hennessy, Kathy Martone, Sandy Miranda Robinett, Tricia Grame, and Lindy Lyman to the resonant poetry of Michele Arista, Andrea Nicki, Annie Finch, Jean Feraca, Bridget Saracino, Nancy Caronia, Gael Belden, Nancy Cosgriff, Elizabeth Cunningham, Judy Millyard-Maselli, David Hatfield Sparks, Giana Cicchelli, Lê Pham Lê, Lori Coon, and Elizabeth P. Sikie; from Max Dashu's textured overview and introduction to the "concept" of Goddess to Leslene della-Madre's personal search for the luminous Dark Mother; from Nicole Margiasso-Tran's pilgrimage to the land of Brigit to Malgorzata Oleszkiewicz-Peralba's exploration of the Romani people's beloved Saint Sara-La-Kali; from Lisa Sarasohn's reclamation of Zeb-un-Nissa, to Solace Wale's messages from the Black Madonna; from Randy P. Conner's article on Diana, witches, and fairies, to Mary Beth Moser's luminous reclaiming of her matrilineal lineage through the lens of clotheslines and inter-generational motherlines; from Laura Amazzone's exploration of the menstrual origins of the kava ceremony of Fiji to Shelley R. Reed's presentation of the Red Mother of the Salish mountains; from Anne Key's exploration of the Mesoamerican clay figurines and priestesses to Nané Ariadne Jordan's discussion of the poetics of the placenta; from Chickie Farella's wry and poignant look at one mother's eschewed relationship with her son and her daughter to Luciana Percovich's spotlight on the renown Goddess herstorian, Momolina Marconi; from Glenys Livingstone's casting of invocations to re-create Her to Donna Henes' creative treatises on Terra Mater and the holy yoni; from Etoyle McKee's remembrances of the lessons learned from her mother's garden okra to the keen insights gleaned from Joanna Clapps-Herman's essays about her mother; from Mischa Geracoulis' powerful narrative on the potency of hair to Catyln Fendler's reminiscence of her experience with the Black Madonna and the labyrinth; from Theresa Gale Henson's moving poem and her story about finding Ixchel to Kirsten Schilling's heart-felt journal entries and my own poems and my fictional account of the tarantata's healing power to transport a mute seventeenth century southern Italian herbalist and painter back to wholeness, encircled in the collective energy of her sister and brother villagers.

We invite you to join us on the spiritual pilgrimage that unfolds in these pages. As you embark on the journey of discovery (and perhaps reunion), it is our hope that you find inspiration, solace, compassion, intellectual stimulation, and personal transformation. May you come to witness and to celebrate that She is literally *everywhere!*

Mary Saracino
Lafayette, Colorado
February 2, 2011

As I write this introduction, I have just returned from a period of caring for and being with my mother, who is recovering from a broken hip. When she fell on January 3 and hit the floor of her dining room, the earth shook for me upon hearing the news. Learning of her progress with reports from my sister, Marlene, and then witnessing her daily improvements in person have inspired me during these tumbling times of change. Will I have her determination when I am 87 years old to meet such challenges? Do I have such courage now to rise up and learn to move in new ways in a changing world? Will we all be able to do the hard work of rebuilding broken structures that no longer sustain life?

My mother has repeatedly thanked me, *"tante grazie, cara fiola,"* endearingly using the Trentino dialect of her mother, but the rewards are also mine. In sharing ten uninterrupted days and nights with my mother in service to her well-being, my rhythm found resonance with hers allowing me to be present in the moment. My body and spirit were fed by the daily dose of light seemingly ever-present in the blue skies of Colorado, my birthplace. I felt a familiarity there, one that evoked the essay that I chose to submit for this anthology. A solid feeling of family and motherline was amplified by the watchful gaze of the Blessed Mother images adorning several walls of her home.

During the day I hung out the laundry in the unseasonably warm February weather. Sun, wind, and low humidity all cooperated to dry the clothes. In mid-afternoon, while my mother rested, I sat outside on her sundrenched back porch reading excerpts of the essays presented here, finding the threads of commonality, and feeling the sisterhood of community.

Co-editor, Mary Saracino, drove from her town almost an hour away to deliver golden roses and to share our simple lunch, blessing my mother and me with her presence. I am gratefully indebted to Mary for her outstanding organization and editing skills, which allowed this volume to come together and move forward. In our gathering of this anthology, Mary carried the heavier load.

During my daily walks, I discovered an urban trail along an irrigation ditch that in summer months carries the precious resource of water through the neighborhood. The dirt path was lined with Cottonwoods, stark and majestic in their winter state. Their presence and beauty nurtured me so I could nurture my mother. On the last day of my visit, I discovered with dismay that a large Cottonwood I had admired along the trail, perhaps 100 years old, had been cut down, considered too dangerous and costly if it fell to earth one day, no longer able to stand.

In the evening, after the simple activities of the day, I would read aloud letters to my mother that she had written to me decades before. I had recently retrieved a large box of them from my garage at home, and at the last minute, pressed two handfuls of letters into my suitcase. Her weekly hand-written or typed letters of family news had sustained me when I married and left my large clan to live in the Northwest. The pages were filled with events of an earlier time, whose vitality seemed to infuse the present. Although we both knew how the story turned out for my younger brothers and sister as they made their way through school and life, we were reminded of the challenges of the everyday and the spiral progress of each one of us, held by the net of clan. The letters were encouraging, honest, and funny. Sometimes we laughed so hard upon hearing the misadventure (usually hers) told in that week's letter that we couldn't stop. Mother's writings also unintentionally documented her long list of service to family, neighbors, and community.

One night as I opened a letter to read it, a two-dollar bill fell into my lap. In reading, I learned that my mother had sent it as repayment for a photo I had printed for her. When I folded the letter back into its envelope, I discovered that the postmark was February 21, the same date as I was reading it, 32 years later, in my mother's presence. The auspicious two-dollar bill will go on my home altar, a precious reminder of this sacred synchronicity. Finding unspent money after decades of maternal support seems to be a message that mothering sustains, that there is a deeper and older maternal matrix that cannot be replaced by a monetary system. The letters allowed me to revisit my relationship with my mother at the age that she was when she was writing to me, to view the wheel of life from the other side. Their contents remind me that it is the everyday events that fill our lives and give it meaning—shared food, good friends, and having fun; adventures and accomplishments; births, marriages, and deaths. It is a gift to see these cycles of transformation and renewal, to look back and see that there is always change.

My mother has mothered, grand-mothered, and great-grandmothered throughout her life. Her nurturing expands far beyond family. Reportedly she had more visitors in a day than most have in a week at the rehabilitation center that became her home for several weeks. She would *never* tally her friends by number. However she does "count her blessings," and proudly enumerates her lineage: seven children, 21 grandchildren, 14 great grandchildren (and still counting).

I am grateful to my mother's caregivers, the professionals who dedicate their lives to helping people walk again. Nearby family, especially my sister Marlene, and friends have readily stepped forward to offer their gifts. There is a natural flow of regular service to my mother by my brothers, John and Tim, and the extended family.

Nurturing males—both named Tom—dwell on either side of my mother's brick home. One of them drives her to a nearby nature park and walks with her. The other Tom, who is caring for his 94 year-old mother, includes my mother in his field of view and volunteers acts of maintenance and care across his driveway to hers. While I was there, Paul, a neighbor across the street, laid his hand on my mother's hip upon learning of her accident and blessed her with a spontaneous prayer.

My mother has been there for people of all ages, to serve them. She has cooked for them, prayed for them, visited them when there were infirm, watched over their little ones, and listened to their sorrows and troubles. I dedicate this book to Lena Moser, the She who is my mother.

Returning home to my studies and completion of this volume, I am immensely grateful for the teachers and students in Women's Spirituality program at California Institute of Integral Studies. In particular, Lucia Chiavola Birnbaum has inspired me and countless others with her presence, guidance, and scholarship. As a visionary, her name surely reflects the seeing eyes of Santa Lucia of Sicily.

May our work, contained within these pages, reach out into the world and find those who need to hear the messages. May the Elders of all species be respected. May the changes in the world, which is crying out for mothering instead of materialism, bring justice, compassion, caring, and sharing, the values of the Dark Mother communicated so clearly by and embodied by Lucia, and reflected in this volume of She Is Everywhere.

Mary Beth Moser
Vashon Island, Washington
March 4, 2011
New Moon

A Tribute and a Note about Future Editions of *She Is Everywhere!*

Le Comari Laboratorio sign in Lucia Chiavola Birnbaum's
dining room; Photo © 2011 Mary Beth Moser

The anthology series *She Is Everywhere!* would not be possible without the generous financial support and nurturance of its founding mother, Lucia Chiavola Birnbaum.

Lucia's contributions to womanist/feminist scholarship in women's spiritualities are unparalleled. Her ground-breaking work has literally birthed a new way of remembering/reclaiming our most ancient memory of the Divine Female.

Simply put, Lucia has helped usher in a new generation of scholars who keenly and astutely reclaim Her through the lens of embodied scholarship. Equally important is Lucia's inclusion of creative writers and artists in this ongoing conversation, inviting into the circle resonant voices that might not otherwise have been given a broader platform.

In Lucia's dining room hangs a sign from a Sicilian ceramics shop, gifted to Lucia by the women owners, of four apron-clad women with the caption: *Le Comari Laboratorio,* the godmothers' laboratory.

This fitting image perfectly encapsulates the essence of who Lucia is and the many gifts she brings to the world. While the Italian title, *comare,* is conferred upon a woman who is a godmother, its connotation is more vast and deep, reaching back to the time when circles of wise women convened to provide village counsel, working to ensure the greater good for their families and their communities.

The *comari* were sages, healers, counselors, social activists, and archivists of the wisdom traditions. As keepers of the ancient ways, they were/are invaluable points on the wheel of memory refusing to let humankind forget its ancient, sacred roots.

Ever the 21st century *comare,* Lucia's *comari laboratorio* has given birth to the *She Is Everywhere!* anthology series—and this compilation of womanist/feminist scholarship, creative writing, and artwork is, perhaps, one of Lucia's most significant achievements.

On a personal note, Lucia has touched our lives in deep and transformative ways. Both of us have been privileged to have participated in multiple Dark Mother Study Tours with Lucia, travelling with her to Sicily and to Sardegna. We share a common Italian heritage with Lucia and an abiding passion for the Dark Mother.

Mary Beth has had the honor of pursuing a Ph.D. under Lucia's mentorship at the California Institute of Integral Studies. Lucia has been a loving and inspiring presence in Mary's life as well, providing *comare* support to Mary's novels, memoirs, and poetry.

We are grateful to Lucia for the opportunity to contribute to her legacy by co-gathering this third edition of *She Is Everywhere!*

While Lucia's tenure at the California Institute of Integral Studies has come to a close, her influence continues and her legacy will continue to grow and thrive. As a professor emerita, she will write books and articles, speak, travel, and present at national and international conferences. The vision she launched with the *She Is Everywhere!* series will continue to provide a forum for scholars, creative writers, and artists with future editors and subsequent volumes of *She Is Everywhere!*

With Lucia, we share the hope that past and future editions of the anthology will continue to mark and accelerate transformation.
Blessed Be!

Mary Saracino & Mary Beth Moser
Co-gatherers
She Is Everywhere! Volume 3

Healing Wells and Sacred Fire: A Pilgrimage to Brigit's Land

Nicole Margiasso-Tran

In 2007, I ventured on a pilgrimage to Ireland in search of the goddess Brigit. During my six-month journey, I visited several of Her sacred sites and experienced profound feelings of connection to this ancient goddess. In this paper, I draw upon my journal entries to share my experiences from my first visit to Brigit's sacred land, Kildare, where it became clear to me as both goddess and saint, Her following is vibrant and thriving.

Brigit's Eve

Today, January 31, 2007, marks my thirtieth birthday. I am two and a half weeks into my pilgrimage in Ireland. A cloudy, grey morning sky hangs above. Sitting on the bus, I am ready to depart Galway, an old western fishing town that I have claimed as my home, and venture to Kildare. Brigit,[1] an ancient Celtic goddess of healing, smithcraft, and poetry, has also been honored as a Christian saint since the fifth century CE.[2] As a saint, She is known for Her loving connection to nature, pacifism, hospitality, and for the abbey that She established in Kildare. The Irish contend that Her two guises as goddess and saint cannot be separated. With both titles, She is associated with sacred fire, the sun, serpents, craftsmanship, agriculture, healing wells, cows, and milk products.[3] She is the only Celtic deity that survived the Christianization of Ireland. Mary Condren in *The Serpent and the Goddess* attests that Brigit is the "most powerful religious female figure in all of Irish history."[4] Today I will be joining in the celebration of this great figure at *Féile Bríde*, an annual week-long festival in honor of Brigit that includes a peace and justice conference and rituals at Her sites.

Spirituality plays a foundational role in this journey. Philip Cousineau, in *The Art of Pilgrimage,* defines pilgrimage as "a transformative journey to a sacred center . . . an act of devotion to find a source of healing . . . a journey of risk and renewal."[5] This journey began seven years ago, while I was in my Masters program at the California Institute of Integral Studies in Women's Spirituality. This program taught me to critically analyze history and religion in order to study and understand the Divine Feminine[6] more comprehensively. This entails researching with a feminist lens[7] and a keen eye to depict where, how, and why the sacred feminine has been overlooked, suppressed, or misinterpreted. Through this form of research, I came upon the goddess Brigit.

Within the realm of Women's Spirituality,[8] I specifically identify with the spiritual path of Wicca. It is a tradition that honors the sacred in both female and male forms, celebrates the cycles of the earth, moon, and sun, and is tied to the indigenous religions of my European ancestors.[9] It is with this perspective that I have embarked on a pilgrimage to Ireland.

In the first semester of my Masters program, I was given the assignment of researching my "Motherline" heritage. I learned my matrilineal ancestors are rooted in Ireland. My great, great grandmother traveled from Dublin, Ireland to New York City, in 1891, at the age of sixteen. On both sides of my family I am the descendent of European ancestors who came from poor economic conditions and immigrated to the United States for a better quality of life. As a middle-class woman, with a degree in higher education, I am grateful that I have had the economic opportunities to create a self-determined life. Here I am with the freedom to journey alone through the land of my foremothers.

Along with learning the location of my ancestral homeland, I also discovered a matrilineal connection to a goddess. My grandmother, Patricia Hand, explained to me that she named my mother, "Bridget," after St. Brigid of Ireland. This became fascinating news as I learned that St. Brigid is a Christian figure closely tied to the ancient goddess Brigit.[10] I also realized a synchronicity between our birthdays and Brigit's sacred day: I share my birthday, January 31st, with my grandmother and our birthday falls on Brigit's Eve, the beginning celebration of Brigit's most sacred day, Imbolc. Though my connection to this goddess seems clear now, it still took quite some time to understand and honor the fact that I could have a personal relationship and connection to a goddess. Seven years later, I am sitting on a bus six thousand miles from home, traveling to Brigit's holy sites.

As the bus meanders through narrow country roads, we pass numerous farms surrounded with sheep, cows, and horses. This is my first time venturing out in Ireland since my arrival. It is exciting and challenging to explore this country where I do not know anyone. Nonetheless, I trust that I am in the safekeeping of Brigit. I repeat the mantra in my head, "Brigit to enfold me, Brigit to surround me, Brigit to comfort me. For I am under the shielding of good Brigit each day. For I am under the shielding of good Brigit each night. Each early and late, every dark, every light. Brigit is my comrade. Brigit is my maker of song. Brigit is my healer, my choicest of women, my guide."[11]

I arrive in Dublin and have a two hour wait until I transfer to the last bus which will take me to Kildare. Kildare is located in the region of Leinster, the eastern section of Ireland. Its Irish name, *Cill Dara*, means Church of the Oak. Historical lore tells that St. Brigid, born circa 480 CE, established Her monastery beside a sacred oak tree. This tree marked an ancient Druidic site[12] where people lit ritual fires to invoke the goddess Brigit for protection of their farm animals and for prosperous crops.[13] On this spot, Brigit built Her abbey and a formal fire temple, thereby bridging Celtic spiritual practices and Christian worship.

Brigid was appointed as Abbess circa the fifth century CE and headed a double monastery for men and women that grew to be renowned throughout Europe. With this success, Kildare grew to be a vibrant center for education, culture, and religion up until the sixteenth century. All the while, Her perpetual flame was kept alit by the Brigidine nuns.[14]

Early practices at Kildare, though nominally Christian, included ancient pagan practices that resembled other goddess cults in Europe. The tending to sacred fire was also a practice of the Roman goddesses Minerva and Vesta, and the British goddess Sul.[15] Brigit marked Her land at Kildare by spreading Her cloak, which magically grew to cover almost five thousand acres, thus defining the boundaries of Her sacred land. This method of marking boundaries parallels acts of the ancient Irish goddesses Macha and Tephi.[16] Brigittine scholar, Mary Condren, asserts that there may have been an order of vestal virgins in Kildare, resembling other orders in Europe.[17] These fire keepers would have been the first "nuns" of Brigid's order.

Over the centuries, Brigit's church endured several destructions and recreations due to Nordic pillagings, the Protestant Reformation, and Irish uprisings against Protestantism. Unfortunately, in 1632, the weight of religious persecution and patriarchy took their toll and Brigid's flame was extinguished. Twelve hundred years of continuous rituals sacred to Brigit in Kildare came to an end.[18]

In 1807, Daniel Delany, Bishop of Kildare, appointed six women and reinstituted the Sisterhood of St. Brigid. Delany was not beginning a new order, but reinstituting the ancient order of Brigid.[19] To convey this, he planted an oak sapling in the Tullow convent ground, where the six Sisters resided.

In 1992, two Brigidine Sisters moved to Kildare to establish a "centre for Celtic Spirituality, in the spirit of Brigid of Kildare."[20] They named their community *Solas Bhríde*, which means Brigid's Light/Flame. In 1993, the Sisters re-lit Brigid's sacred flame in the town's center where it still burns today. The Brigidine Sisters affirm that they primarily honor Brigid as "Prophetess, Earthwoman, and Peacemaker."[21] The Sisters attest that this relighting of Her flame has resulted in much interest, activism, and artwork in the figure of Brigit all over the world.[22] My journey to Kildare is a testament to Her global influence.

Finally aboard the third and final bus, I depart from Dublin. It is taking longer than expected to get to Kildare. I will now be arriving in the evening and I am preoccupied with making it in time for the Brigid's Eve Ritual. It will be held at Her two wells and will start in one hour. A local man on the bus is curious about my coming to Kildare. I explain to him that I am attending the *Féile Bríde* festival. He warns me, "Be careful, don't walk around at night by ye'self." Nervously, I recite the Brigit prayer in my head. We arrive in Kildare and this same man kindly sees me to my hotel. I am safe.

While checking into my room and unpacking my things, I notice that I feel timid about meeting Brigit in Her homeland for the first time. I am walking on Her sacred ground, the place where Her wells and ancient fire temple reside. I feel like I am about to meet someone I have been dating online for seven years! I look at my watch and realize I have a half an hour before the ritual begins. I catch a cab and ask the driver to take me to the Japanese Gardens parking lot where the ritual will begin.

Luckily, I arrive on time. The lot is full with people carrying candles. I walk towards a large group encircling a blazing fire. One of Brigit's attributes is sacred fire and the flame is a physical expression of Her. Spiritually, fire is associated with purification, activation, and the hearth. In many depictions, Brigit is shown with Her red hair aflame. Coincidentally, in the first six months of my introduction to Brigit, my hair caught on fire twice.

There are about seventy-five people here, more than I expected. The walkways and the circle around the fire are lined with candle-filled jars. Orange-lit Chinese lanterns hang in the trees. I find a spot on a small mound that elevates me enough to see what is happening inside the circle. Several Brigidine Sisters are in the center, leading the group in singing celebratory songs in praise of Brigid.

This event and all of the events of the *Féile Bríde* festival have been organized by *Solas Bhríde*, which has now grown to include four Brigidine Sisters. They are Christian, yet they welcome "all who honour the name of Brigid."[23] The Brigidine Sisters begin the ritual with invoking the directions,[24] which is also a Wiccan practice. Being gathered around a fire and singing songs in praise of a saint is not like any Christian event I have ever attended, but more like a pagan ritual. I am open and excited to see how these Sisters will weave this ritual. They address us as "pilgrims" and I feel my journey has been acknowledged. I am in the right place.

One Sister enters the circle and stands near the fire. She begins to weave a St. Brigid's cross. This cross is equilateral in shape and usually made from local grass. Lore tells us that Brigid made a cross out of straw to teach a local chieftain about Christianity. This cross, however, symbolizes the sun and first came to Ireland between 100 BCE and 100 CE.[25] Brigid's crosses are still used today as amulets of Brigit's protection for the home and farm.[26] Mary Minehan, in *Rekindling the Flame,* explains the cross is placed above the front door "to bless all who come in or go out, and to gain protection of the household from fire and disease."[27]

As the Sister weaves the cross, another Sister asks us to think of our deepest desires, dreams, and prayers. She explains that these thoughts will be woven into the cross and will become part of the working ritual. My eyes float up to one of the hanging lanterns. Standing there in this full circle, a state of bliss fills my body. It is one of those moments when I am conscious that every cell in my body is alive. I am exactly where I am meant to be. I know this blissful state is fleeting so I let myself experience it fully and express gratitude for the magic I feel tonight. The woman continues to weave the cross and I invoke my intentions; I wish for personal wholeness, physical well-being, and clarity on my spiritual path.

The Sister, holding the completed Brigid's cross in front of her, leaves the circle and leads us to Brigid's Wayside Well. In order to understand the significance of Irish wells, it is important to consider how the ancient Irish viewed the Earth. The people of this land come from an indigenous worldview of honoring the earth as the living Goddess and mother to us all.[28] Wells were considered to be wombs of Mother Earth, the source of life. Walter and Mary Brenneman, in *Crossing the Circle at the Holy Wells of Ireland*, explain, "the spring has a hole in the bottom, which is itself a threshold providing entrance into the body of the goddess and allowing her nurturing blood/milk/water to emerge in an endless and continual stream for the benefit of us, her children."[29] The well as a constant spring of fresh water is honored as a source of nurturance, abundance, wisdom, fertility, renewal, and healing.[30] The wells of Ireland are still actively used today. I posit that this use represents the continuity of the Irish people's spiritual connection to their land, their local holy places, and the concept of the sacred as immanent in the earth.

I am humbled to be standing amongst the locals at this well, which is known as the "pagan" well.[31] Candles encircle and light the well, which spans about four feet in diameter. The Sisters begin singing songs about coming to the water. They sprinkle us with leaves that were dipped in the well. My fellow pilgrims, after being blessed, make the sign of the cross on their bodies. I respond a little shocked, having forgotten that I am surrounded by people of the Catholic faith. Further, I am probably the only self-declared Wiccan person present. This is a new and exciting experience for me. I am honored to be partaking in the rite amongst these Irish folk whose ancestors have been honoring this holy day for thousands of years.[32]

We leave the Wayside Well and process across the street and down a narrow road toward the second well. Although I know no one in the large group, I feel safe and comfortable. I walk contentedly, breathing in the cool night air. We cross a little wooden bridge to enter the site of St Brigid's Well. There is a beautiful bronze statue of Brigid, a trickling stream, prayer stones and the well, all lit with candles. We gather around the prayer stones. The Sisters tell us stories about Brigid's life: She was an "Earthwoman, a woman of the soil, who loved animals." The Sisters impress me with how smoothly they lead this ritual, incorporating pagan and Christian practices and language. The combination of Celtic spirituality and Catholicism has a fascinating blend here. Patricia Monaghan, in *The Red-Haired Girl from the Bog*, asserts, "it is possible to be fully Catholic and fully pagan [in Ireland] at the same time."[33]

The Sisters continue to talk about the significance of Brigid's teachings in our lives today. I notice that they refer to Her only in the past tense, which is different from how I speak of Her. There is a difference here in pagan and Catholic spiritualities. For pagans, Brigit is always alive and accessible to us. She is not only a model from the past for us to remember and try to exemplify. When we invoke Her, we actually conceive of Her being with us in that moment and it can be a very intimate experience.

Towards the end of the ritual, the Sisters present a baby oak sapling that will be planted in Kildare. It has been taken from the mother oak in Tullow, where two hundred years ago, to the day, Bishop Delany reinstituted the Order of the Brigidine Sisters. They conclude the peaceful evening with a flute song. I listen, taking in all that the night has offered. I realize, standing on the wet grass, that this is the first time my feet have touched Irish soil since arriving. It feels good.

Imbolc Day

I awake bright and early, ready to spend a full day in Kildare. I have my pilgrimage map, created by *Solas Bhríde*, which shows me how to get to Brigid's sites. As I walk through the town, it is clear that Kildare is certainly Brigit's land. Her crosses are everywhere, even on garbage bins. Many here work in Her service and they identify with the community name, *Cáirde Bhríde*, which means Friends of Brigid. They work to promote justice, peace, and reconciliation, qualities associated with Brigid.[34]

Today is St. Brigid's Feast Day, formerly known as Imbolc. Imbolc is an ancient Celtic fire festival that marks the beginning of spring. Brigit's aspects as an ancient Mother Goddess are especially apparent on this day. Imbolc means "in belly" and refers to the pregnancy and lactation of domestic animals. All mother's milk was believed to have healing powers and was given great value in ancient times.[35] Brigit, as both goddess and saint, was said to have been reared by a red-eared sacred cow, with udders that never emptied.[36] It was common for Irish folk to pour milk upon the hills or toss pats of butter into holy wells in religious offering.[37] I posit that the spiritual relevance that is given to the lactating animals and to dairy products today are remnants of an ancient religion when Brigit was revered as a great Mother Goddess.

I pass these full-bellied sheep as I make my way to Brigit's pagan well, which I reach within a half hour. No one is here. What luck I have, considering this is the spring that the local people have been using on this day for a very long time. I slowly approach the well taking in the beauty of it all. It has a perfectly round shape, encircled with stone slabs, containing shallow crystal clear water. Bright green moss grows snugly between the stones. Lush plants and trees hang over the wall leaning towards the water. The chirping birds are my only company. As I inch closer to the well, I see that it reminds me of a womb, the womb of Mother Earth. I feel the holiness of this place and it humbles me.

I sit down on the stone bench that surrounds half the well. I want to get closer, so I lower myself to the stone slab next to the water, not caring if I get wet from the ground's moisture. I pause momentarily, allowing myself to become fully present. With a deep sense of peace, I feel ready to speak to Her. I profess, "Dear Goddess, I have come from very far to be here. I am in deep awe of the beauty of your sacred place and am filled with deep contentment." I sense Brigit's energy alive and present. Comforted with a sense of safety, lovingness, and peace, I feel Her respond, "My dear child, I am so proud of you. Leave your worries here and use this water for healing. Drink of me."

I take a sip of Her cool, quenching water. I invoke healing for my body. I imagine Her healing water flushing through my womb, cleansing me of residual wounds. The water, energetically, pours out of me and onto the stones. I invoke healing for some of my loved ones. Then, I ask Her for clarity about the role of a priestess. She explains to me that it is a position of service with a commitment to honor Her will. One must follow through with given tasks and, occasionally, sacrifice personal comforts. I realize it is a heavier role than I had glorified it to be. Nonetheless, I take a leap of faith and consent to what feels like an offer and intuitively anoint my forehead with Her water.

I sit with this experience, letting my body absorb this new information. Suddenly, I see several small bubbles come up to the glass-still surface of the water in the center of the well. In such shallow ground I am not sure what would have caused this, but I feel it is an affirmation from Brigit.[38] I take three more sips of the water so that I may receive all of Her blessings. I place a spiral silver earring and an American penny, representing smithcraft and pilgrimage, into the water as offerings. I place my hands together in prayer and kiss them. I have fulfilled a significant part of my pilgrimage in connecting with Brigit here. Still, I am reluctant to leave. I am in the presence of a divine Mother and She is fulfilling a deep longing inside of me. For some reason, I have this desire to lie naked on Her stones and rest in the cradle of the goddess. I feel I have come home, though I am at a place I have never been. I make a solemn oath that I will return to this well before I leave Ireland.

I cross the road and make my way to Brigit's other well. Suddenly, school children surround me. They are on fieldtrips for the holiday. I smile knowing how lucky I was to have had the other well to myself for all the time I needed. This well, St. Brigid's Well, has more Christian characteristics in comparison to the pagan well. People have come and left flowers, prayer notes, and hand-made Brigid's crosses in the arms of the bronzed Brigid statue. I take a turn at each prayer stone asking for special blessings from Brigid. I leave another silver earring and an American penny in this water.

I return to the main road and decide to take the long way home. I am walking through the *Curragh* or Brigid's Pastures. This is the land that Brigid acquired for Her monastery with the magical toss of Her cloak. As I walk down the long country road, I pass the animals that are sacred to Brigid: cows and sheep. On this first day of spring, I admire the bright green grass. Having walked for over an hour, I am aware of the physical aspect of the pilgrimage. It has been a full day and I return to the hotel with deep contentment.

Day after Imbolc

It is my last day in Kildare. There are two more places I must still visit: the cathedral grounds, which contain the fire temple, and *Solas Bhríde*, the Celtic spirituality center and home of the Brigidine Sisters. I first make my way to the Cathedral, the place where Brigid built Her abbey. I walk around the Cathedral sunwise before entering.[39] After spending twenty minutes in the church and not feeling much connection with the space, I decide to leave. Outside, I use my map to find Brigit's ancient fire temple. To my excitement, I find it in the churchyard. The temple is a rectangular stone structure about ten feet long, with a few steps that descend into a gravel-covered floor. This is the last remaining structure from Brigid's lifetime as a saint. It was at this location that a total of twenty women, including Brigid, tended a perpetual fire that was "inextinguishable."[40] Upon Brigid's death, nineteen fire keepers remained. On the eve of the twentieth day, a nun would say, "Brigid, keep your own fire, for the night has fallen to you."[41] Sure enough, every twentieth day the fire would remain alit and that fire was maintained for twelve hundred years!

I descend into the temple and sit on the stone steps. I feel a strong holy presence like I did at the well. I think about how many devoted women must have walked this ground. I put my hands on the stone and draw its energy into my body. Feeling present with Brigit again, I say, "Sweet Brigit, I am sitting in your temple. I express great honor for the history of this place and for all who have served You here." I am suddenly inspired to participate in ritual with other women in this space. I wonder if any ritual is held here. I will have to talk to the Sisters about this. I leave the church grounds, deeply satisfied, and ready to visit the Sisters' home.

I knock on the door of *Solas Bhríde*. I am nervous to meet the Sisters, whom I consider to be the guardians of Brigit's sacred sites. Sister Phil and Sister Mary warmly welcome me in. Even though they are bustling with all the festivities they have coordinated for *Féile Bríde*, they make time for me. I relax and tell them where I have come from and about my two days in Kildare. They emanate loving energy and invite me to browse around the center. They have a "Brigid room" that contains a beautiful altar, which seems very pagan to me. I sit on the floor and admire the altar. Green and yellow fabrics are pinned to the wall creating a colorful backdrop. Several straw Brigid's crosses scatter across the fabric. Numerous objects, symbolizing Brigid, are placed about. A small black and white cow statue rests on its legs. A small globe brings attention to Brigid's care for all of humanity. Images of Her as a saint are interspersed with candles. On the floor I notice a glass box containing a lit yellow candle. It is Brigid's sacred flame that has been burning since its resurrection in 1993. All that I have experienced in the last twenty-four hours is almost too much to take in.

Sister Mary walks over to speak with me. I ask her if the fire temple is still used. She explains, "No, but sometimes we light a fire in it on Imbolc." I do not respond, but feel excited and inspired to possibly participate in future rituals in the temple. Sister Mary tells me of the future of *Solas Bhríde*. Due to the increasing number of pilgrims that come to visit Brigid's sites every year, they are planning to build a new hermitage center in Kildare. They have already purchased the land for the center, which is located just a few miles away near the wells. It will cover three and a half acres and is planned to be an ecologically sustainable center. The design will include four hermitages, an exhibition space, a spirituality education and library area, a meditative garden, and a labyrinth.[42] Participating in *Féile Bríde*, witnessing all of the activities in honor of Brigid, and now learning of the plans for this new hermitage center, leave me with the evidence that Brigid's following is flourishing in Kildare and the larger world.

I leave *Solas Bhríde* with an expanded perspective. There are many others like myself who feel a deep connection with this divine figure, whether they regard Her as a saint or a goddess. She has remained close to the hearts of the Irish over the centuries, surviving dramatic cultural changes while retaining much of Her ancient identity. She is a rare figure in this sense. As Europeans, we have largely been severed from our indigenous spiritual traditions. Brigit is one figure who still connects us to an ancient worldview, one in which the sacred was honored in female, as well as, male forms and the Earth was revered as a Great Mother. By honoring Brigid today, people are keeping that link alive. As an ancient Earth Goddess, one can still connect with Her through the natural elements of water and fire, where She offers Herself as a source of healing, maternal love, and ancient wisdom.

With a full head and heart, I arrive at the town square where I will catch the bus back to Galway. In the center, I notice a tall metallic structure that rises about fifteen feet high. At the top there is an acorn-shaped formation. Inside the acorn, something flickers. I realize it is Brigid's sacred flame burning brightly in the center of Her sacred land. Humbled, I stand beneath the flame of this great goddess and powerful Christian saint. I acknowledge the end of my journey in Kildare and the beginning of a deeper journey with Brigit.

Notes

1. I will use the term "Brigit" to refer to the goddess figure and the term "Brigid" to refer to the saint figure.

2. In reference to centuries, I will use the non-denominational terms CE for "Contemporary Era" and BCE for "Before Contemporary Era."

3. Mary Condren, *The Serpent and the Goddess: Women, Religion and Power in Celtic Ireland,* 2nd ed. (Dublin: New Island Books, 2002), 65-6.

4. Ibid., 55.

5. Phil Cousineau, *The Art of Pilgrimage: The Seeker's Guide to Making Travel Sacred* (Berkeley: Conari Press, 1998), xxiii.

6. I use the term "Divine Feminine" in reference to any aspect of the sacred in the female form.

7. A feminist lens strives to analyze history, religion and culture, with equal inclusion of women and men.

8. I use the term "Women's Spirituality" to refer to the modern movement of women who seek a feminist approach to their religions/spiritual paths.

9. See Starhawk's writing "The Burning Times: Notes on a Crucial Period of History" for an in-depth analysis of the Christian suppression of European indigenous spiritual practices in her book *Dreaming the Dark: Magic, Sex and Politics* 3rd ed. (Boston: Beacon Press), 1997.

10. Condren, *The Serpent and the Goddess,* 65; Rita Minehan CSB, *Rekindling the Flame: A Pilgrimage in the Footsteps of Brigid of Kildare* (Kildare: Solas Bhríde Community, 1999), 12.

11. This prayer is adopted and rearranged from the "Brigid's Forge/Brigid's Well Ritual" created by Robin Dolan, Kate Pennington, and Martha Storm. I performed in this ritual at Pantheacon in San Jose, California in 2006.

[12]   Druidism refers to the priestly class of the Celts.

[13]   Minehan, *Rekindling the Flame*, 26.

[14]   Patricia Monaghan, *The Red-Haired Girl from the Bog* (California: New World Library, 2003), 151.

[15]   Condren, *The Serpent and the Goddess*, 57.

[16]   Ibid., 67.

[17]   Ibid., 68.

[18]   Monaghan, *The Red-Haired Girl from the Bog*, 151.

[19]   Minehan, *Rekindling the Flame*, 14.

[20]   Ibid.

[21]   Ibid.

[22]   Ibid., 14-15.

[23]   Minehan, *Rekindling the Flame*, 7.

[24]   This is a pagan practice of creating sacred space by calling in the cardinal directions of East, South, West, and North.

[25]   Condren, *The Serpent and the Goddess*, 66.

[26]   Minehan, *Rekindling the Flame*, 29.

[27]   Ibid.

[28]   Walter and Mary Brenneman, *Crossing the Circle at the Holy Wells of Ireland* (Charlottesville: The University Press of Virginia, 1995), 11.

[29]   Ibid., 19.

[30]   Ibid.

[31]   Monaghan, *The Red-Haired Girl from the Bog*, 158.

[32]   Brenneman, *Crossing the Circle at the Holy Wells of Ireland*, 19.

[33]   Monaghan, *The Red-Haired Girl from the Bog*, 145.

[34]   Minehan, *Rekindling the Flame*, 14.

[35]   Condren, *The Serpent and the Goddess*, 58.

[36]   Monaghan, *The Red-Haired Girl from the Bog*, 148.

[37]   Brenneman, *Crossing the Circle at the Holy Wells of Ireland*, 97.

[38]   Walter and Mary Brenneman, in *Crossing the Circle at the Holy Wells of Ireland*, explain that these bubbles are "Bubbles of mystic inspiration . . . which themselves are evidence of the living force and the presence of wisdom in the water." Brenneman and Brenneman, *Crossing the Circle at the Holy Wells of Ireland*, 27.

[39]   It is traditional Celtic practice to circle sunwise, which is considered to be the "harmonious" direction of the universe. Minehan, *Rekindling the Flame*, 42.

[40]   Minehan, *Rekindling the Flame*, 26.

[41]   Ibid.

[42]   Solas Bhríde, "Development," *Solas Bhríde Center and Hermitages*, http://www.solasbhride.ie/development.

Bibliography

Brenneman, Walter and Mary Brenneman. *Crossing the Circle at the Holy Wells of Ireland.* Charlottesville: The University Press of Virginia, 1995.

Condren, Mary. *The Serpent and the Goddess: Women, Religion and Power in Celtic Ireland,* 2nd ed. Dublin: New Island Books, 2002.

Cousineau, Phil. *The Art of Pilgrimage: The Seeker's Guide to Making Travel Sacred.* Berkeley: Conari Press, 1998.

Minehan, Rita, CSB. *Rekindling the Flame: A Pilgrimage in the Footsteps of Brigid of Kildare.* Kildare: Solas Bhríde Community, 1999.

Monaghan, Patricia. *The Red-Haired Girl from the Bog.* California: New World Library, 2003.

Solas Bhríde. "Development." *Solas Bhríde Center and Hermitages,* http://www.solasbhride.ie.

Starhawk. *Dreaming the Dark: Magic, Sex and Politics,* 3rd ed. Boston: Beacon Press, 1997.

Brigit's Wayside Well, Imbolc 2007, Kildare, Ireland; Photo
© 2007 Nicole Margiasso

The Meanings of "Goddess"

Max Dashu

So much confusion has been sown about Goddess reverence. Even the word "goddess" is contested today. It's considered blasphemy by the Abrahamic religions that define religion for billions of people, while in popular culture it has been totally desacralized, stripped down and trivialized. People talk about a pop star as a "sex goddess" or diva—which means "goddess" in Italian, but is now used to describe performers with overinflated egos. "Goddess" has no cultural standing in mainstream society, except as a negative. Few people are conversant with the rich and ancient history of goddess reverence. Instead they see press reports about finds of an "8,000 year old sex goddess." Even fewer understand what spiritual feminists mean when we speak of Goddess or goddesses.

Schools still teach the patriarchal Greek and Roman archetypes: the vain and capricious Venus, male-identified Athena, jealous and vindictive Hera. These goddesses are of the most patriarchal vintage, out of a narrowly Eurocentric worldview. Further up the educational ladder, it's risky to talk about goddesses, except when ridiculing feminist "ideology" or "utopianism." Resistance to seeing any sacral value in ancient female icons has been a particular sticking point in academia, where theoretical frameworks typically ignore the pervasive sense of sacredness in aboriginal cultures. Most intellectuals think sardonic and cynical readings of Goddess are hip, and dismiss the female Divine as an illusion with no possible relevance in a post-modern or hi-tech world.

In recent decades, scholars have dropped some of the more offensive descriptions of the ancient female figurines—"dancing girls," "concubines." But "fertility idol" is still much-used, even preferred, while saying "goddess" has become the scholarly equivalent of walking onto a target range, at least in Anglophone universities. (European and

Asian scholars often use the term, and many have no problem identifying female figurines as religious icons.) "Fertility idol" is a step-around where sacral significance is clearly involved but it's considered unacceptable to say so—in other words, to say "goddess." Naming the figurines as "idols" evokes a load of negative cultural associations going back to the biblical ban on "worshipping stocks and stones." It perpetuates the ancient religious bias against traditions considered to be Other, "primitive" and "superstitious." The reductive "fertility" tag is also problematic; as Paula Gunn Allen pointed out, it demeans and trivializes both aboriginal religion and women's power.[1]

It might be argued that at least "idol" concedes a religious context, but often that is exactly what is being denied. Many scholars seem determined to go to great lengths to deny that the ancient female icons were sacred. They've proposed that the abstract marble sculptures of women from the ancient Cycladic islands were toys—in spite of their size and weight, or the fact that they remain stylistically consistent over a period of eight centuries and were buried in concentrated deposits. Another popular explanation treats the ancient figurines as pornography. This idea really does bear the marks of modern assumptions. Its proponents don't bother to explain the frequency of figurine finds in burials, shrines, and among ritual items. They're unable to imagine that female culture-makers created them as embodied female self-expression, for their own ritual purposes. Instead it's back to the tired assumption that women are sex, are reproductive function, are objects manipulated by and for men.

Goddess talk has a forbidden charge in all kinds of settings. Marxists and materialists want no part of it. (And yet the new physics, in showing that matter consists of nothing but energy and space, immeasurable and indeterminate, has erased the scientific foundations of materialism.) Even in Women's Studies, examination of Goddess-oriented culture and history is generally stigmatized as "utopian" and regarded as an embarrassment that detracts from the acceptability of a field already under siege. By contrast, the patriarchal religions still carry a venerable aura of time-honored tradition, and have roared back into currency in recent decades. Scholars tread this ground much more cautiously: these constituencies must not be offended, even when they embrace foundational myths and structures that heavily privilege the masculine. In fact, these scriptures and institutions originate in times when the transmission of Goddess veneration was being interrupted, severed and broken.

Something precious and important was negated in that cultural break, in each time and place where it occurred: the honoring of the Female as creative, sovereign, and potent in her own right, as transcendent and immanent. This is not to over-idealize the ancient pagans, many of whom had become patriarchal as well, but simply a recognition that paganism retained a very ancient cultural freight, including female spiritual leadership. The new patriarchal institutions attacked and bitterly fought down the pagan priestesses, and the early Christian ones too: the Montanists of Anatolia, the Sicilian and Breton women who officiated at Mass, and the "heretical" Kollyridian women who worshipped Mary with loaves.

Male-dominant religions adopted two primary strategies to conquer Goddess reverence: they forbade it outright, or they mythically colonized it. This feminine veneration was derided as "idolatry" and "whoring after false gods," attacked as "heresy" and "blasphemy" and "*shirk*,"[2] persecuted as "devil-worship," and finally stigmatized and dismissed as "superstition" and "cult." In successive stages, a wealth of spiritual observances enacted by women were lost or buried, in a repression spearheaded by social elites. After a long struggle, goddess veneration lapsed into invisibility, as if wiped out, but its marginalized vestiges persisted among the common people.

Mary Ford Grabowsky described the cultural remainder of this process as "the crushed feminine."[3] A French historian of the witch hunts characterized the abased condition of women in 17th century Europe as *la femme vaincue*: "the vanquished woman."[4] European torture trials led to this cultural outcome of "women possessed" even as they redefined folk goddesses as the devil.[5] It was out of this long cultural dispossession and exile in "Western civilization" that women rose up to reaffirm Goddess. We refused her relegation to heresy, to the unspeakable—and that goes for both women's oppression, and female power.

The Goddess movement recognizes the political uses of male-supremacist religion, and undermines its dominionist foundations. We challenge theologies that make females stand for the "inferior" material realm, reduce us to sex, decree our submission to male privilege. We repudiate hierarchy of all kinds, including the demonization of matter, of bodies, of darkness in patriarchal religion. We recognize how the twisted ideas of diabolism not only degraded women in the witch hunts, and inculcated hateful ideas about human sexuality, but at the same time demonized dark peoples and indigenous religions.

In Starhawk's words, we value power within, and power with, not power over. We disavow ideas of superiority/inferiority, the idea of us down here under him or even her "up there"—anything that smacks of pompous authoritarianism. This is why many prefer "spirituality" to the notion of "religion," which has become so deeply stained with dominance behaviors and institutional rigidities. (Originally, however, *religio* meant "bound together.") Some say "earth-based religion," saying that even "spirituality" implies a rejection of earthly sacredness, as in dominionist religion.

Goddess feminists understand that religious symbolism is not irrelevant happenstance, but a deep encoding of values. Subordination in this sphere, or exclusion from it, has consequences all along the cultural line. It shapes attitudes, behavior and human relations. There's a reason why religion has been a pivotal battleground in deepening systems of domination. In modern cultures, mass-market advertising also utilizes the power of symbolism to maximum effect, deploying it to manipulate human feeling and motivation in sophisticated ways. To ignore these forces would be foolish.

All the controversies over goddesses boil down to conflicting views of what is real and significant. Humans are more than rational beings. The mind is powerful, but the heart is greater. We live swimming in a dreaming consciousness of the numinous, where our awareness of ourselves arises. So do our values and the ways we connect with each other. If in this dream-realm of the symbolic, the female is deprecated and subjugated, is ruled out from being named and pictured as divine, creator, or source of being, the effect on girls and women is negative and demoralizing.

While intellectuals hedge about whether goddesses have any significance, the Catholic hierarchy goes on insisting that the maleness of god and christ is non-negotiable. (Hmmm: even as I write, the software keeps trying to make me capitalize those titles.) The popes say the priest must be masculine because he stands for christ—who therefore represents maleness as well as divinity. The Virgin Mary represents the female, but Church doctrine vehemently insists that she is not goddess, is beneath the heavenly father, and must never be worshipped.

Of course, other methods have been used to mythically subjugate the female, as in pagan Greek and Norse mythology, Babylonian scriptures, or Indra's attacks on the dawn-goddess Ushas in the Rg Veda. Patriarchal Hindu theologies retain the goddesses but portray them as *pativratā*'serving their husbands, dutifully rubbing their feet, or plastered to their sides like clinging vines. But other voices in the multi-stranded web of culture called "Hinduism" uphold female sovereignty. These voices say that Devi is the ultimate Reality, that Shiva cannot even move a limb without Shakti. These voices say that Brahma, Vishnu and Shiva are like tiny flakes of red *kumkum* in the *bindi* dot on Devi's forehead. Tantriks say that all women are Devi herself and that to harm any woman is to do violence to Goddess.

The deep stream of Goddess veneration also resurfaced in Christian Europe as the Black Madonnas and Our Lady of the Local Animist Sanctuary. Their divinity is very different than the virgin-vessel-handmaid-of-the-Lord propagated by the theologians. Over many centuries, these strands coalesced to a greater or lesser degree, but folk reverence never yielded to the priestly prohibitions against worshipping Mary. Many of its goddesses-in-disguise re-emerged as apocryphal saints. Later, diasporic Africans adopted the Catholic terminology of the saints in order to smuggle their own *orishas* or *loas* into the churches. The Maya and Peruvians did the same.

"Saint" itself simply means "holy one," from Latin *sanctus*. So much comes down to language, with all its limitations (to say nothing of translation). It's also important to grasp the variation in cultural approaches to the sacred. The Dineh/Navajo speak of the "holy people" rather than gods and goddesses. Indigenous people seem more likely to speak of "Our Mother," or of "Mothers," who can be ancestors, forces of nature, law-givers, or primordial creators. It's illuminating to reflect on names for spirit—*neter, manitou, kami, orisha* or *loa, akua, teotl.* All have their own flavor and range, which encompass natural powers.

The further back we look into the roots of common words for the Divine, the more they resemble concepts in aboriginal philosophies. For example, *deity, divinity,* and the latinate names for "goddess" (*dea, déesse, diosa,* and so on) all spring from a Proto-Indo-European root—*deiwa (f), *deiwos (m)—that meant "shining." From this same root comes the word for "day" in various European languages, and the names of the Latin goddess Diana and Greek Dione. Over 3,000 years ago, the earliest Greek inscriptions in Linear B show Di-wi-ya, "Goddess." In India her exact linguistic equivalent is Devi, praised in litanies as Divyaa, "shining."

The English word "Goddess" is a feminine latinization of the Germanic "god." It comes from the proto-Germanic root *gudhan (dh standing for a slashed đ). Its original meaning is still debated, but both of the proposed roots point to ritual. Most linguists favor *ghau, "to call on, invoke," while the alternative *gheu* means "to pour libation." Because of the long history of persecution of pagans, English and most European languages have a limited vocabulary for shamanic concepts. This is why they borrowed words like *shaman* (from Evenk, Siberia) or *mana* (from the Pacific languages). Europeans too once had drum rituals, trance dancing, even ritual sweathouses: the ancient Portuguese *pedras formosas*, the Irish *teach-an-alais*, the Russian *bozhena* ("divine"). For Lithuanians, the bath-house was sacred to the goddess Laima and a place of women's ritual, and the Finns also had their Sauna-Mother chants.

"The Mothers"

Isis notwithstanding, many academic writers deplore the "essentialist" concept of a "mother goddess." The current trend is to dismiss "mother goddess" as an irrelevant modernism—and a purely "biological" one at that. Lotte Motz insists that there was never any Mother Goddess, going so far as to claim that "mother" has nothing to do with Kybele's titles of Great Mother (Magna Mater) and Mother of the Gods (Mater Deum).[7]

"Mother of the Gods" is no isolated incidence, however. This title recurs in a deep and broad swath of cultures: for Neith in ancient Egypt, Athirat in the Ugaritic scriptures (Syria), Aditi in the *Rg Veda* of India, Teteoinan and Coatlicue (Aztecs), Nana Burukú (Dahomey, and beyond), Allat (Arabia), Ninhursag (Sumeria), Kiririsha and Mashta of the Elamites (Iran). The Chamacoco of Paraguay name Kasogoanaga "mother of the spirits." Some peoples call their primordial goddess Grandmother: Hannahanna of the Hurrians (Asia Minor), and the Grandmother Creator of the Shawnee, Kokomtheyna.

The title Mother of All also gives a rich yield: Nyame of Ashanti (Ghana); Terra Ops (ancient Latins); the Gnostic goddess Barbelo (as Mother of *the* All); Amaná of the Calinya Caribs (Surinam); Aluna of the Kogi (Colombia). In Australia, various cultures give this title to Ngalyod, Mutjingga, and Kunapipi, who is called "one mother for all people everywhere."[8] Along similar lines, Uralic peoples speak of the Mother of Nature, and the Chinese of Wu Sheng Lao Mu ("Primordial Venerable Mother"). More conceptually, the *Dao De Jing* calls her "the creating Mother of whatever exists under heaven."

Such titles could be multiplied, with considerable overlap. The Yoruba sea goddess Yemanja is Mother of the Orishas, and also called Mother of All. The Laguna writer Leslie Marmon Silko talks story about Thought

Woman as Mother Creator—and with her three sisters, Mother Creators.[9] Of course "mother" is not the only signifier of Goddess. There are creator goddesses, fates and lawgivers; immanent powers of land, sea, and sky, of fire or clouds, of animals and birds; and goddesses representing divine principles, cycles, or planets. But "mother" mixes freely and frequently with other attributes—including some, such as warrior or destroyer, that conflict with more conservative conceptions of "mother."

If we look to indigenous religions, Mother is a truly expansive concept, and a divine one. In aboriginal philosophies, it is extremely common to name spirits and deities as "mothers." South Americans often describe them as mothers of waters, of animals, of special power places. In Brazil's upper Xingu river, the Kamayura speak of *mama'é*, the mother spirits of animals, fish, and food plants. The Tupí say that that every animal has its own spirit mother, *cy*, and that Putcha Cy is the "mother of animals," who follow her thunderous roar. She protects them from hunters. Putcha Cy lives in the springs at the headwaters of rivers, and often takes the form of a tortoise or coatá monkey.[10]

In Colombia, a song of the matrilineal Kogi (Kagabá) praises a divine Mother as the source of everything:

> The Mother of Songs, the mother of our whole seed, bore us in the beginning. She is the mother of all races of men [sic] and the mother of all tribes. She is the mother of the thunder, the mother of the rivers, the mother of trees and of all kinds of things. She is the mother of songs and dances. She is the mother of the older brother stones. She is the mother of the grain and the mother of all things. She is the mother of the younger brother Frenchmen and of the strangers. She is the mother of the dance paraphernalia and of all temples, and the only mother we have. She is the mother of the animals, the only one, and the mother of the Milky Way. It was the mother herself who began to baptize. She gave us the limestone coca dish. She is the mother of the rain, the only one we have. She alone is the mother of things, she alone . . . [11]

For the Kogi, a Great Mother is the origin of everything. She is Aluna, which translates as spirit, vitality, awareness, reality, and the primordial sea. Their eloquent chant flatly contradicts pronouncements that no culture ever conceived of a Great Mother.

In the Quechua language, Mama ("mother") translates in sacral contexts as "goddess," and Tata ("father") as "god." So Peruvians invoke and make offerings to Pachamama, Mother Earth; Mama Quilla, Mother Moon; Saramama, Corn Mother, and so on. Further south, the Mapuche pray to the Grandmothers and Grandfathers of the Directions. The Guaraní of Paraguay venerate Ñandecy, "Our Mother," who lives in the east, beyond the sea, in the Land Without Evil. She is First Woman, and also appears as a green snake. After the Spanish invasions, Ñandecy inspired successive Guarani movements seeking liberation from European domination.

The Calinya Caribs speak of Amaná, a self-conceiving Mother whose essence is Time, existing through eternity, and who has borne all beings. Amaná lives in the waters of the heavens, in the Pleiades, in the form of a woman-serpent. She renews herself continually by sloughing off her skin, and can take any shape. Shamans commune with her and with the mothers of rocks at the headwaters of rivers for visions and healing. Amaná governs all spirits of the waters, and as mother of all species is called Wala Yumu, "spirit of the kinds."[12]

In the far north, the Inuit speak of Takanakapsaluk, the Sea Mother, who created the great ocean mammals, and the Caribou Mother, who created land animals by speaking magical words of power. She made their skin from her own leather breeches.[13] These Mothers are also elder beings, like the primary female spirit of the Cheyenne, Old Woman. The monolithic stone women scattered across the steppes of Central Asia are known as *bülbül*, "grandmothers." Sacred mothers also persisted in parts of Europe, most dramatically among the incompletely-christianized Latvians. They venerated over fifty *mâtes*, "mothers" of natural powers: earth, forests, and fields, sea, waves, rivers, rain, fog, and wind, as well as threshing houses, markets, gardens, roads, linen, wine, flowers, and the dead.

In India, every village has its goddess. This local Gramadevi "is perceived as the local manifestation of the cosmic mother-goddess."[14] Even great cities are named for goddesses of place: Mumbai (Bombay) and Calcutta (Kalighat, the "river-steps of Kali"). The pervasive Goddess veneration of India is rhapsodized by seers such as Ramakrishna of Dakshineswar: "The Mother projects the entire world, moment by moment, from her own ecstasy. Simply remember that all comes from her, belongs to her, abides in her, and disappears into her . . ."[15] (But this is not "goddess monotheism"; the same tongue praised other forms of deity.)

In the African stronghold of mother-veneration, the Yoruba speak of *awon iya wa*, "our mothers," who exist on a continuum of deities and ancestors. *Awon iya wa* is "a collective term for female ancestors, female deities, and for older living women, whose power over the reproductive capacities of all women is held in awe by Yoruba men." People call these mothers "the owners of the world."[16] In a patriarchal world, their wrath must be placated through the masked *gelede* dances.

African women's rites of the mothers underlie female identity and empowerment, even in patrilineal and patrilocal societies. In Igbo country, as Onitsha women married out, they brought with them shrines to "the mothers," and made conical clay mounds for the Oma spirit of nurturing and maternity to inhabit. [17] Ifi Amadiume describes how an indigenous Igbo matrilineage preserved veneration of its ancestral goddess under "patriarchal incursion." In Nnobi oral histories, the hunter Aho-from-the-wild met the divine woman Idemili near a stream and married her. Idemili had more powerful influence than her husband, "and so she spread her idols everywhere." Over time, as the Igbo shifted to a patrilineal and patrilocal order, conflicting themes of female subordination arose: "Thus, the all-powerful goddess Idemili was domesticated and made the wife of a less powerful god, Aho." (And a junior third wife at that.) Their much-courted daughter married out, taking a ritual pot with her, and she too spread her shrines around. In spite of the patrilocal "domestication" of these female powers, they remain the central mythic figures of the region, with important political ramifications.[18]

The Gouandousou statues of the Bamana display diverse and multivalent meanings of Goddess, including the kind many academics reject as untenably "essentialist" because of their connection to body mysteries: menstruation, pregnancy and lactation. This is "dangerous" terrain, both in animist terms and in the sexual politics of patriarchy. In Bamana culture (as for countless others) it is a terrain of female potency. "For them these statues represent either Mousso Koroni the supernatural female creator, Gouandousou the gifted and powerful historical figure, or female ancestors as a collectivity." The images also carry meanings of mother, milk-giver, protector, and worker.[19]

Senufo thought envisions a comparable spectrum of spiritual beings: deities, ancestors, and wilderness spirits. Anita Glaze has described the powerful female forces in this cosmology: "Central to Senufo religion is the conception of a bipartite deity called Kòlotyölöö in its aspect of divine creator, and Màlëëö or Kàtyelëëö in its aspect of protective, nurturing being." The last two names mean "Ancient Mother" and "Ancient Woman." The creator divinity is remote and cannot be approached directly, only through other deities.[20]

Linguistic indicators point to a shift that masculinized the Senufo creator: "There is some evidence to suggest that Kòlotyölöö was originally considered female in nature (*työlöö wii*, for example, means 'woman' or 'wife' in Tyebara), although present usage suggests a neuter or even a paternal image."[21] This change could well date to men's takeover of the Poro society from its female founders, as described in oral histories. Numerous instances are known of a female deity changing to male during a patriarchal culture-shift. Paula Gunn Allen commented on the displacement of Pueblo female divinities, and Tikvah Frymer Kensky tracked the turning of Sumerian goddesses into gods.[22]

The Moving Power of the Mythic

We are mythic beings. However rational we are on the surface, we have numinous dimensions. Carol Christ's insights on the tremendous power of the symbolic and mythic explain why so many experience it as a primary arena of transformation: "A symbol's effect does not depend on rational assent, for a symbol also functions on levels of the psyche other than the rational." She observes that symbols create cultural contexts experienced even by non-adherents, for example at marriages, funerals, and holidays. She makes a most astute comment about how human culture works: "Symbol systems cannot be rejected, they must be replaced."[23] This pivotal principle helps us to understand why attempts to create social change often falter. They have not yet touched the depths where psyche and culture are transformed.

Anthropologists speak of memes, powerful value-forms backed by the collected sum of cultural consensus—or under systems of dominance, by coercion and submission. Memes acquire a force of their own, fed by naming, storytelling, repetition, artistic and ritual enactment. They replicate and spread beyond their original context, long after their creators are dead, and go on to shape new contexts. They have been described as cultural genes or programs, which can be positive or negative, inspired or oppressive—or complex mixtures. Today we swim in a toxic cultural sea of magnetized signs and stories which affect us on multiple levels.

Myth and ritual have transformative power. Ifi Amadiume describes how Igbo women use them in their oaths of solidarity at shrines, in women's strikes and collective actions of calling men to account by making them eat fufu and swear oaths at the shrine of the goddess Ala. The Igbo Women's War of 1929 drew extensively on ritual custom—processions, carrying wands, ceremonial dress of leaves—in mass protests of British colonial taxes and puppet chiefs. (They also tore down telegraph lines and stormed jails to free prisoners).[24]

Igbo women's use of ceremonial regalia toward political ends is one instance of "how metaphor translates into genuine cultural power," as Judy Grahn writes. "In examining the power of verbal metaphor, I began to see that we surround ourselves with living, interacting, physically embodied metaphors." Grahn names these embodied patterns "metaforms," explaining that "Some metaphors are so powerful they become translated into physical form . . ." This goes to the very heart of ritual, whether it is acts or masks or sacred objects or substances that carry that potent meaning. [25]

Ritual is the enactment of symbols, conduits for directing and magnifying energy. Symbolic acts are potentized through chant, drumming, dance, and with lights, paint, oils, incense, libations. Through ceremony—divine Essence invoked and guided through symbol and sacred substance—we wash our minds, harmonize our bodies, revitalize our spirits. Through story and litanies and ritual theater, we affirm what we value and how we are connected in the world. Thus we concentrate awareness and intention, thus we create change and forge connections: the deep calling to the Deep.

The Goddess movement affirms a sacral view of the world, the conviction that we are kin within a whole, a flowing circle. Ruth Barrett writes that for many "the Goddess is not an entity but the web of life itself." Maybe that web, too, is a Being whose totality we can hardly conceive because we are within, like cells in a great body. Some British Goddess folk have expressed this diverse continuum as "the one and the many."[26] Most Goddess pagans don't relate to rigid categories of monotheism vs. polytheism, or transcendent vs. immanent. We have deists and atheists and polytheists and panentheists among us. Each follows the deepest truth she can uncover within herself. There are many approaches: some pray, some invoke, some take the deities as symbols, others as beings, or

Being. Still others ride the currents of mystic bewilderment, recognizing the impossibility of condensing their experiences into language.

Some simply say Spirit: the divine spark present in all beings. Another way of putting it is Essence: the source of being from which we all arise. Feminists with Buddhist leanings call it Mother Essence or the Ground Luminosity. Mary Daly called it Quintessence: that which permeates all Nature, the Spirit that gives life to the universe, the "real source." In ancestor religion, Essence includes the human mothers living and dead, and the mother within us, who swells in our breasts and wombs and blood, whether we have biological children or not, or even have wombs or breasts anymore. This experience of the body as sacred and filled with vital force (Indic *ojas*, Chinese *jing*, and 10,000 other names) has nothing in common with the theoretical construct of "essentialism." It belongs to animist philosophy (animism: another "spirit" word).

Most spiritual feminists conceive of Goddess as a continuum, encompassing living beings, ancestors, spirits, essences, qualities, and vast governing principles like Maat, Tao, and Wyrd—all names for divine Law, Nature. We see parallels in the pagan Gothic Halioruna ("Holy Mystery") and the Great Mystery of Native North America. These Mysteries are far from the mystification practiced in authoritarian institutions. Our reverence has nothing in common with abasement, with the submission demanded by doctrines of dominance. It flows toward what is valued and admired, what causes awe: a rushing river, wind moving through a great forest, the fire-patterns in embers. It is roused by powerful music and beautiful art, incantation and drumming and dance. There we enter into the Presence where knowing and healing and transformation come.

We affirm the long-reviled Female, now expanding out of ancient cultural confinements. In her liberation males are transfigured too. There is room for the gods, without the taint of lordship and oppression. In the ultimate sense, gender is ephemeral, and in a just world it would not matter, but we live in a world that is severely out of balance, afflicted with male domination to a high degree. So in our invocations it is She. We say that this She is found in our own inner fire, a spark of the entire Vastness, and a gateway to it. We say She rather than It, rejecting the impersonal object in favor of a numinous and melodic approach to consciousness. In the same spirit, many of us prefer to say Goddess rather than "the Goddess," which carries a sense of A Thing or construct, rather than

Essence and Presence. Our conception of Goddess is expansive. For us Nature is holy, ultimate Reality, and the fount of wisdom.

We address what we hold sacred through this mirror of Goddess, however she is understood, whether she is experienced in body-knowing, or relational, or conceptual ways. She is rising now, through us. We are recreating the arts of invocation, of incantation, of drumming and sacramental dance. Countless women are "resacralizing the female body through Goddess spirituality," in the words of Wendy Griffin.[27] It's all a remembrance, a return of the spiral, with the old kinds of veneration taking on new forms.

The resurgence of the female Divine is creating a profound transformative impact on the patriarchal empire we live in. This expansive cultural shift restores balance, and answers a deep hunger for truth and justice.[28] This longing is felt beyond pagan circles. For more than a century, prophecies of the re-emergence of female sovereignty have circulated among the original peoples of North America. A cry is now rising, a call mounting from women within and without the majoritarian religions, propelling a movement transcending the traditional religious boundaries. The meanings of Goddess speak to what we revere and what we are reaching toward, and how we know the ultimate nature of reality in our deepest core.

Notes

1   Paula Gunn Allen, *The Sacred Hoop: Recovering the Feminine in American Indian Traditions* (Boston: Beacon, 1986), 14. For more discussion, see Max Dashu, "Icons of the Matrix" (2005) http://www.suppressedhistories.net/articles/icons.html

2   *Shirk* is an Islamic concept of blasphemy that means "ascribing partners to Allah," and more broadly, goddess veneration.

3   See Mary Ford Grabowsky, *The Sacred Feminine: Essential Women's Wisdom Through the Ages* (San Francisco: Harper, 2002).

4   Robert Muchembled, *Sorcieres, Justice et Société aux 16e et 17e Siecles* (Paris: Editions Imago, 1987), 8.

5   *Pativratâ*: a woman who is "vowed to a lord" and, as prescribed, worships her husband "as a god

6   Max Dashu, "Secret History of the Witches," http://www.suppressedhistories. net/secrethistory/secrethistory.html, publication in print forthcoming.

7   Lotte Motz, *The Faces of the Goddess* (New York: Oxford University Press, 1997), 120.

8   Peggy Grove, "Myths, Glyphs and Rituals of a Living Goddess Tradition," in *Revision*, Vol 21 #3 (Winter 1999), 12

9   Leslie Marmon Silko, *Yellow Woman and A Beauty of Spirit: Essays on Native American Life Today* (New York: Simon and Schuster, 1996), 63-64.

10 Otto Zerries, in *Pre-Columbian American Religions*, ed. Walter Krickeberg et al (New York: Holt, Rinehart and Winston, 1968), 260-1.

11 Erich Neumann, Erich, *The Great Mother* (Princeton University Press, 1972), 85.

[12] Zerries, *Pre-Columbian*, 245-6. For more detail on these South American goddesses, see Max Dashu, "Mother and Origin: South American Goddesses," in *Goddesses in World Culture* (Santa Barbara CA: Praeger, 2010)

[13] Knut Rasmussen, Report of the Fifth Thule Expedition, 1929, 69-70, in Franz Boas (English language translation) Volume III: 122.

[14] Devdutt Pattanaik, in Nagar, Shanti Lal, *The Universal Mother* (Delhi: Atma Ram & Sons, 1988), 152.

[15] Lex Hixson, *Great Swan: Meetings with Ramakrishna*, (New York: Larson, 1997).

[16] John Pemberton, "The Carvers of the Northeast," in *Yoruba: Nine Centuries of African Art and Thought*, eds. Henry John Drewel et al. (New York: Harry Abrams, 1989), 210.

[17] Ifi Amadiume, *African Matriarchal Foundations: The case of Igbo societies* (New York and London: Karnak House and Red Sea Press, 1995 (1987), 19.

[18] Ibid., 59-61, 39.

[19] Pascal James Imperato, *Buffoons, Queens and Wooden Horsemen* (New York: Kilimi, 1983, 42-43.

[20] Anita Glaze, "Woman Power and Art in a Senufo Village," *African Arts*, Vol 8, No. 3 (Spring, 1975): 29.

[21] Ibid., 64.

[22] Gunn Allen, *The Sacred Hoop*, 41. See also Tikvah Frymer-Kensky, *In the Wake of the Goddesses: Women, Culture and the Biblical Transformation of Pagan Myth* (New York: Ballantine, 1993), passim., whose book criticizes Sumerian patriarchy but glosses over the Biblical.

[23] Carol P. Christ, "Why Women Need the Goddess," in *Womanspirit Rising: A Feminist Reader in Religion* (San Francisco: Harper Collins, 1979), 274-275.

24   This union of spiritual and political is common. My slideshow *Rebel Shamans: Indigenous Women Confront Empire* (2006) gives many examples: http://www.suppressedhistories.net/catalog/shamanliberators.html.

25   Judy Grahn, *Blood, Bread and Roses: How Menstruation Created the World* (Boston: Beacon, 1993), 19.

26   Ruth Green, in the British pagan journal *Wood and Water*, Vol 54 (1996): 4-7; also Asphodel Long, "The One or the Many: the Great Goddess Revisited," Dublin 1996, at http://www.asphodel-long.com/html/the_one_or_the_many.html.

27   Wendy Griffin, "Crafting the Boundaries" in *Daughters of the Goddess: Studies of Healing Identify and Empowerment,* ed. Wendy Griffin (Walnut Creek CA: Altamira, 2000), 76-77.

28   This essay is condensed from an article published in Goddess Pages (www.goddess-pages.co.uk/). Links to the full three-part series are at www.maxdashu.net/articlesinter.html.

Soror Mystica:
New Myth for a Changing Earth

Gael Belden

During the Earth's first turning
(whereby the one became two,
the two became three, and the
three became 10,000 things),
there were only metals and minerals.

Older than the Earth itself, these elements
came from stars. They came from
before the before and they painted
the earth with red ore, blue copper, and yellow sulfur.
Then everything cooked itself.

There was a furnace and everything glowed red,
the heat unimaginable—everything hot, hot!
There was no air to breathe, and no breath to breathe it.
The atmosphere reeked with carbon dioxide,
and there was nothing to breathe.

Four billion years ago this happened.
Four billion years ago water vapor condensed
and fell to the earth.
And rivers carved out features, and the below
rose up and created from itself the above.

And the water above ran to the lower,
taking minerals from rock.
And thousands of oceans were born.
Because when matter and water enter
into their sacred contract no life form is exempt.

When the three became 10,000 things
Eventually two-leggeds came to be.
Four *million* years ago humans, the result of cells dividing,
came forth from the water.

And everything changed.

And everyone forgot that we came from
stardust, minerals, metals, and heat.
Everyone forgot that we came from being cooked
down, down in the Great Below.
Cooked in the Great vessel we forgot that this *temenos* is *alchemical.*

But Persephone didn't forget. Nor did her twin.

Her name was Demeter/Persephone and she told the story.
She told the story about the need to remember how
marvelous our origins are. She told the story of the
first descent, and then of the movement into breath.
And of water, and of the infusion of ore, sulfur and heat.

The fertile darkness is our Mother; the moist darkness,
he is our father. We are divine sparks in a dark field.
And we benefit from a four-billion-year-old bequeathment.
What is held in matter is divine. It is the *prima materia.*
And there is no part of it that we are not.

Across our planet one river in ten no longer flows to the sea.
Across our planet one mammal in four, one bird in eight, and
one amphibian in three, are threatened. In sixty short
years we have done more to impact the earth than the
combined ages of all that came before.

In sixty short years three-fourths of our fishing waters are
exhausted. We are shaping the earth in our image. And one
major river in ten no longer flows to the sea.
The earth is our alchemical vessel. It is our home and
the rivers no longer flow to the sea.

Her name is Demeter/Persephone and she is black, red, yellow,
and blue. Her name is Mystic Sister, or *Soror Mystica,*
and she has been called by Hades, that old man of fathomless depths, to
pick the narcissus and fall into the hole. Because to do this is to
remember, to fall into the hole is to remember. And so the Mystic Sister
summoned Hades.

Their home was the Great Below. The Mystic Sister was un-moored and
adrift and she became Queen of the Great Below.
Who cares? She thought.
The Mystic Sister was too smart to be taken in by titles.
The Queen was too much part of the *hidden* mystery
to be taken in by titles.

And so the word, *Eleusinian* rolled off her tongue.
Along with one, red, berry.

She knew she was being cooked and that her gift
was to remember this cooking.
And that the function of the King and Queen,
whatever the landscape is to birth the new.
And so she learned what she learned and she called on Mercurius. She
called on the god Mercurius:
Get me out of here! She said.

Have you reconciled death? He asked.

I am the Mystic Sister, said she.
And through the sisterhood that is I myself,
the grail everyone is seeking is revealed.
The divine is unearthed from matter. The peacock tail is fanned,

and the mystery drops its veil. This is the Way of Change.
This is the Way of Change and the *Imago Dei*. And *everyone* dies.

The polar ice caps are 40% thinner than they were 40 years ago;
The polar ice caps are 40% thinner than they were 40 years ago
And still the Milky Way moves around 10,000 galaxies.

We have birthed the Self from below. It is very useful
to remember that we birthed the Self from below.
When Mercurius held out his hand, the Mystic Sister grabbed on.
When Mercurius held out his hand the message from the underworld
was unequivocal.

The Mystic Sister reminds us to go below this hollow earth.
The Mystic Sister reminds us to go to the Great Below in order to
grasp the impermanence of life and its god-sent beginnings.
This woman is covered with ore. This woman is deep into it.
This woman and her lover want us to be intimate with the miraculous
journey where heat came first.

When Demeter/Persephone and Dionysis/Hades move together
in consort, the earth shakes. When Demeter/Persephone
and Dionysis/Hades join forces the Great Vessel heats up
reminding us of the original plan.
And the Vessel is stained red.
And the Vessel is made from beginnings and endings.

And it gave birth to the 10,000 things; all beginning, all ending . . .

The Mystic Sister wants us to remember our origins.
The Mystic Sister wants us to remember our origins
so we know where home is.
The Mystic Sister wants to bow to the ground with gratitude
so that in this gratitude rivers will flow to the sea once again. And so that
one-half the world's forests, now gone, will be replenished.

The *Soror Mystica* is in the center of our hearts.
The *Soror Mystica* resides in the center of our hearts.
We are The Great Vessel and *we* are The Great Below.
And we come from stars.

We are beautiful and we come from stars.

Our planet, our home, is heartbreakingly beautiful,
and we come from stars.

The Luminous Dark Mother

Leslene della-Madre

I am deeply interested in the true origins and beginnings of the spiritual life of humankind. This interest has, over time, become a passion as I have expanded my awareness and understanding about our human story—most of which is not told in history books. As a long-time student of Goddess thealogy and spirituality, I have woven into the fabric of my life the inspirations and insights that have come from teachers, elders, and sister travelers who also share this same passion. I have also made spiritual journeys in search of ancestral wisdom about how our ancestors revered the most ancient and primal deity—the Great Mother, also known by some as the Dark Mother. I have found myself propelled into finding answers to the questions: "Who is She?" and "What significance does She hold for all of humanity?" I realized that I have had a profound inquisitiveness about, and yearning for, the Dark Mother for a very long time while not really knowing it, because I had no language for this longing until the Goddess spirituality movement became a reality for many women. From vision quests on mountaintops, to using sacred hallucinogens, to studying numerous Goddess cultures from around the world and traveling to sacred sites, I have been on a long quest—one that has taken me to the heart of the Goddess.

In 1998, I went on pilgrimage to Malta, Egypt, and Crete on the trail of the African Dark Mother who was carried in the hearts and minds of very early peoples migrating from the African continent into other parts of the world. My longing for this communion with the Dark Mother was also further deepened when I attended a conference in San Francisco on the Goddess at the California Institute of Integral Studies, in the late 1990s, honoring the work of the late archaeomythologist and linguist Marija Gimbutas. There I met cultural historian Lucia Chiavola Birnbaum, whose work has focused on the origins of Goddess culture and spirituality originating in Africa, and the subsequent diaspora. I was enthralled with her research and could deeply understand her passion for educating people about the Dark Mother. Her wisdom ignited something deep within me. Perhaps it was more of an awakening—a remembrance bubbling up from my very cells. When Lucia planned a pilgrimage to Sardegna in May/June of 2004 to explore African migration paths and the Dark Mother, I jumped at the chance to travel with and learn from her.

I had been fascinated by astronomer Vera Rubin's discovery of dark matter (the word "matter" comes from "mater" or "mother"). Dark matter comprises about ninety percent of the matter in the universe (which I like to refer to as the "yoni-verse," as "uni" is a cognate of "yoni") and yet, is invisible. It is thought by astronomers and physicists that the gravity of dark matter shapes galaxies and holds them together. I had begun to think of this as metaphor and to consider what sacred meaning this metaphor might hold for humanity as a reflection of macrocosm in the microcosm. In other words, what is the correspondence between the Dark Mother of space and the Dark Mother in our human experience?

Lucia's work sheds light on this mystery. Her work cites research by noted geneticists revealing that African DNA is found in all races of people, and that humans—our species homo sapiens sapiens—originated in Africa. Her research has revealed that the worship of the Dark Mother followed African migrations after 60,000 BCE, first moving west into Asia and then spreading out across the rest of the world. From this evidence, supported by archeologists and other cultural historians, she boldly asserts that we are one race of people, originally African, and that we are all people of color!

Evidence of early African migration can be seen at the site of the oldest religious sanctuary in the world, Har Karkom, created in 40,000 BCE in the Sinai Peninsula, later known as Mt. Sinai. In Lucia Chiavola Birnbaum's seminal work, *dark mother: african origins and godmothers*, she notes that this ancient site is known as the geographic origination of Judaism, Christianity, and Islam.[1] Yet long before the emergence of these recent religions, in Paleolithic times, the site served as "an open air museum of a sacred place with altars, megaliths in alignment, and a cliff art record of peoples who have lived there."[2] Their religion was centered on a female divinity, which would have been African and black, millennia before the rise of patriarchy.

My interest in learning about the Dark Mother has grown like a glowing ember, fanned by the wisdom of people like Lucia Chiavola Birnbaum, who has inspired me to think of the implications of being originally African, and to find sacred meaning in the microcosmic experience of the Dark Mother. The first homo sapiens sapiens mother passed her mitochondrial DNA to her children and her daughters passed it to their children, and their daughters to their children. The mitochondria in DNA is the "powerhouse" of the cell—the organelle at the center of enzyme activity producing the storehouse of chemical energy, the power molecule ATP, or the vital power the cell needs to live. This mitochondrial DNA, shaped in the form of a double helix, is only passed by the mother. There is no corresponding genetic material which is passed from father to child. Therefore, the vital cellular energy of all people on the planet came from the first African homo sapiens sapiens mother—the original Dark Mother of our current human species. In *dark mother*, Lucia cites geneticist L. Luca Cavalli-Sforza who refers to the double helix as "the symbol of the evolution of the universe . . . the unlimited possibilities of becoming."[3]

In the word mitochondria, "mitos" means "thread." My own view is that this thread relates to the "superstring" in modern astrophysics theory, which asserts that subatomic phenomena are actually manifestations of vibrations of fundamental, one-dimensional strings. As emanations of consciousness in form, humans are connected to a primary source through our cellular threads. Just as dark matter (mother) in space shapes galaxies, and holds them together, we are shaped and held by the African Dark Mother who has given us Her life force, and resides in the very depths of our being, where the macrocosm is literally reflected in the microcosm—creating an unbroken, ecstatic, (I prefer to think of the constant creation in the yoniverse to be of an ecstatic nature rather than a violent one, as is so often assumed in the patriarchal scientific rhetoric), luminous, cosmic weaving connecting mother and daughter, which is really more of a cosmic dance of continuous, whirling motion. This original "matriarche," as I am calling it, is completely inseparable from the greater body/yoniverse/source and beyond. In my view, and in this context, the term "matriarche" differs from the term "matriarchy," which most commonly defines a social system of culture (though is no doubt based on the macrocosmic reality). Some common definitions of matriarchy include: "a family, group, or state governed by a matriarch," and "a system of social organization in which descent and inheritance are traced through the female line." [4] There are also feminist definitions, which I think are much more accurate, one of which is offered by philosopher, scholar, and director of the Matriarchal Studies School, Heide Gottner-Abendroth. Her comprehensive work on the subject, spanning some thirty years, redefines matriarchies more inclusively: "they are all gender-egalitarian societies, and many of them are fully egalitarian. This means they have no hierarchies, classes nor domination of one gender by the other."[5] While Gottner-Abendroth does include the spiritual in her redefined view of matriarchy, which is too extensive to fully discuss here, my use of the term "matriarche" is closer to the core meaning of the truest essence of what I am presenting as an expression of yoniversal spiritual Presence. "Matri" means "mother"[6] and "arche" means "the underlying source of the being of all things,"[7] so, taken together, "matriarche," for me, conveys "mother as the underlying source of the being of all things." *She* is the yoniversal primal reality from which all is birthed. Thus, She is everywhere.

I am also profoundly intrigued by the recent discoveries in astrophysics of dark energy and dark flow. With the discoveries of these dark phenomena in space, I see a reflection of the sacred trinity of the Goddess/Dark Mother of our ancestors—creation, preservation, dissolution—which was co-opted and twisted by the church, resulting in the patriarchal reversal known as the christian trinity. Dark energy is said to be responsible for accelerating the expansion of the yoniverse. Dark flow, the most recent discovery, is believed to be a kind of unseen force, pulling on us from perhaps another yoniverse outside of our own, over 14 billion light years away, which can be detected in a clear patterned direction displayed by certain galaxy formations. Here is the dark trinity—right there in astrophysics! From my perspective, dark matter, dark energy, and dark flow seem to be a part of something so great and truly mystical—a vast energy that gives birth to Herself. The "Mother Universe" theory of Princeton cosmologist J. Richard Gott suggests that we live in a multiverse that has always been here—a Mother universe that gives birth to daughter universes, eternally. This theory, as I see it, reflects the early parthenogenetic Goddess of Paleolithic ancestors—The Great Mother/Dark Mother. Dr. Gott says "The mother universe, which is sustained by energy from the quantum world, creates itself and makes the first matter in some way we will never be able to know."[8] Maybe our ancestors did know.

I am also equally intrigued by the recent acknowledgement by astrophysicists and cosmologists of the possible functions of black holes.

Though little is known about these mysterious beings, some theorists now consider them to be centrally responsible for the creation of galaxies, since most galaxies have one at their core—the Dark Mother is at the core of every galaxy giving birth from Her great womb/cauldron of stellar creation! And some theorists go so far to say that because of their enormous energies black holes could be responsible for creating "baby universes."[9]

The darkness clearly holds all possibilities. It is not something to be feared; rather, it is a mystery to be lived. Understanding the meaning of being held and shaped by the invisible Dark Mother can give us insight into the true nature of our being, and can help us remember what we have lost when we have strayed too far from Her embrace. I believe women are the original and primal species of our kind, giving birth, just as the yoniverse gives birth. We are held in this deep mystery, which I believe is intrinsically, unequivocally female at its core. She simultaneously rocks us in the cradle of chaos and order.

What Lucia and others are telling us is that, contrary to modern belief, human nature has not always been violent. No evidence of warfare or weaponry in the artifacts and iconography in these early civilizations has been found. The work of the late archaeomythologist Marija Gimbutas has shown the peaceful and creative nature of the early cultures of Neolithic Europe. In her monumental volumes, *Language of the Goddess* and *Civilization of the Goddess*, her discoveries about the peaceful and female-centered Goddess cultures are exquisitely detailed. Now, Lucia's work reveals the origins of European culture in a single source, the African Dark Mother, whose worship conveys peace, justice, and compassion. She inspired the creation of cultures of beauty and celebration on all continents. As the very early African rock carvings and paintings show, life was celebrated and enjoyed by our early ancestors.

Lucia's work demonstrates that at the heart of Goddess spirituality is the Dark Mother Herself—which is the living soil/soul of the Earth, the spinning matter/mother and mysterious unseen forces of the yoniverse, source of us all—peaceful and beautiful. It is my belief that, when we remember who we really are, and from whom we come, peace will once again reign as our birthright. When women are returned to our proper place of respect in the greater scheme of things, it will be very difficult to imagine a world full of violence, hatred, and war.

When women are loved, all life is loved, and from this organic flow, people will naturally revere life, as they did so many millennia ago. This lack of evidence of warfare and violence in the archeological evidence from many early cultures gives us new material to teach to our children. I think it is imperative that we teach them about the peaceful nature of early humans, as this will help change their entire orientation to life. In these very difficult times, we are witness to a collective desperate longing of our souls to come home. I see this desperation reflected in the violence our society perpetuates against women and children, and now, children against children—usually males against others. It is no wonder that our children, at this time, are experiencing a devastating despair and loneliness, fueled by an insatiable hunger for violence and destruction. The only culture they have known is founded on premises that promise equality for all—if you happen to be male and white.

This kind of arrogant exclusivity is taking a psychic toll on all of us, as well as the planet. Our so-called founding fathers modeled much of their constitution on the Iroquois Federation. However, I feel they left out the most important premise on which the Iroquois based their agreement—that the council of grandmothers and clan mothers was the governing body that determined who embodied the virtues of female wisdom enough to become chief—virtues of peace, compassion, and kindness! This council had the power to remove any chief who did not hold these values sacred. The Iroquois placed the highest authority into the hands of women—of wise grandmothers. To me, these grandmothers were the embodiment of the Dark Mother, and were respected as such. The Iroquois knew that human life comes through women, and so women must be revered in order for all life to thrive. We have forgotten this. And when people collectively forget this very basic truth, there is a high price to pay for their (our) amnesia. It is the wisdom of the grandmothers that needs to govern our lives once again. When the wisdom of the Dark Mother is denied, we spiral downward into a deep abyss of carelessness, confusion, violence, and a profound sense of separation from the living Earth as we witnessed with the 2010 oil catastrophe in the Gulf of Mexico. I feel it is imperative to bring to our children the truth about our real history—herstory—in order for them to find a positive life experience that allows them to look forward to growing into their wholeness.

In Malta and Gozo, I felt the presence of the African Mother in the fantastic megalithic temples—the first one constructed over 5000 years ago, and in the Hypogeum, a labrynthian-carved structure in the limestone earth some thirty feet deep, with curved and round, egg-shaped niches for burial. The Hypogeum felt to me like a large womb, once holding the remains of about 7000 people. There is evidence that a temple once stood on top of the ground, indicating that rituals of life and death, as well as perhaps healing, were all enacted in a sense of wholeness/holiness. The Maltese structures are the oldest free-standing structures in the world, pre-dating the pyramids by about 1000 years. The megalithic temples are built in the shape of a large-bodied woman, so that upon entrance, one enters the body of the Mother through her yoni/gate. They are "double temples," with two shapes of the female body, side-by-side, indicating perhaps, shared leadership, mother-daughter relationship, and/or lesbianism, and perhaps, even, the double helix.

The temple-builders were migrants out of Africa, apparently first arriving in Sicily. I was amazed at how some of the rock construction of these temples reminded me of the natural rock formations in Philae in southern Egypt surrounding the Temple of Isis, the black African Goddess. Was there a memory of these amazing rock formations in the minds and hearts of the Africans who migrated to Malta?

Philae in southern Egypt, home of the Temple of Isis, was, itself, a very popular pilgrimage site in the millennium preceding Jesus and continuing several centuries beyond his death. Isis was a female deity with origins in central Africa, or Nubia, and was known as a compassionate mother. In *dark mother*, Lucia cites the work of leading nubiologist and archeologist, William Y. Adams, who considers Isis worship to be "one of history's most important ideological transformations."[10] Adams further writes that Isis worship became "the first truly international and supra-national religion"[11] because pilgrims of all classes and nationalities, including Meriotes, Egyptians, Greeks, Romans, and desert nomads alike flocked to Her temple for healing and spiritual guidance. Isis veneration spread as far east as Afghanistan, to the Black Sea, as well as to what is now western Europe in Portugal and as far north as England. It is Her legacy that has been inherited by christianity as revealed in the icons of the Black Madonnas found all over Europe; Isis and Her son Horus suckling at Her breast are most likely the prototypes for Mary and Jesus.

The Dark Goddess of Africa is the same Dark Goddess of India and the Far East—all with different names, but with the same power. Kali is a well-known Goddess from India, though we often hear Her name associated with the aspect of destruction. She was actually the Dark Goddess of India in all Her aspects—creation, preservation and dissolution. Why is it that Her destructive aspect seems to be more visible in literature and in many myths than the others? It seems to me that associating the Goddess or Dark Mother only with destruction instills fear in people, and yet this is common. We have learned to fear Her power, the dark and death, with men in particular fueling this fear because of their own separation from the Dark Mother.

This separation is a result of the fear of the power of the Goddess that, for some reason, grew in men over time. The vast creative power of the Goddess, the Sacred Female, began to be taken as a threat by the male mind some 5000 years ago, and because of this fear, the need to "conquer" became the chosen acceptable heroic behavior for men in order for them to become "real men." To me, however, these men suffer from "PMS," or the Patriarchal Mind Set, which has only served to cause further separation and alienation of men from their source—the vast watery womb of the Dark Mother, who cannot be controlled.

The obsession to control and dominate has created a deep psychic split between mother and son, which is the only reason why rape exists. At the core of rape is a monstrously distorted compulsion to control, which comes from deep-seated feelings of being out of control, alone, and isolated from life and beauty. The projection of this fear of the Sacred Female onto women has created devastating destruction of the Earth and all her living children. The Dark Mother's message to us is that we must address this destruction—face the huge shadow that humans have created by denying Her. The shadow is all that has been split off and denied in our psyche, all that longs for attention and is, often, rarely seen. People act out what is in their shadow; often it is our children who carry the heavy burden of the unhealed collective wounding, with no idea of what it is that pains them so deeply in their tender psyches. Every day in the news, we see violent acts carried out by younger and younger people—mostly despairing boys and young men (though not all are young) whose souls ache from separation from the Mother.

In 1999, in Littleton, Colorado two desperate boys opened fire on students and teachers at Columbine High School, killing twelve students and one teacher before ending their own lives. Prior to that, in the Montreal Massacre in 1989, a twenty-five year old man, who claimed to be "fighting feminism," killed fourteen women at Ecole Polytechnique in Montreal, Quebec before taking his own life. And more recently, in China, there have been several horrific attacks by middle-aged men using meat cleavers and knives on beautiful little school children, killing sixteen children and one teacher before killing themselves. These heinous, unspeakably brutal crimes, which have become a cross-cultural, global phenomenon, would never happen in a culture where the Mother is revered. *Never.*

When a society idealizes and romanticizes war and violence, how do we expect our children will behave? We don't need scientists, sociologists, and psychologists to hypothesize about whether or not violent media affects our kids. How could it not affect the open bright minds of our children? Imagery is a powerful force—the root of "magic" is contained within it. We must be responsible for the magic we give to our children. If we give them glitzy Hollywood movies, such as *Star Wars*, then they will grow up thinking violence is a neat adventure—full of excitement and power. Most of these kinds of movies are imagined in the minds of men, from Walt Disney to George Lucas. The visions in the minds of women are very different indeed, as is evidenced by early woman-centered cultures, which were notably characterized by the organization of community around the mother-child bond, egalitarianism, peacefulness, and an absence of weaponry. As Lucia notes, "The harmony of ancient mother-centered civilization is shown in that in Paleolithic Africa there was no division between sacred and profane and no division of self and other—the mother and her nurture of all life were one."[12]

We often refer to the negative experiences in our life as "dark." As a sweat-lodge facilitator for women, I have learned that the dark is not a fearful place. In a sweat lodge, it is so dark inside that one cannot see one's hand in front of one's face. What I have come to experience sitting in this dark womb space is the incredible light that emerges from the deep dark—at times so bright, so luminous, that I couldn't tell that I was even sitting in the dark. I would like to offer that the dark is actually a nurturing place—just like the dark earth surrounding the tender seed, encouraging it, in full darkness, to sprout. If the seed is exposed to the light too soon, it will die. If the seed is not rooted in the dark, damp, rich soil, it will die. The darkness is necessary for life to take root! In that context, I would like to reclaim the dark, and refer to our negative experiences as something else—perhaps just "negative"—and let the dark emerge for us as the Dark Mother who holds us together and shapes us, just as a potter shapes her clay. The dark place of growth, Her womb, holds us and keeps us safe while providing us with nourishment.

Women carry the dark womb space within our bodies. To be in touch with our womb-wisdom is to know the wisdom of the Dark Mother. In my previously-mentioned journey to Egypt, I was led off-the-beaten path to the temple of Sekhmet, the fierce lion-headed goddess considered to be an aspect of Isis or the Goddess Hathor. Though Sekhmet's temple is not easily found, nor seems to be considered that important for tourists, for me She was an awesome treasure. I was not interested in the grandiose pharaonic temples. I found them imposing and suffocating. Carved in black granite, Sekhmet was a regal and daunting presence. She was truly a magnificent embodiment of the Dark Mother. A solar disc rested on top of Her head and She held in Her hands a staff topped by a lotus, which perhaps was symbolic of the sacred yoni and/or the psychotropic blue lotus. After quieting my mind, I sat quietly on the temple floor and simply allowed myself to feel Her energy. She felt strong, protective, fierce, and peaceful. I felt that if I embodied the energies She was representing, I would be in touch with my own deep female strength and power. The fact that She was black made me feel even more in touch with the dark womb of the Earth and cosmos.

Several weeks after I returned from my journey to Egypt, Malta, and Crete, I participated in a teaching-transmission of the Tibetan Black Dakini, who is seen as a black lion-headed goddess, Simhamukha. Although She is Tibetan, Her energy and Her attributes felt the same to me as those of Sekhmet—fierce and powerful. It was the same archetype. I was truly awestruck by the similarities between these two goddesses, and felt Lucia's work resonating in my heart. I could see the arms of the original African Dark Mother reaching out across the planet, embracing Her children and encouraging them to come close to Her—to come back home.

In these desperate times, we need the healing power of the Dark Mother who is not afraid to cut through the egoic structures/strictures of dualistic thinking with ruthless compassion. Women especially need Her image to help us shed the heavily imposed patriarchal layers of definition by a mind that does not really see us—a mind that is only interested in controlling us and making us "behave." This healing power is a primal transformative force emerging from the depths of women's wisdom, which is, as we now know, genetically passed on to all of us. Men need this image in order to face their fear of the feminine, which they have learned to hate and which they have internalized as the hatred of women and of themselves. With the Dark Mother by their side, men can allow themselves to go into their deep feelings and not be ashamed to bring forth those frozen tears that often turn to bullets or violent attack. They can once again reclaim their heritage of being the loving sons of the Mother who has shared Her womb and breast with them to give them life. No longer will they need to conquer and dominate. With the Dark Mother's embrace, all people will be able to once again live in Her bountiful peace, beauty and celebration. Without Her, we will perish.

With a deep and profound reverence for our ancestors, and to the foremothers that have literally given birth to all of us, I offer a prayer in closing:

In the spirit of peace, beauty, compassion, kindness and love, let Her wisdom once again guide us out of our own mind-made prisons of distortion so that we may once again feel Her exquisite embrace and gracefully move our feet in dance to the rhythm of Her beating heart and come to know within the blessing of Her ecstatic joy. BLESSED BE.

Notes

1   Lucia Chiavola Birnbaum, *dark mother: african origins and godmothers* (San Jose: Authors Choice Press, 2001), 45.

2   Ibid.

3   L. Luca Cavalli-Sforza, *History and Geography of Human Genes* (Princeton University Press, 1994), quoted in Lucia Chiavola Birnbaum *dark mother: african origins and godmothers*, (San Jose: Authors Choice Press, 2001), xxxvii.

4   *Merriam Webster*, "Matriarchy," www.merriam-webster.com/dictionary/matriarchy.

5   *International Academy HAGIA*, "Matriarchal Studies," www.hagia.de/de/matriarchy/matriarchal-studies.html.

6   *The Free Dictionary*, "Matri-," http://www.thefreedictionary.com/matri-.

7   Simon Blackburn, *The Oxford Dictionary of Philosophy* (Oxford University Press, 1994, 1996), 23. www.amazon.com/Oxford-Dictionary-Philosophy-Paperback Reference/dp/0192831348#reader_0192831348.

8   Roy Abraham Varghese, *The Wonder of the World*, www.thewonderoftheworld.com/Sections7-article83-page1.html.

9   Ibid.

10   William Y. Adams, *Nubia*, 338, quoted in Lucia Chiavola Birnbaum, *dark mother: african origins and godmothers* (San Jose: Authors Choice Press, 2001), 14.

11   Ibid.

12   Birnbaum, *dark mother*, 6.

Story, gifts, standpoint, and methodologies of feminist cultural history

Lucia Chiavola Birnbaum

A note on style: The formatting of this article reflects Lucia Chiavola Birnbaum's preference for downcasing, a decision based on her dislike for capitalization, which, as an historian, she views as a custom that perpetuates the hierarchy of nation states and dominant cultures in the modern era. In that regard, typically proper nouns are capitalized and words that are used as adjectives are written in lower case.

Author's Note: *In January 2011, I thought about the most appropriate article I could offer to this volume of the continuing anthology I helped to found . . . She is Everywhere! In May 2011, I transitioned from teaching in the Women's Spirituality program at California Institute of Integral Studies (CIIS) to another phase of my life in which research and writing become my uppermost concerns. The following is chapter one of my manuscript (on its way to french and italian publishers):* the future has an ancient heart: african legacy of caring and sharing on world migration paths: case of the mediterranean.

This first chapter of the future has an ancient heart *follows a prologue wherein I point out that, perhaps, the most significant variables in my work as a feminist cultural historian are two liminal experiences. The first was in 1970, outside Palermo in my ancestral maternal region of the Mediterranean, wherein I viewed the mountain at Erice as a pregnant and sleeping woman covered by a mantle of african dark wheat and red poppies. I learned later that dark wheat connoted african Isis and red poppies referred to semitic Astarte. In 1988, during easter week in Trapani, on the west coast of Sicily on a major primordial path out of Africa, I was deeply moved watching the procession of the black madonna, followed by a dream vision of my mother as a black madonna, and a few days later learning that my sicilian american mother was dying.*

I am accustomed to introducing myself at academic conferences by saying I am a sicilian-american woman who received the doctorate in the cultural history of the United States and Europe at the University of California, Berkeley in 1964, who today sees her work as a feminist cultural historian as not only dismantling untrue assumptions of the West but offering historical knowledge to sustain the work of ending wars and other violence. In my view, telling the truth is healing.

Interested in origins, I consider feminist cultural history to be the story of human beings starting with *homo sapiens sapiens* 100,000 BCE in Africa and their first communities of caring and sharing in South and Central Africa in which women were spiritual centers of the family and first human communities, a legacy transmitted by african migrants—women and children, men—who reached every continent by 70,000 BCE. "Civilization" today is being reconsidered by biologists, and others, to encompass animal studies, as well as human sources not dependent on the written word.

My book, *the future has an ancient heart* is grounded in the books I have written and the research I have conducted since 2001 when my *dark mother: african origins and godmothers* was published ... continuing to track the african legacy of caring, sharing, and (later) healing in the DNA, as well as in rock art, rituals, stories, and icons on african migration paths around the world. My research after 2001 has focused specifically on on-site research in the mediterranean region, with cases in point: islands of the mediterranean Sicily and Sardinia and areas of the african mediterranean regions later called Italy, France, and Spain.

The form of *the future has an ancient heart* has been shaped by the spiral theory of history. I have taken steps backward into what has, inaccurately, been called "prehistory" as well as into my personal story, to amplify the large story since the beginning of human civilization. Steps backward, in my case, are also suggested by negative periods in my own story, e.g., the many rejections at the end of the 1990s of my manuscript *dark mother, african origins and godmothers* by white male editors in the United States, including two cases of acceptance by women editors at university presses subsequently reversed by white male editors. This was not a matter of competence since, in the period at hand, I had published in the United States and internationally. The continuing experience of two steps backward, which interpolates my "successes," has always been accompanied by emotional depression, meditation, and many questions that have stimulated this book.

Ethnicity, deeper indebtedness, and standpoint of a feminist cultural historian

A sicilian-american feminist cultural historian with a Ph.D., my many stays in Europe, travel across the world, intercultural research in the United States, and elsewhere, and first-hand research in the Mediterranean have accompanied an underlying desire to reach the shores of my ancient and contemporary african-sicilian grandmothers/foremothers and their beliefs.

Let me count my gifts (academically called acknowledgments) along this journey. Major spurs to my research have been italian feminists, notably Simona Mafai of Sicily and her values. A grandmother, she put her political career on the line when she successfully carried the bill legalizing abortion through parliament in the late 1970s in catholic and communist Italy. In the 1980s, she, and other italian feminists, transformed both communism and catholicism, in the first case, placing into the protocols of the italian communist party that religious and spiritual beliefs are prior to political beliefs, and that the way to socialism is non-violent. A founder of Rifondazione Comunista, the communist party of Italy today does not aim to win elections . . . but to be a party of opinion educating the electorate about principles of justice and equality without the divisive wedge issues that have kept the italian parliament in paralysis for more than a decade. In the case of catholicism, putting divisive issues like abortion to one side, this enables catholic and communist women to work together on projects to promote human well-being. This last has also made Italy a powerful secular voice against war and the death penalty.

My research with italian feminists in the 1970s and 1980s has enabled me to see U. S. feminists more clearly. U. S. feminists, largely from northern Europe who identify with the "West" and, implicitly, with whiteness, have been impressed by Marija Gimbutas, lithuanian archeologist, whose large trove of archeomythological evidence for Old Europe confirms that woman divinities preceded, by eons, icons and images of male divinities. Gimbutas' findings relate to "Old Europe" and to a eurocentrism now

52

being challenged by more holistic views of women from, or who identify with, the south of the world and who relate origins of feminism to women-centered societies in paleolithic Africa and/or the "south" of the world. In my case, this means working with women in Africa, who today have retrieved the world torch for justice, equality, and peace.

Concurrently, I am deeply indebted to Genevieve Vaughan, feminist of Texas and Rome, whose concept of the gift economy modeled on mothering coincides with african genetic and cultural history. Gen, who has given away a family oil fortune encouraging feminists of the south of the world, is an authentic woman who sleeps on floors in the budget sections of airports. I am also indebted to Heide Gottner-Abendroth, feminist of Germany who works with Gen Vaughan in a world network of feminists researching "matriarchies." For Heide, matriarchy means mothers in the beginning and mother-centered cultures as the way to societies of equality.

Feminists of Italy after 1968 cooked a combustible mixture of unedited marxism and unedited judeo-christian beliefs, into which they later have added asian buddhist and hindu beliefs, producing an ancient/anarchist perspective of a world "without bosses and without wars." Feminists in other countries of Europe, supported by a viable left with strong labor unions and many left parties, live in an environment of social democracy which seems not to have bruised contemporary european feminists as badly as they have been hurt elsewhere, e.g., in the United States where the environment and democratic rhetoric in a society where domestic inequality has worsened and an unacknowledged U.S. empire has sprung up, negating the founding principles of "liberty and justice for all," not to speak of human rights.

Feminists of the non-westernized world seem to be energized by more awareness of the ancient and indigenous stories of humans and, today, are willing to challenge the privileges and myopias of western feminists; yet, for the most part, they are willing to recognize that feminists of the West are impelled by good will. The willingness to work together—and the creativity of women of both the south and the north of the world—have become apparent to me in world conferences.

My particular angle of vision, extensive research in Italy, and participation in international conferences, may have given me a comparative view of my own country, and its women's movement in particular. After a period of intense research after 1969 looking for my sicilian grandmothers and finding them in Africa, accompanied by the hope of the european anti-war movement, my return sojourns to the United States reminded me that whatever my origins and cosmopolitan identifications, I am a citizen of the United States, where our children, grandchildren, and great grandchildren live. And this is the place I need, not only to study the world, but to change it.

Trying to map out where I have been since the 1990s, lighthouses in choppy waters have been personified in Elinor Gadon, cultural historian of women's art and founder of the Women's Spirituality program at California Institute of Integral Studies in San Francisco, who first invited me to teach in the program. Joseph Subbiondo, president of CIIS, who has navigated the cutting edge graduate university to flagship status in higher education, has been a figure of strength and encouragement in this often-chaotic time of transition. Judith Wexler, academic vice president of CIIS, initiated a Faculty Research Committee, in which I have participated for a decade, helping me clarify my own methodologies, learning in this committee to make the "implicit explicit."

Joseph Subbiondo and Mara Keller, then director of the women's spirituality program, launched my controversial book, *dark mother: african origins and godmothers* (San Jose, New York, Shanghai, iUniverse, 2001) in the spring of 2002 with a feminist art exhibit. That same year, *dark mother* received from Serpentina, independent feminist network of the San Francisco bay area founded by Judy Grahn and Dianne Jenett, the Enheduanna Award for excellence in Women Centered Literature.

In 2003, I was given a Founding Mother award by the Women's Spirituality program of CIIS "for ... visionary co-creation of the Women's Spirituality M.A. and Ph.D. programs at CIIS, the first Women's Spirituality M.A. and Ph.D. programs in the world." Alice Walker, contemporary great african-american mother of world literature, hailed my research and *dark mother* in a large public gathering, thanking me for "showing us Her signs . . . you are doing the work that truly turns the tide."

Other gifts, acknowledged in previous books and in the prologue of *the future has an ancient heart* were from Luca Cavalli-Sforza, perhaps the greatest geneticist alive, who confirmed in the DNA that africans reached all continents after 50,000 BCE (updated by his student Spencer Wells to 70,000 BCE). Luca has encouraged my research in feminist cultural history, calling it "courageous."

Later, particularly after studying the french Annales school of historians, I have come to see my work as part of the cultural historian's task to recognize the *"the long endurance of beliefs."* This last premise was earlier stimulated by my study of psychology for the outside field for the doctorate in cultural history at U. C. Berkeley (one independent studies project in psychology was "a history of the soul") as well as personal study of depth psychology in the writings of Sigmund Freud and Carl Jung and, later, the work of african theorists Frantz Fanon, Cesaire Aimee, Cheikh Anta Diop, and Bernadette Muthien.

Molefi Asante, father of afrocentrism, who early supported my work, introduced me to Salomon Mezepo, major african publisher in Paris, who has published and distributed my work in Africa and the Caribbean. Asante and Mezepo are major african-american and african theorists who have supported my controversial research, which like theirs erodes racism, sexism, homophobia, and other forms of violent ignorance, with the truthful story of humans.

As a woman scholar who is aware that women have largely been left out of (and have rarely written) cultural history, I have been inspired by many significant women theorists, especially Mary Daly, Barbara Mann, Luisah Teish, and Arisika Razak who have rescued women from the distortions of dominant western male history. Alice Walker is the towering african-american feminist who has encouraged a generation of world feminists to tell and write truthful history, while witnessing, as public intellectuals, to the world's injustices. Always taking the ethnic story and culture into account, Alice Walker never allows ethnic affiliation to descend into othering.

My work of african origins and legacy has coincided with that of male scholars whose scholarship subverts the dominant paradigm of western violent white male supremacy. This is exemplified by my encounter with Emmanuel Anati. On one of many research trips to Italy, I rang his door bell at the Centro Camuno di Studi Preistorici at Capo di Ponte, in Italy near Brescia. Jungian world expert in prehistory studies, and jewish in heritage, Anati wrote a major early work on the ancient common story of Palestine and Israel. Anati has independently confirmed, in rock art, Cavalli-Sforza's genetics documentation of african migration paths throughout the world, notably the first sanctuary in the world at Mt. Sinai, 40,000 BCE, the founding place of judaism, christianity, and islam. (See Anati, *Museo Immaginario*). Early on, he asked me to present papers on my research of signs of african mothers (pubic V, color ochre red, menhirs, and dolmens) to the Centro Camuno's annual international conferences on prehistory. Centro Camuno launched the italian edition of *dark mother*, published as *La madre o-scura* in 2004 by the italian feminist press, Media Mediterranea, in Cosenza, Italia. The publisher of this press, Nadia Gambilungo, a slav-italian, wrote a moving preface on everyone's ultimate african mothers and the significance of mothering. Rose Romano, Italian-american exmatriate to Italy, deepened *La madre o-scura* with her insights as a lesbian mother.

African-american educators (many women, notably Dr. Pat Adelekan and Ida Dunson) and afrocentrist male scholars, especially Molefi Asante, welcomed my work in the period when white male editors were rejecting my *dark mother*. Most white feminists, fighting off their own slings and arrows for challenging white male supremacy, met the book with silence; most well-meaning feminist friends, bruised by their own battles for recognition in academic and other patriarchal structures, early counseled me not to tilt at fortified windmills.

After *dark mother: african origins and godmothers* was published late in 2001, Molefi Asante called me from Europe to invite me to present a paper to his annual conference in Philadelphia in homage to Cheikh Anta Diop, major african theorist who, after world war two called for a true history of Africa . . . and thereby, a true history of the world. In subsequent participation in afrocentrist conferences of Asante's Ankh Institute in Philadelphia, I learned about the work of a generation of african/american scholars excavating the truthful history of the world that begins in Africa. Asante and the Ankh Institute (whose name suggests his acknowledgment of the significance of women in the world story) have awarded me certificates of scholarly advancement, as well as personal support: "Your work on the African origins of homo sapiens sapiens, that is, the genetic origin of modern humans in South and Central Africa, particularly . . . the aniconic signs of veneration of the African dark mother, is exciting research."

Salomon Mezepo, whose Editions Menaibuc in Paris is the major african publisher in Europe, contacted Maurice Akingeneye, a young frenchman (who is active in the recent renaissance of french/africans, identifies with his african roots, and works helping the children of war-torn Rwanda) to translate *La Mere Noire*, which Maurice did with deep understanding. Salomon Mezepo invited me to yearly conferences in Paris sponsored by Editions Menaibuc, a press that dubbed me Scribe Royal of Kamit in 2006. In 2007, Editions Menaibuc published my *dark mother* as *La Mere Noire* and gave me an award in 2008: "Grande Protectrice des Nations Negres . . . *pour son engagement e son travail en rue de La Renaissance Kamite* . . . ." Menaibuc is publishing my newest book. *The future has an ancient heart*, in a french edition with distribution in Africa and the Caribbean.

A mother-centered and Africa-centered feminist cultural historian

After 2003, I was alternately lifted to world recognition and sometimes bruised in the United States by U.S. feminists in an environment of mounting anxiety at worsening world conditions, fewer financial resources, and the need to protect some hegemonic beliefs. In this environment, I sought to figure out my own self-definition. I may be considered a sicilian-american feminist cultural historian educated in western white male schooling who was awakened by african theorists and the african-american civil rights movement in the early 1960s to the necessity, and possibilities, inherent in sweeping away the omissions and deceptions of conventional dominant history, to research the true history of the world . . . . and to change it. I have tracked my sicilian great grandmothers to Africa and am drawn to the possibility that everyone may take hope in the legacy of african mothers who carried values of caring, sharing, healing, as well as great art, to all continents of the world by 70,000 BCE and, subsequently, carried this hopeful legacy to the present in cells, story, art, healing, and ritual. This large story is today being written by many scholars . . . that often foreground the african and african/american gift of music to the world. Here, I need to honor Bill Barlow, white student revolutionary in the work for ethnic justice and world peace, at San Francisco State in the 1960s. Bill, subsequently professor at Howard University, and a great scholar of african-american music, was felled by a stroke, a casualty of the ongoing struggle.

I owe a very large, and continuing, debt to every student who has crossed my path. I have acknowledged this debt in previous writings as well as in the text of my book, *the future has an ancient heart*. Here, I note only those in my immediate foreground in 2011: doctoral students, In Hui Lee, Pairin Jotisakularatana, Mary Beth Moser, Laura Truxler, Annette Williams, Marion Dumont, and Damaur Quander; as well as gatherers of the published volumes of *She Is Everywhere!* Josephine MacMillan, Kalli Halvorson, and Laura Amazzone . . . Karen Villanueva and Annette

Williams . . . Mary Saracino and Mary Beth Moser; and the gatherers of future volumes of *She is Everywhere!* Laura Truxler, Sara Salazar, Vivian Deziak, May Elawar, Marilyn Nebolsky, In Hui Lee, and Randy Conner.

Faculty colleagues at CIIS have created a unique environment of freedom to differ and creativity. In my foreground, in addition to Joseph Subbiondo and Judith Wexler, are Constance Jones, Richard Shapiro and Angana Chatterji, Mtumbo Mpanya, Ian Grand, Matthew Bronson, Jim Ryan, and Steve Goodman. Charlene Spretnak advised me that every Balkan capitol has a black madonna. Mara Keller gave me african violets and said that her grandmother grew them. Arisika Razak, in a Women's Spirituality workshop, commissioned african dancers who celebrated me.

Caring and sharing

Caring and sharing were characteristic of first human settlements, notably of the KhoeSan after 100,000 BCE in south and central Africa, a legacy that is documented in the master's thesis of south african feminist Bernadette Muthien, herself a descendant of the KhoeSan, as is world statesman Nelson Mandela. I came to know Bernadette as part of the Gift Economy delegation to the 2007 World Social Forum in Nairobi, Africa and at subsequent international conferences on the Gift Economy. Her grace and determination to tell the truth are stunning, as is her ease in welcoming feminists of the west when these privileged women are able to see their own campaigns in the truthful context of the world story.

Cultural history of caring, sharing, healing on african migration paths

The pattern of african migrations out of south Africa, confirmed by Cavalli-Sforza in the DNA, has been augmented by Spencer Wells, pushing african migrations back to 70,000-60,000 BCE, tracking the Y chromosome of the DNA (see Wells' video, *Journey of Man*), tracing the journey of african migrants out of Africa to west Asia and far Asia, a migration that turned back into Europe after 40,000-35,000 BCE. This last datum has been interpreted by Cavalli-Sforza as the predominantly asian inheritance of europeans. This asian origin is confirmed by the very early migration of africans into west Asia and the indian subcontinent, around the littoral of India and, thence, into the Pacific and islands of Oceania, reaching Australia. On the northern route, african migrants walked into far Asia, crossed the Bering Straits, and migrated down through north and south America. (See L. Luca Cavalli-Sforza's map in *dark mother*, see Spencer Wells' map of the Y chromosome in the DNA in his book and video, *Journey of Man)*. The Bering Straits view is contested by Native Americans Vine de Loria and Barbara Mann, who hold primary their own community's creation myths, as do some israelis, as well as many protestant fundamentalists of the United States. In any event, contemporary archeological research is demonstrating african presence in the new world a long time before the Bering Sea crossing.

Biography and the long endurance of beliefs

My recent scholarship may be regarded as that of a feminist historian, who without institutional affiliation after San Francisco State fired me in 1969 for joining students in demanding a black studies department, as well as for activism with millions of others in the world who opposed the U. S. imperial war in Vietnam, has been trying to work out methodologies of feminist cultural history for myself. This perspective was influenced by my childhood and youth in a sicilian-american family in Kansas City, Missouri, by refugee jewish professors at the University of Kansas City, by a spiritual search first shocked into awareness by the 1945 images of the jews killed or starved during the holocaust and by horrific images of japanese killed or burned by the atomic bomb dropped by the U.S. In the late 1940s, I was drawn to Gandhi's non-violent political struggle for the liberation of India.

Meeting my life partner, Wally, at the end of world war two has had an incalculable effect on my scholarship, which he has always supported. Of conservative jewish heritage, Wally's beliefs are those of an agnostic scientist, a physicist. Our mutual realization that his jewish grandmothers and my catholic grandmothers were very similar has been confirmed in recent scholarship, notably that of christian thealogian, Elisabeth Schussler Fiorenza, that christianity may best be understood as a reform movement within judaism. Daniel Boyarin has carefully researched this tangled story.

In the early 1960s, my spiritual itinerary was punctuated by the african-american civil rights movement when we helped to found the Peace and Freedom party allied with the Black Panthers of Oakland who provided breakfast to black children while asserting black power. After I was fired at S. F. State at the end of the 1960s, I went to Italy in search of my grandmothers . . . while my own country descended into assassinations of black leaders Malcolm X and Martin Luther King, Jr . . . . and leaders thought to threaten the military-industrial complex, John and Robert Kennedy.

In Italy, studying the ancient geography of the mediterranean sea, I learned that my ancestral island of Sicily was part of the continent of africa up until the time the ice melted (ca. 10,000 BCE) leaving the narrow strait of water, the Canal of Sicily, that today separates my ancestral island (and paternal birthplace at Ragusa Ibla) from the continent of Africa. The point I am making is that Sicily was a part of the african continent until 10,000 BCE and, thereafter, a major hub of everyone who crossed the mediterranean, coming out of, or returning, to Africa. (See the chapter on the Strait of Sicily in *the future has an ancient heart*). First sea migrations out of Africa reached Sicily and /Sardinia. Italy cannot be understood without taking into account that its first inhabitants were Africans. All of Europe and of Asia, similarly, cannot be understood without acknowledging first migrations of africans who became ancestral tribes . . . from the celts to the saami to the semites . . . and return migrations of semites, and others, to Africa.

My recent research focus has been on primordial and continuing direct and return migrations out of Africa to mediterranean islands and regions of south Europe where I have a genetic-biographical connection. My book information was deepened by research on-site (often with students) on the islands of Sardinia, Sicily, and Malta, where the archeological and cultural research of Willow LaMonte has been path-breaking and Jennifer Berezan's deeply moving music is unforgettable.

Mediterranean islands and regions, regions primordially reached by african migrants into the region later called Asia and Europe, is a very large subject encompassing Palestine and Israel to Cyprus and what we call today the "Middle East." In *the future has an ancient heart* I have limited my purview to *close analysis of conferences in which I have participated* in the region of the Mediterranean, where I have done on-site research, as well as relevant conferences in the United States, notably feminist, afrocentrist and italian-american gatherings.

For revisiting my italian roots, I have learned from the insights of Chickie Farella, Louisa Calio, Fred Gardaphe, and Gian Banchero, on-site learning with Sandy Miranda and Mary Beth Moser in Sardinia, with on-site learning in Sicily with Mary Saracino, who later wrote a novel on Ibla whose tongue had been cut out. Among the sequellae of my many research trips to Italy is my contemporary burning desire to uncover the largely suppressed muslim story of Italy

For the convergence of my views with contemporary afrocentrist scholarship, see above and see the 2007 Ankh conference on "Classical Africa: Foundations for Postmodern and Post-Western Renewal." My work also converges with cutting edge asian comparative studies, a field that has attracted my students, as well as latin american studies, a region just now being reinterpreted from indigenous sources.

My theme of the significance of primordial african migrations into the region called Europe, has large implications not only for Europeans—who consider Europe their "white" continent—but for descendants of europeans in the United States, many of whom (not all) perpetuate the socially-constructed notion of whiteness, a subject touched on in this volume of *the future has an ancient heart*, and pursued in-depth in research for volume two of *the future has an ancient heart*.

My ultimately close african origin (as well as the ultimately african origin of everybody) has been substantiated in archeology, genetics, geography, and cultural historical research, and recently in biological research on my blood type: african "O" as well as Rh-negative blood type. This blood type is characteristic of african enclaves in Europe, e.g., Sicily, Italy, and the basque country of Spain and France, where african beliefs of caring, sharing and healing (also great art) were early brought by african migrants, life-sustaining beliefs that have endured to the present, offering hope in a bleak time.

Today it seems crucial to me, in what appears, in the west, to be a suicidal thrust of dominant anxious elites toward the extinction of the planet and its inhabitants, that we realize there are other ways to live . . . that everyone on Earth has a genetic as well as a subaltern legacy of caring, sharing, healing, ultimately from everyone's african mothers who gave the gift of life to everyone and transmitted this knowledge over the centuries not only in genetic predisposition but in rock art, story, myth, ritual, icons, and many other ways of knowing.

For the culture of the Mediterranean, where all of my grandparents as far back as I can track, and my father were born, I am indebted to the french Annales school of historians who emphasize not boundaries of modern nation states, but regions of the Earth whose creation is ancient. For the larger sicilian region of the Two Sicilies, comprising Apulia, I am indebted to Giuseppe Goffreddo who invited me a few years ago to participate in a seminar entitled, *the Mediterranean—"shores of god the mother."* The poster of this conference suggests the African-mediterranean mother's body as half bird, half snake; the poster has been mounted above my desk at California Institute of Integral Studies, another is in our home in Berkeley, and another is the cover of my book, *the future has an ancient heart.*

Research strategy—cultural history grounded on science and other ways of knowing

Deepening my earlier study of U. S. and European cultural history with particular study of the cultural history of Italy, then of Africa, then of the region of the Mediterranean, my particular study combines science, on-site research, and major indebtedness to Antonio Gramsci, italian marxist who pointed out that beliefs of subaltern cultures differ from beliefs of dominant cultures. Subaltern refers to the disinherited or lower classes, and, in my view, to all those subordinated and humiliated, including women.

My own education has been multi-disciplinary and intercultural which has helped me appreciate the significance of a variety of ways of knowing, notably genealogy, ethnic history, the social sciences as well as the humanities. I regard history as both in the humanities and informed by the empirical methodologies of social science, biography, and the myriad ways of knowing—some of them considered heretical (e.g., astrology)—of our grandparents. This last has led me to the open-ended subject of heretics—who dance in the margins of all my work.

Beyond The Symbol, VIII

Tricia Grame

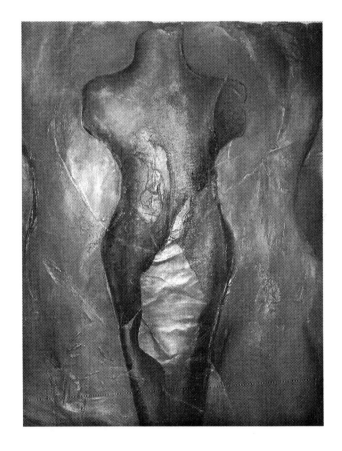

Original artwork, 50" x 38", acrylic, mixed media on paper;
© 2009 Tricia Grame; Photo by Tricia Grame

Isis

Tricia Grame

Original artwork, 54" x 54", acrylic on canvas;
© 2010 Tricia Grame; Photo by Tricia Grame

The Interconnectedness of All Being: A New Spirituality for a New Civilization

Claudia von Werlhof

When I had become an activist against globalization in 1998, a colleague of mine told me that if I was going to try to fight globalization I was only going to make a fool out of myself. I was very surprised. I did not understand. He said: "You cannot fight the multinationals. Trying to do that is absurd. You cannot actually achieve anything struggling against these people".

Shortly after this conversation, however, the MAI treaty—the Multilateral Agreement on Investment of the OECD-WTO—did not get signed because of the emergence of a huge worldwide anti-globalization movement in 1998 which caused the French government to withdraw from the treaty (Mies, Werlhof 2003). In the meantime even the WTO itself has been at the brink of failing, too, because the worldwide movement succeeded twice in blocking its summits (Seattle, Cancún). The next step was the struggle against GATS, the General Agreement on Trade in Services, of the WTO which is still on the table (Barlow 2001).

What seems undeniable is that the paradoxical politics of *profitable destruction* (Chossudovsky 1996) that these treaties are an expression of have by now produced their own boomerang, in other words: the consequences of the destruction are coming back to haunt us, as shown, for example, by the various natural disasters we have recently been witnessing. At this point it will not suffice to think about what to do in the future, once everything has collapsed and vanished. We need to think about how to oppose the destruction that is happening here and today.

There is no alternative to the search for an alternative. We need a vision of what to do now and how to do it.

In this context, Renate Genth (2002) says that we need a new "politics of civilization", since we are experiencing a "civilization crisis". This new politics of civilization has to focus on a new relationship to nature, a new relationship between the sexes, a new relationship between the generations, and a new relationship to "the transcendent". The transcendent generally means religious needs and our relationship to death. I would say that the relationship to the transcendent is the relationship to *earth spirituality*.

The goals of this new politics of civilization, according to Genth, are based on the "five political senses", the sense for community, the sense for justice, the sense for equality (as in: material equality—not spiritual or emotional equality), the sense for freedom, and the sense for responsibility. This implies that diversity is possible—yet there exists a common base.

From this point of view each living being is born free and equal by nature. The first "natural right" is defined as the old mother right that is based on the understanding that everything that has come to life has an innate right to live. Mutual respect is the foundation of all. Society always has to be accountable for what it does.

But, how do we get there? And what all is in our way?

As dreadful as globalization is, it is at least making clear what is actually happening. It seems to have become impossible to ignore what is at stake here. It is now more obvious than ever. Still, next to deep-rooted concepts like Genth's, we hear suggestions about trying to help "shaping" globalization rather than opposing it. Me, however, I am an uncompromising opponent to globalization because what is happening under its banner can never be reconciled with a notion of a world of justice, freedom or equality. That is why I regard the somewhat pretentious notion of "participation in shaping the course of globalization" (Attac) as inappropriate. This notion will lead and has already led to a split in the anti-globalization movement.

What we need is truly radical opposition, meaning: an opposition that targets the roots of the problem and embarks on a fundamentally different path of thinking and feeling. Which leads me again to my main question: How will this be possible?

As long as we keep on believing that our civilization, and what it has brought to us, is in any way superior to other civilizations, or that our culture is in any way superior to other cultures (past or present), as long as we keep on believing this—and many people generally critical of globalization still do—we cannot find common ground. We have to realize that we are indeed facing a crisis of western civilization and that this concerns not only capitalism and modernity, but the entire patriarchal endeavour—in other words: the socio-political order with which the whole problem began (Werlhof 2007).

Since I have been actively involved in the anti-globalization movement for some time now, the search for the "what to do?" equalled a personal crisis that was not bereft of pain. What is, in fact, the key to an effective movement against this global madness?

I have been part of many movements, and already in the 1970s, some feminist friends and I developed the "subsistence perspective" through our own experiences in the periphery, where people had already been reflecting on the unsatisfying state of the world—or the part of the world they live in—for decades (Mies, Bennholdt-Thomsen, Werlhof 1988, Bennholdt-Thomsen, Mies 1999). The subsistence perspective means a notion of community that is based on local involvement and engagement, and a related notion of an economy that is based on the forces (both materially and non-materially) and natural potentials of a specific place without trying to exploit them. Meanwhile, different terms have been coined to describe this perspective: Helena Norberg-Hodge calls it "localization", Vandana Shiva speaks of a "living democracy", and people in Porto Alegre (where the worldwide anti-globalization movement began to gather annually as the "World Social Forum") speak of an "economy of solidarity" (Bennholdt-Thomsen, Faraclas, Werlhof 2001).

There is also the term "sustainability", but this term remains within the logic of the system. It does not fully recognize that we really do need a different form of civilization, not just an economic reform. We need a different culture, because *cultura* means nurturing. The question always is, of course, what are we nurturing? Right now, we nurture machines rather than community. We nurture violence rather than love. This renders our culture useless. It needs to be changed (which, of course, does not exclude saving certain aspects we might recognize as useful).

We need far-reaching, global, perhaps even further-extending notions and terms that are tied into a way of thinking, acting and feeling that is able to confront globalization with the possibility of success. Yet, success ought not to be *expected*, since this would instantly lead us back into a modern, rationalizing, calculating way of thought. When it comes to calculation, we are inferior to "them". In the same vein, we cannot *"participate"* in anything. The gender movement is wrong in the assumption that women's future is determined by the logics of becoming sex-less, male or patriarchal. Under conditions of globalization such theories have all become irrelevant and lead nowhere. Christina von Braun (2000), for example, says that there is no possibility for transformation at all anymore because she assumes that we have already been so alienated from ourselves by patriarchal conditioning that is has become impossible to return (or progress) to non-patriarchal forms of community. This kind of pessimism is also prevalent in the gender movement, and translates into the quasi-optimistic notion that we can at least still go somewhere *within* the system of capitalist patriarchy. It is always this *failure to leave* the confines of the system that divides all social movements. In other words, making compromises with the system by taking it for granted will always lead us back into it.

In patriarchy, everything is separated: the material from the spiritual, men from women, the lower from the higher, etc. This becomes expressed, on the one hand, in the form of a materialism that regards matter as spiritless, and, on the other hand, in the form of an idealism that regards matter as not important. When comparing to this the notion of *subsistence* I realized that the reason why so many people still do not understand subsistence must also lie in the fact that we, who propose subsistence as an alternative, have forgotten something or have not thought it all the way through. That is exactly the point.

What needs to happen is that our notion of subsistence which is materialistic in the sense of focusing on what materially shapes our existence, has to be explicitly complemented—not by idealism, but by an explanation of how the material relates to the non-material, to mind and soul, to the spiritual. In other words: we also have to explain mind and soul, the spiritual, through our notion of subsistence. The connections exist anyway—the separation is always but a fictitious and imagined one. All things are connected. This has to be made explicit. This is why I speak of "earth spirituality".

As a next step, I concluded that it is not enough to call for a relationship to nature that is simply not antagonistic anymore but caring, or that is also spiritual and not only material, etc. It is also not enough to say that we want to "co-operate" with nature or that we want to "be part of a network". These are all *"cold"* terms. They are rationalistic terms that always miss something. When we speak of co-operation we have a guideline for action—since co-operating means acting with—but we do not address any emotional or spiritual dimension. The biggest problem with rationalism is that it tries to extinguish our feelings, or tries to turn them into their opposites: for example, love into hate. I believe this is the main problem of our rationalistic society. The problem is amplified by the history of National Socialism that has abused our feelings violently and still leaves the question: how can we rehabilitate our emotions without arousing suspicion of becoming susceptible to a new form of Nazism or fascism?

But we cannot shun the problem because as humans we are sentient beings. If we do not feel, we cannot think. Thinking and acting and feeling are intrinsically linked. In our society, we have separated the three. We think differently to how we feel and act. Native Americans know the term K'OP—a term that expresses the understanding that acting, thinking and feeling belong together and correspond. We have lost this understanding through the permanent processes of separation.

I then reflected on *"wilderness"*. What is wilderness? I have always been looking for a term to substitute "nature" with. The term "nature" has been abused and become abstract. I realized, while reflecting on wilderness as the original and first expression of nature, that we need a notion of a "spirituality" that is linked to the wild!

Basically, spirituality is a notion that is always related to wild nature, and that does not see nature as exclusively material, but also as mind and soul—we could also say: as *alive*. Spirituality is embedded in the vitality of nature. This is my notion of spirituality, hence "earth spirituality".

But, how can we express this without championing just another "cold" term on the one hand, or, on the other, without reproducing a notion of spirituality that is purely idealistic and knows of no relationship to matter, leave alone of political reflection and activism?

Eventually, I did find the answer.

We need a term that is not just cold, but that expresses the *affection* that is inherent in life. The term is: *"interconnectedness of all being"*! This has become my central term in the search for what it actually is that we need to be based on in order to confront the madness of globalization and to get a sense for where to actually go.

When I speak of the interconnectedness of all being, I am not only talking about connectedness as an opposition to separation, but about intrinsic links between everything there is. Everything is tied together;

everything is connected with each other. We are not in the world as human beings alone.

Systems of ethics do not suffice to explain what that means, however. They mostly negate the relationship to nature (Jonas 1979). Religion does not work as a term either, because it does not want to reconnect us with the wild and is based on the separation that has occurred.

My point is: There is no separation—it is purely fictitious. That is how I came to the notion of interconnectedness as the truth about our reality, if we want it or not.

The notion of interconnectedness of all being is a notion that is very comprehensive—a notion that guides us back to the unity that truly exists underneath all. The notion of interconnectedness is a notion in which *love and knowledge belong together.* Contrary to rationalism which distances itself from nature—particularly evident in the machine-logics of a computerized rationality that systematically eradicates all feelings of love and belonging—the notion of interconnectedness embraces everything.

Interconnectedness means that we are connected and feel mutually bound in solidarity in a decisively caring environment to which we belong. In English we have the terms "solidarity," "bonds," and "ties." In Spanish we use *"apego,"* which is a term expressing closeness: the child who discovers the world still attached to its mother, or *"lazo,"* which translates as connection and bond. In German I call it *"die Verbundenheit allen Seins."* These terms are rather more poetic than analytical. I find them very useful to provide some kind of an orientation within the diversity of being, including the diversity of social movements. Because when one feels connected to all being—and I mean really from the leaves of grass to the universe—there is no end to this feeling. And it is precisely then when one will actually find solid ground under one's feet.

With the concept sketched above, we will have a point of reference which will tell us what it is that we do, what it is that we shall and can do, and what it is that we cannot do. And it is by way of this that we will find a holistic way of thought that does not omit anything: not the animals, not the elements, not the planet. We will find a holistic way of thought that will not allow for gaps, since true interconnectedness knows no gaps either. *Nature has no gaps.*

Furthermore, the concept requires a call for action, namely to take a stand for the defence of all being and its interconnectedness, and I mean on all levels. Only through this will we be able to feel and take on responsibility. With the return of the emotional, the passion to defend that which is alive will return as well. Our feelings will regain their place. They will be able to flourish again without being abused. Because, on the basis of the notion of the interconnectedness of all being, it is impossible to be corrupted or seduced or confused.

At any rate this is my thesis.

Because if nature is alive and not just machine or resource, or whatever these patriarchal terms replacing nature are, then she is neither merely object nor no object at all, but subject, meaning: she is telling us something, she speaks to us, she communicates with us, she is sending us messages, and we can turn to her, *we can ask her what we shall do.* We can ask where it was that we have erred and where to go from here.

We not only have to regain our senses and our sensitivity, but we have to expand them, also in the terms of Günther Anders (1987) who always demanded that. In order to expand our senses, to let them grow above us, we have to "deploy" antennas of perception and realization of the interconnectedness, but not in any super-sensual terms (*übersinnlich*: that which goes beyond the senses), but in *trans-sensual or cross-sensual* terms (*transsinnlich* and *quersinnlich*), which will allow us to also perceive the senses of others, not only our own. My energies are not only isolated and ego-logical ones, exclusively focused on me, but they are connected to other energies and forces that support me, just as I support them.

I know that this is the way it is. I have experienced it. If we open ourselves to the interconnectedness of all being, then all energies are with and behind us, and they will guide us, and we will be their advocates and voices.

We have a calling in this world, namely to prevent the destruction from continuing. This also leads us close to Gandhi's notion of *ahimsa*, which is always translated as non-violence, but which also means *innocence*. Ahimsa is a way of action that does not follow self-centred goals and the interest to *be personally successful,* but that follows the bonds of life and that thereby offers new possibilities of acting and resisting and creating alternative ways of living. This way we can finally leave ego-centrism behind us and become channels of and for mother earth.

Only such a way of feeling, thinking and behaving makes it possible to act without rational calculation and unnecessary compromises. *Compromises will be made, but not with society.* We will gain a truthfulness of action, and even though the web in which we act will be large, it will always be possible to have an orientation and to act very concretely in each specific case. This is an outstanding experience since so far we have not had many possibilities (and were prohibited from having them) to unite theory and practice in such a way.

Acting, thinking and feeling along the lines of the interconnectedness of all being also creates a *"mimetic sphere"*, meaning: a mimesis which allows for the extended and conscious exchange of energies with other living beings, since we will establish always more contacts with them and will thereby also create common ground and orientation.

For me all this means the possibility to escape the one-step-at-a-time character of the alleged alternatives offered—from above, from the west, from the left—so far, their temporality and weakness, their incompleteness, and their lack of vision and orientation. But this happens without needing a "political program" or "technological project", not to speak of new forms of domination.

What we have instead is a way of perceiving and thinking that follows the interconnectedness of all being and that knows as its base the depth of this interconnectedness—I call it *"deep feminism"*.

There will also be no more separations in action and thought. There will be no *nihilism* that denies life, any more. The interconnectedness of all being teaches us that there are no ruptures and gaps, but that there is always a connecting *rope* that guides us and that we can hold onto.

The main challenge that remains probably is: how can we turn this awareness into appropriate action *in each specific case*? How can we exchange the experiences we are making on this path? How can we know that we do the right things in order to defend mother earth? And how do we know that we are really on the way to another civilization?

I consider the development of a spiritual understanding in the way outlined above for absolutely necessary and, in the end, I consider it to be the only possible way to find an adequate response to globalization and to develop alternatives to it that will not lead us astray once again.

Bibliography

Anders, Günther, 1979, Die Antiquiertheit des Menschen, München

Barlow, Maude, 2001, "The Last Frontier," in The Ecologist, Feb., London

Bennholdt-Thomsen, Veronika, Faraclas, Nicholas, Werlhof, Claudia von (Eds.) 2001, There is an Alternative. Subsistence and Worldwide Resistance to Corporate Globalization, London

Bennholdt-Thomsen, Veronika, Mies, Maria, 1999, The Subsistence Perspective: Beyond the Globalized Economy, London

Braun, Christina von, 2000, "Gender, Geschlecht und Geschichte," in Braun/Stephan (Eds.), Gender Studien. Eine Einführung, Stuttgart-Weimar

Chossudovsky, Michel, 1996, The Globalization of Poverty, London

Genth, Renate, 2002, Über Maschinisierung und Mimesis. Erfindungsgeist und mimetische Begabung im Widerstreit und ihre Bedeutung für das Mensch-Maschine-Verhältnis, Frankfurt—New York

Jonas, Hans, 1979, Das Prinzip Verantwortung, Frankfurt

Mies, Maria, Bennholdt-Thomsen, Veronika, Werlhof, Claudia von, 1988, Women, the Last Colony, London

Mies, Maria, Werlhof, Claudia von (Eds.), 2003, Lizenz zum Plündern. Das Multilaterale Abkommen über Investitionen, MAI—Globalisierung der Konzernherrschaft und was wir dagegen tun können, Hamburg

Werlhof, Claudia von, 2007, "Capitalist Patriarchy and the Negation of Matriarchy. The Struggle for a Deep Alternative," in Vaughan, Genevieve (Ed.), Women and the Gift Economy. A Radically Different World View is Possible. The Gift-Economy Inside and Outside Patriarchal Capitalism, Toronto: Inanna, pp. 143-157

Unfamiliar

Bridget Saracino

Author's note: Unfamiliar *refers to the subjugation of ancient cultural Feminine Divine and the subsequent domination of power by different monopolies—in this case, Christianity, BP. Oya and Sedna are two different Goddesses, both associated with water, fertility, death, transitioning, and rebirth. They share quite interesting cosmologies well worth exploring. Sedna is the crux of this poem and since both Goddesses claim the oceans as their home, I found it important to touch upon the Gulf Oil Spill.*

Unfamiliar
Dreams of baleen and parallax
And falling
Across the sky of my mind, the infinite sky
Of the Sea
This *skin*
Of the World.
That I am drowning in
Drowning in
Puddles of oily Christmas dreams of—
Ghosts
And thorns
And
warm
wet—
blood
On hands
Between thighs
And all
This

Guilt
And honesty
And honestly
My atomic number doesn't compute with the number of protons—
I have
Built ships of bone
Of black burnt
Turtle shells
With sails of shoelace shirts and dollar
Bills
To navigate the treacherous
Clinging
Puddles.
Will the ebony ivory baleen boards
Whisper to me
Yesterday
Lost
SubjuGAtiondisrespECT
And this amazing
Lush
Fertile
Power
Where is Oya? Sedna?
The Raven.
Will He
Turn my kayak into the icy arctic sea?
My vessel is made of sacrificial whalebone
Fingers
And pioneered
Piloted through phalange infested waters of dream
Soup
Bathe me
And
I
Will
calm

Anubis

Bridget Saracino

Author's note: *I believe that the different representations of the Divine, from culture to culture, are in fact different manifestations of One Great Creator. Perhaps a cleaner way to describe this would be to say that different Divine Beings are simply different personalities of One Being, though that is not simple at all. In this poem and the meditation session that inspired it, the jackal-headed Egyptian deity may or may not have the physical presence of a male. To be honest, I cannot clearly remember the gender that "his" presence inspired. In ancient Egypt, Anupu had a female counterpart represented exactly the same. Her name was Anput. This poem is based on one or two meditation sessions, and Anupu refers to the more widely known Anubis. (Anubis is the Greek word while Anupu is the Egyptian.) Anupu was the protector of the dead and the color of his coat refers to the black Egyptian soil in the Nile river valley—the soil that is so widely known for its fertile properties—and thus to rebirth.*

Anubis
Visited, stood above and looked through my skin like water
Like fire.
To think I would entertain a God
Of Death!
I was stiff as I lay on the floor
Cold Savasana
Corpse pose it's called.
I tried not to meet His eyes
His welcoming
His Death Eye
The optic nerve rolling like the sun around the sky
Just as bright
And just as knowing

Trying to tell me
To tell me that I—
And my cousin
My long lost cousin—escaped
from the sterile white room, white plastic
Halls that smell like
Alco—
Halls that smell like
My beautiful cousin
lost, flew away
Seen last on a blue Summer Sunday
But she
Came in with Anubis
Danced in and held my hand and
Dreams came
I came
To become
Of my dreams of—
The round moon falling like a comet
Pregnant with meaning
Through the tearing sky
She dropped down the drop
I cried
Tears
Of boiling sea
And I remember . . . .
I woke with tears on my pillow
Perfect tears
Like salty sea brine
So miserable
And all I'm doin' is lookin' for love
For my long past lost moon love who fell from the sky and doesn't
No she doesn't
Visit me with Anubis . . .

Strawberry Lullaby

Bridget Saracino

Author's note: *This poem refers to a prophecy that the Haudenosaunee have for the end of the world and to the ancient practices of medicinal plants.*

Strawberries
Are the very strongest
Medicine
But even they can't stop the end of the world
Now
Can they.
Can they?
If she stood on the snout of the serpent he couldn't gnash his dagger
teeth
And if she didn't whisper so soft and sweet in his ears he wouldn't cry his
dragon tears
Oh and if she just sealed her lips with a golden key and
sang lullabies through
stopped chops
Maybe
Maybe
Maybe . . .
Maybe the world wouldn't have to end
The serpents wouldn't
bleed and
fight to shred
each others' skin beneath the organs
the skin of the soul
all the nations wouldn't stare aghast

At the carnage and
The crazy woman
Laughing
Crying
Sobbing hysterically as she destroys everything she loves
Hugging her arms
wrapped tight round her barren belly, suffocate her life
Snuff out the light from the dancing comet as it burns a hole in the sky
so final
So—
And strawberries fall from her gasping mouth as the sea empties out of
her eyes.

Lisa & Zeb-un-Nissa

Lisa Sarasohn

She may be everywhere, but if she wants to tag me with a clear directive, she'll snag me at the library or in a book store. Whoever's lurking in the aisles—a gang of Greek Muses, the Celtic Brigid, the Vedic Saraswati?—She's goddess of the written word. The books she chooses for me tip off the shelf, into my hands.

Just so: Twenty years ago, I left a used book shop in Bennington, Vermont carrying a blue cloth-covered volume dressed in a tattered red dust jacket—*The Diwan of Zeb-un-Nissa*. The book presents fifty of Zeb-un-Nissa's poems, rendered from the Persian into English by Magan Lal and Jessie Duncan Westbrook. The text includes Ms. Westbrook's introduction and a glossary of Persian names, places, and terms.

Zeb-un-Nissa: her name means "the glory of womankind." I'll tell you what I know about this 17th century Sufi poet and her life as the eldest daughter of Aurungzebe, the last politically powerful Moghul emperor in India. I'll show you some of her poems, discuss my process of crafting new versions of them, and share some of those new versions with you.

But first I must describe the book itself—as artifact, icon, a talisman of the belle-lettered belle.

The book itself

My *Diwan* is five inches wide and seven inches high; it rests easily in the hand. Published in the United States in 1913 by E. P. Dutton and Company, New York, it's printed by Hazell, Watson & Viney, Ld., London and Aylesbury. Its 112 pages are thick, felt-like.

Was it printed on a letterpress? If so, a typesetter put each metal letter in place, preparing to stamp lines of type into paper. I can feel the impression each letter makes upon the page.

The text fills seven signatures of sixteen pages. (Seven and sixteen: two of Her favorite numbers.) Were the signatures hand-sewn? If so, who made the four inch-long stitches in the center of each signature that hold the pages together? Who assembled the signatures, discreetly labeled by letter to indicate their order?

John Murray, Albemarle St. W., London commissioned the *Diwan* and published it in the United Kingdom in 1913. Founded in 1768, this company has a reputation for pushing the envelope of intellectual history—for example, with the publication of Charles Darwin's *On the Origin of Species* in 1859. The *Diwan* is one of 122 volumes in the publisher's "Wisdom of the East" series, initiated in 1905, introducing English readers to the philosophy and poetry of India, China, Japan, Persia, Arabia, Palestine, and Egypt.

Written a hundred years ago, the series editors' note remains timely. Editors L. Cranmer-Byng and S.A. Kapadia declare their intention: to promote "a revival of that true spirit of Charity which neither despises nor fears the nations of another creed and colour." The goddess of the written word favors the multicultural.

I must have paid $2 for this book—that's the price marked in pencil in the upper-right corner of the flyleaf. That page also bears this inscription in strong, graceful, stylish strokes:

> To Maliha
> from Razzack
> in grateful remembrance
> of all your kindness.
> October 20 | '52

Maliha means "beautiful, graceful, strong." *Razzack* likely means "devotée." They are names from India, Africa, the Middle East. The book is a gift, an expression of gratitude.

About Zeb-un-Nissa

There's a reason why the historical record concerning Zeb-un-Nissa is contradictory and incomplete. Here's what may be true about the woman:

Born in 1638, she was the eldest daughter of Aurungzebe, the last Moghul emperor wielding significant power in India. She was a direct descendant of Genghis Khan and Tamerlane (Timur Lenk), Mongol warriors who conquered most of Asia and Eastern Europe in the late 12th and early 13th centuries.

Persian was her mother tongue; she learned Arabic in four years. By the age of seven she was reciting the Koran by heart. Encouraged by her father, she studied mathematics, astronomy, and military strategy; she also began writing poetry at an early age.

As her father permitted, Zeb-un-Nissa gathered a circle of poets from India, Persia, and Kashmir around her and she gained fame as a poet. She excelled in a kind of literary contest called *mushaira*, answering another poet's line with one of her own, using the same meter and rhyme.

Enjoying an unusual degree of freedom in the palace, Zeb-un-Nissa used her own fortune to support writers and scholars, often critiquing their work. She established a library and more than one scriptorium, employing expert calligraphers to copy manuscripts for her on paper of the finest quality.

As the Empire's leading lady, Zeb-un-Nissa took an active role in her father's court. She advised the Emperor on administrative appointments and served as his diplomatic representative. She frequently resolved disputes taking place between those belonging to the Sunni and Shiah sects of Islam.

Although she was a Sunni like her father, she did not share his orthodox beliefs and practices. In contrast, Zeb-un-Nissa identified herself with the mystical Sufi path of Islam. Versed in Islam and familiar with Hinduism, she asserted that God is gracious enough to be known through both religions and too great to be confined to either.

The woman had no luck in love. Her father poisoned one suitor, the son of a political rival. Another man, perhaps mistaking Zeb-un-Nissa for a servant, insulted her with a crude remark; she sent him packing. A third, meeting Zeb-un-Nissa in secret and surprised by the Emperor's unexpected visit, hid in a large vessel used for cooking. He perished when—without Zeb-un-Nissa's objection—the Emperor ordered servants to put the pot on the fire.

In 1681, Zeb-un-Nissa's brother Akbar attempted to usurp their father's position as Emperor. Aurungzebe prevailed, Akbar fled to safety, and the Emperor accused Zeb-un-Nissa of betrayal, based on her correspondence with her exiled brother. Although he reconciled with Akbar, the Emperor imprisoned Zeb-un-Nissa in the fort at Salimgarh. He held her captive for the twenty years until her death in 1702.

Zeb-un-Nissa continued to write poetry through the years of her imprisonment. Following her death, her writings scattered. But by 1750, more than 400 of her poems had been collected and published in Persian. *The Diwan of Zeb-un-Nissa* presents fifty of these poems in English.

Because Zeb-un-Nissa was *persona non grata* at the Emperor's court, none of the record-keepers dared to chronicle her life. That's why the historical record is so sketchy.

Yet the image remains: The Moghul Emperor imprisons his daughter in the fortress. The imperious mogul incarcerates the woman in the tower. Could there be a clearer image of patriarchal alienation from and subjugation of the feminine?

Zeb-un-Nissa's God

Was Zeb-un-Nissa's spirituality particularly a womanist or feminist spirituality?

The *Diwan*'s dedication reads "In the Name of God, the Compassionate, the Merciful." The qualities of compassion and mercy inform *Rahman* and *Rahim*, two of the many Sufi names for God. Both words carry the sense of womb, the divine love that radiates from the center of being, the energy of creation: birth and re-birth.

Although Lal and Westbrook give "God" a masculine pronoun in most of the *Diwan*'s poems, they personify divine Love and Wisdom as womanly in two instances:

> XII
> I follow on where Wisdom's feet have led,
> And firmly hold,
> The while this hard and thorny path I tread,
> Her garment's fold.
> XLIX
> . . . O breezes, free to stray,
> Back to her garden find your way,
> And greeting to my Love convey.

Westbrook's introduction includes another poem of Zeb-un-Nissa's with reference to the feminine divine:

> No Muslim I,
>   But an idolater,

> I bow before the image of my Love,
>   And worship her:
>
> No Brahman I,
>   My sacred thread
> I cast away, for round my neck I wear
>   Her plaited hair instead.

Dedicated to the Sufi path of devotion, Zeb-un-Nissa often addresses God as the Belovèd in her poems. She is the Lover who seeks union with Him. She plays the polarities of masculine and feminine, mosque and Hindu temple, sun and moon, long-billed songbird and rose to point to the consciousness that arises from, and goes beyond, the merging of dualities.

Zeb-un-Nissa's sense of God is more complex than a simple sorting into "his" or "hers." When *God* appears on the page in the English translation of her poems, we don't know which word Zeb-un-Nissa has chosen to name the divine. If Zeb-un-Nissa has written *Allah*, she's chosen a name that joins the sounds of yes and no, fullness and emptiness, into one word. *Allah* is the name that points to God as all-encompassing, a reality shimmering beyond our conceptions of this-and-that.

She is everywhere, beyond categories of gender and conventions of grammar.

Zeb-un-Nissa's poems

To place Zeb-un-Nissa's writing in the historical continuum of some well-known Sufi poets: Rumi wrote in the 13th century, Hafez in the 14th, Kabir in the 15th, Zeb-un-Nissa in the 17th, and Ghalib in the 19th.

Zeb-un-Nissa wrote her poems as *ghazals*. A ghazal (pronounced "guzzle") is a series of self-contained couplets. The first couplet establishes an end-rhyme. The second lines of succeeding couplets continue this rhyme. The last couplet addresses the poet by name and provides some kind of personal instruction. In the final lines of Zeb-un-Nissa's ghazals, the poet calls herself Makhfi, meaning "the hidden one."

A ghazal usually contains no more than eighteen couplets, thirty-six lines. Lacking a clearly stated, unifying theme, the poem engages the reader in searching for the larger context in which the whole may have meaning. The form of the ghazal ushers the reader into the unknown—in essence, a spiritual quest.

A diwan is a sequence of groups of ghazals, ordered according to their rhyme. The first group of ghazals rhymes with the first letter of the alphabet, the second group rhymes with the alphabet's second letter, and on down the line.

Collaborating across divides of time

When the *Diwan of Zeb-un-Nissa* dropped into my hands twenty years ago, I'd been reading—imbibing—Robert Bly's *The Kabir Book: Forty-Four of the Ecstatic Poems of Kabir*. Mystery surrounds the identity of Kabir. It might be true that Kabir was a 15th century Muslim and/or Hindu poet. As his words reveal, he defied religious convention, drilling down to the essentials that make such conventions irrelevant.

Working largely from the Bengali translation of a printed Hindi text, Rabindranath Tagore and Evelyn Underhill translated Kabir's odes into English. Working from their *Songs of Kabir*, published in 1915, Robert Bly crafted new versions, updating their Victorian-era English into a modern American idiom.

Now you can access the Tagore-Underhill *Songs of Kabir* on the Internet. In the late '80s, though, I was lucky to find a copy of the book at the local library. I found two poems in *Songs of Kabir* that did not appear as new versions in Bly's book. Working from the Tagore-Underhill translations, I made new versions of those poems myself. And I loved the process:

> Collapsing distinctions of time, distance,
> ethnicity, language, and culture.

> Sinking down through words to the kernel of a
> knowing that words in any language can barely
> convey. Then rising up, surfacing, trailing new
> words that hint at what I've seen and felt.

> Stretching out threads of empathy, tendrils
> of inquiry, until I'm buzzing with the initial
> impulse of the poem. Reeling in those threads
> and arranging them in a form that resonates
> with the original.

Perhaps my years of practicing yoga, qigong, meditation, and bodywork plus my general sensitivity to light and sound equipped me for this process.

When the *Diwan* came into my hands, I thought that someday I'd play with Zeb-un-Nissa's poems in the same way: making new versions, updating diction and rhythm, making her work accessible to women and men in this day and age.

That someday is now.

Why has it taken me this long? With all respect to Magan Lal and Jessie Duncan Westbrook, the way these Persian poems morphed into Victorian-era English makes them difficult for me to read. The rigid rhyme schemes, monotonous rhythms, and convoluted syntax put me off. Within any sentence, the subject seems miles apart from its verb, separated by a bevy of convoluted prepositional phrases.

Three events got me started. First, a demonstration of the possible:

In June 2009, I attended poet and critic James Longenbach's lecture on poetic tone at Warren Wilson College in Swannanoa, North Carolina. Longenbach is on the faculty of the college's MFA program in Creative Writing.

The very first item on his handout put Herbert Giles's Victorian-era translation of a Chinese poem next to Ezra Pound's free verse adaptation of that translation. Here's the juxtaposition:

Herbert Giles's translation of "Liu Ch'e"

The sound of rustling silk is stilled,
With dust the marble courtyard filled;
No footfalls echo on the floor,
Fallen leaves in heaps block up the door.
For she, my pride, my lovely one, is lost,
And I am left, in hopeless anguish tossed.

Ezra Pound's adaptation of Giles's translation:

The rustling of silk is discontinued,
Dust drifts over the court-yard.
There is no sound of foot-fall, and the leaves
Scurry into heaps and lie still,
And she the rejoicer of the heart is beneath them:

A wet leaf that clings to the threshold.

The Giles treatment of the Chinese poem is so similar to Westbrook's treatment of the Persian poems. And Pound's adaptation is so gorgeous. I was heartened, inspired by this demonstration of possibility.

Second, no alternative:

I like to do crossword puzzles, the Sunday *New York Times* crosswords in particular. They make me blend logical thinking with intuitive leaping. They exercise memory, guesswork, pattern recognition. I can feel various parts of my brain lighting up and nerve impulses shuttling between brain hemispheres.

I especially like to do a crossword as I'm sitting in my kitchen, keeping my washing machine company, on hand to check the water isn't overflowing at any point in the cycle.

Not long after the Longenbach lecture, I was in the kitchen with my washer but without a crossword. Bereft of a puzzle, I retrieved the *Diwan* from a dark corner and began with the first poem.

My first step was simply to untangle the words into straightforward sentences. What were these words trying to say at the simplest level of communication?

Then I felt my way into the poem. I bought my ticket for that state of being in which time and space are fluid, permeable, detached from any fixed coordinates.

Having read the story of Zeb-un-Nissa's life in Westbrook's introduction, I already felt a sense of kinship with the poet. Now, as I sat with the first poem, that sense of connection intensified.

I felt an oscillation in time, saw the split-screen image of parallel lives: the 17th century Muslim woman writing these poems in a prison tower and the 21st century American woman, complete with her own limitations, sitting with the poems at her kitchen table.

Third, structure and format:

I saw "Julie & Julia," the movie. Talk about parallel lives. Here's Julie Powell whipping up the 524 recipes in Julia Child's *Mastering the Art of French Cooking* in 365 days, with a blog to go, intercut with Julia Child writing and rewriting that cookbook and seeing it through to publication.

If I'm going to get something done, I need a due date. A public forum adds to the pleasure. I created a blog at 50ghazals.wordpress.com and a timeline: 50 ghazals in 52 weeks.

A sampling of poems

Here is a sampling of poems, the Lal-Westbrook translations followed by my new versions. I suspect there are mysteries and meanings embedded in the meter, rhymes, cultural references, and images of the original Persian that have been lost in translation. I hope they can be sensed, by resonance, in the energy surrounding the poems now.

May the mother of us all and the goddess of the written word be pleased, or at least amused, by this tribute. May these words honor my mother, Shirley Sarasohn, the woman who weekly tipped the books she chose for her daughter off the library shelf, into a toddler's hands.

I

      To Thee, first,
From the clouds of Whose mercy is born
The rose of my garden, I look!
Let the praise of Thy love the beginning adorn
Of the verse of my book.

      A thirst
For Thy love are my body and soul;
Like Mansur the grains of this clod,
My body, cry out—They are parts, Thou the whole,
Themselves they are God.

      The waves
Of Thy deluge of love o'er the boat
Of mortality roll;
No Noah could lift from the deeps till it float
My love-drownèd soul.

      As slaves
The powers of the darkness for me
Will obedient fly;
If a word of my praise be accepted by Thee,
Like Suleiman I.

      And now
No more do the ready tears start

As laments from my tongue,
For like pearls the blood-drops that are drawn from my heart
On my lashes are hung.

      Bear thou,
O Makhfi, with patience thy pain,
It is endless, and leave thou the night
Of thy passions; for then shall not Khizr attain
Such a spring of delight.

I

Nothing without your love.
Your mercy mixes with
garden soil,
moistens the seed. It's the
atmosphere
unfolding rosebud into rose.

Body and soul thirst for
your love;
every blessed cell cries out
for home.
Typhoon waves flood this
boat, drown
this soul. It sinks too deep
for rescue.

Accept one word of praise
from me,
you make me sovereign;
angular phantoms flee
at my command.

I used to speak my grief,
then weep. Now my heart's
the source of tears. They hang
from my lashes like pearls.

Be patient, Makhfi, with
your pain.
It is endless.
Put suffering aside. Look:
The angel of immortality

is pointing.

II
O Thou Who all things mortal and divine
Hast fashioned, and by Whom alone we live,
May there still shine
The torch of hope that Thou to us didst give!

Within us stirs the leaven of Thy love,
As streams of water of Thy mercy run.
Look from above
And bless Mahmoud and all that he hath done.

Whether it be in Mecca's holiest shrine,
Or in the Temple pilgrim feet have trod,
Still Thou art mine,
Wherever God is worshipped is my God.

The morning I shall greet with tears and sighs,
And from my heart that burns with holy fire
A breath shall rise
To burnish thus my mirror of desire.

Give me thy tears, O Makhfi, let them rain
In quenching torrents on my burning heart;
So hot its pain
At every sigh I breathe the flames outstart.

II
You've created everything
that does and doesn't die,
we only are because of you.
You've given us a torch of
hope—

may it always be the light by
which we see.

Your love's the buoyancy
within our blood,
your mercy, a flowing stream.
Bless all who walk the path
and all that they have done.

Whether pilgrims praise
your name
in Kali's temple
or bow to you in Mecca's
most holy shrine,
the act of worship is my God.

My days begin with tears, heart
a conflagration of holy fire,
breath the pressure-pulse
that lengthens longing.

Makhfi says: I give you my
tears in torrents,
let them drench my burning
heart.

This heart-pain's so hot that
every breath
fans the flames higher,
skyward.

VIII
From the glance Thou bestowed, O Belovèd,
    flows beauty no words can express;
My life—it were little to offer in thanks for Thy
    bountifulness.
How shamed were the pious assembly, how
    grieved in their hearts when they heard
That for love of Thy fluttering tresses the utter-

91

most nations were stirred.
My heart is riven in fragments, ravaged by tears
    of my grief,
But to one whom Thy lashes have wounded never
    there cometh relief.
At Thy feet, O haughty Belovèd, I lay down the
    pride of my brow,
I am near to Thy heart as Thy raiment; why
    sayest "A stranger art thou"?
O Makhfi, walk boldly like Majnun in the valley
    of grief undismayed,
Girt round with thy new dedication, the promise
    of love thou hast made.

VIII
Beauty flows to, through
whatever you gaze upon;
no words can describe it.
Your gifts are infinite,
my life's a small gesture of
gratitude.

The ones whom the pious
call *sinner* truly love you.
Seeing that shames their
righteousness—
they fear for their own
salvation.

Tears of grief tear my heart
to shreds,
shatter it to sharp-edged
fragments.
Yet you've never wounded
me.

Bowing my head at your
feet, I find relief.

Now I'm as close to you as
your clothing.
Why, then, call me a stranger?

Makhfi, walk boldly through
the valley of grief,
girdled with new dedication
and wrapped in your promise
to love.

IX

O Saki, do thy task;
Into this moon-like goblet pour
The golden wine that, shining like the sun,
From out the dusky flask
Comes till my goblet bubbles o'er,
As from the clouds the dawn when night is done.

Behold my luckless heart,
So broken, so dissolved by pain,
It even flows in tears between my lashes;
And yet how can I part
With it, while still to me remain
Its shards—I wait till it is burnt to ashes.

I knew long, long ago,
Your promises were less than naught,
I blotted them forever from my mind.
Why was I born to know
An age above all others fraught
With love ungrateful and with fate unkind?

But grasp thy joy; who knows,
Makhfi, what may to thee befall?
The firm foundations of the earth may shake,
The breeze that blows
May, if this empty life be all,
The bubble of our vain existence break.

IX
You who serve the wine, do
your job!

Your flask is the color of
twilight, your wine
is gold, fluid sunshine. My
cup's the shape
of the crescent moon. Fill it,
spilling the wine
over the brim: dawn disperses
the cloudy night.

Pain's the liquid that rims my
eyelids.
Look at my luckless heart:
it's broken.
Holding onto the splinters, I
can't release it.
But as soon as it's burned to
ashes, I will.

I knew from the start your
promises
were worthless. I made sure
to forget them.
We live in a time that
specializes
in stingy fate, ungrateful love.

Makhfi, take hold of joy.
Anything can happen:
foundations fall apart,
fabrics unravel.
The morning breeze
evaporates illusion,
breaks through the vault of
our vanities.

Bibliography

Barks, Coleman. *The Soul of Rumi*, (New York: HarperCollins, 2001).

Bly, Robert. *The Kabir Book: Forty-Four of the Ecstatic Poems of Kabir*, (Boston: Beacon Press, 1977).

_____. *The Winged Energy of Delight*, (New York: HarperCollins, 2004).

Disse, Dorothy. Zeb-un-Nissa /Zebunnisa /Makhfi (1638-1702), http://home.infionline.net/~ddisse/zebunn.html (accessed October 30, 2009).

Douglas-Klotz, Neil. *The Sufi Book of Life*, (New York: Penguin, 2005).

Krynicki, Annie Krieger. *Captive Princess: Zebunissa, Daughter of Emperor Aurangzeb*, (New York: Oxford University Press, 2006).

Lal, Magan and Jessie Duncan Westbrook. *The Diwan of Zeb-un-Nissa*, (New York: E. P. Dutton and Company, 1913).

National Library of Scotland. The John Murray Archive, http://www.nls.uk/jma/ (accessed October 30, 2009).

Tagore, Rabindranath and Evelyn Underhill. *Songs of Kabir*, (New York, The Macmillan Company, 1915).

Roaring Red River

Judy Millyard-Maselli

Young woman, old woman,
Seen woman, hidden woman,
Laughing woman, crying woman,
Daughters held in loving arms.

In every moment—joy or pain
we connect over time
suckling daughters
at the Creatrix's breast.

I live in herstory.
I dream in her language.
Her symbols—my touchstones,
Her breathing in and out—my breath.
Her truth—my truth
All memory—lost and reclaimed,
SHE—torch bearer in the dark.

In this place of power,
This sacred territory of soul, mind and spirit,
I stand with all those who have come before
With their cracked and calloused hands,
Their unspoken words & their unsung songs,
Their shoeless feet and their broken dreams.

Strong Worker woman,
Unknown Silent woman,
Wise Mother woman,
Delicious Whore woman,
Lovers of wolf and dove

Lovers of children & lovers of men
Lovers of women
Bird and berry
Cat and cow . . .

Holding hand and heart,
All together—
Our stories untold.

Old women in the shoe with too many children disappeared
Wailing women—life ripped from their wombs—
All Lover Women we, come again and again,
Daughters of Lilith and Eve
Dancing on this sacred breast
Howling to this sacred moon
Bleeding her blood, our blood
In a roaring red river of remembering.

The Fairy and the Dragon

Lê Pham Lê

Author's note: These poems reflect the significance of goddesses, female ancestors, and my mother in my experience.

I was told
we Vietnamese are *dong bào*.
In the time before records
born in a sac
of one hundred eggs,
we became the children
of the Dragon *Lac Long Quân*
and the Fairy *Âu Co*.

Their honeymoon over,
like fire and water,
this married couple
could no longer live together.
Irreconcilable differences
between goddess and god.

Half of their children
left for the mountains,
with their mother,
to her fairy home.
The others with their father
seaward journeyed,
to his dragon kingdom.

Con Rong, cháu Tiên
Children of Fairy, descendants of Dragon!
That's who we are.
Gourd and pumpkin vines
climb the same trellis,
always connected,
forever different.

Hát River

Lê Pham Lê

Dedicated to the Trung sisters (c. 12-43 CE), women warriors who repelled Chinese invaders

It was in Mê Linh village
where she swore a sacred oath
witnessed by rivers and mountains,
blessed by heaven and earth.

Sharpening swords under moonlight
practicing battles night by night.
Her own sister, fellow warrior, at her side.
One word she uttered, thousands replied.
Who says women are delicate
willow branches/*phan lieu bo?*

Willows can survive strong winds
as she once proved. The very first
among countless Vietnamese heroes.
sweeping Chinese troops from our land,
Lady Trung opened the first chapter
of Viet Nam's history!

Conquerors' ambition was a bottomless well.
One attack after another, shocking like earthquakes.
Have ants ever defeated elephants?
Can willow branches survive harsh storms?

Laying down arms was never her option.
At Hát River, icy water
concluded Trung's life.
Viet Nam forever owes its endurance to her.

For thousands of years,
The drum of Mê Linh village
has echoed in the hearts of the Vietnamese.

Journey to Langbian Mountain

Lê Pham Lê

A foggy dawn
in a plateau city,
after hours squeezing on a bus,
I arrive at the foot of Langbian Mountain.

Slipping several times on the muddy,
upward path, I continue to climb
until reaching the top
of this giant mountain at noon.

Impatiently awaiting Quan Âm*
until her subtle image emerges from
a cluster of clouds.
I am convinced her spirit is everywhere
in this bamboo forest at this moment.
The time and space seem to pause
in a strange tranquility.
Kneeling down, I bow my head and pray
as many others do.

At fourteen years, I follow
fellow Buddhists to discover the mystery
on the other side of this mountain.
Like a monkey, I hold the wild vines
That wind around the ancient trees
tightly, moving down carefully.

Yet a dry branch once fails me.
Like a leaf caught in the storm,
I roll down quickly
until my feet touch a stone
of the mountain wall.

Perhaps the *Goddess of Mercy* protects me
from this fatal fall.
I find myself rejoining others
at the foot of the mountain,
where a peaceful silver stream curves.

I drink the stream's clear, sweet water
as if I had never drunk water before.
Washing my face with it, hoping its miracle
will help me see things clearly.

I sit still on a grassy edge for a moment,
closing my eyes, praying for my parents'
good health and long life.
Here she is—Quan Âm appears
holding a willow branch and holy water
that flows into my being.

Suddenly, the sound of a bird singing
nearby brings me back.
I climb to the mountaintop and then return
to the starting point of my journey
to meet my companions
before the sun fades in the West.

I carry home with me
small bamboo branches, heavenly-fragrant.
My mother lights a candle,
burns incense to Quan Âm
and prays at her altar for her blessings.

*Buddhist *bodhisattva*, saint, or goddess; also Guanyin, Kuan Yin.

The Dark Goddess

Lori Coon

I am called by the Black Madonna.
She of a thousand names
who walks with the burdens of the world,
who suffers our sins.
She who caresses our bodies and eases our pain.
She who roots our souls to the earth
and beckons release in thunderous ravaging change.
She who expresses the eternal Mother of us all.

I kneel before her.
My soul knows her sound.
I wait.

"Arise!" she says,
"Lay yourself upon my bosom.
Dissolve into the dark, rich soils below.
Seep deeper into the vital essence of my being.
Be not afraid of the things you will see there
for I Am with you
and they are but the Mystery
guiding you
shaping you
into form and formlessness."

The red river delivers me then,
crashing upon the jagged shores.
My body broken

My name forgotten
A swirling mass of bones
surrendering
expanding
welling up
emerging.

And the Dark Skies rage in wind-swept torment.
And the earth moans
cracking open—
hallowing my name
while tides plunge
downward
consumed
and I must follow
until silence spills into empty spaces
and the dark calming waters wash over me
anointing me with a healing balm,
fleshing me out,
re-membering me
as I remember who it is I serve.

Earth Mother; Sculpture
© 1995 Lori Coon; Photo by Lori Coon

Making the Gyonocentric Case: Mago, the Great Goddess of East Asia and Her Tradition Magoism[1]

Helen Hye-Sook Hwang

This study documents and interprets a substantial body of primary sources concerning Mago [麻姑, also known as Magu or Mako] from Korea, China, and Japan. Much of this material has never been brought to light as a whole. In working with these various and sundry data including folklore, paintings, arts, literature, poetry, toponyms, rituals, historical and religious records, and apocryphal texts, I encountered an organic structure that relates these seemingly unrelated materials and named it Magoism. Magoism refers to an anciently originated gynocentric cultural and historical context of East Asia, which venerates Mago as supreme divine. Although "Magoism" is my coinage, its concept is not new. Magoism is referred to as the Way of Mago, the Origin of Mago, the Event of Mago, Reign of Mago, Heavenly Principle, or simply Mago in historical sources. In the West, its partial manifestation is known as the cult of Magu within the context of Daoism. One of the earliest verified records, the *Biography of Magu (Magu zhuan)* written by Ge Hong (284-364) dates back to proto-Daoist times.[2]

Nonetheless, "Mago" remains largely forgotten and misrepresented to the world especially in modern times. More incisively, her sublime divinity is made invisible despite strong evidence. No scholarship in the West has treated Mago as a topic in her own right. Mago's multiple identities ranging from the cosmogonist to a grandmother, from the progenitress to the Daoist goddess, from the sovereign to a shaman/priestess in Korea, China, and Japan remain unregistered in modern scholarship. When mentioned, her transnational manifestation is not recognized cogently. She is often lumped together with other parochial goddesses from China. Other times, she is fetishized as a Daoist goddess of immortality. She is also known, among other representations, as the giant grandmother (goddess) who shaped the natural landscape in the beginning of time among Koreans. In any case, Mago is not deemed on a par or in relation with Xiwangmu (the Queen Mother of the West in Chinese Daoism) and Amaterasu, (the Sun Goddess of the Japanese imperial family), both of whom represent the East Asian pantheon of supreme goddesses to the West.

I hold that the paramount significance of Magoism lies in the fact that it redefines the female principle and proffers a gynocentric utopian vision to the modern audience. Its utopian cosmology is no free-floating abstract idea but imbedded in the mytho-historical-cultural reality of East Asia. I suggest Magoism as the original vision of East Asian thought. Put differently, Magoism is an East Asian gynocentric testimony to the forgotten utopian reality. In the sense that Magoism presents an East Asian gynocentric symbolic system, this study is distinguished from Western and androcentric discourse. In other words, its gynocentric universalism should not be subsumed under the discourse of Western or patriarchal universalism. Magoism prompts an alternative paradigm of ancient gynocentrism that redefines major notions of the divine, human, and nature in continuum. Mago, the great goddess, is the unifying and at the same time individualizing force in this system. Magoism enables a macrocosmic view in which all individualized parts are organically co-related and co-operating. As a religious system, it is at once monotheistic and polytheistic. That is, Mago is the great goddess in her multiple manifestations. Underlying the patriarchal edifices, the Magoist principle is the Source from which the latter is derived.

My task is to explicate the Magoist utopian vision within its East Asian context. Difficulty is manifold. Complexity and immensity warrant an open-ended ongoing assessment. To say the least, this project explores uncharted territory. I draw upon feminist studies, religious studies, and goddess studies and link them with the area studies of Korea and East Asia. Thus, this study is necessarily interdisciplinary and cross-cultural. I have named this study the mytho-historical-thealogical study of Magoism.[3] One may call this an experimental study that tests out new possibilities seen from an East Asian feminist perspective. This paper discusses the following three issues: Unveiling Magoism as a trans-patriarchal and transnational reality, reconstructing Korean Magoist identity, and claiming the *Budoji* (Epic of the Emblem City) as a principal text of Magoism.[4]

Unveiling Magoism as a Trans-patriarchal and Transnational Reality

I begin with defending the legitimacy of naming Magoism as a transnational mytho-historical-cultural system. I argue that at the core of the issue is the gynocenric symbolic system that Magoism embodies. In other words, Magoism is a system that attributes the gynocentric principle represented by Mago to the (pro-)creative force from which human civilizations are derived. Mago is both the progenitor and cosmogonist. Magoism encodes the Origin Myth in which Mago is portrayed as the progenitor and the cosmogonist at once. The story of Mago's beginning is the Archaic Memory that humans from all times must not forget for their survival and prosperity on Earth.

The hard fact is that the Magoist female principle is made invisible in modern scholarship. However, the dynamic is reciprocal: The Magoist principle knows of neither the patriarchal ideology of female subordination nor modern Western hegemony. More to the point, Magoism ascribes the female principle to power, intelligence, and equilibrium in ultimatum. Mago is the Way, Heaven, and Source. As such, the Magoist gynocentric principle is antithetical to the patriarchal mind where female is defined as dependent and derivative. In this regard, it is not surprising that the large corpus of primary data concerning Mago has been left in the dark.

The name "Mago" is the primary defining factor to identify her transnational manifestations in Korea, China, and Japan. This name crisscrosses otherwise seemingly unrelated data including folklore, arts, literature, poetry, and religious and historical records. Such toponyms as Mt. Mago, Rock of Mago, and Cave of Mago presently extant in Korea, China, and/or Japan further substantiate the transnational context of Magoism. However, like her multiple manifestations, "Mago" has many derivative names. While "Mago" is the most frequently used, she is also referred to as "grandmother" (*halmi*) or "female immortal/transcendent" (*seonnyeo*). "Mago" is also called "Hwago" (Huagu, flower goddess), "Maego" (Meigu, plum goddess), and "Seongo" (Xiangu, transcendent goddess), all of whom are better known as Daoist goddesses.[5] Korean folkloric sources avail us of other derivative names such as Magu, Magui (demon), Nogo (ancient woman/goddess), Nogu, Gomo (goddess mother), Seolmundae, and Samsin (triad deity). These names are distinguished from others in that Mago is depicted in them as the nature-shaper or progenitor. Like her name, her toponyms have multiple derivatives such as Mt. Nogo and Mt. Goya. Some other names reflect her negotiated and mutated identities. Dense and yet fluid, her many names suggest the enduring and adoptive qualify of Magoism.

In modern times, she is reduced into a cultural fetish associated with immortality in China. This perception proves to be problematic, however, given a close investigation. Mago's origin or identity remains unknowable among the Chinese throughout history. In fact, partial aspects of Magoism are fairly well-documented by a group of Daoist scholars in the West. It appears that these scholars whose assessments I will discuss below have paid close attention to the topic of Mago within the context of Chinese Daoism. However, they all arrive at the conclusion that Mago's origin or identity is unknown. Wolfram Eberhard details the list of topological centers such as Mt. Magu or caves of Magu across China as well as fragmented folkloric data to say that even her legends "do not help much in identifying her."[6]

Edward H. Schafer goes further to describe "the cult of Miss Hemp" in his book dedicated to Ts'ao T'ang, poet of the Tang (Dang) Dynasty. Nonetheless, his assessment does not elucidate its pre-Dang history, as it states:

> Indeed, a personal cult of Miss Hemp [Mago] flourished in T'ang times, associating her with rocks, mountains, mysterious grottoes. On the level of popular religion her name was given to a cliff at Mount T'ien T'ai, the holy mountain of Chekiang: The Precipice of Miss Hemp (Ma Ku Yen) was believed to be the very place where she condescended to visit the home of Ts'ai Ching, and in Sung times there was still an old statue of her standing in a grotto there. But in the arcana of Highest Clarity her petrological associations were even more refined: The twenty-eighth of the thirty-six "lesser" grotto-heavens, called "Heaven of the Cinnabar Aurora" (Tan hsia t'ien), was believed to lie beneath the mountain in Kiangsi that bears her name, on which the commemorative stele with an inscription composed by Yen Chen-ch'ing was placed.[7]

Schafer's brief sketch helps recognize a host of Mago data from China within the context of Daoism. What Schafer spells out above is indeed resourceful to assess the coherency of Magoist transnational data, a discussion to be made in a separate space.

Robert Ford Campany also provides, among other data, some legends from which he observes that her cult is attributed to its existence in Chin times (221 BCE-206 BCE) and even older times. Campany estimates that Magu was possibly "a theriomorphic deity (snake-headed) who gradually metamorphosed into a human being."[8] This suggests Magu's origin in the Stone Ages as animal headed deities are thought to originate in those times. It should be noted that contemporary scholars' assessments of Mago's origin and identity only echo what the ancient Chinese text of Magu represented by Ge Hong (284-364) and Yan zhenqing (709-785) conveys.[9] In other words, the Chinese have adumbrated but not articulated her non-measureable origin and identity. Furthermore, it is in fairness to say that the Chinese have anguished to know about her mysterious origin and identity throughout history.

The Daoist approach to Magoism is ultimately limiting in that "the cult of Magu" antecedes the foundation of Daoism. It may as well be said that Mago has never been fully entrenched in Daoism. Daoism could neither embrace nor eliminate the supreme divinity of Mago. Her situation parallels the Christian conundrum of the supreme divinity of Mary, which could neither be embraced nor eliminated by the church. Unlike Christianity, however, Daoism coped with this dilemma by forging a different name for the great goddess, Xiwangmu, whose origin is also unknown.[10] Thus, that early Daoist schools extensively borrow the central premises of Magoism goes undetected.

Translated as the "Miss Hemp" or "Hemp Maid" in English, "Mago" (麻姑) is further diluted in the West. The logographic meaning of "Hemp Maid" misdirects one's perception to some sort of a parochial deity from China. Linking hemp with Mago leads the researcher to a meandering dead end. Wolfram Eberhard rightly concludes that hemp is not directly associated with Mago.[11] Logographic meanings of a word are often irrelevant to the meaning of the word. It is common that specific Chinese characters are taken to express the sound of the word not its meaning.[12]

An etymological discussion of "Mago" is rather prolix.[13] In sum, I posit that "Mago" is an old word referring to the great goddess: "Ma" in "Mago" refers to "mother" or "goddess" and "go" to "goddess" or "woman." Reinstating "Mago" as the great goddess sheds light on the hidden or forgotten meaning of a series of female-identified words. When the old meaning of a female-connoted word is discovered, it in turn brings back the once highly deemed status of women. For example, "go" is known as a female sibling of father or "mother-in-law" for modern East Asians, it is elevated to a goddess-referral within the context of Magoism. This suggests the idea that women in the family were once deemed as divine-like beings.[14] Magoism also re-apotheosizes the Korean word "halmi," a favored epithet of Mago. Known as "grandmother" or "crone" for modern Koreans, "halmi" is the old referral to the great mother (*hal* means great and *mi* means mother). This suggests the idea that "grandmother," "crone," and "goddess" were closely co-affiliated terms in ancient times.

Reconstructing Gynocentric Korean Identity

Scholars in the West, upon assessing a religion or deity of the non-Western world, tend to pair the topic with a modern nation. Thus, they often project their modern knowledge of the nation or culture onto the indigenous religion or deity they study. Such a methodology betrays the assumption that the modern notion of national identities is time-proven and bias-free. In this process, one's perception of other people's cultural expression is molded by Western-made modern knowledge of that people. This kind of knowledge loses ground outside the Western mind. Some go further to point out that the religious expression of a non-Western country in point is colored by the air of nationalism that is culturally on the rise in that country. This kind of assessment suggests the idea that a cultural expression fostered by nationalist zeal is inauthentic or impure and therefore of less value for study. While such approaches are not necessarily wrong, I find them misguided. Done so, they prepare the ground for Western scholars to wield the authority of Western hegemony over the non-Western world. Precisely, they are blind to the fact that no cultural expression in modern times is free from nationalist ethos. Modern life is inherently shaped by the shade of nationalism whether it is in a non-Western world or a Western world. In my view, the question to be asked is: How can we assess a religious expression of a people beyond the modern notion of national identities? Or, how can we go beneath the modern notion of national identities in order to assess a religious expression of a people?

I hold that the modern category of national identities in particular causes harm to the study of the goddess. Modern nationalities go hand in hand with the impetus of patriarchal religions that do away with the female principle. There is an unmistakable difference between the male divine and the female divine when their manifestations are found cross-nationally. It is generally assumed that exchange of cultures between nations allows the male divine to be disseminated from one people to another. It is true that patriarchal religions have traveled around the globe and disseminated their gods into other nations. When it comes to the goddess whose worship is widespread across nations, such as the case of Mary in the West, however, this kind of reasoning proves to be inadequate. Antithetical is the idea that patriarchal religions actively promote the transmission of the great goddess from one nation to the other. Thus, the very perception of the transnational goddess is systematically thwarted in the realm of patriarchal religions. Androcentric researchers may choose to either dismiss as anomalous the topic of the goddess whose manifestation is found cross-nationally or treat her as a local deity severing her from her transnational context. This has been done to the topic of Mago.

While Mago's manifestation exists across the national boundaries of Korea, China, and Japan, it differs in nature, density, and complexity in these countries. Likewise, primary sources also show different traits according to the country. Korean sources surpass her Chinese counterparts not only in number but also in density and complexity. Mago's supreme divinity is essentially affirmed in Korean sources, whereas it is treated as unknown in Chinese and Japanese counterparts. More to the point, the *Budoji*, the principal text that re-emerged in Korea in 1986, asserts that Koreans were the defenders of Old Magoism (Magoism in pre-patriarchal times) against the pseudo-Magoist Chinese regime. How can we understand the primacy of Korean Magoism without resorting to the modern notion of nationalist identities?

To this question, the *Budoji* offers a compelling reading: Korean Magoist identity precedes the formation of nationalist identities. Its mytho-historical account forges Korean identity within the context of Old Magoism. The Magoist universalist principle is predicated on the idea that individualized group identities (polities) co-exist as a unified force on account that Mago is the origin of everyone and human civilizations. Consanguinity of all peoples is at the root of Magoist universalism. According to the *Budoji*, tracing Mago's genealogy was a means to uphold Magoist universalism. Mago's genealogy was constructed to affirm the consanguinity of all peoples and their languages in pre-patriarchal times. Being the primal genealogy of the human kind, it reifies the Magoist universalist principle proclaiming the Origin of Mago. The *Budoji* continues to warrant that ancient Koreans were the orthodox compliers of Magoist chronology.

In the Magoist mythological schema, responsibility and leadership are given to the eldest of the community. The eldest devotes her life to the cause of Magoism. One's sacrificial love for the whole is the hallmark of Magoist leadership. The *Budoji* focuses on Hwanggung, the eldest grandchild of Mago, the common ancestor of East Asians. Hwanggung is the primal Magoist leader/shaman who set her life as a paragon for forthcoming East Asians to become the oldest civilizers of Magoism.[15] Owing to the leadership of her and her successors, Magoist East Asians were able to become sea voyagers, teachers, philosophers, missionaries, diplomats, astrologists, musicians, mathematicians, and linguists in pre-patriarchal times. They carried out the Magoist mandate to bring all peoples of the world under the unified banner of Magoism. Nonetheless, this undivided identity of East Asian Magoists came to an end in time. Korean identity was perforce forged as the defender of Old Magoism, as Chinese rule rose to overthrow the traditional rule of Old Magoism.

The *Budoji* makes it possible for us to distinguish Old Magoism from Later Magoism. Standing at the epochal junction from Old Magoism to Later Magoism, the *Budoji* bemoans the advent of a degenerative time. In this schema, Koreans are identified as the primary and last witness to the universalist rule of Old Magoism on Earth. Ancient Koreans are the ones who remembered their ancestors as the civilizers of Old Magoism (Magoism in pre-patriarchal times). The hallmark of Old Magoism lies in its political agency. Old Magoist polities held theocracy, which I call magocracy (societies ruled by Magoist shamans). Old Magoism gradually declined due to the expansion of the Chinese pseudo-Magoist regimes. The birth of ethnocentrism, colonialism, or nationalism, offshoots of patriarchal rule, characterizes the era of Later Magoism. Although Magoism as a political system disappeared into the shadow of history, its memory lived on East Asians for centuries to come. The nostalgic ethos that longs for Mago or Magoism, sentimentalized in many texts and arts from Korea, China, and Japan epitomizes Later Magoism. Later Magoism conveys people's wish to be comforted in the memory of Old Magoism. As history ran its course, new cultural, religious, philosophical, literary, and artistic tropes began to develop. Later Magoism was widely favored and sustained by spiritualists, intellectuals, and the populace not without the exception of individual rulers and aristocrats.

The *Budoji* deplores the course of history that runs to degeneration. According to its mytho-historical narrative, two epochal catastrophes respectively brought an irreversible regression in history.[16] The first catastrophe is called "the disaster of five tastes." This is the mythic event referring to eating grapes (living organism) by a member of the primal community of Mago's descendent demiurges. Soon after joined by his/her sympathizers, this event brought a series of consequences. Those who ate grapes left Mago's Citadel out of shame but soon regretted and longed to return. However, they did not know how. As they dug the ground in search of the milk spring, which had been the source of nutrition for the divine family of Mago, the milk spring was destroyed. All peoples now had to eat some form of living organism for food. They eventually lost the state of immortality and had to depart from the paradisiacal residence for the four corners of the world. In this context, Hwanggung, eldest grandchild of Mago who is the common ancestor of East Asians, made an oath to Mago that she would bring all peoples to the knowledge of Mago's Origin. To remind everyone of this original event and to build unity among peoples of the world was the political and religious purpose of early Magoist polities.

The second catastrophe refers to the rise of Yao's rule, better known as one of the legendary Chinese emperors of highest antiquity. The *Budoji* depicts Yao as an imposter who imitated the principle of Magoism for his own ambition. Yao's rule aimed to thwart the unified forefront of Magoist polities. This resulted in a confrontation between the traditionally united force of Magoist Koreans and the newly risen pseudo-Magoist Chinese regime. Yao with his successors in time succeeded in disturbing international relations and caused havoc to the lives of ancient peoples. This brought a dispersion of Koreans into peripheral regions in the subcontinent of East Asia.[17] In my view, the *Budoji*, without regards to modern feminist discourse, makes a gynocentric argument against the rise of patriarchal rule in East Asia. The *Budoji* continues to state that, as Magoism lost its political power in East Asia, Magoist Koreans were cast to the mythic realm of the bygone era.

Claiming the *Budoji* (Epic of the Emblem City) as a Principal Text of Magoism

The *Budoji* (Epic of the Emblem City) stands out from other sources for its systemic and refined mytho-historical account of Old Magoism. Alleged to have been written in between the late fourth and early fifth century of Silla Korea (57 BCE-918 CE), the *Budoji* is the Sillan testimony to the history of Budo (Emblem City), a replica of Mago's Citadel. It is a book that summons ancient Koreans to remember the glorious history of their Magoist ancestors particularly Budo, better known as Dangun Choson Korea (2333 BCE-232 BCE). Budo's construction and administration in East Asia for nearly two millennia are attributed to the leadership of Imgeom or Dangun. She is the third of the triad sovereigns of Old Magoism after Hanin and Hanung. Designating the civilization of Budo as a direct successor of its previous civilization Sinsi (Divine Market) attributed to the leadership of Hanung, the *Budoji* traces the Magoist pedigree of pre-patriarchal civilizations ultimately back to Mago and her paradisiacal community, Mago's Citadel.[18]

Composed of thirty-three chapters, its epical narrative is replete with unheard but resonant concepts and symbols such as cosmic music, triad, parthenogenesis, mountain paradisiacal community, genealogy, and so on. Among others, the *Budoji* unleashes one of the most fascinating cosmogonic accounts yet-to-be-known, the story of Mago's beginning.[19] Mago, emerged by the cosmic music alongside the stars in the primordial time, began her procreation. Then she initiates the natural process of self-creation. She had her offspring to procreate and asked them to administer the paradisiacal community in Mago's Citadel. She is the cosmic being who listens to the rise and fall of the cosmic music. The primary task of Mago's community was to produce Earthly musical resonance that corresponds with the music of the universe. The sonic balance between the universe and the Earth is absolutely essential to the survival and prosperity of the earthly community.[20]

The *Budoji* not only makes it possible to recognize a large corpus of transnational primary sources as coherent within the context of Magoism but also enables the researcher to understand erosion, variation, and mutation wrought on individual data in the course of history. *Budoji's* mytho-historical framework is particularly crucial in assessing the large number of folkloric and topological data that are otherwise seen anomalous or corrupted. For example, the stories that Mago lived in a rock or Mago carried large boulders on her limbs and built megalithic structures find resonance in *Budoji's* narratives. Its accounts concerning rocks and landmasses are too complex to present here. Some examples are: Mago began her act of creation by moving and dropping a heavenly landmass and into heavenly water; Magoist sovereigns became rocks that made resonating sounds upon death. In short, Magoism animates pre-Chinese history of East Asia otherwise labeled as "primitive societies." It entertains the idea that animism and shamanism are not isolated practices but the older religious forms of Magoism.

Nonetheless, the *Budoji* has an issue of verification for its original account is found nowhere else today. Alleged to have been written by Bak Jesang (363-419?), the *Budoji* re-appeared in the mid-1980s in Korea in the Chinese written language alongside its Korean translation.[21] According to Bak Keum, its modern scribe and descendent of the last preserver, the original *Budoji* was lost or made inaccessible due to the outbreak of the Korean War in 1950 and the subsequent division of two Koreas up until today. He further states that the *Budoji* is the first book of the fifteen books called the *Jingsimrok* (*Literature of Illuminating Mind/ Heart*) whose authorship is attributed to the same author.[22] The *Jingsimrok* had been handed down in different families including the family of the author throughout the generations. Bak was able to reconstruct it almost identical to the original text from his memory of childhood reading of it as well as his translation work of it. According to Bak, he and his forefathers grew up reading and hand-scribing the *Jingsimrok*. Later during the Japanese colonial period (1910-1945), he translated the *Budoji* but was unable to publish it.

Having that said, I hold that the issue of unverified authorship does not diminish the present *Budoji*'s value for the study of Magoism. In my view, it is unlikely that modern authors would have written the origin myth of Korea in such a full-fledged gynocentric narrative. More to the point, the mytho-history of pre- and proto-Chinese Korea is not unique to the *Budoji*. It is supported by the *Handan Gogi* (Old Record of Han and Dan Korea) and other "apocryphal texts."[23] Even the foundation myth of Korea, also known as the Dangun myth, bears witness to the Magoist pre-patriarchal mytho-history of Korea albeit in a much coarser and simplified manner.[24] It is unfortunate that the history of Budo better known as Dangun Choson is treated as a myth that lacks historicity by mainstream historians. In fairness, we may call the *Budoji* an apocryphal text and its mytho-historical framework a hypothesis. Then, my study takes the task of proving that hypothesis. When Magoism remains invisible in modern scholarship, it is only a corollary that Magoist texts are labeled as apocryphal texts.

To me, the silent treatment given to the *Budoji* by the majority of Koreanists appears to point to something else. What is tacitly objected to is not its unverifiable authorship. It appears that what is rejected is its untamable content of Korean Magoist identity as well as its historical contention that ancient Magoists laid the foundation for East Asian civilization before the arrival of the Chinese patriarchs. Thus, that Magoism is an antithesis to the Sinocentric and androcentric views of East Asia remains a non-topic for mainstream Koreanists. However, many seem to overlook or ignore the fact that this text is a gynocentric book. The *Budoji* subverts modern knowledge about East Asian history and culture from a gynocentric perspective. The *Budoji* is subjected to double biases for its mytho-historical content and gynocentric implication.

I also argue that one's dismissal of the *Budoji* on account of accuracy is groundless. Bak Keum himself does not pretend for its mechanical accuracy. He admits a minimal degree of discrepancy is included in his work. Such discrepancy is, however, not unexpected, given that, as Bak denotes, the *Jingsimrok* was hand-copied and studied by its preservers throughout generations. In this regard, it is probable that some renditions occurred prior to its 1986 edition. When it comes to the female-related referrals, I detect some inconsistency in the *Budoji* to a minor degree and conjecture that previous scribes struggled over the gender implication of the text and altered female-specific concepts and terms into male or neutral counterparts. For this reason, a gender exegesis remains unsettled even in my work. What I draw from this is that these modifications are systematic rather than accidental, which makes it difficult for a gender critic to discern specific gender renditions. At any rate, the *Budoji* as a whole gives the impression that, while ascribing supreme authority to the Mago triad, Mago and her two daughters, male-gender rose as a major player in the mytho-history of Magoism from the third generation of Mago's genealogy. In my view, this is a misguided interpretation that needs more comprehensive gender hermeneutics, a complex topic to be discussed elsewhere.

Notes

1   I dedicate this article to Mary Daly (1928-2010) who has walked with me for the last sixteen years of my journey as Friend and Sister-Sojourn. Her influence is enormous in the formation of my thought on Magoism. I wrote this article in her presence that death can't diminish. Thank you Mary and I love you as always.

2   Ge Hong's account of Magu is neither the earliest nor the original. It is unknown how much of the *Magu zhuan* (Biography of Magu) written in the *Shenhsien zhuan (Hagiographies of Immortals)* by Ge Hong is originally attributed to his authorship. As to its earlier versions, Robert Ford Campany suggests three fragments from the *"Arrayed Marvels*, a late-second or early-third century collection of anomaly accounts credited to Cao Pi (187-226)." See Robert Ford Campany, *To Live as Long as Heaven and Earth* (University of California Press, 2002), 268.

3   See Helen Hye-Sook Hwang. *Seeking Mago, the Great Goddess: A Mytho-Historic-Thealogical Reconstruction of Magoism, an Archaically Originated Gynocentric Tradition of East Asia.* (Ph.D. dissertation: Claremont Graduate University, 2005), 35-67.

4   Keum Bak. *Budoji* (Epic of the Emblem City), tr. by Eunsu Kim (Seoul: Doseo Chulpan Hanmunhwa, 2002).

5   These names are crucial in assessing how Magoism is partly filtered through Daoism.

6   Wolfram Eberhard. *The Local Cultures of South and East China.* Leiden: E.J. Brill, (1968), 123-6.

7   Edward H. Schafer, *Mirages on the Sea of Time: The Taoist Poetry of Ts'ao T'ang* (University of California Press, 1985), 94-95.

8   Campany (2002), 269-70.

9   Hwang (2005), 335-342; 354-6.

10   A cross-examination between Xiwangmu and Mago as well as an in-depth study of Daoist Magu sources is an interesting topic to be discussed elsewhere. I have discussed in part in my dissertation. See Hwang (2005), 353-372.

[11]   Eberhard (1968), 125.

[12]   For more detailed discussions, see Hwang (2005), 18.

[13]   See Hwang (2005), 19-25. Linguistic evidence strongly suggests that "Mago" is associated with ancient Korean people and culture. The phonetic of "ma" not its meaning (hemp) is, according Jungpyeong Noh, derived from "sam" in Korean, a homonym for "three" and "hemp." This deliberation hinges on the ideas that Mago is also known as the Triad, Samsin (Triad Deity), and that the etymology of "the Triad" linguistically precedes "Mago." Noh Jungpyeong. *Go Choson ui Jonggyo Hyeokmyeong (Religious Revolution of Old Choson)*. Seoul: Daehan (2003), 41. While Noh's theory that "ma" comes from the homonym "sam" is plausible, it fails to note that the stem "ma" is shared in "mama" or "mother." Scholars maintain that the stem *ma* indicates not only mother but also goddess. The mother-syllable, "ma," is found in many names of goddesses from around the world. Barbara G. Walker. *The Woman's Encyclopedia of Myths and Secrets*. San Francisco: Harper & Row (1983), 560-1. Matilda Joslyn Gage goes further to say, "The word 'ma' from which all descendants of those peoples derive their names for mother, was synonymous with 'Creator.'" Matilda Joslyn Gage. *Woman, Church and State*. Chicago: Charles H. Kerr & Company (1983), 23. The link between mother and "creator" is corroborated in Magoism whereby Mago is the cosmogonic goddess.

[14]   In the Korean language, "ma" or "mama" is a referential term to respect a person of the royal family or high status. Such words are *sanggam mama* for the ruler, king, *daebi mama* for the mother of king, and *ma nim* for a noble lady. See *the Hangukhak daebaekkwa sajeon (Encyclopedic Dictionary of Korean Studies)*. (Seoul: Eulyu munhwasa, 1991, c1972), 468.

[15]   I view that the early Magoist leaders/shamans/sovereigns are female. However, other scholars see them as male. I argue that assigning female gender to early Korean forebears recounted in the *Budoji* is a more cogent measure that befits the gynocentric principle of Magoism. This requires a separate space to discuss.

[16]   I have discussed these mytho-historical events in detail in Chapters 4, 5, and 6 in my dissertational research. See Hwang (2005), 128-244.

[17]   It is estimated that pre-nationalist Magoist Koreans began in mainland China and gradually migrated eastward to the Korean peninsula in remote antiquity due to the rise and expansion of the Yao (堯) regime. See Hwang (2005), 241-244.

[18] For a more detailed discussion of the mytho-history of Magoism, see Helen Hye-Sook Hwang, "Issues in Studying Mago, the Great Goddess of East Asia: Primary Sources, Gynocentric History, and Nationalism" *The Constant and Changing Faces of the Goddess: Goddess Traditions of Asia* ed. Deepak Shimkhada and Phyllis K. Herman (London: Cambridge Scholars Publishing, 2008), 10-32.

[19] *Budoji*'s cosmogonic account is distinguished from other oral narratives from Korea. Folktales, while describing Mago as the nature-molder, are fragmentary in nature. Nonetheless, central motifs are highly reminiscent of *Budoji*'s account. This is a discussion that requires a separate space.

[20] I have treated *Budoji*'s cosmogonic account in an article. See Helen Hye—Sook Hwang. "The Female Principle in the Magoist Cosmogony." In *Ochre Journal of Women's Spirituality*. Fall (2007) [http://www.ciis.edu/ochrejournal/index. html], 10-19.

[21] The first edition of the *Budoji* was published in 1980s by two publishing houses, Gana (Seoul) and Girinwon (Seoul).

[22] Bak Keum states that the fifteen books are organized to the three volumes. He recalls the titles of thirteen books. These titles indicate the *Jingsimrok* is an encyclopedic compendium that includes such topics as history, language, calendar, religion, astrology, geography, natural science, music, and medicine. For details, see Hwang (2005), 101-102.

[23] Among these books, the *Handan Gogi* and the *Gyuwon Sahwa* (Historical Account of Gyewon) are counted. While both books are highly debated for their authenticity, I have discussed part of the *Handan Gogi*. See Hwang (2005), 115-127.

[24] The lineage of Hwanin, Hwangung, and Dangun centralized in the Dangun myth is concurrent in the *Budoji* as well as other apocryphal texts including the *Handan Gogi*. There is a substantive discrepancy between historians and the general public in Korea as to ancient Korean history. While historians continue to treat the Dangun myth and Dangun Choson as a legendary state, the general public has accepted it as a history.

Three Goddess Icon Spirit Banners
Crow Mother

Lydia Ruyle

Crow Mother is the mother of all the katsinas who are spirits of the Hopi universe. The Hopi, which means peace, believe all beings in the universe carry energy. They are one of the oldest living pueblo cultures and reside on three mesas in northern Arizona. Crow Mother appears during the Powamu or Bean dance, which opens the ritual year. She offers corn to sustain life and switches for discipline and protection. She stands on a rock art labyrinth symbolizing the human journey of life. Black crows hang out around humans and love corn; Artwork ©1998 Lydia Ruyle; Photo ©2007 Pat Alles.

Source: Katsina. Painted Wood. N.d. Hopi. Museum of Northern Arizona. Flagstaff

Isis

Lydia Ruyle

Isis of Egypt sits on her lion throne nursing her sacred son Horus. Her head is crowned with the sun, a snake, and horns, all three symbols of regeneration. Many theories in both art and science suggest humans first came from Africa and a universal black mother. Black Isis is the great mother of Egypt. She symbolizes the black mud of the Nile and its yearly renewal of life as it floods. Isis is often depicted in black basalt. All Pharaoh rulers are crowned seated on Isis' lap as a throne and she guards over their journey to the afterworld at death with her outstretched wings. The mysteries of Isis were strong in the Mediterranean for thousands of years. Isis and Horus become models for the Virgin Mary and child. As it gained power, Christianity absorbed earlier myths and made their stories its own; Artwork © 1996 Lydia Ruyle; Photo ©2007 Pat Alles.

Source: Bronze sculpture. C. 600-400 BCE. Egypt. Leiden Museum. Netherlands

Palden Lhamo

Lydia Ruyle

Palden Lhamo is the fierce protectress of Tibet and the Dalai Lama. She rides a mule standing on the five Chomo great mother mountains of the Himalayas. The mule has an eye of wisdom on her rump and Lhamo sits on a tiger skin. She holds a sword to cut through ignorance and carries a skull bowl filled with blood, the substance of life. Palden Lhamo is a dark blue, ample, nude crone with five skulls on her head and more hanging around her neck. A crescent moon crowns her flaming hair. One earring is a snake, the other is a lion, both worldwide Goddess symbols. The only thanka, prayer flag, which the Dalai Lama took with him when he fled the Chinese takeover of Tibet in 1959, was Palden Lhamo. Since then, she travels with him wherever he goes; Artwork ©2000 Lydia Ruyle; Photo ©2000 Pat Alles.

Source: Bronze sculpture. 9th CE, Tibet; British Museum. London

Saint Sara-La-Kâli:
The Romani Black Madonna

Malgorzata Oleszkiewicz-Peralba, Ph.D.

Is my black Mother Syama really black?
People say Kali is black,
but my heart doesn't agree.
If She's black,
how can She light up the world?
　　　—Kamalakanta Bhattakarya

Yes, I am black! And radiant—
　　　—*The Song of Songs*

For many years I have been studying topics related to femininity and blackness in different cultures. I researched these subjects in various countries of the world, including Spain, Poland, Lithuania, and Russia, Brazil and Cuba, as well as Mexico and "Greater Mexico" in the USA, and compiled my findings in a recent book.[1] The more I knew on this subject, the more I was pointed in the direction of southeastern France and northeastern Spain, where a great accumulation of Catholic sanctuaries to Black Virgins has been documented (see Huynen 168, Begg 150). In this region I found yet another active worship of a Black Madonna empowering and protective figure—the unofficial Romani Saint Sara-La-Kâli, possibly a blend of the Catholic Virgin Mary and the Indian goddess Kali/Durga/Sara.

Curiously, the area in question corresponds to where the Occitan civilization flourished in the Middle Ages, a region which extended from Béziers to Toulouse, Foix, and the kingdom of Aragon (present day Spain). Its language, the Provençal or Occitan, from which the Catalan derives, is used to this day. Within this civilization, which respected the equality of men and women, freedom, and tolerance, the Cathar religion thrived. The Cathars were Christians who did not accept the authority of the Pope and Rome, and who predicated a very simple and humble lifestyle, for which they were called *bonhommes* and *bonfemmes* or "good men" and "good women." They believed in reincarnation, refused to eat animal products, and lived according to the gospels, similar to the early Christian Church. Like some of the Gnostics of the first centuries of Christianity, they admitted women to the priesthood (Begg 136). Catharism spread in the Languedoc among all social classes and by the early thirteenth century was probably the majority religion. The Cathars were wiped out by subsequent crusades to the region, starting in 1208, with such examples as the massacre at Béziers in 1209, where the whole population of the city was burned at the St. Magdalene church,[2] through the cities and castles of Minerve, Aude, Termes, Toulouse, Carcassonne, Montségur, Quéribus, and Peyreperteuse, among others. It is estimated that one-half million people, Cathars and Catholics alike, were massacred in the area at that time ("Cathars and Cathar Beliefs"). Although it is said that Catharism was completely destroyed by the end of the thirteenth century, after the massacre at Montségur in 1244, this may not be the complete truth, as dispersed groups persisted until the early fifteenth century, and vestiges exist even today.[3] Moreover, many Cathar ideas continued among Protestants. The Cathars venerated Mary Magdalene, who allegedly lived in the region for over thirty years.

The above is the background of the Occitan area in the Middle Ages, but we have to go back to the first years of the Christian era, and beyond, in order to understand the context of the topics in question. According to various legends, around the year 42 CE a boat without sails or oars, carrying Mary Magdalene, her sister Martha, her brother Lazarus, as well as Sedonius, Maximus (Maximin), Mary Jacobé, and Mary Salomé, among others, escaping persecutions in Palestine, arrived at the coast of Camargue in southern France, near the place where the town of Les Saintes-Maries-de-la-Mer stands today. The group later spread through Provence, Christianizing the region. But, they did not come into a void, since the river Rhone's mouth area had a long history as a holy site. Celts and Romans inhabited this region, Celts venerating the triple mother-goddess Matres, that coexisted and was blended with Roman worship of Artemis, Cybele, Isis, and Mithras. Already in fifth century BCE documents, there was a mention of the town Oppidum Priscum

Râ, which had a holy spring (Coppens), and was a flourishing port in the Camargue. In fact, there was a sanctuary of the Egyptian sun god Râ on the island of Petit Rhône, and the Camargue used to be dedicated to the this god (Marie-Madeleine en Provence). These sacred sites were further integrated into Christianity, and in the fifth century AD there existed a Christian sanctuary, and in the ninth a church, on a small island, Santa Maria de Ratis (Râ became Ratis—"Vessel"[4]). In the twelfth century the place was renamed Notre Dame de la Mer or Our Lady of the Sea (Hari 24), and in 1838—Les Saintes-Maries-de-la-Mer or Holy Maries of the Sea. To this day, there stands a prominent pagan stone altar from the fourth century BCE in the left-front side of the Saintes-Maries-de-la-Mer church. There also is a walled-up "Lions door" on the opposite side, a vestige of the goddess Cybele. She was often represented flanked by lions as the supreme deity of Gaul, and publicly honored there through the fourth century AD (Begg 57). In addition, in the middle of the church, not far from the entrance to the crypt, there is a freshwater well, probably an ancient holy spring. Different legends attest to the identity of Saint Sara. The main Catholic Church version is that Sara was an Egyptian servant to Mary Jacobé and Mary Salomé and was not allowed in the boat, until the Maries threw a coat, thanks to which Sara could join them and arrive in Provence; another legend says that Sara was a local who helped them to disembark. She may have been an Egyptian priestess of the god Râ's sanctuary, or a Celtic goddess. In Brazil, I recently heard the Romani version of the legend which says that Sara was a local Gypsy who received the arrivals.[5] There are even speculations that she was the daughter of Mary Magdalene and Jesus Christ. How then did she become the patron saint of the Romanies?

The first record of the presence of the Romanies at Les Saintes-Maries (Notre Dame de la Mer) comes from CE 1438 (Hari 20), but in 1415 there already is a mention in Perpignan of a single Gypsy, Thomas of Saba, who obtained a letter of recommendation in Catalan from Alfonso of Aragon (later King of Aragon). According to Kenrick, and based on linguistic analysis, the Romanies migrated from India to Persia between 250 and 650 CE, and through Armenia they spread to eastern and then to western Europe in the fourteenth and the fifteenth centuries. They withstood 600 years of slavery in Romania until the nineteenth century. They received permission to participate in Catholic pilgrimages, and since 1407 they were in Western Europe as pilgrims and religious refugees fleeing alleged forced conversion by the Turks (29-34, 55-57). Thanks to the official letters they carried, initially they were well received and even given sustenance, but gradually, they were told not to come back, or not let into the European cities altogether.

Today, the Gypsy pilgrimage at Les Saintes-Maries-de-la-Mer is among the most important to them. As many as 10,000-15,000 Romanies gather here yearly to honor their patron, Saint Sara-La-Kâli (Sara the Black). They stay as long as two weeks celebrating in social gatherings, trading, renewing family traditions, and performing baptisms and marriages. Although the Church tries to use these pilgrimages for evangelization, in my visit to Les Saintes Maries in 2008, I did not see one single ritual of this kind, and almost all of my Gypsy interviewees stated that they only come for Sara and not for Catholic worship. Their devotion to Sara is indeed very strong—they gather in the thousands and participate in the Masses, the processions to the sea and other ceremonies, as well as in the music and dance. But the most important part of the gathering is their private time with Sara who is profusely dressed, touched and kissed. They perform private rituals, tell her about their joys and sorrows, and ask for protection and favors. Sara's multiple, always renewed, cloaks attest to the devotion of her worshippers, who offer her their own pieces of clothing or specially prepared cloaks so they can be imbued with Sara's magical energy. But why is Sara so popular among Romanies? Her color, unlike that of Mary Jacobé and Mary Salomé, the two saints also venerated at this occasion, is very dark, like their own original color. She is small and apparently insignificant, being relegated to a status of a pseudo-saint, and to the subterranean crypt of the church. But here we can't but stop and remember that most of the dark Maries were also found in and have a sanctuary in a grotto, and the goddess Cybele's "name is etymologically linked to the words for crypt, [and] cave" (Begg 57). Apparently, the crypt was also where the bones of two women, allegedly Mary Salomé, Mary Jacobé, were found in 1448 (Hari 25),[6] and where a pre-Christian sanctuary stood. In addition, the relics of Saint Sara remain quietly guarded in a box on the left side of the crypt, while those of the two Maries are placed in a large case covered with painted scenes, high above the altar of the church, and are ceremoniously lowered to the ground on 25 May, the day of the two Maries, among fervent exclamations of the congregation. Nevertheless, there is no question that the subterranean vault where Sara is located is the place of highest energy, continuously visited and lit with hundreds of candles brought by the tireless worshippers. We also have to remember that whatever worship was taking place at this site in ancient times it was certainly performed below ground where the crypt is located today, as the crypt represents the sacred womb of the earth, where all life comes from, and to this day some of the most important Virgin Mary sanctuaries are located in or next to a cave, a mountain, or a holy spring, water being the life-giving element. In fact, the black Sara is the one with the power of tremendous attraction at Les Saintes-Maries, as the other two pilgrimages to this place in October and in December, dedicated to the two Catholic white Maries only, are much less famous and numerous. In addition, Sara's cult spread around the world. Since 1998, there has been an analogous Romani sanctuary and pilgrimage to Kali Sara in Vancouver, and she has also found her way to the United States, Mexico, Brazil, and Australia.

While examining other religious festivals, we may be stricken by the similarity of the main events, dedicated to Sara-La-Kâli, especially the procession to the sea and the immersing of the statue into the waters, with the most important Hindu festival, the Durga Pooja. During this festival, the maternal fierce warrior, Durga of the Hindu religion, is taken in procession to a body of water, totally immersed, and left in it. The difference here is that Sara, as well as the two Maries (the following day), are taken to the sea and then back to the church. This practice suggests a syncretism or a parallelism among the Hindu and the Catholic traditions, as it is customary for Catholics to parade their holy statues, which always find their way to the original church, but very seldom are immersed in water. The Virgen del Carmen of Spain, patroness of fishermen and sailors, is one of the exceptions, as she is not only paraded through the streets of coastal villages, but also taken on a boat-ride in Malaga. In addition, the city's scuba diving club placed a permanent image of their patroness in a nearby location at the bottom of the sea (O'Shea).[7] The fact that this tradition takes place in the southern coast of Spain is not without significance, as a great number of Spanish Gypsies inhabit the southern province of Andalusia, which is widely known for their flamenco singing and dancing.

Durga Pooja (Bengali: "Worship of Durga") is an annual Indian festival, most popular in West Bengal, in honor of the fierce but benign divine mother goddess Durga, a multi-armed, warrior-mother-protector. Her celebration, traditionally held in the month of Chaitra (April-May) and in Ashwin (September-October) is a very important socio-cultural event ("Durga Puja"), similar to the festivals at Les Saintes Maries, which are also held in May and October. In India, Kali is also called Durga and Sara, who are aspects of the same goddess. Therefore, we can see that either consciously or subconsciously, the ancient Hindu divinity is venerated in the figure of Saint Sara-La-Kâli (Rishi, "Sati Sara" 4-7; Lee, "The Romani Goddess") who to a degree has been accepted and incorporated by the Catholic church (and from here the title of "Saint"), but who also preserves the Hindu names of Sara Kali. Therefore, we can conclude that Durga/Sara/Kali has been blended with the energy of a local goddess/Black Madonna in order to assure continuity of worship for the Romanies, in a similar way that in Brazil and Cuba the African gods and goddesses, such as Iemanjá/Yemayá—the *orixá/oricha* of the oceans—has been blended with the figure of the Virgin Mary.

While conducting interviews at Les Saintes Maries, I found out that—thanks to Marquis Folco de Baroncelli, an aristocrat from a Florentine family that settled in Provence and who "offered" the town to the Gypsies for ten days each year—the procession to the sea in honor of Saint Sara was instituted in 1935. Nevertheless, the first mention of Romanies in the region dates from the year 1438, and that of Sara in the "Legend of the Saint Marys" of the Arles manuscript, from 1521 (Hari 25). In addition, in spite of the fact that the most important figure on the presumed boat escaping persecutions in Palestine was Mary Magdalene, she is consistently omitted from all the recounts and ceremonies at Les Saintes-Maries. The local silence surrounding her persona is all-pervasive, but the observant eye will notice, in the church, a prominent portrait of a woman with an alabaster jar, clearly Saint Mary Magdalene, above the statues of the two other Maries in the boat. In fact, if we follow the route north, in the direction of Marseilles, to Saint-Maximin and La Sainte Baume, we will be rewarded with finding major traces of Mary Magdalene. The sleepy town of Saint-Maximin is dominated by the imposing medieval basilica dedicated to her, in which one can find an abundance of precious works of art and books on Mary Magdalene, and most importantly, her skull and other relics, guarded in a fourth century crypt, which was discovered in 1279. According to Bridonneau, at that time there were still traces of a sect that worshipped Mary Magdalene, probably related to the Cathars. The crypt also contains four sarcophagi from the fourth and the fifth century CE: presumably that of Mary Magdalene, Saint Maximin, Saint Sedonius, Saint Marcellus, and Saint Suzanne. Mary Magdalene's tomb can be considered the third most important of Christendom (44, 55). Covered with a golden mask, the alleged Mary Magdalene's skull and relics are paraded in a procession through the streets of Saint Maximin on her feast day every 22 July. Some thirty kilometers further, at the Sainte Baume mountain range, "sacred to the Greco-Marseilles cult of Artemis" (Bridonneau 16), one arrives at the cave where she presumably spent thirty years as a hermit, only covered by her long hair, as portrayed on many paintings. The same place is still visited today by couples imploring for fertility, as it was before the time of Mary Magdalene when people came there to pray to Artemis, the virgin goddess of fertility, pregnancy, and childbirth. Interestingly, the same qualities are attributed to Saint Sara-La-Kâli. In this single example we already notice a connection between feminine divine figures, such as goddesses and saints, regardless of culture, place and time.

The persona of the unofficial Saint Sara-La-Kali is especially fascinating, because she stands on the margins between the Catholic Church's official acceptance and sanction, while being the patron of one of the most dispossessed and persecuted minorities on Earth. No wonder she has been the object of attention of other subaltern groups, such as the Indians in Mexico, who identify her with the Virgin of Guadalupe, as well as mixed-blood Brazilians, who also pay homage to her. In fact, while attending the Catholic Mass for Saint Sara at Les Saintes-Maries on 24 May 2008, just before her procession to the sea, I was astonished to realize how similar this ceremony for the Gypsies must have been to the Catholic Church efforts of Christianization of the Mexican Indians in the sixteenth century. In the sermon, in the church brochure, as well as in several chants during the Mass and the procession, the Romanies were addressed in a patronizing way, as little children, and every occasion was used to glorify the "official" Maries as well as Jesus Christ. A common exclamation, heard over and over again, was:

> Vive Saint Sara!
> Vivent les Saintes Maries!
> Vive le Christ ressucité!
> (Long live Saint Sara!
> Long live the Saint Maries!
> Long live the resuscitated Christ!)

While conducting interviews at Les Saintes-Maries, I was also surprised by the fact that people from different extractions identified Sara with the "Black Madonna" or the "Virgin Mary." When asked about it, it was obvious that they referred to a similar energy and function—that of motherly help and protection of a subaltern, dark icon—rather than to the official Church images. Is then Sara a product of the collective imagination, of the yearning for an all-accepting feminine divinity? Let's remember that all the main Virgin Mary statues and images, such as the Guadalupes of Mexico and Spain, Fatima of Portugal, Lourdes of France, Regla (Chipiona) of Spain, Aparecida of Brazil, and del Cobre of Cuba were "found" or "discovered" by humble, dispossessed individuals: shepherds, fishermen, Indians, and children. It appears that the small, dark statue of Saint Sara, appropriated by the marginalized Romanies, is part of this continuum. At many famous places of pilgrimage, including those in southern France and northern Spain, as at other locations, we can observe a strong continuity attached to the worship of Dark Virgins, connected to caves and waters—symbols of the womb—at such places as Montpellier, Rocamadour, Meymac, Le Puy, Nuria, Solsona, and Montserrat (Begg 135, 150; Huynen 168). These have been places of adoration of dark female divinities for millennia.

The festival at Les Saintes Maries is an all encompassing, all accepting people's festival, where different social and economic groups, as well as many world traditions and nationalities intermingle. They are all welcomed by Saint Sara, a small dark figure, standing in the crypt of the Catholic Church, without access to an official status. Therefore, she can be considered the "saint" of the dispossessed, the persecuted, the nomads, the travelers. In view of the strength of her uncertain origin cult's attraction, the Church with precaution incorporated her into their own ceremonies in order to bring "new souls" to the religion, to prevent a parallel worship from developing, and the town—to attract pilgrims and tourists. Such is the economy of religious celebrations and pilgrimages, and although the number of Romanies in 2008 was much smaller than usual—presumably around 3,000[8]—there were still crowds of people everywhere for the whole duration of the festival, including nomads from Kenya, neo-pagans from England, anti-globalization youth from Spain, and a great number of very engaged tourists. In fact, most of the people dancing and parading in traditional Gypsy attire were non-Romani, *gadje*[9] enthusiasts from other countries, i.e. informed tourists and sympathizers. What was different about this colorful, international gathering was the fact that there were little to none mere onlookers or "consumer tourists." Everyone was a participant, if not wearing a special outfit or dancing, then walking in the processions, and attending Mass. People seemed to have arrived there consciously prepared, neither for the first nor for the last time. The festival of Saint Sara is all-accepting of social classes and national origins. Moreover, its magnetism spread to other lands, and today such festivals are practiced on several continents.

As the Sara-La-Kâli ritual in France has many analogies with that of Durga Pooja in India, it also reminds us of the "national goddess" of Brazil, Iemanjá, the *orixá* of the salty waters, whose places of worship are located close to sea, and who is celebrated in profuse ceremonies. On 31 December and 2 February, thousands of Brazilians at different locations arrive at the beaches at midnight, immerse themselves in the waters, and offer her presents and flowers, in a similar way that this is done in France and Brazil for Saint Sara and in India for the goddess Durga. All above divinities—Saint Sara-La-Kâli of the Romani tradition, Durga/Kali/Sara of the Hindu tradition, Iemanjá of the Afro-Brazilian tradition, as well as the Catholic Virgin Mary—are protective and nurturing patrons of fertility, guardians of gestation and childbirth, connected to grottos and waters, to the primordial moisture from which all life comes, to the waters of the womb.

Notes

[1] *The Black Madonna in Latin America and Europe: Tradition and Transformation* (University of New Mexico Press 2007 and 2009).

[2] Curiously, when trying to visit the church in 2008, I found that it was continuously closed, contrary to the announcement on the posted sign. When I inquired about this at several locations, I was repeatedly given the run-around, with no credible explanation or positive result.

[3] While visiting Montségur in 2008, I found fresh flowers at the monument to the Cathars, which seemed to be an active site.

[4] The vessel was one of the symbols of the goddess, and "[i]n Egypt, the sun god's diurnal death and rebirth placed him on a boat that represented mother Isis, whose temples featured boats carved in stone . . ." (Walker 121).

[5] Kellymask Ramirez. This version is incongruent with the time of arrival of the Gypsies to this area, which was identified as the fifteenth century of the Common Era.

[6] Another version of this story says that the bones of four women, including those of Mary Magdalene and Sara, were found there.

[7] A similar permanent underwater monument was established for the Virgin of Guadalupe off the Pacific coast of Mexico in 1958 and was replaced by a new one in 2002 ("Nueva imagen submarina").

[8] In 2009 the number of attendees increased again to 40,000 (Olga Seoane Paulus).

[9] Denomination given by Gypsies to non-Gypsy others.

Bibliography

Begg, Ean. *The Cult of the Black Virgin*. 1985. London: Arkana Penguin, 1996.

Bottaccini, Giannina. "Kali Sara Comes to Canada." *Kali Sara in Canada*. 14 Sept. 2007 <http://home.cogeco.ca>.

Bridonneau Yves. *The Tomb of Mary-Magdalene Saint-Maximin-la-Sainte-Baume Christianity's Most Important Tomb*. Aix-en-Provence: Companie des Éditions de la Lesse, 2006.

"Cathars and Cathar Beliefs in the Languedoc." *Cathars and Cathar Beliefs in the Languedoc*. 14 March 2008 <http://www.cathar.info/>.

Coppens, Philip. "The Gypsy Goddess of Saintes-Maries-de-la-Mer." *The Gypsy Goddess of Saintes-Maries-de-la-Mer*. 31 July 2008 <http://www.philipcoppens.com>.

"Durga Puja." *SurfIndia*. 4 Aug. 2008 <http://www.surfindia.com>.

Hari, Albert. *A Short Guide to the Church of Saintes-Maries-de-la-Mer*. Transl. Oliver Todd. N.p.: Éditions du Signe, 2002.

Hawley, John S. and Donna M. Wulff, eds. *Devi: Goddesses of India*. Berkeley: University of California Press, 1996.

Huynen, Jacques. *El enigma de las vírgenes negras*. Trans. R. M. Bassols. 1972. Barcelona: Plaza & Janes S.A., 1977.

Kamalakanta. "Is My Mother Really Black." Transl. Rachel Fell McDermott. *Poet Seers*. 18 Sept. 2009 <http://www.poetseers.org>.

Kernick, Donald. *Gypsies: From the Ganges to the Tames*. Hertfordshire, Gr. Brit.: University of Hertfordshire Press, 2004.

Kinsley, David. *Hindu Goddesses*. 1986. Berkeley: University of California Press, 1988.

Lee, Ronald. "The Romani Goddess Kali Sara." *The Romani Goddess Kali Sara.* 14 Sept. 2007 <http://www.home.cogeco.ca>.

_____. "The Rom-Vlach Gypsies and the *Kris-Romani.*" *Gypsy Law.* Ed. Walter O.Weyrauch. Berkeley: California University Press, 2001. 188-230.

Marie-Madeleine en Provence. Dir. Georges Combe. DVD. CLC Productions/ KTO, 2006.

McDermott, Rachel Fell and Jeffrey J. Kripal, eds. *Encountering Kali: In the Margins, at the Center, in the West.* Berkeley: University of California Press, 2003.

"Nueva imagen submarina." UNIVISION.com. 2 Feb. 2003 <http://www.univision.com>.

Oleszkiewicz-Peralba, Malgorzata. *The Black Madonna in Latin America and Europe: Tradition and Transformation.* 2007. Albuquerque: University of New Mexico Press, 2009.

O'Shea, Teresa. "Virgen del Carmen." *The Virgen del Carmen Festival en Andalucia.* 13 August 2008 <http://www.andalucia.com>.

Ramirez, Kellymask (Kelli Cristine Lopes Rego). Personal interview. Rio de Janeiro, 7 June 2009.

Rishi, W.R. "Roma." *Roma* 1 (1974): 1-23.
_____. "Sati Sara Consort of God Shiva." *Roma* 3 (1977): 4-7.
_____. "St. Sarah (Goddess Durga/Kali): Ancient Indo-French Cultural Link." *Roma* 25 (1986): 4-8.

Sanctuaire des Saintes-Maries-de-la-Mer. *Livret du Pelerin.* 1976. N.p. : Éditions du Cloître, 2005.

Seoane Paulus, Olga. Electronic communication. 31 May 2009.

The Song of Songs: A New Translation. 1973. Transl. Marcia Falk. New York: HarperSan Francisco, 1993.

Walker, Barbara G. Dictionary *The Woman's Dictionary of Symbols and Sacred Objects*. New York: HarperCollins, 1988.

Wiley, Eric. "Romani Performance and Heritage Tourism." *The Drama Review* 49 (2005): 135-158.

Saint Sara-La-Kali;
Photo © 2008 Malgorzata Oleszkiewicz-Peralba

Devotees light candles and leave ex-votos at
Saint Sara-La-Kali's statue;
Photo © 2008 Malgorzata Oleszkiewicz-Peralba

Case containing Mary Salomé´s and Mary Jacobé´s relics,
ceremoniously lowered to the ground every May 25th;
Photo ©2008 Malgorzata Oleszkiewicz-Peralba

Messages from the Black Madonna

Solace Wales

Over the past 20 years I have been privileged to be in the presence of a number of Black Madonnas, mainly in Italy. While meditating in front of Her, messages have come to me in the form of thoughts. These thoughts often address issues I am currently grappling with, but always seem to also apply more generally. At moments of doubt or grief—whenever I feel overwhelmed—I return to these messages and am strengthened. Below are some of the messages I received and the sites that inspired them. (Note: Except for Einsiedeln, which is in Switzerland, and Chimayo, which is in New Mexico, all of the sites below are located in Italy.)

Sommocolonia—Main Church; *Santa Maria del Carmine* (wooden statue):
Stay mindful of the sacred in each moment—now.

Do what you can each day, however little—do it with joy and a sense of completeness and it will be enough.

Spello—San Andrea Church (fresco):
Be tender with your child, whatever his or her nature.

Spoleto—Cathedral; *La Santissima Icone della Gran Madre di Dio* (The Most Sacred Icon of the Great Mother of God; painting):
You will have the strength to rescue one of your own.
and
You will have the strength to rescue one of my own.

Manfredonia—Cathedral (painting):
> **Cultivate wisdom by accepting grief, smiling all the while**
> **at the discoveries of the child.**
>
> **Come into your age with full womanliness.**

Foggia—Cathedral; *Madonna delle Sette Vele* (The Madonna of the Seven Veils is a painting literally covered with veils so that all you see is a black oval where Her face would be against a white ground of embossed silk):
> **Even when not visible, I am fully present.**
> **Appreciate my seven veils, but know that**
> **my mystery is infinite.**
> **You must do the unveiling nonetheless**
> **in order to meet 'the dark eye of the self.'**

Bari—Cathedral (painting):
> **Be joyous! Revel in festivity and fruitfulness!**

Assisi—San Rufino Church (relief sculpture over the portal):
> **Provide that circle of space in your life**
> **Where introspection is primary—**
> **for it is there, within the encompassing Mother arms,**
> **that the holy child is fed.**

Einsiedeln, Switzerland—Benedictine Monastery; *Our Lady of Einsiedeln* (wooden sculpture):
> **Be certain of your motives—**
> **then proceed with sobriety, kindness <u>and</u> lightness.**

Siena—Cathedral; *Madonna del Voto* (Of the Vow; painting):
> **You need only bring a pure heart.**

Montenero—sanctuary near Livorno (whitened painting):
> **Be thankful for life's abundance and its sanctity.**

Lucca—Santa Maria Nera Church; *Madonna di Loreto* (statue):
> **Do not shy away from power.**
> **If you can seize it with unfettered spirit,**
> **then use it to heal the Earth and its inhabitants.**

Borgo a Mozzano—San Jacopo Church (sculpture in high niche):
> **Wear humility, not with submissiveness and passivity,**
> **but with power which originates from an inner sense of**
> **beauty with no eye to outer effect.**

Chimayo, New Mexico—*La Madonna di Guadalupe* (fresco):
> **Always welcome your frightened child.**
> **Bring her with you so that she may be heard**
> **and comforted. Then, with her fully present,**
> **act with great courage.**

Palmi—Cathedral; *Madonna della Sacra Lettera* ("Of the Sacred Letter"; painting):
> **My meaning is elusive:**
> **To arrive at it, one must have great perseverance**
> **And pursue an arduous path.**

Seminara—Cathedral; *Maria Santissima dei Poveri* (Maria Greatest Saint of the Poor; statue):
> **You must bring your faith into the world—into action.**
> **You will picture it and find the way.**

Cagliari—Chiesa di Sant'Agostino (St. Augustine's Church; statue):
> **The richness of the black earth is**
> **the richness of your soul touching eternity.**

Mater Dolorosa

Jean Feraca

I

Mother most sad
Mother most silent
Mother afflicted
Mother demented
Mother transfixed with grief
Mother given to the Lutherans
Mother bereft of her children
Mother left to die alone

Mirror of patience
Seat of wisdom
Well of calm
Smiling tiger
Lady from Niger
Eye of the storm

We children, that you might hear us
We children, that you might spare us
We children, that you might bring us with you into heaven
    to share in the company of your mother
    and your sister and your brother and our father

From your wrath, deliver us
From your scorn, deliver us
From your mop and pail, deliver us
Mother, have mercy

Mother, have mercy
Mother, have mercy
Remember us, O Mother
Now and at the hour of our death.

II
Grassy Mound
Chicken Little
Clammy brow
Mother of the clean sheet
Hole where I came out
Hole where my sister came out
Hole where my brother came out
Mouth that my father kissed
Mexican Hairless
Font of bliss

Blue Rose
Baby rose
Pressed rose
Primrose
Rock rose
Rosey the Riveter

III
Steam iron
Sweating kettle
Rising scum
Rocking cradle
Boiled egg
Rusty ladle
Mother of vapors and rubs
She who kept us alive
She who did not dash our brains out.

Broken tooth
Pearly gate
Bloody root

Mother of maggots and moths
We praise you, we bless you, we call your name.

Mother of liniments and cloths
Mother of iodine
Mother of gauze
She who bound up our wounds
She who painted our thumbs
Mother of ovens and stoves
Rubber glove
Mother of cloves
Mother of the clean steps
Hear me, look on me, remember me, O Mother
Now and at the hour of our death.

IV
Rosy ghost
Vapor trail
Baby's breath
Face veil
Freight cargo
Motherlode
Flashgun
Silver bullet
Screaming Mimi
Loose cannon
Shining path
Vacuum cleaner
Third rail

Nursing My Child
Through His First Illness

Jean Feraca

Basilicata, 1974

1
Sleepless he rages, fists on the rails
howling for hours . . .

This, the old dream to be martyred
the calling denied
floats up, a kidney in a bowl
carried to the altar, St. Agatha's breasts
Ophelia's face

the procession of virgins advances, she carries
a candle
she wears a white dress

a thimble rolls out of my grandmother's coffin
I am bound on the hoop sewn into my hem

This is the way, each moment
I mount
ever higher, the life
of the flesh
falls away

knock knock knock

upstairs, the invalid thumps with his cane
from the bed

knock knock knock

in his three-legged
crib, the infant stands up.

2

I live alone on the edge of town
I keep my father's house

Remember, O most gracious virgin mary
never was it known that anyone who fled to thy protection
was left
unaided . . .

Skull-bald, these mountains hang over us
massive and terrible
leaning like great-aunts over an infant's cradle.

3
teeth descend from the cave roof in rows
Mouth
under the Mountain

O mother of the world incarnate
before thee I stand
sinful and sorrowful

a tower extrudes from a hill
salt
laps at the edge, uneasy

my darling, I'll croon to you, I'll coo
I'll carry you for hours
your wails
splash my sides like a tide of acid
you wear me away all white

the sea sucks up, shudders
subsides to a hiss
starfish slide
dead crabs float
belly up
the moon spins upside down
I'll croon, I'll coo, I'll carry you for hours

all the rock pools give up their ghosts
in the sun
white algae heaps up in pockets
airy
weightless
I drift I rove, I carry you for hours

O Mountain, O Rose, O Gold

knock knock knock

pocked, pitted, this blister of rock

white algae heaps up in pockets
despise not my petition
hear me, O Mother
Answer.

Crossing the Great Divide

Jean Feraca

Your real country is where you're heading
not where you are.
            —Rumi

1

Hooked in this pace between sea and sky
like a hammock
pitched from a cliff
I stare out at the day, death in the corners of its eyes.

Only the goat-hoofed, the cloven
survive in this place
scrambling for toe-holds, hanging in the crags.

The gecko clings with tacky feet to the stucco wall.
Stupefied at noon,
he curves around a roofbeam
abandoning his long body to its love for the hot dark.

I let myself down, inch by inch.
On the ledge, white wine withers in the glass.
I live in the holes.

Life slows to a lizard's pulse
a hot stone,
I hold the quick between my thumbs, stroking its throat.

2

The sea asleep, brassy serpent
sullen in the shadows now
a muddy swell
slithering through trees below.

I shall live out my life rejoicing
ribboning under the jagged shadow of the hawk.

There is no reason for this joy
eagle-bald, knifing through me like a canyon.

There is nothing in this landscape that defines me.

3

Freed from the priest's hands
we are grails
crossing a great divide,
below us, the abyss, ahead, the dense glass—
Believing we will crash, we are passed
whole
through the rose
the blue
the needle's eye of God.

—Maratea, Basilicata

The Black Madonna
and the Labyrinth

Catlyn Fendler

Author's Note: *A version of this article first appeared in the Conference Reader for "Awakening the Energy for Change: The Black Madonna and the Womb of God," a conference created and directed by China Galland, Professor-in-Residence at the Center for the Arts, Religion, and Education at the Graduate Theological Union's Pacific School of Religion, Berkeley, California, June 18, 2005. (For a description and discussion of the conference, see the report by Galland in She Is Everywhere, Vol. 2.). I would like to gratefully acknowledge China Galland, Lucia Chiavola Birnbaum, and the Rev. Dr. Lauren Artress, whose work and teachings have and continue to guide and inspire me on my journey with this work.*

Several years ago, I made a pilgrimage to Chartres Cathedral in Chartres, France, located about one hour west of Paris. Chartres Cathedral stands beautifully preserved, a wonder of the medieval period, although its origin dates back to the 5th century when she first came into being as a small church built by early Christian settlers. As a sacred site, her roots go even farther back, for the original church was built on a hill, next to a sacred well where Druids had worshipped from time unknown.

I was traveling there to walk the labyrinth, an exceptional one, one of the oldest surviving labyrinths in one of the greatest Gothic cathedrals ever built. The labyrinth is an ancient pattern found in numerous cultures around the world. Some of the oldest forms, carved onto stones, date back over 3,000 years. A labyrinth is not a maze—there are no dead-ends or mind-teasing paths that keep us guessing which way to go or how to reach the end. A labyrinth has only one path that weaves to its center, and then back out to the entrance again. No choices are necessary, so the mind is free to relax, grow quiet, turn inward, and open. Today there is an on-going, global awakening of interest in walking the labyrinth as a path of self-reflection, transformation and connection to sacred source.

Both the Black Madonna and the labyrinth arrived in my life within a few years of each other. Although they came to me in different places and under different circumstances, I sensed a strong connection between the two. From the beginning of my relationship with each, I have felt compelled to explore and understand them not only for their separate and unique teachings, but also to explore where and how they are interconnected, each enhancing and expanding the great wisdom the other has to offer. What particularly drew me to the labyrinth at Chartres is that the cathedral is also home to not one, but two Black Madonnas: Notre Dame du Pilier: Our Lady of the Pillar, and Notre Dame de Sous-Terre: Our Lady Underground.

It is my experience that the labyrinth and the Black Madonna share many qualities that express similar wisdoms and complement each other profoundly. Just as the qualities of the Black Madonna are expressed in the Dark Mothers of many cultures, labyrinths, in their many forms, also are shared by cultures the world over. As the Black Madonna and the Dark Mothers express the sacredness of the feminine, so, too, is the labyrinth a physical expression of the feminine principle.

From their earliest forms as ancient spirals and Great Mothers, labyrinths and Black Madonnas have been with us throughout the ages, and they share a history of being particularly important in Western Europe during the Middles Ages. Hundreds of Black Madonnas, in the form of icons, statues and paintings, have been found in churches, cathedrals, chapels and shrines. The Feminine was celebrated as Divine, a source of wisdom, comfort and strength. The Dark Mother was present and available to people on a daily basis. In many places She also was the sacred destination for pilgrims who traveled far and wide to open their heart to Her. She was counsel and guide for all: men, women, children, the royal as well as the poor.

During this same time, labyrinths were placed in numerous cathedrals, particularly in northern France, as a destination for pilgrims who were unable to make the Church-encouraged journey to Jerusalem. Those who came to Chartres could make a pilgrimage to both the Black Madonna and the labyrinth, each a powerful archetype of wholeness, the life force, both sacred and divine.

The Black Madonna tells us that all who come to Her are welcome, that no one is to be excluded. She is the source of life, the fertile darkness of the Earth itself, nourishing us, celebrating diversity, creativity and the deep mysteries of birth, death and transformation. She is the archetype of wholeness that is accepting, healing and compassionate, binding all of us together in love.

The labyrinth, too, is an archetype of wholeness. The path of the Chartres labyrinth is contained in a great circle, the oldest and most enduring expression of the feminine. The circle reflects the cycles of the seasons, the phases of the moon, the rhythm of sunlight and darkness, the interplay of these holding the great cycle of life, death and regeneration.

When we walk the labyrinth, we are held in Her circle. As in the energy and spirit of the Black Madonna, all are welcomed into the labyrinth; no one is excluded. We walk as individuals, alone with our own thoughts and experiences, while simultaneously walking in equality with one another, all members of the human family. The meandering path suggests a metaphor of life's journey, with all of its unexpected surprises and turns. Arriving at the center, we are given the opportunity to connect with our own center, our experience of Source, Divinity, Ground of Being. Here we may receive wisdom and inspiration, or perhaps offer a petition, or a pardon, or a prayer. We might express gratitude or simply experience the profound healing of a moment of inner quiet and peace. As we return to the entrance, taking with us our experience of the walk and our time in the center, we return with those insights and gifts to share with the world.

The labyrinth and the Black Madonna are both archetypes with which we can interact, literally, physically, with full body, mind and spirit. We can share the gaze of the Black Madonna, sit with Her, touch Her image, while opening our heart and mind to what She has to offer. On the winding path of the labyrinth, we place our whole being into the experience. As the mind quiets, intuition can open, receive; creative thoughts and inspirations may arise. On the labyrinth we can walk, crawl, sit, dance, place our feet and hands on its sacred ground. Each is an archetype that offers many opportunities for insight and learning that literally help us to connect with the energy we need for change.

The labyrinth offers a sacred space, a special time out of the ordinary, where transformation occurs. The Black Madonna, too, offers us a ground for deep growth and change, for I have been told that one of Her greatest miracles is the transformation of the human heart. Both the labyrinth and the Black Madonna are builders of community and connection. As we experience each, we are joining the great human community of all who have come before, opening our hearts and minds to the wisdom offered there, joining with them to use this energy to build a future and a world sustained by compassion, justice and inclusion, bound together in love.

In France, farther west, and north of Chartres, I have visited another convergence of the Black Madonna and a labyrinth. In northern Brittany, in the bustling little town of Guingamp, a Black Madonna stands amidst candles and flowers, presiding over a small, circular labyrinth beneath an outside porch of the cathedral. People passing by stop in and pause awhile to sit on the stone benches next to the labyrinth, for it is somewhat obscured by the banks of candles above which the Black Madonna stands. Still, I was able to walk most of the curving path, one quite similar to that of the Chartres pattern. Unable to walk the complete pattern, I am reminded that there is no right or wrong way to walk a labyrinth. Further, another part of experiencing the labyrinth, an important one, can be that of simply sitting by the labyrinth, witnessing, journaling, meditating or praying, or just enjoying a quiet moment of being.

Under this little portal in Guingamp, next to the Black Madonna and Her bank of candles, sat a table containing material about the cathedral, indicating that there also is a statue of Mary inside the church. The information noted that some people prefer to pray to Her indoors, while others prefer to be with Her outside. This reinforced for me the way in which both the Black Madonna and the labyrinth are deeply connected with nature and place.

There are many stories in which a Black Madonna originally was found outdoors, perhaps under a bush, in a tree or in a stream. Sometimes a church would be built around Her in the very space where She was found. Sometimes She would be taken to another place and a church built for Her there. Sometimes she would find a way to become just too heavy for any man or beast to move Her from the spot where She was found, indicating indisputably where She wants to be. She is part of nature and teaches us to respect its importance and power. She reminds us of our inseparable part in the great web of being, and leads us to be stewards of nature, honoring and respecting its rhythms and diversity. Rather than exerting power over nature, we are instructed to participate with Her, learn Her teachings, and use Her gifts with thoughtful respect.

Curled within the pattern of the labyrinth is an expression of one of the oldest and most familiar shapes found in all of creation, the spiral. Some of the farthest and oldest star systems observed are in the shape of a great spiral. It is a shape found everywhere in nature. We see it in the whirlpool's eddy, the uncurling of a fern, the opening of a rose. Closer to home, in our bodies, we have the spiraling tissue of the brain, the winding of the intestines, the path our blood makes as it swirls through the heart. Our uniqueness is expressed in the spiral of our hair at the crown of our head and in the print on the tip of our thumb. The labyrinth bone in our ear helps us keep our balance. Lift up the double helix of our DNA, and the code of our being forms a spiral. It is a shape that is deeply familiar to us, one we seem to find pleasing, comforting, even calming. The spiraling pattern of the labyrinth reminds us that we are part of nature, an inseparable part of the life force itself.

In Brittany, along with labyrinths, Black Madonnas, and numerous sacred landscapes of standing stones and circles so deeply rooted in our Earth and the presence of our ancestors, there is a religious tradition called the pardon. One of the most famous is the Pardon of St. Anne, echoing to us the matrilineal heritage of the feminine as sacred. Once a year, at different times in different communities, people gather together and walk. In the labyrinth tradition, there is a popular quote attributed to Augustine: "It is solved by walking." In the tradition of the pardon, people make a pilgrimage together, sometimes lasting several days. They ask for forgiveness and offer it to each other as well.

In this practice resides the most ancient heart of the sacred feminine, breathing, as ever, holding us. Whether seen or unseen, whether remembered or not, nonetheless She is carried forward, and still She is carrying us. She lives in the spirit of walking the Earth together, in silence, in celebration, in mutual recognition of our frailties and strength, in mutual pardon, and in mutual responsibility to each other and our planet, our mother, the life force who sustains us.

People make pilgrimages to Black Madonnas and Dark Mothers the world over. The pilgrimage may take a few steps, to a place known only to our private heart as sacred, or it may last days or weeks. People also make pilgrimages to labyrinths, whether across town or half a world away. Walking the labyrinth is, in itself, a kind of pilgrimage. Honoring the Black Madonna is a pilgrimage, too. For in each of these acts, the Black Madonna and the labyrinth can take us to our deepest heart, opening us to the transformative energies of compassion and love.

Rebirth

Kathy Martone

This tapestry captures the image of a Native American shaman who first showed up in a dream of mine and then began visiting me on a regular basis during my daily meditations; Artwork © 2008 Kathy Martone; Photo © 2008 Paul Gillis, www.artworkphotography.net.

Gathering Forces

Kathy Martone

This woman appeared in several dreams as an artist and actress. During my active imagination sessions, she asked to be the subject of my next tapestry and strongly encouraged me to add the animal images from my previous dreams. She even suggested the tapestry's title; Artwork © 2009 Kathy Martone; Photo © 2009 Paul Gillis.

Hymn to Ma of Ephesus

Elizabeth Cunningham

I sing to the mother of all
she whose heart is honeycomb
who follows the spiral flight of bees.

I sing to the mother long bereft
to the one who is leaving me
for the far high reaches of light and air.

When you are gone, will you be my road?
When you are gone, will you show me the stars?
When you are gone, will I find your face in my own?

I sing to the mother who is more than mine
to the girl grown ancient gathering eggs to her breast
to the abandoned mother who has never, never left.

Author's Note: The Virgin Mary "Ma" is reputed to have lived in the hills above Ephesus in her old age while worship of Artemis of Ephesus was still going strong.

Ave Matres

(with gratitude to the Hail Mary)

Elizabeth Cunningham

Hail all mothers
graceful or not
God or goddess is with you, believe it or not.

Blessed are all women
and blessed are the fruits of our wombs
whatever names, ridiculous or not, we choose for them
and even when they're acting rotten.

O mothers
holy human mothers
all our children are divine.

Long after they leave us
they will curse us and pray to us
now and in the hour of our death
now and in the hour of their need.

The Tarantata

Mary Saracino

Note: "The Tarantata" is an excerpt from Mary Saracino's novel *The Singing of Swans* (Pearlsong Press 2006).

The Magistrate's soldier returned Ibla to her village of Alberobella late in the evening after the jail in which she had been incarcerated had collapsed to the ground, a mass of cinders and smoldering ash. The Magistrate's wife had demanded that Ibla be set free, even though the Magistrate wanted to throw Ibla into a jail cell in nearby Castellana. His wife insisted that the fire had been the doing of the Black Madonna of the Flames. Her proof was that Ibla had exited unharmed. The jailer's dog had not been as fortunate nor had the two drunkards who occupied the cells adjacent to Ibla's. Although the Magistrate dismissed his wife's ramblings as nothing more than silly superstition, he acquiesced to her wishes. He realized that he would have to provide Signore Martelli with a better excuse than that of a miracle for why he had set Ibla free. Not a religious man, the padrone harbored no patience for those who followed spiritual ways. What plausible excuse the Magistrate might concoct would have to wait, for his wife would not cease her harping until he had agreed to her request.

The same soldier who had claimed Ibla the prior day escorted her back to Alberobella upon her release. When the jailer's wagon arrived in the piazza, Fiora emerged from the shadows to meet them. She had sensed that Ibla would return that evening and so had walked to the center of the village in expectation. As she waited by the well, she gazed at the moon rising in the evening sky, thinking of all that had transpired. She pondered the power of Cybele to reassert Her presence. The others think it is the Black Madonna, Jesus' dark-skinned mother, who has proclaimed her disfavor at the jailing of my Ibla, but they misunderstand. It is none other than the Divine She. Although in truth, it matters not what they call Her. My people have waited years for the balance to be righted. For so long the unjust have ruled the Earth, raining down indignities upon the people, conquering their spirits and their bodies, stealing their livelihoods, trampling their pride and worth. Perhaps the time has come for the meek to inherit the Earth, as their Christ proclaimed.

In the distance, Fiora discerned the rumbling of wheels crushing dirt and stone as they hurried along the roadway. She turned to watch the prisoners' cart approach. When the wagon rolled to a stop, the mule pulling its weight brayed then snorted. Fiora reached out to pat the animal, offering a soothing touch of thanks for carrying her daughter safely back to her.

"Get out!" the soldier ordered Ibla.

"There is no need for such disrespect," Fiora said, addressing the Magistrate's guard.

"You and your heathen daughter can rot in hell for all I care," the man spat. "She cast a spell on the jail. That is how it burst into flames. Just to save her sorry life."

"Do not speak of that which you have no understanding," Fiora cautioned.

"Watch your back, Witch. You have not seen the last of me or the Magistrate."

The soldier slapped the reins against the mule's sweaty back and the cart lurched off, filling the evening air with dust.

Fiora waved away the cloudy residue of dirt that stained the air. "Filthy deeds breed filthy outcomes," she said.

Ibla reached for her mother's arm and fell into her embrace.

"Are you all right?" Fiora asked, tears streaming down her cheeks.

Ibla nodded.

"Come, let's go home. I have made some soup for you to eat. I am sure they did not feed you well in that horrid hole of a jail cell."

*   *   *

Life resumed its normal pace for Ibla and Fiora and the rest of the village. The two herbalists tended the sick and the dying. They attended births, applying their midwifery skills in the service of the women of their town. They cultivated their herb garden and harvested its bounty. They prepared healing potions and salves. Ibla continued to paint pictures of flames and brilliant-red tongues, adding ochre-colored triangles and other symbols to her images. Above all, they honored the Dark Mother, Cybele, each day, praying before the small altar they had erected for this purpose in the corner of their kitchen.

Word spread of the miracle at the jail and Ibla's release. Neighbors came to welcome home the freed painter. The farmers brought olives and almonds, figs and fava beans from their gardens. Signore Fornaio brought two loaves of dense, warm bread. His wife, Inez, greeted Ibla with a bouquet of the ruby red flowers. "Like the tongues of flames of your paintings, the fiery eyes of the Madonna," she said. Ibla and her mother feasted with their friends and planned a big celebration to honor the miracle and the Black Madonna who had instigated it. There would be a parade and revelry to rival the grandest of carnavales—floats and people dressed in costumes, dancing and music of all kinds. They planned to hold it on the 15th of August, the day of the Virgin's Ascension into Heaven. They still had two months to prepare for the festivities.

One afternoon, when no patients had come to call and Ibla was unmotivated to paint, she decided to write a letter to her father, the Archbishop. She had been inspired to do so after he had interrogated her when he had arrived in Alberobella to question her about the Black Madonna emerging from the painting she had created for the now-destroyed church. How he had acted that day had unsettled her. Ibla disliked how he had disrespected her mother and how he had disassociated himself from his biological ties to her. More than that, however, she had sensed a churning within his breast, the rumblings of a disease, as if his heart was floundering in a vat of poison and was choking for breath. She thought to ask him to return to Alberobella so that she could prepare herbal remedies for him. She sought to save his life.

The Archbishop received Ibla's letter and read it in his study one evening, after having finished his supper of roasted chicken, artichoke hearts and red wine. He was alone, preferring the company of his books. Surrounded by shelves of scholarly and theological tomes, he slit open the envelope and withdrew the sheet of paper on which Ibla had written her note. He scanned the page, reading her offer to treat him, then scoffed. *Arrogant Witch! Thinks she can discern illness without the proper medical knowledge. There is nothing wrong with my heart.*

He stood and paced before the window, pausing long enough to gaze onto the moonlit courtyard that lay beneath the balcony of his chambers. An owl screeched twice and two cats hissed at one another, the larger mangy one boxing the ears of its smaller, tabby-colored brother. He turned away from the window, picked up the letter once more and re-read it. Angry, he crumbled it in his fist then flattened it once more before holding it over the candle flame to set it on fire. *Potions indeed! Poison is more like it! No doubt she would concoct a serum to suck the life out of me. She is against me for I did not sanction her supposed miracle. She knows of the potency of Belladonna. The strega means to kill me with that Deadly Nightshade if I return for her medicinal advice. I will teach her not to threaten a man of my authority.*

A week later, a messenger arrived at Ibla's door, carrying a small unidentified parcel bearing her name. Fiora took the package, asking its deliverer who had sent it.

"I do not know, Signora," the young man replied.

Fiora presented the box to her daughter, cautiously. "Be careful, Ibla. Who knows what it contains."

Ibla unfastened the string that bound the package and opened the lid. Inside, beneath a loosely strewn bed of straw, emerged a large tarantula. Its furry legs reached for the rim and crept over the side. Ibla opened her mouth to scream but her tongue-less mouth was able only to exert a muffled cry. She dropped the parcel to the floor. She could not move, so frightened was she. Fiora grabbed a broom to sweep away the insect, but as she approached her daughter with the bristled end of the tool, ready to swat, the tarantula had already scurried up Ibla's leg and bit her, injecting its venom into her thigh. Ibla swooned and fell. The tarantula hurried off toward a chink in the kitchen wall, where it rushed inside, safe from harm.

Fiora quickly flew to her pharmacy of medicinal herbs. With great haste she prepared an antidote to the spider's poison, administering the concoction in order to save her daughter's life. She put her daughter to bed afterwards and, while Ibla rested, Fiora rushed to tell Augusto and Inez about the incident.

"Who do you think sent the spider?" the baker asked.

"Enzo," Fiora replied, referring to the Archbishop by his childhood name.

"But why would he want to harm her?" Inez questioned.

"She sent him a letter, offering medicines for his heart condition," Fiora explained.

"I didn't know he was ill," Augusto replied.

"He didn't either," Fiora said. "Ibla sensed it when he was in Alberobella."

"And so she offended him by offering to help him?" Inez asked.

"He is not a trusting man," Fiora told her. "It is the way of the life he has chosen. He is always on the alert, thinking someone is out to assassinate him, usurp his power and his position."

*　　*　　*

The following morning, Ibla's health had been restored and she began to paint images of the large, black insect. Giant tarantulas filled the spaces of her canvases. Where once had appeared luminous tongues of fiery red, now emerged fuzzy-legged creatures baring golden fangs. She painted with the frenzy of one possessed. She danced as she applied long strokes of pigment onto the white muslin background. She tossed back her head and opened wide her mouth. She wept because she could not proclaim with words the passions that now consumed her body.

For days, Ibla continued her fevered pitch. She did not eat. She slept only long enough to rest her weary arms, rising at dawn to paint, painting until midnight, collapsing into bed only to rise once more. Fiora questioned whether the antidote to the spider's poison had worked, for her daughter was consumed by something she would only explain as a frenzied insanity, something she associated only with the bite of the tarantula.

"I am puzzled as to what to do," Fiora confided in Signore Fornaio and Don Marco.

"Perhaps your medicine released the poison's hold on her body, but not her soul," Augusto said.

"There is but one thing to do," the priest suggested. "We must call the community together for the ritual dance."

"Ah, yes," the baker concurred. "The Tarantella!"

*　　*　　*

So it came to be that on the twenty-ninth of June, on the feast of St. Paul, the townspeople gathered in the piazza, in the center of Alberobella, with their tambourines, their guitars and their accordions. For this sacred and solemn occasion, they dressed in traditional costumes. The women of the village wore white, long-sleeved blouses with close-fitted, black vests, buttoned from top to bottom. Two stripes of golden fabric accented the ruffles of their bright red skirts. Over their skirts they donned red-patterned aprons, bedecked with gold ribbing. The men sported red hats, white shirts and black vests, left open to catch the breeze. Gold-colored cloth kickers and long, red stockings completed their outfits. In their strong and sturdy hands they carried tapered banners of red cloth adorned with gold and red streamers.

The festooned men and women created a circle in the center of the piazza, into which Ibla entered, led by Fiora and Don Marco.

"This woman has been bitten by the dreaded tarantula," Don Marco announced. "She is a Tarantata. The poisonous spider has induced in her a frenzy from which she has not been released, even though her mother, the healer, had administered an antidote. It is up to us, her community, to free her, retrieve her soul, call her back to the sanctity of the village and reunite her with her family, friends and neighbors, once more."

With that pronouncement, the music began. The tamburelli, the tambourines, shimmered first, clapping their silver jangles against the still air. They were joined by the sonorous voices of the guitars' sorrowful strings, then by the bellowing gaiety, the brash frivolity of the accordions. As the chords rang across the piazza, the music infected Ibla's bones. Her muscles began to move to the rhythm of the instruments. It was a melody as old as time, as ancient as memory. Lively and graceful, the music swept Ibla into its arms and off she sailed, stepping to its beat. Light, quick steps mixed with passionate gestures. Hers was the dance of the spider. Ibla moved and swayed around the circle emitting an abbastanza mosso tempo, keeping 6/8 time.

The musicians and the costume-clad couples accompanied Ibla as she moved about the piazza. Their first step was a jump—emulating the spider's initial bite, reflecting back to Ibla her experience of the tarantula as it crept out of the box and up her leg. Next came the swaying of hips and the erotic undulating of arms as the dancers and the dance shifted into a trance state, ebbing and flowing, ebbing and flowing. Ibla closed her eyes and tumbled into the rhythm, spellbound. The vitality swelled then waned, then swelled again. Over and over the music rose and fell, the bodies of the dancers, Ibla's body, too, swirled and swayed, stomped and pranced to the mysterious cadence.

Was it unrequited love that their bodies enacted? The rancid grief of repressed desire? The potent sorrow of loss? The sweet promise of redemption?

As the tempo of the music soared, Ibla began to rage, shaking her fist at the heavens. She opened her muted mouth to howl at the injustice that had been thrust upon her. The rhythms of the music mirrored her movements, inviting an improvisation of melodies and sounds that transported her into a nether world of disorientation. Her dance and the songs become the poison's antidote, the serum she needed in order to suck the venom from her soul. The community of dancers, the ring of red and gold-clad couples, contained her frenzy, inviting her to release the ills that possessed her, eradicate the rage, and return once more to the assurance and acceptance of their circle.

On and on they danced, for hours, Ibla, the tortured Tarantata, stomping and twirling, shaking and shivering to the tambourines' shimmering siren-call. Up and down, over and around she flew, her body a mass of lava, oozing, burning, leaving a molten path in her wake. She trod past men and women, children and animals. None could cease her fury; none could contain her. They let her spill, for spilling was the reason for this sacred rite. Spilling was her release, her salvation, her road back. She erupted, flinging her arms at the sky, stomping her feet upon the cobblestone pavement. She thrust her head about, shaking it, loosening the curls that hung tightly around her furious face.

Ibla was a woman on fire. A dancer of flames and fury. The music spiked to a fevered pitch She rode its wave in ecstasy. Hers was a choreography of pain and joy, of freedom and mourning. She grieved her severed tongue, she mourned her father's arrogance, she wailed at a world that despised those who lived in poverty, she raged at the soldier who imprisoned her, she raged at the Magistrate who ordered her incarceration. She raged at the silencing of hope, the starvation of her people, the kidnapping of their souls.

Ibla danced until she could no longer take another step. Exhausted from her own ferocity she collapsed, surrounded by the shimmering red folds of dancers' skirts, the comforting red of dancers' leggings.

"The demons have been released," the dancers proclaimed. "She is cured, free to return to the life she was meant to lead. We welcome and embrace her."

Ibla opened her eyes and gazed upon the men and women who encircled her. She felt a peace in her heart that had been lacking since the day Alberto had cut out her tongue. Speech formed in her mouth, in the space where her tongue used to reside. She parted her lips to thank the dancers and musicians for this gift they had given her. A muffled sound emerged. She gritted her teeth then opened her palms and lifted them toward the cloudless sky. From her pocket she pulled a slip of paper upon which she had written a note. She handed the page to Fiora who became, as she had for so many years, her daughter's instrument of speech.

Fiora began:

"In the time before this era in which we now live, when the men and women of the Earth lived in peace and harmony, there was no need for wars and violence. People had no desire to own one another or take from their neighbors what did not belong to them. Peoples everywhere were free to speak the truth that reigned within their breasts. They were not denied their voices. And yet, each voice could ring with dissent as well. For there was no need for a singular melody; there was a great appreciation for the beauty of the chorus. Speak out, beloved friends. Do not let yourselves be silenced. For silence is more potent than the poison of the tarantula. There is no antidote for voicelessness."

As Fiora read loud Ibla's message aloud, Don Marco slipped away from the crowd to retrieve the painting of the Black Madonna of the Flames. When he returned to the piazza, he bore high the image, raising it above his head. The men and women of the circle parted to make way for his procession of one. When he was enfolded into the center, the circle closed once more.

"Ibla," the priest began. "This patron of our village has come to us because of you and your courage. Although you have been silenced in speech, your message and its meaning have reached our ears."

"There is much about our lives in this small village that is hard," Fiora added. "But we have proven one thing for certain. The devil is nothing more than those who would seek to harm us. And there is much more that is mightier than the sword of injustice. We are all the Mother's children. She distinguishes not from rich or poor. She cares not what color is our skin. She does not abandon us, unless we abandon ourselves. In Her arms we are continually embraced. This is what we have discovered. She lives in each of us, and us in Her."

"Amen," Don Marco stated.

"Amen," the villagers echoed.

Ibla rose from the sun-heated stones of the piazza that afternoon in June and stared into Don Marco's cinnamon-brown eyes. She smiled at him, standing tall among the villagers, proclaiming the glory of the black Mother. Something stirred inside her, some feeling of affection or admiration or both, which took her by surprise. If she could have spoken she would have thanked him, told him she loved him. Instead, she bowed her head and walked home in silence with her mother beside her. She slept for three days, exhausted from the effort of the Tarantella dance. When she awoke, she went to her pigments and her canvases and began to paint. From that day forward, she would never again treat patients or concoct a cure or a potion for she sensed another purpose to her life, one that would be revealed in time.

The painting of the Black Madonna of the Flames continued to watch over the villagers. The townspeople eventually built a new church to house the image and named the building in honor of its patron. It became known as the Chiesa della Madonna Nera di Fuoco, the Church of the Black Madonna of the Fire.

Don Marco, too, had sensed something in how Ibla had looked at him, after she had risen from the cobblestone streets of the piazza the day of the dancing. He did not understand at first, that feeling of longing and love, but he pondered it until it grew and became clearer. That he loved Ibla startled him, for he was a man of the cloth, one who had taken a vow of celibacy and, unlike others of his profession, had kept it all these many years. What he felt for Ibla did not resemble the affection he felt for other women in the parish, for those emotions were more in keeping with friendship and companionship. The fire that was ignited in the piazza on the day of the Tarantella now blazed inside the priest. He dreamt of kissing Ibla, of making love with her, holding her in his arms, gently with great care. He told no one of this, not even his confessor, for he felt great shame. He also felt something stronger, something that compelled him to one day, visit Ibla and her mother.

Don Marco stopped by Ibla and Fiora's house, under the guise of asking Ibla if she needed more pigments for her paintings. Fiora greeted him at the door and invited him in. She made some tea, but left after she had served it to her daughter and the priest. She told them she had a patient waiting when, in fact, she sensed what was to transpire. In Fiora's absence, Don Marco set down his teacup and reached for Ibla's hand. Without thinking, for if he had stopped to consider his actions he would not have proceeded, he cradled Ibla's fingers in the palm of his hand and kissed them. He stood to approach her. Ibla stood as well. Their eyes met and a spark ignited, propelling them into each other's arms. Lips met lips and in a moment they kissed deeply and passionately.

With the moist scent of Ibla's lips upon his face, and emboldened by Ibla's eager return of his affections, Don Marco spoke, "Ibla, I do not fully understand what has overcome me, but I must tell you that I love you. It is crazy, I know, for I am a priest and I mustn't behave in such a manner."

Ibla placed her finger upon Don Marco's lips to silence him. She shook her head and stepped in closer to kiss him once more. Without words she told him that she too loved him, that she cared not that he was a priest, that their love required no marriage ceremony, no blessing of the church.

Don Marco remained a priest in his Catholic Church, living in his small church-provided rooms, serving the spiritual needs of his parish, but he and Ibla shared their lives as if they were wed. Fiora blessed their relationship and while, initially the tongues of the town's gossips wagged furiously, in time all came to accept the arrangement. Within a year, Ibla gave birth to two twins, Paradisa, a daughter, and Arcangelo, a son—both born with the sacred caul of the strega upon their infant faces.

Fiora and Ibla rejoiced, as did Don Marco.

As her grandchildren grew, Fiora reveled in teaching them the ways of the herbalist. She gathered them up and took them to the fields to learn about the medicinal plants. She instructed them in the ways of Cybele and in the art of midwifery. They grew to be intelligent and caring healers, serving the people of Alberobella after Fiora's passing at 98.

Under the influence of his children and his lover, Don Marco began to acquire the ways of the Dark Mother, transforming his devoting to the Black Madonna, the mother of Jesus, into a veneration of a more ancient female Deity. He retained the persona of his Catholic obligations, presiding over Mass on Sundays, hearing confessions on Saturdays, officiating at the festivals of each of the various saints throughout the church's calendar year, but his heart belonged to Ibla and to Cybele. Even as he said the prayers of the Catholic Mass, he did so standing before the altar of the Black Madonna, not the altar of Jesus. His parishioners did not question this, for they, too, had accepted Her as their town's patron and were beholden to Her for the miracles she had bestowed upon their village and for the strength she had endowed them with when they struggled against

Signore Martelli, the padrone. Their faith in Her was great and strong, their acceptance of Don Marco's choice to honor Her was unequivocal.

Don Marco died ten years after the dance of the tarantella. His heart gave out and he passed over, gently in his sleep one night. Ibla and her children wept with great grief, for he had grown to be a man of deep compassion and lasting tenderness. The baker Fornaio paid for a proper funeral for the priest, with whom he had become close friends. Fiora anointed his body with the finest of fragrant herbs and applied a henna to his hands and feet, a sacred ritual often reserved only for priestesses of the Divine She. She knew that Don Marco had embraced the divinity of the Black Madonna, knowing Her not merely as God's humble servant but as a powerful Deity in her own right. And so, she sought to honor him in the old ways.

Fiora passed away two years later. She was nearly one hundred years old. Ibla, with her beloved mother and her lover gone, lived out the remainder of her days a near recluse, visited only by her son and daughter and their children. And, every now and then, by Inez, Augusto Fornaio's wife. In her self-imposed exile, Ibla subsisted off roots and berries she could forage in the forest near her home until the day she drew her last breath. Paradisa and Arcangelo stood at Ibla's side when she crossed over.

Some called Ibla a saint. Others a prophet. All who knew her rejoiced in her living and wept for their loss.

Ibla flew into the open arms of Cybele on the morning of her last day. As her skin was kissed by the loving touch of the Dark Mother's embrace, Ibla began to sing. Her tongue restored, she praised the Dea Madre with every fiber of muscle, every vibrant coil of energy that coursed through her Earth-loving and ethereal bodies.

Ibla's daughter and son heard the music of their mother's voice for the first time and wept, for it rang with the clarity of one who had known her truth and had lived it. In spite of everything. Paradisa and Arcangelo would remember, always, the voice of the mother they had so dearly loved, the voice of the woman who had no tongue.

Sicily

Mary Saracino

How was I to know I'd be coming home
when first I tasted the salt sea air
of your sun-stained shores?

Isola Bella, something rattled my DNA
dislodging its memory
awakening its forgotten longing.

Isola Madre, something birthed voice
erasing a long silence
that which had been lost
suddenly reclaimed.

In Erice, the homeward-seeking doves
soar back to Africa each spring
released by those who remember
how true blood sings for its Mother.

In Ragusa Ibla, St. George could not slay
the Amazon hunters or their ebony strength.
The dragon of memory loomed fiercer
than his shining sword.

In Tindari, the Dark One reigns still
Her benevolent eyes
welcome pilgrims of every hue

seeking solace, affirmation
in Her declaration: "I am black and beautiful."

In Trapani, Siracusa, Custonaci, Enna, Palermo—
over hillsides littered with ruins
through valleys bleeding
with stark red poppies
across mountains erupting
beside turquoise seas swelling
we remember our First Womb
marked as we are by
Her ancient imprint.

Sicily's salty air whispers
a mournful dirge
a litany inviolable
the eternal archive of names—
women & men, young & old
native-born & foreigner
living & dead—who see everything
hear always
speak unfailingly
releasing their long
soulful sighs
into the waiting
watchful wind.

Holy Mary

Mary Saracino

Holy Mary in the water

Holy Mary in the trees

Holy Mary in the sunshine

Holy Mary in the breeze

Holy Mary up above me

Holy Mary deep within

Holy Mary down below me

Holy Mary in my skin

Sing a song of Holy Mary

Blessed is Her holy blood

Blessed is Her name, forever

Holy holy, ever more

Mary outward

Mary inward

Mary shining ever-bright

Light the way through deepest darkness

Deep inside the still dark night

Where the silent mirror shines

Where the heart's desire thrives

Where Her blessings bless our lives

Holy Mary ever-true

Help us to remember always

Help us to be just and wise

Goodness flows from tears of sorrow

You in me & me in you

Of Diana, Witches, and Fairies
An Excerpt from *The Pagan Heart of the West*

Randy P. Conner, Ph.D.

They, the feminine ones, are coming back from far away, from forever, from 'outside,' from the heaths where witches stay alive.

> Hélène Cixous and Catherine Clément, *The Newly Born Woman*

No Such Thing as a Dianic Cult . . . ?

In 1925, in *The History of Witchcraft and Demonology*, the eccentric Anglican clergyman Montague Summers insisted, in a tome chock-full of bizarre data in which he sincerely believed, that there had never been a "Dianic cult," that "nothing of the sort ever survived," that it was "utterly imaginary."[1.]

In 1972, in *Witchcraft in the Middle Ages*, Jeffrey Burton Russell argued that the "reverence of Diana and comparable chthonic deities does seem to have had special significance" in the Middle Ages, "but there is no evidence of any Murrayite Dianist cult."[2] As I reread this statement, I remember a Bible verse that reads, *"For where two or three are gathered together in my name, there am I in the midst of them"* (Matthew 18:20, KJV).

Present-day academics and writers including Ronald Hutton, Diane Purkiss, and Joanne Pearson generally hold that neither a Dianic cult nor a cult of Witchcraft ever existed.[3] I find their strident objections fascinating, especially in light of the myriad cults proliferating from Late Antiquity through the Renaissance—Barbeloites, Bogomils, Brethren of the Free

Spirit, Cathars, Flagellants, Hussites, Lollards, and Taborites, to name only a few.[4]

On the other hand, Hans Peter Broedel (2003) argues ever-so-cautiously for a "pagan cult" of Diana and/or of fairy:

It is remotely possible that the consistent references to Diana indicate the presence of a relict pagan cult . . . Although they are scattered over several centuries, taken together these accounts suggest a reasonably consistent body of belief, closely related to the rural European "fairy cults" . . . In its medieval form, the tradition centered upon a belief in troops of spectral women, led by some specific but variously named mistress which visited houses at certain times of the year and brought either good fortune or ill, depending upon their reception. These beings might also determine a person's fate at birth, and claimed a certain number of people, sometimes up to a third of humanity, as their own . . . . I will . . . refer to them as the *bonae res*, the "good things," a term used by the Dominican Inquisitor Stephen of Bourbon (d. 1261).[5]

Diana and Her Tribe, Fifth through Eleventh Centuries C.E.

One of the earliest descriptions of "witches," not counting Greek, Roman, or Biblical literature, is found in a tale concerning St. Germanus of Auxerre (a.k.a. St. Germain, d. 448). One night in France, after he'd finished dining and was about to retire, he noticed that servants were busily preparing another table. When he asked who would be dining so late, the servants responded, "the good women that walk by night." Later, he watched as many persons arrived and sat down to eat. He learned, however, that this was a gathering of spirits or what we might at present call "astral bodies," as it happened that at the same hour he witnessed the guests dining, they were, in terms of their physical bodies, asleep or in trance in their beds.[6]

"The cult of Artemis," Frank R. Trombley relates, "proved exceptionally difficult to eradicate."[7] Diana continued to be revered in the Middle Ages, roughly, from 500-1500 CE, in places in Europe influenced by Romans.[8] In some cases, it is difficult to say whether Christian authorities were troubled by the cult of Diana or of a local goddess who reminded them of her. The Church's tendency to discuss the reverence of Diana (or, alternatively, a local goddess the Church found synonymous with, or identified as, Diana) in connection with wise women or witches—whether to compare or contrast them—appears to have commenced sometime around the sixth century CE.

St. Caesarius (d. 543), Bishop of Arles, complained that many peasants continued to worship Diana in sixth-century France.[9] She was especially revered at that time by women seeking successful childbirth.[10] Offerings to her included "sandals, headband[s], a scented lock of hair, [and] belt[s]."[11] St. Samson (d. 565), bishop of Dol, Brittany, witnessed a troop of women, led by a hirsute sorceress holding a hunting spear—undoubtedly a reference to Diana—who seemed to be flying through a forest.[12] Gregory of Tours (*c.* 539-594) bemoaned the fact that many persons persisted in worshipping Diana in Trier, on the banks of the Moselle River in Germany.[13] A shrine to her there was destroyed by St. Wulfilaich (d. *c.* 594).[14] St. Eloi (or, Eligius, 588-659/660), bishop of Noyon, France likewise condemned the worship of Diana.[15] The missionary bishop St. Kilian (d. 689) was greatly troubled to find that "Diana was the chief goddess of Würzburg" in what is now Germany;[16] he was martyred as he tried to convert the east Franks "from their worship of Diana."[17]

According to Geneviève Saint-Martin, Diana continued to be worshipped in the late eighth or early ninth century CE in the Auvergne region of France, especially in the vicinity of the Cantal Mountains and the Santoire Valley. The village of Dienne appears to have been named after the goddess.[18] In the vicinity of the village is the Rocher Laqueille, where a temple of Diana is believed to have stood until the reign of Charlemagne (768-814), when he ordered its destruction.[19]

Robert Muchembled notes that worship of "the pagan goddess Diana . . . was still quite widespread in the eleventh century."[20] In the mid-eleventh century, Bulgarians who lived not too far from Mt. Athos in Greece—they had probably first settled there in the late seventh century—were discovered worshipping at what appears to have been the site of a shrine or temple to a goddess, probably Artemis/Diana, possibly conflated with a Slavic goddess. The Christian priest George the Hagiorite (d. 1065), setting out for Constantinople, was extremely troubled when some of the men who worshipped this goddess approached him and allegedly told him, "If you wish to prosper in all your affairs, ask the goddess that she would help you with the emperor."[21] George pretended that he would do so, if the men would show him where they worshipped her. They took him to where a marble statue of the Goddess stood, at which point he asked them if he might be left alone with the statue the following morning so that he might commune with the Goddess. The next morning, together with two other men, he used a hammer to break the statue "into little pieces," despite the cries and curses of the Goddess' devotees, who had learned too late of the priest's true intention and who arrived at the site as the statue was being destroyed.[22]

The Significance of the *Canon Episcopi*

Reverence of Diana appears to have escalated dramatically during the early tenth century. In or near 906 CE (according to one significant source, the date appears to be closer to 877-879 CE), an official document that has come to be known as the *Canon Episcopi* or the *Decretum*,[23] recorded by Regino of Prüm (who claimed it originated in 314 CE, at the Council of Ancyra, an assertion now doubted) and later by Burchard of Worms (d. 1025), St. Ivo of Chartres (*c.* 1040-*c.* 1117, bishop of Chartres 1090—*c.* 1117), and Johannes Gratian (fl. *c.* 1150), this document was very widely known by the mid-twelfth century.[24] The document reads in part:

[S]ome wicked women [and men {mentioned in another part of the document}] . . . believe and profess that, in the hours of night, they ride upon certain beasts with Diana, the goddess of the pagans, and in the silence of the night traverse great spaces of earth, and obey her commands as of their lady, and are summoned to her service on certain nights . . . . [A]n innumerable multitude believe this to be true . . . and [thus] return to the error of the pagans.[25]

The *Canon Episcopi* greatly enhanced controversies regarding belief in witches and punishment of both alleged witches and those who believed in them. Although some continued to think that more harm might be done by acknowledging the existence of witches and burning them, more and more Christian authorities and Christian(ized) rulers came to argue that as exemplary of paganism, belief in witches should be condemned, as, in "reality," these women were deluded followers of the Devil and not devotees of Diana (or other pagan deities and/or spirits), and, moreover, alleged witches should be burned or otherwise suffer capital punishment because, in falling into Witchcraft, they had become instruments of the Devil. Those Christian authorities who followed the *Canon Episcopi* insisted, on hearing from an alleged witch that she had worshipped a goddess or a goddess and god (or Fairy Queen and Fairy King), that she had in fact worshipped the Devil. Moreover, in order to prove himself a good Catholic, the Inquisitor found it necessary, generally speaking, to transliterate her words concerning such encounters into a stereotypical narrative of a Satanic sabbat. In this way, the *Canon Episcopi* ultimately served to promote the burning of alleged witches and to promote the notion that Witchcraft did not represent a manifestation of Goddess reverence but rather a manifestation of Satanism.[26]

Not wishing to malign her work in the way that Hutton and other present-day academics do, I do think that Margaret Murray goes astray not so much when she theorizes the existence of a counter-religion of witches[27] but when she fails to grasp the potent significance of the *Canon Episcopi*. By not fully comprehending that, due to its powerful role in promoting Church officials to insist that narratives of Diana and other goddesses and women's meetings to revere her be transmogrified into narratives of the Devil and the Sabbat, Murray makes certain significant incorrect assumptions. As Carlo Ginzburg notes, Murray "uncritically accepted the by now consolidated stereotype of the Sabbath as a basis for her interpretation."[28] The most important of these is her assumption that the Devil must be a cover for a pagan *male* deity. Had she fully realized the significance of the *Canon Episcopi*, which, again, branded as heretical mere belief in Goddess-revering witches and which insisted that this belief be transformed into that of perverse women imagining celebrating with the Devil, Murray would have realized that in many cases, the Devil probably refers *to Diana or a local goddess rather than to a male god.* This causes Murray to stress the role of the god and to lessen the importance of the Goddess. Further, by not accounting for the significance of the *Canon*, she accepts, at least template-wise, the Church's construction of the Sabbat.

It should be noted that in the twelfth century, certain versions of the *Canon Episcopi* also named Minerva alongside Diana as a patron of witches or else the focus of a Goddess-revering cult, one which Christian authorities interpreted as demonic.[29]

Although the work of George Lyman Kittredge is now considered controversial, in *Witchcraft in Old and New England* (1929), he makes a very interesting remark about the *Canon Episcopi*:

> The *Canon Episcopi*, we observe, has in and for itself nothing to do with Witchcraft. The [sin of the] women whom it contemplates . . . consists in their faith in a heathen goddess . . . In short, they have relapsed into paganism. But they are not witches, even in intent . . . . In the mind of the folk, however, the coursers with Diana became crossed or confused with . . . the *striges* [i.e., destructive "witches"] . . . . [I]n

Regino [of Prum]'s book, [they] . . . are brought into close connection
with Witchcraft . . . [30]

Witchcraft, a Cult of the Goddess, and/or a Cult of Fairies: Medieval and Renaissance Controversies

Alleged incidences of persons, primarily women, traveling at night to
meet with Diana rose dramatically from the eleventh through the fourteenth
centuries, "calling for earnest repression" by the Church.[31] In eleventh-century
Belgium, the prince-bishop of Liège condemned persons in the Ardennes
Mountains who continued to revere the goddess Diana.[32] In the mid-twelfth
century, the English scholar-priest John of Salisbury (c. 1115/1120-1180)
condemned belief in the cult of Diana. In the late twelfth-century
Anglo-Norman *Penitential* of Bartholomew Iscanus, one finds:

They who . . . believe and profess that they go or ride in the service
of her whom the stupid crowd call Herodias or Diana with a countless
multitude and obey her commands shall do penance for one year.[33]

During the thirteenth through the fifteenth centuries, the ancient
goddesses Hera/Juno and Venus—together with the pagano-Biblical
figure of Herodias—also experienced a dramatic renascence and came
to be linked to Diana and Minerva in regard to Witchcraft and/or a
Goddess-revering cult; moreover, a host of regional and local goddesses
and/or female spirits and, to a lesser extent, male divinities, appeared on
the spiritual radar of Europe at this time, divinities virtually unknown until
this time, reflecting pagan innovation in spite of official Christianization.
These divinities included Habundia, Holda, Nicneven, Dame Dark, and
many others.[34]

An investigation ordered by Pope John XXII (1249-1334; pope,
1316-1334) indicates that Diana was still thought—as a demoness, of
course—to exist by authorities of the Church and that she was thought to
be able to manifest in multiple. In 1318, John ordered an investigation of
a group of magicians who were believed to be having sexual intercourse
with various manifestations of Diana.[35]

An event that conceivably hints at reverence of Diana occurred in
1351, when Bishop Grandisson of Exeter reprimanded the Prior of
Frithelstock for building a chapel near the village full of earth-centered
and sexual imagery: the statues "reminded one more of the proud and
disobedient Eve, or the shameless Diana, than of the humble and most
submissive Blessed Virgin Mary."[36]

Some of those who believed in the existence of a Goddess-revering cult argued that it should be distinguished from the emerging sect of "Witchcraft." Their chief reason for doing so, however, appears to have been motivated by a desire to punish these practitioners with even greater ferocity than those accused of "Witchcraft."[37]

Regarding a cult of fairy veneration, despite Chaucer's (1343-1400) remark in "The Wife of Bath's Tale" that fairies had vanished long before his day,[38] evidence indicates that a cult devoted to the fairies arose and became widespread in the Middle Ages and Renaissance—demonstrating pagan innovation in spite of official Christianization—and in some places persisted for a long time thereafter. Increasingly, Diana came to be identified as, or conflated with, the Queen of the Fairies; moreover, Diana, fairies, and witches were increasingly linked, and perhaps not only in the minds of nostalgic poets and fearful Christians. Reginald Scot relates in *The Discoverie of Witchcraft* (1584):

[T]he witches themselves, before they anoint themselves, do hear in the night a great noise of minstrels, which fly over them, with the Ladie of the fairies, and then they address themselves to their journey.[39]

In the mid-fourteenth century, the Spanish Dominican theologian and Inquisitor Eymeric insisted that while practitioners of "Witchcraft" indulged primarily in sorcery or destructive magic, the followers of Diana, by way of offering both *dulia*, ritual acts of lesser reverence that were to be performed only in honor of angels and saints, and *latria*, acts of worship that were to be performed only in reverence of the Biblical God, the cult of the Goddess was "to be treated, not as sorcery [i.e., not as "witchcraft"], but as heresy, the same as worshipping Mahomet [i.e., Mohammed];" "the followers of Diana are heretics, to be punished as such."[40] This may be one reason why Diana, in her manifestation as the Fairy Queen, is called both the 'Queen of the Jews' and the 'Wife of Mohammed.'[41] The notion that Diana and Mohammed were linked in a significant way appears to have been bolstered by a misinterpretation among Christian crusaders that the crescent appearing on Islamic standards represented the goddess of the moon.[42]

In spite of the insistence that the accused must not speak of Goddess reverence, or at least that Christian authorities not record it as such, certain women, especially Italian women, it would seem, continued, in spite of the lethal danger they placed themselves in by doing so, to describe ceremonies celebrating a goddess. For example, near the end of the fourteenth century, two highborn Milanese women, Sibillia Zanni and Pietrina de' Bugatis, claimed to revere a goddess, apparently embodied by a priestess, named Madonna (or, Signora) Oriente. This was a lunar goddess, synonymous with Diana. At this time, the Goddess also appears to have gained the moniker of *Domina Ludi* or *La Signora del Gioco*, the "Lady of the Game," *Dona del bon zogo*, the "Mistress of the Good Game."[43] It is conceivable that this attribution of the "game" to the Lady signifies the playing of the game of "*moccola di Benevento*," associated with paganism and Witchcraft, and/or to an association between the reverence of Diana and *Ludus Amoris*, the "game of love," familiar to both courtly lovers and Christian mystics.[44]

Maurizio Bertolotti, in his microhistorical analysis "The Ox's Bones and the Ox's Hide: A Popular Myth, Part Hagiography and Part Witchcraft," demonstrates the increasing demonization of the ceremonies of the followers of Diana or a local goddess by Christian authorities in regards to practices occurring in northern Italy. During the first phase of several, the Goddess preserves her "original characteristics." In the second phase, she becomes a more ambivalent figure with increasingly sinister characteristics. In the third phase, she "has not disappeared, but the devil has taken her place at the center of the sabbat." With the arrival of the fourth phase, "the Lady exits definitively from the scene."[45]

In early fifteenth-century France, the Council of Amiens (*c.* 1410) forbade women to profess that they rode to meet Diana, Herodias, or Bizazia (i.e., Bona Socia), for "this is a demonic illusion."[46] In this manner, Goddess reverence was increasingly transformed by the Church into Satanist "witchcraft." There was absolutely no room for acknowledging the reality of religious pluralism. Should priests or other Christian leaders "find a man or woman follower of this wicked sect [they should] eject them, foully disgraced, from their parishes."[47] Indeed, those who believed that they traveled, or who were believed to travel, to meet with Diana were increasingly characterized by Christian officials in Italy, France, Spain, and elsewhere neither as the devotees of a goddess nor as misguided victims of hallucinations but rather as evildoers going to meet the Devil at sinister, very tangible, sabbats.[48]

Near 1458, Nicolas Jaquier differentiated "Witchcraft," which he considered a new sect, from the cult of the Goddess, which he considered to be far older.[49] Alphonso de Spina (d. *c.* 1491) wrote in *Fortalicium Fidei* (wr. *c.* 1458-1460, pub. 1494):

Therefore what wicked women believe and profess, that with Diana the pagan goddess and Herodias and great multitudes of women they ride at night . . . is false, and whoever believes this is without doubt an infidel and worse than a pagan. And since such women are too abundant in Dauphiny and Gascony [in southeastern France], where they assert that they assemble by night on a desert plateau where there is a boar on a rock which is commonly known as "el Boch de Biterne" . . . many of them, arrested by the inquisitors, have been burnt.[50]

In early sixteenth-century Italy, near Modena, women continued to insist that they revered Diana at nocturnal gatherings.[51] In his 1504 *Summa*, Mazzolini Silvestro Da Prierio (a.k.a. Sylvester Prierias, *c*. 1456—*c*. 1523/7) determined that followers of Diana were heretics because, whereas practitioners of "Witchcraft," that is, the *secta strigarum* (or, *stregheria*), a name given to Italian "Witchcraft," by way of worshipping Satan as the enemy of God, at least inadvertently acknowledged the Biblical God, followers of Diana did not, focusing their attention instead on a female deity. Satan, after all, was a fallen angel, not a god; thus, practitioners of "Witchcraft" could revere him without accepting the absolutely heretical notion that "there [could] be deity outside of [the Biblical] God."[52] Thus, in his view, "witches" or practitioners of *stregheria* were ultimately to be considered less heretical than those who claimed to revere a goddess. The cult of the Goddess was especially heretical, he insisted, because: 1) the Goddess was perceived as an authentic non-Christian deity and not just an illusion created by, or a manifestation of, the Devil; 2) Her devotees believed that they traveled great distances to convene with each other and Her; 3) Her devotees believed in the possibility of actual metamorphosis of humans, animals, etc. that was neither performed by the Biblical God nor a Satanic illusion or hallucination; and 4) worst of all in his way of thinking, her devotees believed the Goddess to be "good."[53] At least, in his opinion, those who practiced the *secta strigarum* believe none of [these things], but say [that] the spirit appearing to them is the devil. [They do not believe in] a good goddess, nor are they summoned to the service of any goddess.[54]

Likewise, Silvestro Da Prierio insisted that practitioners of the cult of the Goddess be categorized as apostates. Moreover, he argued that those who took practitioners at their word should also be viewed as apostates: those who did so would be involved in pagan error, believing also in [a] deity besides God, [believing] that these things are done by a good spirit, and [for believing] that a creature has the power of transformation . . . [55]

In or near 1510, an inquisitor at Como, Italy, Bernard de Como (fl. 1510) likewise insisted that those who believe in the existence of the cult of the Goddess "are truly apostates, idolaters, and heretics . . . *perfidas et infideles* [i.e., unfaithful ones and infidels]."[56]

On the other hand, in his 1514/ 1518 *Summa*, Johannes Cagnazzo de Tabia (fl. 1515), a Dominican priest who taught at a convent in Bologna, in taking what was indeed a highly unorthodox position, seemed to make room for a kind of "bi-religiousness" or spiritual hybridity which could acknowledge both the Biblical God and Diana. In elaborating on the differences between adherents of the Goddess and adherents of the *secta strigarum*/"Witchcraft," he argues that although both sects promote "voluptuous pleasure," they share little else in common. Whereas practitioners of "Witchcraft" "work much evil" including causing illness and death, followers of Diana do "none of these things." Whereas practitioners of "Witchcraft" or *strigarum* abjure Christianity, followers of Diana do not.[57]

According to Bartolommeo della Spina (or, Bartholomäus Spineus, 1465/1474-1546), the Goddess of Italians at this time was also identified as, or synonymous with, Diana, Minerva, the Lady Sibylla, and/or the Queen of the Fairies.[58] Divination, magic, and animal sacrifice allegedly took place at her rites. This was a miraculous form of animal sacrifice; after the animals were slain and eaten, their bones were collected and they were born anew.[59] In Bartolommeo della Spina's case, we find an example of someone who may have shifted his opinion as to, or else heard contradictory reports concerning, whether or not witches attended gatherings in the flesh or instead attending them astrally while in a trance, dreamlike state.[60] We also find, in Bartolommeo's case, an example of someone who appears to have shifted his opinion as to whether or not the cult of the Goddess constituted Witchcraft. At one point, he appears to have thought that Goddess worshippers should not be equated with witches, whereas at another, he insisted that since no such goddess existed, and that the entity the women worshipped was in fact the Devil, then they should be considered and tried as witches. Whichever the case, for their admission of revering the Goddess, they were to be executed.[61]

Near 1530, Martin de Castañega, deploying euhemerism in a negative manner, insisted that Diana and Herodias had been human women who were wicked and who had turned against Christianity and that hence to attribute divinity to them was blasphemous:

. . . Diana and Herodias were two normal women killed and not resuscitated. To say that live women converse with the dead . . . is an error, a public deceit, and an illusion of the devil. Second, Diana and Herodias were wicked and faithless women when they lived. To affirm they were goddesses or that there was some divinity, power, or grace in them is a manifest error and blasphemy.[62]

If—as some present-day academics insist—no women or men were revering Diana or Herodias in Spain at the time, in 1530, that is, one must wonder why de Castañega found it necessary to both reiterate and expand upon the *Canon Episcopi*. After all, his is not meant to be a work of literature or history; it has the purpose of locating witches/heretics, trying them, and punishing them.

Near 1536, the Italian jurist Paulus Grillandus insisted that those who worshipped the Devil were not nearly so heretical or duped as those who worshipped the Goddess. At least those who worship the Devil, he argued, "know [him] to be inferior to God."[63]

Johann Weyer (1515-1588) reiterated the associative chain of Diana, Minerva, Herodias, and witches:

[S]ome poor femmelettes, servants of Satan, seduced by illusions and phantoms of devils, believe, and attest that they go by horse in the night with Diana of the Pagans, or with Herodias, or Minerva.[64]

The philosopher Giordano Bruno (1548-1600), burned at the stake as a heretic, describes Diana as "she who is the being and truth of intelligible Nature." "Very few are those," Bruno relates, through the persona of Mariconda, "who arrive at the font of Diana." [65] One should not underestimate the significance of Diana in Bruno's work. In *Eros and Magic in the Renaissance*, Ioan P. Couliano states: "Giordano Bruno . . . becomes, in London, a fervent adherent of the obscure cult of the goddess Diana."[66]

From her ebony statue in ancient Ephesus onward, Artemis/Diana has frequently been depicted with black skin, suggesting an African origin or African heritage.[67] As a "dark mother," to borrow a term from Lucia

Chiavola Birnbaum, Diana was often represented in Renaissance art as an African woman.[68] This suggests that during the period of the witch trials, the divine patroness of a cult of Goddess reverence, Witchcraft, and/ or fairies may have been perceived as a dark-skinned woman of African heritage, which cannot but have elevated the horror that Inquisitors and other Christian authorities held for practitioners.

The years 1594-1597 are especially intriguing in regard to England's relationship to Diana, fairies, and witches. Near 1594-1596, Shakespeare penned *A Midsummer Night's Dream*. In this play, Diana, in her manifestation as Titania, appears as the Fairy Queen (elsewhere, Shakespeare associates the Queen with Mab, a variant of the Celtic Maeve[69]).[70]

In Cheapside, northwest of London Bridge, a large Christian cross stood, allegedly set up in the late thirteenth century. Attached to this cross was a pieta of the Virgin Mary cradling Jesus as well as images of the apostles and the Pope. In the sixteenth century, the cross and sculpture were defaced, possibly by Protestants, and repaired numerous times. Around 1596, a rather surprising addition to the site was added; John Stow (1525-1605), in his *Survey of London* (1598, 1604), explains that there was "then set up a curiously wrought tabernacle of grey marble, and in the same, an image alabaster of Diana, and water conveyed from the Thames, prilling [i.e., flowing] from her breast for a time."[71]

In *Daemonologie* (1597), King James I (r. 1603-1625) insisted that the Fairy Queen was the current avatar of Diana, frequently conflated with Hecate, and the object of a cult. "That kind," he observes, "the Gentiles . . . called Diana, and her wandering court, [which] amongst us [is] called the Phairie [i.e., Fairy, or Faerie]."[72] According to King James, the cult is widespread.[73] The King reports that the fairies are ruled by a "King and Queen of Phairie," who possess a "jolly court" with whom they ride and feast "like natural men and women."[74] He suggests that contact with the fairies is thought to be attained after votaries fall into a trance, not unlike a shamanic trance; in this state, votaries' "senses [are] dulled . . . as [if] it were a sleep . . . their bodies being senseless."[75] He blames Catholics for not succeeding in stamping out, and the Devil for encouraging, belief in fairies.[76] He describes those who honor the fairies as "sundry simple creatures" on the one hand, and as demonically possessed on the other.[77] Like other witch-hunters, he insists that wisewomen and second-sighted men who communicate with fairies, as well as those who rely on such persons, should be "as severely . . . punished as *any other Witches* [italics mine], and rather the more" since they claim to be practicing the magical arts for beneficial purposes when, according to James, they are doing the work of the Devil[78].

Also at this time, Tomaso Garzoni (1549-1589), in *La piazza universale di tutte le professioni del mondo* (*The Universal Piazza of All the Professions of the World*, 1585), found it necessary to reiterate the words of the *Canon Episcopi* in order to remind readers once more that "certain accused women" claimed that they revered the goddess Diana, or else Herodias, rather than Satan.[79] In 1599, Martín Del Río argued that there are two primary kinds of witches: the first are those who practice healing, divination, and/or magic, but who do not renounce the Biblical God; whereas the second are those who renounce the Biblical God and worship Diana or another earth-centered deity, whom Del Río identifies with Satan. These latter are heretics.[80] Like many other Christian authorities, Del Río conflates the reverence of Diana and/or the fairies with that of Satan, and Goddess-revering/fairy gatherings with the Sabbat.[81] In the early seventeenth century, Strozzi Cicogna (1568-1613) and Pierre De Lancre (1553-1631) argued that witches who worship non-Christian deities have been taught to do so by demonic spirits who "[lead] them to believe that other gods beside God [are] to be found."[82] That Cicogna and De Lancre felt compelled to remind judges and other religious and secular authorities of this claim suggests that as late as the seventeenth century, some women accused of Witchcraft believed that they worshiped Diana or a kindred goddess rather than Satan.

Displacement, Persistence, and Metamorphosis of the Reverence of Diana

From the Middle Ages and Renaissance onward, Diana and her reverence experienced deicide, masking, and hybridity, as with her being displaced by the Virgin Mary and Saints Agnes, Artemidos, Hubert, Lucy/Santa Lucia, Sabina, and Yllis of Dôle, among others.[83]

She and her reverence were also, however, recalled and transformed over the centuries that followed. In 1850, the naturalist and political rebel Henry David Thoreau (1817-1862) praised Diana:

My dear, my dewy sister, let thy rain descend on me . . . . Thy dewy words feed me like the manna of the morning. I am as much thy sister as thy brother. Thou art as much my brother as my sister . . . . O my sister! O Diana, thy tracks are on the eastern hills. Thou surely passed that way.[84]

In other places, her reverence continued as it had for centuries or even millennia. For example, in Transylvania, Moldavia, and Wallachia,[85] celebrations of the goddess or "fairy" Sânziana have continued into the present, with the name of Sânziana deriving from Sancta Diana.[86] The Romanian goddess Dragaica, also revered into the present, has also been identified with Diana.[87] Also in Romania, the *calusari*, male dancing ritual specialists of Romania, who seem to mix elements of shamanistic-like practice with healing, magic, and Goddess reverence, continue into the present to invoke "their guardian goddess," Irodeasa (or, Arada, Aradia, Herodiada, Herodias, Irodiada) or Doamna Zinelor, the Fairy Queen, whom, Mircea Eliade argues, constitutes "the Romanian metamorphosis of Diana."[88]

As neo-pagan movements and traditions emerged in the late nineteenth and early twentieth centuries, among these was the Adorateurs de la Lune, also known as the Phoebéphiles, founded in Paris in 1912 by a Bulgarian named Arpad Pradjick. The group celebrated the Goddess by dancing for her, sometimes "skyclad," during the new moon of August or September, in the Bois de Boulogne, an activity for which, on one such occasion, they were arrested. In 1954, five years after the death of Pradjick, the group was renamed the Témoins d'Artémis and continued for some time as a salon, with adherents chanting to the Goddess before a statue of her.[89] Also commencing in the mid-twentieth century, the religion of Wicca (or present-day Witchcraft) has embraced reverence of the goddess Artemis/ Diana, including within all-female Dianic covens.[90]

Not counting the thousands of years that the goddess Artemis/ Diana (together with local variants) was worshipped prior to the official Christianization of the Roman Empire—and granting that Church leaders, lawyers, scholars, and King James I should probably not be viewed as nothing more than paranoid fools, as some present-day academics would have it—it would appear that some form of Dianic reverence both persisted and experienced innovation and metamorphosis for seventeen or so centuries. The foregoing also suggests that further exploration of, and perhaps also consideration of the deployment of, the terms "witch" and "Witchcraft" need to be undertaken.

Notes

[1] Summers, *History of Witchcraft*, 43.

[2] Russell, *Witchcraft in the Middle Ages*, 60-61.

[3] See Hutton, *Witches, Druids* and *Triumph of the Moon*; Purkiss, *Witch in History*; and Pearson, Wicca, Paganism.

[4] See, for example: Cohn, *Pursuit of the Millennium*; Fichtenau, *Heretics and Scholars*; Frassetto, *Heretic Lives*; Lambert, *Medieval Heresy*; Loos, *Dualist Heresy*; Martin, *Gnostics: The First Christian*; Peters, *Heresy and Authority*; Roach, *Devil's World*; Stoyanov, *Hidden Tradition*.

[5] Broedel, *The Malleus Maleficarum and the Construction*, 102-104. In a similar vein, Gary K. Waite, *in Heresy, Magic, and Witchcraft in Early Modern Europe (2003)*, in which he describes the process by which Christianization and its tactic of demonization transformed "pagan ritual" and the "traditional religion[s]" of people of northern Europe into "demonic idolatry," which "led very directly to the witch trials." He further describes how the same process of "demonological interpretation" was applied by "Christian missionaries [seeking] to convert the New World peoples" (See Waite, *Heresy 100*).

[6] Douce, *Illustrations of Shakespeare*, 238-239.

[7] Trombley, *Hellenic Religion*, 1: 157.

[8] Grimm, *Teutonic Mythology*, 1: 286.

[9] Cohn, *Europe's Inner Demons*, 212.

[10] Trombley, *Hellenic Religion* 1: 157.

[11] Ibid., 1: 157-158.

[12] Rio, *Arbre Philosophal*, 185.

[13] Cohn, *Europe's Inner Demons*, 212.

14   Behringer, *Shaman of Oberstdorf*, 51-52.

15   Bologne, *Du flambeau au bûcher*, 72; Rio, *Arbre Philosophal*, 186.

16   Behringer, *Shaman of Oberstdorf*, 52.

17.   Cohn, *Europe's Inner Demons*, 212.

18   Societé de mythologie française, *France mythologique*, 61.

19   Saint-Martin, *Auvergne: Des monstres*, 131.

20   Muchembled, *Popular Culture and Elite*, 68.

21   Trombley, "Paganism in the Greek," 350.

22   Ibid., 350.

23   Kors, and Peters, *Witchcraft in Europe*, 60-61; Douce, *Illustrations of Shakespeare*, 236 (for 877-879 CE).

24   Douce, *Illustrations of Shakespeare*, 238; Kors, and Peters, *Witchcraft in Europe*, 60-62. See also McNeill and Gamer, *Medieval Handbooks*, 332.

25   Regino of Prüm, quoted in Kors, and Peters, *Witchcraft in Europe*, 62. See also McNeill and Gamer, *Medieval Handbooks*, 332.

26   Among continental Germanic peoples, the Alemannic laws of the early seventh century "forbade the burning of *strigae*"; at this time, "*striga*" was a multivalent term embracing female human followers of Diana as well as vampiric supernatural beings who devoured human males. The burning of *strigae* was prohibited because to burn them meant that they were believed to actually exist, and according to the authors of Alemannic law, they did not. To believe in them constituted a form of heresy. This belief, and the consequent determination to prohibit the burning of *strigae* was seconded by Rothari (*c.* 606-652), King of the Lombards, in 643. In the late eighth century, Christianized Saxons rejected Alemannic law, seeing Goddess reverence and belief in witches as exemplary of persistent paganism and thereby deciding

that both witch and Christian believing in their existence should be burned (Behringer, *Witches and Witch-Hunts*, 30-31).

27   See Murray, *Witch-Cult*.

28.   Ginzburg, *Ecstasies: Deciphering the Witches'*, 9.

29   Lea, *Materials Toward a History*, 1: 181.

30   Kittredge, *Witchcraft in Old*, 244-245.

31   Lea, *Materials Toward a History*, 1: 173.

32   Bologne, *Du flambeau au bûcher*, 70; Adam of Bremen, *History of the Archbishops*, Book 2, sec. lxii (60), pp. 97-98 and Book 4, sec. xxvi (26), pp. 207; Farmer, *Oxford Dictionary*, 385-386.

33   McNeill and Gamer, *Medieval Handbooks*, 349.

34   See Alford, and Gallup, "Traces of a Dianic," 350, 354, 358-359; Bachtold-Staubli, Hoffmann-Krayer, and Ludtke, eds., *Handworterbuch des Deutschen* C-Fr, p. 88; Behringer, *Shaman of Oberstdorf*, 53-56; Caro Baroja, *World*, 62, 64; Dashu, "Tregenda of the Old Goddess," *Suppressed Histories*; Douce, *Illustrations of Shakespeare*, 236; Golther, *Handbuch der Germanischen*; Grimm, *Teutonic Mythology*, 1: 250-254, 266-299, 308; 2: 883; 3: 925-927, 932-934, 949, 1162, 1364; Kloss, "Herodias the Wild Huntress," 101; Lea, *Materials Toward a History*, 1: 175-177, 181, 187-189, 191-192, 271; Maury, *Croyances et légendes*, 376-377; Monaghan, *Book of Goddesses*, 126, 239-240; Motz, *Beauty and the Hag*, 124-125; Motz, "Winter Goddess," 151-166; Pócs, *Between the Living*, 125; Rager, *Dictionnaire des fées*, 748; Reeves, "Shakespeare's Queen Mab," 26; Savli, "Slovenian Mythology"; Scott, *Minstrelsy of the Scottish*, 2: 325-326, 328-329; Thorpe, *Northern Mythology*, 1: 232, 273, 280; Timm, *Frau Holle, Frau Percht*.

35   Lea, *Materials Toward*, 1:159.

36   Rattue, *Living Stream*, 87.

37   Among those who argued that "Witchcraft" was a new sect, possibly emerging in the fourteenth century, which should be distinguished from the persistent cult of Diana were Eymeric (*c.* 1320-1399), Jean Vineti (1400-1470), Nicolas Jaquier (d. 1472), Vincenzo Dodo (fl. 1510), Bernardo di Como (fl. 1510), Gianfrancesco Pico della Mirandola (1469-1533), and Paulus Grillandus (or, P. Ghirlandus, P. Grilandus, Paolo Grillandi, Pauli Grillandi, Paolo Grillando, Paulus Grillandus, b. *c.* 1490-d. after 1536). See Lea, *Materials Toward a History*, 1: 272, 276-277, 367, 372, 383, 405-406 ; Lea, *History of the Inquisition*, 3: 496-498.

38   Chaucer, *Canterbury Tales*, "The Wife of Bath's Tale," ll. 1-5, p. 281; Schildgen, *Pagans, Tatars*, 70.

39   Scot, *Discoverie of Witchcraft*, 106.

40   Lea, *Materials Toward a History*, 1: 212-213.

41   Scott, *Minstrelsy of the Scottish*, 2: 325-326.

42   Comfort, *Saracens in Italian*, 901. Giacopo Passavanti (d. 1357) of fourteenth-century Italy and numerous others continued to condemn the cult of Diana, reiterating the view of the *Canon Episcopi*, that the nocturnal encounters of persons with the Goddess were in fact evil dreams or hallucinations sent by the Devil. It was the duty of Church leaders, the *Canon Episcopi* and related documents explained, to insist that this "innumerable multitude" was *not* worshipping the pagan goddess, but instead, Satan (See Lea, *Materials Toward a History*, 1: 172-173, 182).

43   Bertolotti, "Ox's Bones," 59, 63-64. Although Wolfgang Behringer does bring to our attention the testimony of Margherita Vanzino from Tesero regarding various "games" including that of the Donna del Bon Zogo, he does not stress that her testimony indicates a proliferation of cults during the early Renaissance, a point that I think is extremely significant. Vanzino describes three primary sorts of "games" or rites: those dedicated to the Devil, the Zogo *del diavolo*; those dedicated to ancestral spirits and other spirits 'of the night;' and those dedicated to the Lady, that is, the Goddess. We have seen that many pagan traditions honor the dead. I happen to believe that Satanism has existed in some form for many centuries. Vanzino's important

contribution, it occurs to me, is her emphasis on the division between Satanism and so-called Witchcraft (See Behringer, *Shaman of Oberstdorf*, 59).

44 See Andre, le chapelain, *Art of Courtly Love*; Underhill, Evelyn, *Mysticism: A Study*, 227; Duby, *Love and Marriage*, 57-63; Leland, *Aradia, or the Gospel*, 362. *Moccola*, suggesting a mushroom's top or the stub of a burnt candle, may have included hopping, as in "hop[ping] into another world." Benevento was a seat of Witchcraft.

45 Bertolotti, "Ox's Bones," 63.

46 Lea, *Materials Toward a History*, 1: 189.

47 Regino of Prüm, quoted in Kors, and Peters, *Witchcraft in Europe*, 62.

48 Lea, *Materials Toward a History*, 1: 175, 189-193, 292-297, 365-366.

49 Ibid., 1: 277.

50 Ibid., 1: 291.

51 Bertolotti, "Ox's Bones," 64.

52 Lea, *Materials Toward a History*, 1: 194-195.

53 Ibid., 1: 355.

54 Ibid., 1: 356.

55 Ibid., 1: 357.

56 Ibid., 1: 373.

57 Ibid., 1: 194-195.

58 Cited by Scot, *Discoverie of Witchcraft*, 24, 106.

59   Scot, *Discoverie of Witchcraft*, 24; Ginzburg, *Ecstasies: Deciphering the Witches'*, 226-295; Lea, *History of the Inquisition*, 3: 503.

60   Scot, *Discoverie of Witchcraft*, 106.

61   Duni, *Under the Devil's*, 44.

62   Darst, "Witchcraft in Spain," 306.

63   Lea, *Materials Toward a History*, 1: 406.

64   Weyer, *Histoires, disputes et discours*, 1: Bk. 3: pg. 318.

65   Bruno, *Heroic Frenzies*

66   Couliano, *Eros and Magic*, 82.

67   Begg, *Cult of the Black*, 53; Grimm, *Teutonic Mythology*, 1: 313 n.

68   Kaplan, "Isabella d'Este and Black," 149, 150, fig. 33; Seelig, "Christoph Jamnitzer's 'Moor's Head,'" 205, fig. Giulio Aristide Sartorio (1860-1932) also portrayed Diana of Ephesus as having black skin in *Diana d'Efeso e gli schiavi* (1899). This painting is housed in Rome, at the Galleria Nazionale d'Arte Moderna; see Honour, ed., *The Image of the Black in Western Art: IV: 2*: 184 and 185, fig. 138.

69   Shakespeare, *Romeo and Juliet*, I.4.53-95, pp. 1110-1111.

70   Barkan, *Gods Made Flesh*, 262; Shakespeare, *Midsummer Night's Dream*, ed. Furness, 2; Briggs, K., *Encyclopedia of Fairies*, 401.

71   Stow, *Survey of London*, 261; Wheatley, *London: Past and Present*, 372; *OED*, "prill."

72   James I and Anon., *Daemonologie* and *Newes from Scotland*, 73.

73   Ibid., 73-75.

[74] Ibid., 74.

[75] Ibid., 74-75.

[76] Ibid., 74.

[77] Ibid., 74.

[78] Ibid., 75.

[79] Lancre, *On the Inconstancy* 533.

[80] Ibid., 533.

[81] Scott, *Minstrelsy of the Scottish*, 2: 336-337.

[82] Lancre, *On the Inconstancy* 533.

[83] Brand, *Observations on the Popular*, 1: 362; Lawson, *Modern Greek Folklore*, 43, 51; Blunt, *Vestiges of Ancient*, 57; Weigall, Paganism in Our Christianity, 226; Weyer, *Histoires, disputes*, 1: Bk. 3: p. 334; Hamilton, Pagan Element, 352.

[84] Thoreau, *Journals*, 3: 125-126 (Nov., 1850).

[85] Baciu, Tradiciones en zonas, 16.

[86] Rucsanda, Tradition and contemporaneity, 2 (51): 61.

[87] Baciu, Tradiciones en zonas, 16-17. See also Rucsanda, Tradition and contemporaneity, 2 (51): 61.

[88] Beza, *Paganism in Roumanian*, 45-53; Eliade, Observations on European, 81; Ginzburg, *Ecstasies: Deciphering the Witches'*, 189; Simpson, *European Mythology*, 121, 126.

[89] Breton, *Nuits secretes*, 137-151.

[90] Adler, *Drawing Down*, 45-50; Barrett, *Women's Rites*.

Bibliography

Adam of Bremen. *History of the Archbishops of Hamburg-Bremen.* Trans. Francis J. Tschan. New York, NY: Columbia University Press, 2002.

Adler, Margot. *Drawing down the moon: Witches, Druids, Goddess worshippers, and other Pagans in America today.* (orig. 1979). New York, NY: Penguin, 2006.

Alford, Violet and Rodney Gallup. "Traces of a Dianic Cult from Catalonia to Portugal." *Folklore* vol. 46, no. 4 (Dec. 1935), pp. 350-361.

Andre, le chapelain (a. k. a. Andreas Capellanus), *The Art of Courtly Love (De Arte Honeste Amandi*, 1184-86). New York, NY: Ungar Publishing Co., 1941.

Bachtold-Staubli, Hanns, Eduard Hoffmann-Krayer, and Gerhard Ludtke, eds. 1927-1942. *Handworterbuch des Deutschen Aberglaubens.* Berlin, Germany: Walter de Gruyter.

Baciu, Daniela. Tradiciones en zonas ribereñas: El caso de Dobruja—lugar de diversidad cultural y étnica [Traditions in Riparian Areas: The Case of Dobruja—in Light of Cultural and Ethnic Diversity]. *Universität zu Köln Philosophische Fakultät Zentrum Lateinamerika*, 2010. http://www.lateinamerika.uni-koeln.de/299.html/(accessed Jan. 4, 2011).

Barkan, Leonard. *The Gods Made Flesh: Metamorphosis and the Pursuit of Paganism.* New Haven, CT: Yale University Press, 1986.

Barrett, Ruth. Women's Rites, Women's Mysteries: Intuitive Ritual Creation. 2nd ed. Woodbury, MN: Llewellyn, 2007.

Behringer, Wolfgang. *Shaman of Oberstdorf: Conrad Stoeckhlin and the Phantoms of the Night.* Trans. H. C. Erik Midelfort. Charlottesville, VA: University Press of Virginia, 1998.
_____. *Witches and Witch-Hunts: A Global History.* Malden, MA: Polity Press, 2004.

Bertolotti, Maurizio. "The Ox's Bones and the Ox's Hide: A Popular Myth, Part Hagiography and Part Witchcraft." In *Microhistory and the Lost Peoples of*

Europe, ed. Edward Muir and Guido Ruggiero, 42-70. Trans. Eren Branch. Baltimore, MD: Johns Hopkins University Press, 1991.

Beza, Marcu. *Paganism in Roumanian Folklore*. London: J. M. Dent, 1928.

Birnbaum, Lucia Chiavola. *Dark Mother: African Origins and Godmothers*. San Jose, CA: Authors Choice Press, 2001.

Blunt, John James. *Vestiges of Ancient Manners and Customs Discoverable in Modern Italy and Sicily*. London: John Murray, 1823.

Bologne, Jean Claude. *Du Flambeau au bûcher*. Paris, France: Plon, 1993.

Brand, John. *Observations on the Popular Antiquities of Great Britain*. Rev. ed. 3 vols. Ed. Sir Henry Ellis. London: Henry G. Bohn, 1849.

Breton, Guy. *Les nuits secretes de Paris*. Paris: Editeur à Paris/Editions de Crémille, 1970.

Briggs, Katharine M. *An Encyclopedia of Fairies*. New York, NY: Pantheon Books, 1976.

Broedel, Hans Peter. *The "Malleus Maleficarum" and the Construction of Witchcraft*. New York, NY: Manchester University Press, 2003.

Bruno, Giordano. *The Heroic Frenzies. Athenaeum Library of Philosophy*. http:// evans-experientialism.freewebspace.com/bruno_2nd_part.htm/(accessed March 16, 2011).

Caro Baroja, Julio. *The World of the Witches*. Trans. O. N. V. Glendinning. Chicago, IL: University of Chicago Press, 1975.

Chaucer, Geoffrey. *The Canterbury Tales*. Trans. Nevill Coghill. New York, NY: Penguin Books, 1977.

Cixous, Hélène, and Catherine Clément. *The Newly Born Woman*. Trans. Betsy Wing. Minneapolis, MN: University of Minnesota Press, 1988 [quote, p. 69].

Cohn, Norman. *Europe's Inner Demons: An Enquiry Inspired by the Great Witch-Hunt.* New York, NY: Basic Books, Inc., 1975.
_____. *The Pursuit of Millennium: Revolution, Millenarians and Mystical Anarchists of the Middle Ages.* New York, NY: Oxford University Press, 1970.

Comfort, William Wistar. "The Saracens in Italian Epic Poetry." *PMLA* 59: 4 (1944) 882-910.

Couliano, Ioan P. *Eros and Magic in the Renaissance.* Trans. Margaret Cook. Chicago, IL: University of Chicago Press, 1987.

Darst, David H. "Witchcraft in Spain: The Testimony of Martin de Castañega's Treatise on Superstition and Witchcraft." *Proceedings of the American Philosophical Society* 123: 5 (1979): 298-322.

Dashu, Max. "Tregenda of the Old Goddess, Witches, and Spirits." *Suppressed Histories.* http://www.suppressedhistories.net/secrethistory/witchtregenda.html/ (accessed June 26, 2008).

Douce, Francis. *Illustrations of Shakespeare, and of Ancient Manners.* London: Thomas Tegg, Cheapside, 1839.

Duby, Georges. *Love and Marriage in the Middle Ages.* Trans. Jane Dunnett. Chicago, IL: University of Chicago Press, 1994.

Duni, Matteo. 2007. *Under the Devil's Spell: Witches, Sorcerers, and the Inquisition in Renaissance Italy.* Florence, Italy: Syracuse University in Florence, 2007.

Eliade, Mircea. Observations on European witchcraft. In *Occultism, witchcraft, and cultural fashions: Essays in comparative religions* by Mircea Eliade, 69-92. Chicago, IL: University of Chicago Press, 1976.

Farmer, David Hugh. *The Oxford Dictionary of Saints.* New York, NY: Oxford University Press, 1982.

Fichtenau, Heinrich. *Heretics and Scholars in the High Middle Ages, 1000-1200.* Trans. Denise A. Kaiser. University Park, PA: Pennsylvania State University Press, 1998.

Frassetto, Michael. *Heretic Lives: Medieval Heresy from Bogomil and the Cathars to Wyclif and Hus*. London: Profile Books, Ltd., 2007.

Ginzburg, Carlo. *Ecstasies: Deciphering the Witches' Sabbath*. Trans. Raymond Rosenthal. New York, NY: Pantheon Books, Random House, 1991.

Golther, Wolfgang. *Handbuch der Germanischen Mythologie*. Berlin: Fourierverlag, 2003.

Grimm, Jacob. *Teutonic Mythology*. 4 vols. Trans., ed. James Steven Stallybrass. London: George Bell, 1882-1888.

Hamilton, Mary. The Pagan Element in the Names of Saints. *The Annual of the British School at Athens* 13 (1906/1907): 348-356.

Honour, Hugh, ed. *The Image of the Black in Western Art: IV: From the American Revolution to World War I: 2: Black Models and White Myths*. Houston: Menil Foundation; Cambridge, MA: Harvard University Press, 1989.

Hutton, Ronald. *The Triumph of the Moon: A History of Modern Pagan Witchcraft*. New York, NY: Oxford University Press, 1999.
_____. *Witches, Druids and King Arthur*. London: Hambledon Continuum, 2003.

James I and Anon. *Daemonologie* (1597) and Anon., *Newes from Scotland* (1591). Ed. G. B. Harrison. New York, NY: Barnes and Noble, Inc., 1966.

Kaplan, Paul H. D. "Isabella d'Este and Black African Women." In *Black Africans in Renaissance Europe*, ed. T. F. Earle and K. J. P. Lowe, 125-154. New York, NY: Cambridge University Press, 2005.

Kittredge, George Lyman. *Witchcraft in Old and New England*. Cambridge, MA: Harvard University Press, 1929.

Kloss, Kloss, Waldemar. "The Wild Huntress in the Legend of the Middle Ages, II." *Modern Language Notes* 23 (4): 100-102, 1908.

Kors, Alan Charles, and Edward Peters, eds. *Witchcraft in Europe, 400-1700: A Documentary History.* 2nd ed. Rev. by Edward Peters. Philadelphia, PA: University of Pennsylvania Press, 2001.

Lambert, Malcolm. 1992. *Medieval heresy: Popular movements from the Gregorian reform to the Reformation.* 2nd ed. Cambridge, MA: Blackwell.

Lancre, Pierre de. *On the Inconstancy of Witches: Pierre De Lancre's 'Tableau de l'inconstance des mauvais anges et demons' (1612).* Trans. Harriet Stone and Gerhild Scholz Williams. Ed. Gerhild Scholz Williams. Tempe, AZ: ACMRS [Arizona Center for Medieval and Renaissance Studies], in collaboration with Brepols, 2006.

Lawson, John Cuthbert. *Modern Greek Folklore and Ancient Greek Religion.* Cambridge, UK: Cambridge University Press, 1910.

Lea, Henry Charles. *A History of the Inquisition of the Middle Ages.* New York, NY: Harper Brothers, 1887.

Lea, Henry Charles. *Materials Toward a History of Witchcraft.* Ed. Arthur C. Howland. New York, NY: Thomas Yoseloff, 1957.

Leland, Charles Godfrey. *Aradia, or the Gospel of the Witches* (1899). Trans. Mario Pazzaglini and Dina Pazzaglini. With additional material by Chas S. Clifton, Robert Mathiesen, and Robert E. Chartowich. Foreword by Stewart Farrar. Blaine, WA: Phoenix Publishing, Inc., 1998.

Loos, Milan. *Dualist Heresy in the Middle Ages.* Prague, Czechoslovakia: Academia, 1974.

Martin, Sean. *The Gnostics: The First Christian Heretics.* Harpenden, England: Pocket Essentials, 2006.

Maury, (Louis-Ferdinand-) Alfred. *Croyances et légendes du Moyen Age.* Paris: Honoré Champion, 1896.

McNeill, John T. and Helena M. Gamer, trans., eds. *Medieval Handbooks of Penance: A Translation of the Principal libri poenitentiales and selections from Related Documents*. New York, NY: Columbia University Press, 1938.

Monaghan, Patricia. *The Book of Goddesses and Heroines*. New York, NY: E. P. Dutton, 1981.

Motz, Lotte. *The Beauty and the Hag: Female Figures of Germanic Faith and Myth*. Vienna, Austria: Fassbaender, 1993.

_____. "The Winter Goddess: Percht, Holda, and Related Figures." *Folklore* 95: 2 (1984) 151-166.

Muchembled, Robert. *Popular Culture and Elite Culture in France, 1400-1750*. Trans. Lydia Cochrane. Baton Rouge, LA: Louisiana State University Press, 1985.

Murray, Margaret A. *The Witch-Cult in Western Europe*. London: Oxford University Press, 1962.

Pearson, Joanne. "Wicca, Paganism and History: Contemporary Witchcraft and the Lancashire Witches. In *The Lancashire Witches: Histories and Stories*, ed. Robert Poole, 188-203. New York, NY: Manchester University Press, 2002.

Peters, Edward, ed. *Heresy and Authority in Medieval Europe: Documents in Translation*. Philadelphia, PA: University of Pennsylvania Press, 1980.

Pócs, Éva. *Between the Living and the Dead: A Perspective on Witches and Seers in the Early Modern Age*. Trans. Szilvia Rédey and Michael Webb. Budapest, Hungary: Central European University Press, 1999.

Purkiss, Diane. *The Witch in History: Early Modern and Twentieth-Century Representations*. New York: Routledge, 1996.

Rager, Catherine. *Dictionnaire des Fées et du peuple invisible dans l'occident païen*. Turnhout, Belgium: Brepols, 2003.

Rattue, James. *The Living Stream: Holy Wells in Historical Context.* Woodbridge, Suffolk, England: The Boydell Press, 1995.

Reeves, W. P. 1902. Shakespeare's Queen Mab. *Modern Language Notes* 17: 1 (1902) 10-14.

Rio, Bernard. *L'Arbre philosophal.* Lausanne, Switzerland: Collection Antaios, Éditions L'age d'Homme, 2001.

Roach, Andrew P. *The Devil's World: Heresy and Society, 1100-1300.* New York, NY: Pearson/Longman, 2005.

Ruscanda, Madalina [u/v accent over first 2 a's in Madalina]. Tradition and Contemporaneity in Dragaica [u/v accent over first a in Drag.]. *Bulletin of the Transylvania University of Brasov,* 2009, 2 (51): 61-65.

Russell, Jeffrey Burton. *Witchcraft in the Middle Ages.* Ithaca, NY: Cornell University Press, 1972.

Saint-Martin, Geneviève. *L'Auvergne: Des Monstres, des sorciers, et des dieux.* Paris: Éditions e-dite, 2001.

Savli, Jozko. "Slovenian Mythology." *Carantha: History of Slovenia: Carantania.* http://www.carantha.net/Slovenian_mythology_slovensko_bajeslovje.htm/ (accessed January 15, 2007).

Schildgen, Brenda Deen. *Pagans, Tartars, Moslems, and Jews in Chaucer's "Canterbury Tales."* Gainesville, FL: University Press of Florida, 2001.

Scot, Reginald. *The Discoverie of Witchcraft.* New York, NY: Dover Publications, Inc., 1972.

Scott, Sir Walter. *Minstrelsy of the Scottish Border: Consisting of Historical and Romantic Ballads, Collected in the Southern Counties of Scotland: With a Few of Modern Date, Founded upon Local Tradition.* vol. 2. Ed. T. F. Henderson. Edinburgh and London: W. Blackwood and Sons; New York: Charles Scribner's Sons, 1802.

Seelig, Lorenz. Christoph Jamnitzer's "Moor's Head": A Late Renaissance Drinking Vessel. In *Black Africans in Renaissance Europe*, ed. T. F. Earle and K. J. P. Lowe, 181-209. New York, NY: Cambridge University Press, 2005.

Shakespeare, William. *A Midsummer Night's Dreame*. Ed. Horace Howard Furness. New Variorum Edition. Philadelphia: J. B. Lippincott Co., 1895.

_____. *The Tragedy of Romeo and Juliet*. In *The Riverside Shakespeare*, 2nd ed., ed. G. Blakemore Evans, pp. 1101-1145. Boston: Houghton Mifflin Co., 1997.

Simpson, Jacqueline. *European Mythology*. New York, NY: Peter Bedrick, 1987.

Societé de mythologie française. *La France mythologique*. Sous la direction de Henri Dontenville. Paris: Tchou, 1966.

Stow, John. *A Survey of London* (1598). Ed. Henry Morley. London: George Routledge and Sons, Ltd., 1890.

Stoyanov, Yuri. *The Hidden Tradition in Europe*. New York, NY: Arkana/ Penguin, 1994.

Summers, Montague. *The History of Witchcraft and Demonology* (1925). Secaucus, NJ: Citadel Press, 1974.

Thoreau, Henry David. *Journals*. Ed. John C. Broderick and Robert Sattelmeyer. Princeton, NJ: Princeton University Press, 1984.

Thorpe, Benjamin. *Northern Mythology, Comprising the Popular Traditions and Superstitions of Scandinavia, North Germany, and the Netherlands*. 3 vols. London: Edward Lumley, 1851-1852.

Timm, Erika. *Frau Holle, Frau Percht, und Verwandte Gestalten*. Stuttgart, Germany: S. Hirzel Verlag, 2003.

Trombley, Frank R. *Hellenic Religion and Christianization: c. 370-529*. vol. 1. New York, NY: E. J. Brill, 1993.

_____. "Paganism in the Greek World at the End of Antiquity: The Case of Rural Anatolia and Greece." *Harvard Theological Review* 78: 3-4 (1985) 327-352.

Underhill, Evelyn. *Mysticism: A Study in the Nature and Development of Man's Spiritual Consciousness.* New York, NY: E. P. Dutton and Co., Inc., 1961.

Waite, Gary K. *Heresy, Magic, and Witchcraft in Early Modern Europe.* New York, NY: Palgrave Macmillan, 2003.

Weigall, Arthur. *The Paganism in Our Christianity.* New York, NY: G. P. Putnam's Sons, 1928.

Weyer, Johann, *Histoires, disputes et discours, des illusions et impostures des diables, des magiciens infames, sorcières et empoisonneurs; des ensorcelez et demoniaques et de la guerison d'iceux; item de la punition que meritent les magiciens, les empoisonneurs et les sorcières, le tout compris en six livres* (1568). Paris: A. Delahaye et Lecrosnier, 1885.

Wheatley, Henry Benjamin. *London: Past and Present; Its History, Associations, and Traditions.* London: J. Murray, 1891.

The Birth of Xochiquetzal at 948 Noe St.

(for Gloria Evangelina Anzaldúa)

David Hatfield Sparks

Spirits be still
Spell be spoken
Xochiquetzal now is born
Poetry's circle now is open

From a bricked-up fireplace mantle
hangs your silent bamboo wind chime
hollow tubes—fuchsia, mustard yellow—
its twin swaying isolated in the mirror,
protected from any possibility of breeze.

Wooden Quixote fingers a black rosary
praying with Coatlicue for your return,
pregnant with emeralds and quetzal feathers,
offering new life suspended above Her volcanic altar,
the Fool's dream births a butterfly's love.

Bloomless succulents line shuttered windows
in the still haze of late summer's sunlight,
expectant, hooded figures await the bronze woman,
exiled from her fertile valley.

Here I lay in lover's arms animating your quilted divan
with urgent, percussive strokes,

The Birth of Xochiquetzal at 948 Noe St

a rhythmic offering in this wayward sanctuary,
crossroads where the earth quakes
and ocean mist spins monarch's gold cocoon.

You have silenced your war-like brother
who would, one by one, murder Her stars.
You place the silver orb of your sister
on your breast in hopeful reverence, and
I have seen you wait with brass cymbal, pewter bell
to celebrate her appearance in the Western sky.

Here in the still haunt of your absence,
I inhale rich oil of cedar, sip your herbal brew,
blessed maguey for sleepless nights in this narrow bed,
holy vervain, heady pennyroyal, dried lobelia's flame
and soothing flower of chamomile steam this bay of windows
shuttered against these clanging hills.

An urgent wind begs entrance, rushing past my fading silhouette
and he, our brother Ehecatl, softly strums at silent pipes,
demanding attention from daydreaming shadow,
sits on your humble altar, ready judge for all.

Shivering wooden tones escape his smoking mirror
and its melopoeia intones your true reflection
Xochiquetzal, daughter of Coatlicue,
born of She Who Brings Forth Sun and Fire,
honored by women who live as they please.

Finding greatest joy in the pleasure of her sister's body,
forgive the violence of the Mother
and leave behind seductive Itzpapalotl,
your face, painted patches of colored and white chalk,
is washed clean in the dew of prophet marigold.

You have worn too long the mask of skulls
an obsidian cloth sealing your loins, too long
flown to crossroads of the wide plain,

with ghosts of dark butterflies,
to feast on hearts of deer,
felt the knife of sacrifice deep in your belly.

As you lay in a white shroud,
victim of the surgeon's blade,
I imagine you mist-entombed in Her sacred mountain cave,
Chantico, home of our Lady of the Serpent Skirt,
their winged bodies a woven nest around your troubled spirit.

And I and my brother Quetzalcoatl, savior of gentle loves
kneel here in prayer to Tlazolteotl, She Who Receives Confession,
to Teteu Innan, She Who Fills the Womb and Keeps It Empty,
rattling Her Skirt of White Shells to remember
to ease pain of birth for Her daughter of the earth.

I stain my pale face red,
offer sunflower seeds and honeyed cakes of corn
that you might return—Blue Butterfly Woman,
strong and mobile, bright-winged being
that was once stone chrysalis,
that from your sister-twin, for whom you long,
be given your secret name.

From this your scrying glass of smoking stone, foresee that
She, your Mother-Lover will escort you,
seated on a gleaming Ocelot,
onyx ruler of the First Sun,
sacred quetzal feathers crowning your head,
bringing artful gifts to this Fifth Sun,
two golden flowers, seedlings of a newer age,
woven in sleek black hair.

Thin chains of jewels glowing, stretched across bold cheeks,
for from your mouth come words like sweet flowers—
pink oleanders, orange flamed tongues of jacarandas,
from your mouth come words sharp as obsidian knives—
claw-edged winds, drawing blood, giving life.

The Birth of Xochiquetzal at 948 Noe St

Flowing from bejeweled lips,
questions and signals to cities of quaking earth,
singing messages of the Marigold.
From your petalled Book of Cycles,
telling of life from seed to leafy stem
leafy stem to bud
of bud to flower fully offered to the Sun.

From golden flower, a dying petal.
Its house, womb-pocket of new seed
taking root in thrice-plowed earth
in She, the One Who Lies Beneath All These Dualities—
a petalled Book of Cycles,
the Message of the Marigold.

Suddenly the wind is gone and
this temple throbs with terrible shadows.
From a smoking mirror, in the eye of a moment,
she comes dancing destruction,
in an echo of healing chants,
She rips out my heart
and flings it to the glowing air.
And from your bricked-up fireplace mantle
rush armies of fiery butterflies
bursting in a cacophony of hope.
A flurry of wings falls in sacred spirals,
bouquets of red-gold flame drift toward the shattered ground

And the thin shell of your cracked body
appears, in the opened hearth's raging heat,
spilling the seed of green-gold prophecy,
filling the room with dreams of the Star's Great Queen
bronze Lady enthroned in fertile earth,
dancing Coatlicue's joy
with She who gives birth to all.

Moon is full
Spells are spoken
Xochiquetzal is born
Healing's path now is open

Enough

Theresa Gale Henson

The branded questions are ready to turn to soil,
you must let them fall through your fingers
where they might finally do some good.

You are the promise, the completed sentence,
the lingering chord that brings them home.

Behind the trees lining the shoreline are more trees
and then more, among them are the animals.
Everything is covered with their perfect gazes.

The wild watches itself, desires its own flesh and fiber—
when the wind blows all that passion turns to song.

Under the eternal gleam of the water are miles and miles
of everything at once. It moves with itself; swims inside
one massive body—you belong there, but not yet.

Your motion out over the surface is the call, the achievement
the gesture into life—you are the wild, eternal motion.

I am going into the blue along the green and over the black
I carry my red for the eternal yellow.

The streaks of cirrus clouds are lines on the staff,
the birds are the notes and make a living manuscript
for that which survived the great threshing—

when you said no more to what once held up the fruit,
but was now dead, now suitable for burning.

This has got to go—
you could wrap all that in a loosely woven dream
and see what's fine enough to sift out, what is fine enough
to escape, resist gathering, and stay aloft on invisible currents.

She is all one vessel, all one wilderness ceaselessly alive with itself
and throwing new panoplies of violence and resurrections every day.

Finding Ixchel, Mayan Mother

Theresa Gale Henson

The boat bounced over the deepening blue waves. The white lip of the shoreline receded and the water grew more textured with the motion of larger currents. I gripped the sides tightly as the sea showered my face. I watched the small drops from the vast ocean glitter our small and aging, earnest boat. Everything within me searched for the security point—something solid or some anchor that would make me feel safe. I turned to gaze at the elderly fisherman who was our guide to Isla Contoy, an island bird sanctuary off the coast of Cancun. I continued to scan him regularly for any signs of fear, doubt, or hubris. He was placid and jovial. The boat rose and bounced down another wave.

While the six other passengers chatted merrily, I looked around and saw that the boat had no communications device. I began planning for a disaster. With the shore about a mile away, we could swim. Yes that was it: I had a plan now and we would be fine. I tried to steel my stomach and looked again at our guides. Both the captain of the small vessel and his grandson assistant confidently peered ahead over the ocean as the six other passengers of our small group chatted away like the birds we wanted to go see.

Occasionally one of the two motors would halt and the young assistant would reach down and adjust the gas line, sending the motor growling again. I struggled to feel the solidity of "La Maria" but the odd hole near the pile of snorkel gear hooked my attention. Every time the boat came down over a wave, it seemed the wall went one way and the floor went another. I forced myself to trust that the vessel's blessed namesake would prevail. Surely Maria de Guadalupe, the great mother of Mexico, was watching us.

Of course, she was. But there was a presence more ancient around us—in the glittering blue of the water, the moving waves, the distant shoreline, and the clouds. It was the clouds that lifted my eyes away from the boat. It was the wide cumulous tufts that began to draw me out of my corporeal fear. Their forms moved in curving and angular swirls across the sky. I followed them above the horizon and found a serpent's tail that undulated and then flicked its rattle up toward the sun. Then it dawned on me: These were Mayan clouds. A surge of excitement flashed through me and loosened my grip on the boat. I was gazing at the same clouds that hovered over the ancient Mayans. I felt keenly that we had both shared the view of these clouds. And that we were both inspired by them—for the clouds' white forms subtly reminded me of the Mayan art and architecture I'd seen in photographs.

Then the roar of the boat and the chatting within it faded as a broader awareness took over: I was in the land of Ixchel, Mayan goddess of the moon, and mother of the four directions as well as the guardian of all mothers everywhere. Her presence suffused every drop of the sea and began to lighten my knotted mind. I turned and grinned at the salty captain of our boat. I saw how at home he was on these waters. He winked at me kindly in a detached elderly way and returned his gaze to the small island on the horizon. My fear turned to excitement. I was on an adventure. I was in the hands of Ixchel.

A quick survey of her domain and immediately my trust began to grow. Her powers are in creativity, fertility, transformation, and the waters that can either give life or take it. Sometimes known as "Lady Rainbow," she sends rain to nourish the crops and keeps the oceans vital and full of food. One's relationship with her depends on one's gratitude. Give thanks and the life-giving waters will nourish and lift you. Conversely, an ungrateful heart will elicit floods of destruction. As the captain steered the boat across a large ship's wake, I began to steer my heart away from worry into the sure waters of gratitude.

In her story, though, it is revealed that Ixchel's wisdom and power are hard-won. As a beautiful young woman, she was desired by all the gods. But it was Kinich Ahau, the Sun God, whom she wanted. And yet he was indifferent to her. For years she followed him around, unaware of the havoc she was causing. Her pursuit of him around the world caused the tides to rise and floods that killed the crops. Finally, Kinich Ahau took notice of the beautiful cloth she wove and was smitten. Together they had four powerful sons, the Bacabs, who hold up the four directions.

However, her grandfather did not approve of the marriage and like many mythological patriarchs, displayed a severe lack of anger management. He killed his granddaughter with a lightning bolt and (also like many mythological patriarchs) erroneously thought the matter was over. Dragonflies surrounded her dead body and sang to her until after 183 days, she woke up.

She returned to her lover but their relationship was troubled. The Sun God accused her of having an affair with his brother, the Morning Star, and threw Ixchel out of the sky. The vulture gods took her in and the remorseful Kinich Ahau begged her to come back. But Ixchel quickly learned he hadn't changed and she left him for good; she went into the jungle and became a jaguar whenever he came searching for her. She turned her victimization into empowerment when she found her calling, assisting women with pregnancies and childbirth.

In her focus on what is being born, she develops an intolerance for what is not life-affirming—thus her ability to take away life as well as give it. She has been through too much to tolerate any half-love, any failure to wonder with humility at the mystery, any inability to see that everything is a gift. She herself passed through the portals of death and was given life again by the dragonflies, creatures who represent the ability to dance with magic and pass through illusion. Never again would she pursue anything or anyone outside herself, for in bringing forth her devotion to life she found her power and brought balance and life to the world.

Soon we were drifting in the calm shallows of Isla Contoy. I had began to feel a rugged warmth toward our captain and shrugged as he lightly opened another beer. His grandson began telling us about the island, the reefs, and the safest places to snorkel. Cormorants greeted us from the coastal rocks and frigates circled over the center of the island. "La Maria" pulled up to a long pier that seemed constructed specifically for tropical travel advertisements. I looked over the side of the boat, down into the clear water, and saw starfish and mysteriously beautiful, translucent blue tube fish.

A short walk took us to a lagoon that was a thriving frigate nursery. Amidst watchful parents, our binoculars could make out many a fuzzy profile of the newly born. These warm interior waters provided safety for a great profusion of life. Between the island's isolation and the sanction of the Mexican government, this fertile place would be protected.

We returned to the beach where the captain and his grandson had prepared our lunch. They offered grilled fish, salad, guacamole, rice, and chips. We were overwhelmed with the deliciousness of the food. The food was saturated with skill and care, and the natural beauty of the island held us in quiet peace and beauty that was in vital contrast to our raucous ride on the boat.

After lunch, we met Pamela, the guide of another tour who is a young Spanish scientist drawn to Mexico by her love of the jungle and jaguars. She had received a grant from the United Nations to fund her research, but augmented her income by being a tour guide of both Isla Contoy and the jungles of Quintana Roo and the Yucatan. I asked her how the jaguars were doing.

"Not well," she said. "Not well at all. Development is causing them to lose their habitat and then they go hunting for food on ranches and farms, where they are often shot." I thought of how Ixchel had taken refuge in the jungle as a jaguar when her lover became unbearable. Now the jaguars were being driven out into the hostile hands of humans. Perhaps prayers and offerings would help.

The teacher Angeles Arrien speaks of the "Three Vital Impulses of the Spirit": conservation, reproduction, and evolution (Cirlot, 1962). The ancient Mayans discovered these for themselves in the figure of Ixchel, who embodies these principles as goddess of fertility, creativity, and transformation. At her wise discretion, she tips forward the jar of life, spilling out the nourishing waters. Always, she has with her the serpent, possessing the power to shed old skins and grow into ever-increasing magnificence.

Just days before, I rode out to the southern tip of Isla Mujeres or "Island of Women"—so named by the Spanish explorer Hernández de Córdoba who found numerous sculptures of Mayan goddesses throughout the island. The island is a sliver of land in love with the ocean. Wherever you are, the azure Caribbean is nearby. At the rocky southern point, the churning turquoise sea has sculpted the rocks into pocked striations that descend into pale grottoes.

Hundreds of frigates hover overhead. They sail into the wind, but never leave the end of the island, which also happens to be Mexico's easternmost point: Before the sun illuminates the rest of Mexico, it first pays a now-respectful homage to his lady of the moon. The "Acantilado del Amenecer" or "Cliff or the Dawn" is at latitude 21° 12' 05.2" North, longitude 86° 42' 39" East and is one of two known sites (the other is on Cozumel) where the ancients honored Ixchel.

I stood at her temple, with our offerings and prayers, taking everything in. The wind, Ixchel's silky fingers, moved through everything constantly: the dry grasses, the trees, our salt-encrusted hair. The surrounding waves seemed as deliberate as the embroidered flowers of the Yucatan ladies. The gusts fingered our skirts as we laid down our offerings: sugar, seeds, shells, an original painting. We spoke our gratitude for the recent healthy births in our families and for the flowering of the important projects in our lives. I gave thanks for the healing of my friend David's cancer. We turned and watched the ocean dance around us until we were wet with salted water.

That night I dreamt of the sea and a beautiful house on the white sand of the Caribbean. The house was the color of the turquoise waters and I was inside, enjoying the peace and nurturing presence of the ocean. I woke up with a sun-drenched joy I hadn't felt in years. Though I had had the privilege of attending college in a coastal town, I had spent much of my adulthood so far in cities away from the ocean. And now I realized how much I missed it, how essential the bright shores were to my soul. I woke up to the sound of grackles mating amidst the whispering of palms in the morning wind and wrote this in my journal: "Ixchel returns to you your dwelling, your house of prayer overlooking the placid waters."

As I looked over my hotel's balcony at the sunrise, I wondered at how the rainbows were connected to Ixchel. How did they relate to the water and the moon? I wondered at what unified them all. Later, in the hot afternoon, I learned. I went snorkeling in a bright lagoon near my hotel. The sun shone hot and radiant through the water. My eye caught the dancing lights on the white sand of the shallows. And then I noticed the color. Everywhere the light streaked, shimmered with rainbows. Her lover, the sun, refracted through Ixchel's blue skirts to make rainbows. Their love was alive. The streams of color shimmered over the white sand. The sand held the shape of the waves, as the multicolored lights caressed the soft ridges. Although she retreated into the jungle, and then to the company of women, it is clear: She still loves the sun. Together, they bless their children who find themselves here in their Mayan kingdom, who draw closer to their families and loved ones in the combined presence of these two divinities.

Interestingly, the moon was full and clear when the ferry first took us from Cancun to Isla Mujeres. I watched the swirling, illuminated clouds and let the velvety night breezes begin to work away the Northern cold. As goddess of the tides, she guides how the waves crash over the rocks, where along the beach at this moment the shoreline will find you. She moves massive amounts of water around the globe twice a day. She reminds that there is enough happening right now to keep you overwhelmed with joy, wonder, and gratitude.

As we rode the ferry back to the mainland, and then in the cab to the airport, I realized that my intention to restore was also an implied agreement to transform—from fragmentation to wholeness, from control to trust. What drains is resistance to life. I continually worked to leave my adrenaline-filled agendas, my need to know, and my Apollonian reasoning at home. I had come here to a beautiful land with deep magic and it was my job to get out of its way. The light of the sun held my hands while I surrendered to the lunar mysteries of rest. It was in this acquiescence, that Ixchel's power to change manifested. Within my mind and in all of my relationships, the dark corners were turned out and left to dry like bones in the hot sun. What is bright within me grew brighter. Next to the music of her waves my eyes were cleared of shadows and so I see more, appreciate more than I could before. The green of the palm leaves are radiant against the Caribbean sky.

Ixchel is the Mayan Goddess of the Moon, fertility and weaving among other virtues; Her sanctuary is on Isla Mujeres where offerings were made to obtain good harvests of salt. She is regarded as the Giver of Life and keeper of dead souls. Because of this, She is also the guardian of childbirth and the art of medicine. From Her jar flow the waters of the world. The serpent on Her head symbolizes Her wisdom and power to rejuvenate; Photo © 2009 Theresa Gale Henson

The Stuff of Life: Clay, Figurines and Priestesses in Mesoamerica

Anne Key, Ph.D.

Introduction

The female figure is present throughout the thousands of years of Mesoamerican history, spanning its many cultures and encompassing various mediums, whether formed from clay, carved into stone, or drawn on paper or pottery. Viewing these artifacts with the eye of a researcher and a priestess, I perceive many of these pieces as ritual implements. The evidence seems abundant that women were a dynamic force in the spiritual sphere.

However, from decades of studying these pieces I have noticed a distinct gap between what I view *in-situ* and in museums, and what I read in the academic research. While there seems a great deal of physical evidence of women, there is little research into women's roles and even less of women's part in the encompassing spiritual life of the Mesoamericans.[1]

This essay is only a beginning venture into the proposition of women as spiritual leaders in Mesoamerica. I begin with the idea that women were the artists, the creators, of many of the clay figurines found principally in burials throughout Mesoamerican history. In the second section I take a look at the possible function of these objects as ritual implements. Next, the use of clay and the human figure are contextualized within the Mesoamerican spiritual framework, showing them as powerful tools of creation. Following is an inquiry into ceremony and the tools of ritual. The final section addresses the conundrum of why women have not been considered spiritual leaders.

This winding road takes us through seeing women as artists, and then regarding their creations as ritual tools. With those two in mind, it is possible to envision women as priestesses and leaders.

The Maker-Modelers: Women as creators of figurines

There is evidence that women were the artisans of clay figurines in the earliest eras of Mesoamerican culture. Tate (1999) shows that women were both the potters and paper-makers in the Maya civilization. It was only after the Spanish introduced the potter's wheel that men became potters. She points out that: "The activities of hand building pottery emulate grinding corn, forming corn dough, and cooking it, as the mythical First Mother of the *Popul Vuh* formed the human race of corn dough" (86). Women, associated with the earth and the water, were the ones that formed the shapes from clay.

On a different tack, Marcus (1998) has also concluded that women were the original clay artists. In her examination of Formative Era female figurines from the Oaxaca area, she identified their extravagant hairstyles as markers for social status. When considering the gender of the artist of these clay figurines, she consulted modern hairstylists to see if the maker of the figurine would have to know how to "do" the hairstyle to achieve such realistic results. The hairstylists agreed that Formative hairstyles were depicted in such realistic detail that whoever made the figurines also had to have known how to produce the hairstyle depicted. As it is highly unlikely that men styled women's hair in Formative Era Mesoamerica, it seems logical that both the hair styles and the figurines were produced by women.

Women as clay artisans persist to contemporary times. Women in Chiapas still model small figurines from clay and fire them in the cooking fires. These small painted figures are whimsical, representing daily life and sold to tourists for only a few centavos. In Michoacán, making clay figurines is still today considered "women's work," as it has been traditionally (Isaac 1996).

But, does the gender of the artisan matter? When we study the female figurines, does it make a difference if they were formed by women or men? If we view the figurines in relation to culture, as opposed to looking at the figurines solely in an isolated context, then the gender of the artist is certainly relevant.

When the figurines are regarded as a cultural artifact, the gender of the artists tells us about social formation of society. When the figurines are regarded as ritual tools, then the gender of the artisan tells us about gender-specific spiritual practices. Female figurines crafted by women reflect the spiritual practice of women. What were their rituals like? What was their unique cosmovision? How were the figurines used and why did women make them?

Is it Art? Is it a Tool? The intent behind creating ritual tools

Most ritual tools are also works of art. A link exists between art and ritual tools; both are mediums used to express what can and cannot be seen, uniting and giving form to thought. Further, ritual tools bring the formless into form. One example of this is using a feather to symbolize air. The feather, while not being air, brings some of the qualities of air, such as being insubstantial yet strong. Feathers also move air effectively and, when in their original state on birds, are in constant contact with air, using air to do the seemingly impossible—keep aloft a weight in the weightless atmosphere. Art and ritual tools bring multivalent meaning to a single concrete form.

From a physical perspective, creating art unites both sides of the brain, the left for the skill and the right for the inspiration and vision. The creation of art for sacred purpose brings the spiritual realm into the concrete. When viewed in this light, studying clay figurines as ritual tools allows us, in this century, to see how the women of previous times manifested their relationship to the Divine.

There have been numerous methods of categorizing Mesoamerican clay figurines, the most notable being the system authored by Valliant (1930) based on physical features. Methods of categorization that rely solely on physical, i.e. aesthetic, qualities diminish the possibilities for usage of these figurines, and diminish the possibility that we will look at them as ritual tools. It sets them firmly in the category of something to be viewed as opposed to used.

There is certainly a difference between a clay figurine that a woman will make to sell in the marketplace and a clay figurine that a woman will make as a ritual tool. Both may look the same, and both pieces may be evaluated by the same guidelines whether regarded as a piece of art or as a cultural artifact. However, both of these pieces are not the same, for the intent of their manufacture is completely different. This is especially applicable to objects with a numinous quality. At this point, there is not a recognizable metric for establishing the degree, or even existence, of numinous qualities. Yet, this is exactly the quality that separates an object made solely for aesthetic purposes or commerce from an object made with sacred intent. But, simply because we do not have the metrics for something, simply because we have not come up with a way to measure and quantify the "unquantifiable" does not mean that the "unquantifiable" does not exist or is not intrinsic to the meaning of the object.

One of the reasons that we can view these clay figurines as ritual tools, as objects created with sacred intent, is that they are often funerary objects. Objects which accompany a body in burial, and may presumably accompany that person into her next life, are important. In regards to this, most Mesoamerican objects in museums and collections are funerary-related. As Coe (1975) has observed, there is a "tremendous difference between ordinary artifacts and funerary material" (194). He continues:

> I would, therefore, conclude from this that most of what one finds in art museums is not the stuff of ordinary life but, rather, is another form of scarce goods which have been taken out of circulation for this cult of the dead. (194)

And, while these goods can be used as offerings for a "cult of the dead," these scarce goods can also be viewed as ritual tools.

It should be remembered that the pieces that are the most spectacular, the pieces that we study, the pieces that hold the most meaning, are most often associated with ritual. It is no wonder that the artisans put the greatest effort and intent in creating these pieces. In contrast, there are relatively few ritual tools used in modern Euro-American culture. This can be attributed to the fact that spiritual practice in our culture is highly centralized; most ritual tools reside in churches. In a home-based spiritual practice, such as was common in Mesoamerica, ritual tools would be abundant. Again, in modern Euro-American culture, much of our most spectacular art is created for viewing and sale, not for use in ritual. So, it is no wonder that we overlook the ritual qualities of so much of the art of Mesoamerica.

From earth to form:
The medium of clay and the human, and female, figure

For people, one of the most intimately known and powerful figures is the human form. Humans anthropomorphize the un-embodied or unknowable into something knowable by using the human form. Images of deities are often shown in human form.

The making of human figurines that become the first people is told in the creation story of the Aztec from the *Leyenda de los Soles*. Cihuacoatl (woman snake) grinds bones gathered by Quetzalcoatl from the underworld. She grinds them into flour, puts the flour in a womb-like container, and the gods bleed their penises in a ritual of autosacrifice. In four days a boy is born, and four days later a girl is born. In the Mayan *Popul Vuh*, the Maker-Modeler, the mother-father of life, the midwife-matchmaker, grinds corn and mixes it with water to form humans.[2] The forming of human figures out of a substance, be it corn, clay or ground bones, is the act of creation.

The human form can also be a metaphor. *Milagros*, tiny metal figures for sale in front of cathedrals in Mexico, are often in the form of the human body, or parts of a body. They can symbolize the need for healing for a certain part, say a leg, or act as a metaphor:

> The milagro of the arm might represent an arm itself, and some condition associated with it, such as an injury, or, say, an arthritic condition. It might also represent one's strength, one's ability to work—and hence one's job—or some related concept. It might represent an embrace, and physical demonstrations of affection that involve embracing. Any part of the arm might be the focus of the prayers or the magic, such as the hand, for instance.[3]

In general, concrete objects, especially familiar figures make the intangible tangible and manifest multiple meanings simultaneously in a single object.[4]

The female figure represents creation, fecundity. As the gender that gives birth, women are the repository of life. As a symbol, a female figure represents creation, and the ability for humans to create, which is, in itself, a divine act.

As a material, clay possesses many miraculous properties that make it a staple world-wide. Its plasticity and strength make it easy to work with, and it is readily available. It hardens on its own and fires easily. Clay also has medicinal properties. It is used externally to absorb toxins from the skin while simultaneously exfoliating and improving skin circulation. Ingested, clay is an anti-diarrheal medication that relieves nausea and provides calcium. For these reasons, it is especially helpful for pregnant women.[5]

Clay and female figurines combined create a powerful multivalent symbol. Used in ritual, these figurines would have multiple applications.

Ceremony and the tools of ritual: An inquiry into possibilities

Female figurines are some of the oldest known works of art. By regarding these figurines as ritual tools, works of art made to perform a sacred function, we open the possibility of glimpsing into the oldest rituals performed by women. This, indeed, is an exciting prospect. By researching, unearthing, and discovering women's rituals, we expand our perspective on women and their roles.

Regarding the Paleolithic and Neolithic female from Europe and Mesoamerica, which stylistically share many similar characteristics, the standing interpretation has been that these were fertility objects, possibly used to glorify fertility, to request fertility, or to reflect one's own fertility.

The ideas of fertility and a "cult of fertility" bring to mind many images. There is a vital reason that fertility is the basis of many religions, for there is no life without it. Fertility is the sustenance and rejuvenation of life on this earth. However, when one speaks of a "cult of fertility," especially in the context of modern American culture steeped in Abrahamic religious values, the idea of a "fertility cult" is devalued, associated solely with sex or procreation, or considered a component of primitive religions as opposed to more "advanced" religions. So, at the same time that one regards the obvious fertility aspect of these figurines, it is necessary to define, or redefine, the concept of fertility to include all life and the moral philosophy that underlies the continuance of life, the endurance of fecundity.

There continues to be speculation that these figurines were "stone-age sexual fetish" pieces[6]. This perspective precipitates a male artist, and sees the female model as "faceless." This perspective traps women, again, in the "male gaze," solely as objects of "fertility" and procreation, leading some experts to believe that prehistoric males (the artists) viewed females solely as reproductive mechanisms.[7]

Marija Gimbutas' work in Paleolithic and Neolithic Europe began a much-needed re-visioning of these figures. Of her many contributions, two most heavily impact our view of female figurines and this study. The first is her interpretation of the symbols on figurines and pottery of the Neolithic. These symbols were commonly regarded as decoration, not as language. In *Language of the Goddess* (1991), Gimbutas convincingly categorizes the repeating symbols, presenting them as purposeful ideographs laden with meaning. This is crucial to broaden the discussion around these figurines, to move beyond their descriptive and aesthetic qualities and on to their possible meaning, use, and function. By finding meaning in what was previously considered "decorative", i.e., with only minimal symbolic significance and high aesthetic significance, Gimbutas began decoding the symbolic "language" of the artifact. She has paved the way for the interpretation of meaning.

The second contribution by Gimbutas that impacts this study is her idea of a Goddess-based religion prevalent across many thousands of years throughout Old Europe[8] with many of these figurines as images of a Great Goddess. Her work brought to the forefront an overwhelming amount of evidence that in Old Europe a female deity was honored.

Tedlock (2005) gives another perspective on these Old European figurines, linking them with shamans. Many of the figurines feature dress characteristic of shamans that practiced midwifery. This link to shamanism adds another layer of meaning, connecting the figurines with real women performing real functions. It certainly moves beyond the idea of woman as mere "model," passively procreating, to woman as illustrious figure, immortalized in sculpture.

Mesoamerica figurines have a similar array of meaning attached. Bernal assigns the female figurines as "fertility cult" items, intimately tied to harvest and deity propitiation:

> . . . we see that the groups in the Valley of Mexico practised a fertility cult, related to natural phenomena and fecundity, for which female figurines were modeled in clay with a view to propitiating gods who controlled the harvest. (36)

Peterson links their development to the post-Classic Mesoamerican cosmovision: "The clay women probably represent earth or vegetation goddesses made in connection with agricultural ceremonies. This was an important step in the development of one of the greatest magico-religious cultures in the world" (36). Kocyba directly compares the European Neolithic female images with those found in Archaic and Formative Era Mesoamerica; he attributes the decline in both cultures to the institutionalization of religion. Román Padilla R. and Araceli Jaffer G. broaden the possibilities of the functions of female clay figurines to include: magical protection, an amulet, a votive offering, a toy, a death offering, an offering to structures, an element associated with fertility, to represent deities (166-167).

Marcus (1998) proposes that small, predominately female figurines from Early and Middle Formative Oaxaca (1800-500 BCE) were used in ancestor worship rituals. Marcus (1998) speculates that women created clay figurines of their "recent ancestor," female family members that had died, to be used in ceremonies honoring these ancestors.

In a myriad of ways, female clay figurines can be seen as ritual tools. But what of the women that made them and most likely used them? Why are they not seen then as spiritual leaders?

Women and Shamanism and Academia

Viewing these figurines as ritual tools requires that we understand the underlying spiritual philosophy of those who use them. The set of beliefs termed "shamanism" accurately describes the spiritual philosophy of the Mesoamericans.

A comprehensive definition of shamanism is put forth by B. Tedlock (2005), based on both her academic work as an anthropologist and her personal work training with Mayan and other shamans. In her definition, shamans share these traits: the conviction that all entities—animate or otherwise—re-imbued with a life force and participate in the life energy that holds the world together; the belief that all things are interdependent and interconnected; the vision that the world is constructed of a series of levels connected by a central axis in the form of a world tree or mountain; the belief that societies designate individuals to take on the role of "shaman" for their group; the recognition that extra-ordinary forces, entities, and beings affect individual and events in our ordinary world and that rituals performed in ordinary reality can lead to effects in the alternative sphere. (20-21)

To Tedlock's definition, I add an observation from Sasakia, a specialist in Japanese shamanism: "the role of the shaman is related to the maintenance of the cosmology of the society".[9]

However, there has been an ongoing controversy over the use of the word "shamanism" in the academy. Numerous accusations of over-reaching, or even "sloppy" uses of this word,[10] have led to calls for a strict definition. Though definitions such as the one quoted earlier by Tedlock have been proffered, there remains resistance to their usage.[11] This recent backlash against the use of the word "shamanism" could be due to a number of factors, including: an anti-spiritual bias in academia, based on the general idea that spiritual practice is non-rational (I mean this, of course, in a pejorative fashion) in contrast to the rational basis of academic work. The resistance to viewing spiritual practices in terms of shamanism reflects on the resistance to seeing clay figurines as tools in ritual practice.

Even when shamanic ritual practices are recognized, why are women not often seen in the role of shaman, as spiritual leaders, or as the ones that maintain the cosmology of their society? Part of this may be due to data on tribal societies collected by foreign men who did not have access to women. Part of this is also due to the unfortunate fact that many people turn to Mircea Eliade's work when discussing shamanism. Eliade is widely quoted because he explores unifying concepts applying to many religious expressions. However, his work is hampered by multiple factors, including the fact that his work on shamanism is based solely on anthropological records as opposed to *in situ* observation, which often leave the stories of women untold. Tedlock (2005) and others[12] have performed an excellent service to further the study of shamanism by clearly rebutting many of the tenets proposed by Eliade. The unfortunate fallout of Eliade's popularity as a reference for shamanism is that women as shamans and women's rituals are at best overlooked and at the most egregious are devalued. If we move from an androcentric idea of men as the prominent shamans and embrace the idea of women as shamans and leaders, then we begin to view what we find in their graves, what we find in their homes, as ritual tools.

Women as artisans; art as ritual tools; women as Priestesses: Conclusions

The study of ancient spiritual practice is hugely important. By researching spiritual practices in different contexts and searching for the common threads and the uncommon threads, we are able to see more clearly the self-imposed paradigms of our modern spiritual practice, and when the paradigms of our modern religions are found to be less than "historic" or "natural," the gravitas they have accumulated dissipates and fertile ground for new growth opens to the sun.

This is particularly important for women's place in religion. Certainly in the last 2000+ years in many parts of the world, women's leadership roles in socio-politically powerful religions have been incredibly diminished.[13] When faced with the paradigm that women have not "historically" been spiritual leaders, we must understand the limits of "historic"—and who was writing the history. If the idea of historic is expanded to the pre-historic, which is far, far longer than the "historic," then we certainly see a more comprehensive view; we see women in a far greater, juicier context, not hemmed in by the present paradigm.

The figurines from the long and artistically productive Mesoamerican culture were multivalent and with multiple utilizations. Seeing them not only as dolls and votives but also as ritual tools enhances our scope of understanding the spiritual practices of the artists. Seeing them as created by women, for use in ritual led by women, opens new vistas for our understanding of women's roles in the spiritual lives of Mesoamericans.

Pieces that have been labeled as "pretty ladies" and children's toys might be viewed as numinous objects and ritual tools. Women grinding corn to feed their families and making whimsical toys for their children can be seen as women grinding corn to prepare offering tamales and crafting powerful objects of veneration. Women once considered the silent objects of the male gaze can be regarded as spiritual leaders.

Notes

1   Notable exceptions are Tate (1999) and Marcus (1998).

2   Today, the act of making tamales is considered sacred. The corn is the flesh, the meat is the muscle, and the sauce is the blood.

3   See: http://www.faustosgallery.com/milagros/

4   A figurine is also thought to be a form that "traps" spirit, making it controllable. For a look at Yoruba use of human figures, see Wolff 2000.

5   See Wiley and Katz, "Geophagy in Pregnancy: A Test of a Hypothesis" in *Current Anthropology*, Vol. 39, No. 4 (Aug-Oct., 1998), 532-545.

6   Though these sort of interpretations are usually designated to an older, androcentric time in academia (see particularly Desmond Collins 1978), a relatively new general audience book: *The Prehistory of Sex: Four Million Years of Human Sexual Culture* (1997) by British archaeology Timothy L. Taylor, sports some equally androcentric views of female figurines.

7   See Patricia Rice "Prehistoric Venuses: Symbols of Motherhood or Womanhood?" from *Journal of Anthropological Research*, Vol. 37, No. 4. (Winter, 1981), 402-414, for an excellent, though dated, review of female Paleolithic figurines and their possible symbolic meaning.

8   See especially *Civilization of the Goddess* (1994) and *The Goddesses and Gods of Old Europe 6500-3500 B.C.: Myths and Cult Images* (1982). When the latter was first published in 1974, though the figurines in the book were predominantly female, her publishers insisted that the title be *The Gods and Goddesses of Old Europe*.

9   Quoted from Nakanishi 2006, 236.

10 From Klein, *Current Anthropology* Volume 43, Number 3, June 2002: "It is our position that many of these writers, regardless of their disciplinary base, are using shamanism to provide predictable, easy, and ultimately inadequate

answers to what are often very complex questions about the relationship of art to religion, medicine, and politics in pre-Hispanic Mesoamerica" (383).

[11]   For repartee on shamanism, see *Magic, Ritual, and Witchcraft Journal* Volume 1, Number 2 Winter 2006; *Current Anthropology* Volume 43, Number 3, June 2002; as well as Volume 46, Number 1, February 2005 F 127. For a view of shamanism and modern paganism, see G. Harvey 2000, 107-125.

[12]   Tedlock (2005) gives a comprehensive rebuttal of Eliade's scholarship on shamanism (see especially pages 64-65 and 72-75).Other rebukes of Eliade's work: Carol Christ (1997) *Rebirth of the Goddess* especially 80-86; Heinze, Ruth-Inge. (1991). *Shamans in the 20th Century*; Kehoe, Alice Beck (2000). *Shamans and religion: an anthropological exploration in critical thinking.* For a friendly view of Eliade, see Rennie, Bryan S. 1996. *Reconstructing Eliade: Making Sense of Religion.* Albany: State University of New York Press.

[13]   Though, according to the Harris Interactive Poll, church attendance is higher among women (41%) than among men (31%). http://www.harrisinteractive.com/harris_poll/index.asp?PID=408

Bibliography

Coe, Michael. "Closing Remarks." *Death and the Afterlife in Pre-Columbian America.* Cambridge, MA: Dumbarton Oaks Research Library, 1975. 191-196.

Harvey, Graham. *Contemporary Paganism: Listening People, Speaking Earth.* New York: New York UP, 2000.

Hutton, Ronald. "Mapping the Boundaries" *Magic, Ritual, and Witchcraft.* Philadelphia: U Penn Press. Volume 1. Number 2 (Winter 2006): 209-213.

Isaac, Claudia B. 1996. "Witchcraft, Cooperatives, and Gendered Competition in a P'urepecha Community". *Frontiers: A Journal of Women Studies,* Vol. 16, No. 2/3, (1996): 161-189.

Key, Anne. 2005. *Death and the Divine: The Cihuateteo, Goddesses in the Mesoamerican Cosmology.* Dissertation. Available from UMI Press.

Kocyba, Henryk Karol. La formación de las religiones insitucionalizadas y el surgimiento de las sociedades jerarquizadas en Europa centro-oriental y en el área maya". *Historia comparativa de las religiones.* Ed. Henryk Karol Kocyba. México D.F.: Instituto Naciónal de Antropología e Historia, 1998. 41-68.

Marcus, Joyce. *Women's ritual in formative Oaxaca: Figurine-making, divination, death, and the ancestors.* Ann Arbor: University of Michigan Press, 1998.

Nakanishi, F. "Possession: A form of shamanism?" *Magic, Ritual, and Witchcraft.* Volume 1. Number 2 (Winter 2006): 234-241. Print.

Peterson, Frederick A. *Ancient Mexico.* New York: G.P. Putnam's Sons, 1959.

Padilla R., Román and Araceli, Jaffer G. "Las figuras preclásicas de Temamatla, Estado de México." Homenaje a la doctora Beatriz Barba de

Piña Chán. México, D.F.: Instituto Nacional de Antropología e Historia, 1997. 157-176.

Tate, Carolyn. "Writing on the face of the moon: Women's products, archetypes, and power in ancient Maya civilization." From *Manifesting Power: Gender and the interpretation of power in archaeology.* Ed. Tracy L. Sweely. New York: Routledge, 1999.

Tedlock, Barbra. *The Woman in the Shaman's Body: Reclaiming the Feminine in Religion and Medicine.* New York: Bantam Dell, 2005.

Vaillant, G.G. *Aztecs of Mexico.* Baltimore, MD: Penguin, 1965.

Wolff, Norma H. "The Use of Human Images in Yoruba Medicines". *Ethnology*, Vol. 39, No. 3. (Summer, 2000): 205-224.

The Red Mother
of the Salish Mountains

Shelley R. Reed, M.A.A.T.

Several hundred yards from a major highway in the Salish Mountains stands a basalt cliff painted with a multitude of red pictographs. Pictographs are images made on rock using primarily fat-based paints. Commonly called *rock art* these images are not art in the conventional sense. They did not arise from the whole cloth of creative imagination as art is practiced in Western cultures. Rock art is the visual record of pre-literate peoples who once made their homes upon that land. The images on the rock are experiential in nature, arising from ritual action, community knowledge, unusual phenomenon, and dreams. Pictograph sites are volumes of personal and community history painted onto the landscape.

At the Salish Mountains, a chain-linked fence protects some of the ancient images from graffiti and other forms of defacement. This cliff face is a place of prayers and stories. It is sacred ground. Spirit offerings made from tobacco encased in strips of cloth, known as tobacco ties, are attached to the barrier in various places. These tiny tatters are prayers of supplication or appreciation that have been brought to the resident stone spirits. From behind the metal fence you can see the visage of a female form painted in red ochre looking out at you: you are in the presence of the Red Mother.

The blood-colored woman is painted low on the cliff face. She seems to be floating. Her image is featureless save for a full figure with the rounded belly of pregnancy. A small ball fills the open space between her legs at knee level. The woman on the rock appears to be giving birth. The interior Salish oral tradition cycle also begins with a woman and her supernatural issue. The birth of a nation begins with a single cry.

North America was once the home of over 500 nations and a plethora of ceremonial and spiritual practices. The wisdom traditions of America's first nations were not recorded in books. The community traditions and personal experiences of the tribe were recorded through the arts as symbols and designs on everyday objects like beadwork designs and tipi covers. Significant natural, social and spiritual interactions are carried and transmitted through pictograph, song, dance and story.

Tribal traditions are frequently seen by outsiders as the incomprehensible cultural remnants of nearly extinct people. The songs, dances and stories of traditional peoples are viewed as an entertaining relic of history. These assumptions are incorrect. The traditional life-ways and spiritual systems of pre-Columbian America are alive in post-modern America. Much of traditional life is centered on the social duties and spiritual powers of women.

Women play important roles in the traditional spiritual system and are frequently assigned roles of honor and power. Women are featured prominently in the oral traditions of many tribes who tell stories of Changing Woman, White Shell and Corn Woman, Spider Woman, White Painted Woman, and Thought Woman, to name a few. An example of the female spiritual intercessor is the appearance of White Buffalo Calf Maiden to the Lakota. She was a spirit being who brought the way of the pipe and the seven sacred rites that continue to govern the ceremonial life of modern buffalo pipe practitioners. Maria Chona of the Papago put her concept of feminine power this way:

> Women have power. Men have to dream to get power from the spirits and they think of everything they can, hoping that the spirits will notice them and give them some power. But we have power. Children. Can any warrior make a child no matter how brave and wonderful he is?[1]

The indigenous cultures of North America tended towards equating the feminine with spiritual and procreative powers. Tribes from every geographical region retain oral traditions which feature the significance of local landforms and positive female characters. It is common practice to refer to the earth we live on as our mother or grandmother. In many traditional spiritual systems of North America woman was viewed as both a material creative agent and a spiritual intercessor.[2] Woman is assigned the roles of bearer of human life and the bringer of spiritual wisdom and items of sacred technology.

Interior Salish stories about their genesis tell of first woman and the beginning of the material world. One version of this creation story was recorded in 1865 by George Gibbs in the first extensive collection of northwest Native American mythology. Gibbs reports, "before the world was created, a son was born to a very powerful woman, Skomeltem. The son's name was Amotken, which means 'he who sits on top of the mountain,' for his home is on the summit of the covering of the earth."[3] Skomeltem is hereafter associated with the water and her son with the mountains.

It is unknown if the Red Mother is meant to depict an image of Skomeltem giving birth to Amotken. No public information about an interpretation of these images has been recorded in print. Tribal people who were interviewed about the Kila pictographs have said little about these five associated pictograph sites to western academics and rock art researchers. The image of the Red Mother may be simply the local version of a female fertility icon like those produced by cultures across the planet.

The assumption of academics has been that little has been recorded about the images because there is no one alive who remembers the meaning behind the pictographs. These landscapes are considered abandoned. That may not be the case. It has been the experience of tribal people that what is valuable is taken away. The only way to protect some things is to be silent. Perhaps that is why so little is known about these ancient images.

Notes

[1] Judith Fitzgerald and Michael Oren Fitzgerald, *The Spirit of Indian Woman Sacred World Series* (Bloomington, IN: World Wisdom, 2005) 92.

[2] Fitzgerald and Fitzgerald, x.

[3] Ella E. Clark, *Indian Legends from the Northern Rockies* (Norman: University of Oklahoma Press, 1966) 66.

Determining the gender of a pictograph requires using a combination of deductive logic and cultural knowledge. The red painted figure on granite appears to be a human being as it features two arms, two legs, a head, and stands upright. Adjacent male images are depicted as having elongated linear bodies which feature an oversized phallus or a clan headdress. This round body has neither a phallus nor a headdress which are used to denote male forms; Photo © 2005 Shelley R. Reed

Goddess

Annie Finch

The gravity of goddess moves above
My eyes, when I look up like someone's child.
There is no spoken sentence. All she moves
Will leave. And I will always know she smiled
(she stays, so we both stay quiet and wild).
She looks down until her death is unashamed
Undimming holding like receding caves,
Waving inside this time in grains and waves
Of growing, through the call of ancient names.
She does not take me out from presences—
She stays to go—her presence is the loss.
And now I know each knowing's made of senses,
Looking up or looking down. Or this. Or moss.

October Moon

Annie Finch

The moon has dusks for walls,
October's days for a floor,
crickets for rooms, windy halls.
Only one night is her door.

When I was thirteen she found me,
spiralled into my blood like a hive.
I stood on a porch where she wound me
for the first time, tight and alive,

till my body flooded to find her:
to know I would not be alone
as I moved through the tides that don't bind her
into womanhood, like a flung stone.

With each curve that waxed into fullness
I grew with her, ready and wild.
I filled myself up like her priestess.
I emptied myself like her child.

Flooding, ready, and certain,
I hid her—full, fallow, or frail—
beneath each long summer's rich curtain.
It covered her face—the thin grail

that delivers me now. Now I'm with her.
All the cast shadows come home.
I stand in these shadows to kiss her
and spin in her cool, calming storm.

Now as I move through my own beauty
and my shadow grows deeper than blood,
oh triple, oh Goddess, sustain me
with your light's simple opening hood.

Author's Note: "October Moon" originally appeared in the Fall 2007 issue of the *Journal of Feminist Studies in Religion* (JFSR); www.fsrinc.org/jfsr/.

Eve

Annie Finch

When mother Eve took the first apple down
from the tree that grew where nature's heart had been
and came tumbling, circling, rosy, into sin,
which goddesses were lost, and which were found?
What spirals moved in pity and unwound
across our mother's body with the spin
of planets lost for us and all her kin?
What serpents curved their mouths into a frown,
but left their bodies twined in us like threads
that lead us back to her? Her presence warms,
and if I follow closely through the maze,
it is to where her remembered reaching spreads
in branching gifts, it is to her reaching arms
that I reach, as if for something near to praise.

The Fijian Kava Ceremony:
An Ancient Menstrual Ritual?

Laura Amazzone

Fiji is an island paradise. Lush verdant jungles and pristine beaches make up this country of three hundred islands and atolls across two-hundred thousand square miles in the South Pacific. Despite Christianization over the last 200 years, remnants of indigenous Fijian spiritual culture, including ancestor worship, spirit possession, spiritual ceremonies focused on the ingestion of consciousness-altering substances, and a deep respect for elemental forces have a place in Fijian consciousness and are demonstrated in one of their most significant rituals: the yaqona or kava ceremony. The accoutrements and symbolism found in the kava ceremony are strongly indicative of what author Judy Grahn has termed *metaformic* in her book, *Blood, Bread, and Roses: How Menstruation Created the World.* According to Grahn, "Our ancestresses taught via menstrual instruction, through rituals that embodied ideas based on menstrual information. I call this a metaform, specifically, an act or form of instruction that makes a connection between menstruation and a mental principle."[1] Metaforms that appear in cross-cultural rituals and creation stories such as snake, dragon, octopus, boars' tusks, cods, taboos, plants and roots as menstrual inducers, ceremonial bowls, red flowers, shells, chanting, the Kumari (virgin goddess), dreams, possession and visions, all have their place in the Fijian kava ceremony, and many appear in the creation mythology of the islands. Indeed, the ancient kava ritual and local mythology have much to tell us about female power that has been obscured, but not entirely lost on the islands.

Yaqona and the Ceremony

Yaqona or kava is made from the roots of a shrub called *piper methysticum*. It is part of the pepper family.[2] The roots are dried and then ground into a fine white powder that is mixed with water in a bowl called a *tanoa*. Kava has a body relaxant and mind simulating effect. It produces an altered, yet mentally lucid state. Drinking kava induces vivid dreams and opens one to other worlds. For centuries kava has been used as a ritual accompaniment to important life events: births, deaths, marriages, journeys, as a prelude to tribal war, as a high form of welcome to a dignified person visiting a village, and as an offering to the ancestors and deities during any life crisis.[3] Most significantly it functions as an emenogogue[4] and is a menstrual inducent. However, nowadays only men participate in kava ceremonies and many of the spiritual associations have been lost. Unfortunately, alcohol, introduced by the Europeans, has become a problem on the islands and kava is not always drunk in a sanctified way.

Although women no longer participate in today's ceremonies, my research has led me to believe that the kava ceremony was originally a woman's rite. I contend it was a menstrual ceremony probably initiating a young girl into womanhood and a way for women in menstrual seclusion to become oracles of the ancestors and deities for the community. All aspects of this ceremony are clearly metaforms: from its implements—the tanoa bowl with the face of a snake, attached with cord and cowry shell, and the coconut shell cup—to the emenogogic properties of the kava root and its preparation by a virgin girl, to the ritual practices of clapping, chanting, and invocative and de-vocative incantations. In a kava ceremony, everyone circles around the tanoa bowl. Even in the structure of ritual, one finds the menstrual logic of emulating the moon.

> Almost everywhere, people perform rites after first forming themselves into a circle. This is not a "natural" pattern; few animals make circular formations. Here on earth there was nothing to draw people to the circular shape. The circle was the sky, the light that came and went, the light whose habits and whose shapes the menstruant imitated. Early people devised indigenous methods of studying the circle . . . . The people ate from round plates and bowls, used round mats, round baskets.[5]

The group forms a circle and also prepares the medicine in the round *tanoa* bowl, then drinks from a coconut shell. How much kava one wants to imbibe is described as *half-tide* or *full-tide*. This suggests an acknowledgment of the synchronous lunar pull on the ocean as well as on women's wombs. Bowls or vessels have long been associated with the womb of the Great Goddess in cultures around the world. In Fiji the bowl used in the kava ceremony has the face of a snake. The bowl, itself, is symbolic of the womb, and combined, the bowl and snake face present a double metaform. The relationship between a snake's ability to shed its skin and a woman's monthly shedding of her uterus lining is undeniably metaformic. Vicki Noble writes, "The snake from ancient times has been associated with women and healing regenerative power. A snake shedding its skin is the perfect symbolic image of a woman bleeding each month."[6] Let's look more closely at the serpent, menstruation, the local mythology and accoutrements of the kava ceremony.

Serpent and Menstrual Seclusion

Although there are no living snakes on the Fijian islands, myths of the great serpent Nakavaudra and the creator snake god Degei abound. Degei's home is a cave (a metaform for a woman's vagina) and a curtain of snakes guards the mouth of this cave.[7] Perhaps the origin of this myth leads us back to a time when female menstrual power and the observation of a menstruating women's cycle was a crucial component in creating culture and consciousness.

Certain common themes emerge in creation stories all around the world. Most creation myths begin with a time of chaos characterized by darkness (reflective of pre-human consciousness, then lead to processes of differentiation or separation that illuminate the change of consciousness that has taken place).[8] Distinguishing between light and dark also is popular because it marks the beginning of human perception in many creation myths.[9] Grahn claims that the separation between light and dark forces played a significant role in our ancestors' understanding of human self and other and influenced the development of human consciousness through what she calls "external measurements"[10] of the world.

One of the Fijian creation myths begins with the serpent god sleeping in a *cave* (metaform for vagina) and describes how darkness descended over the world as long as his eyes were closed. The opening and closing of the serpent's eyes bring the separation of morning and night, and earthquakes occurred every time he turned in his sleep.[11] Grahn likens the act of separation of light and dark to menstrual seclusion rites as "repeated separations consisting of metaforms that contain creation stories."[12]

Menstrual seclusion rites characteristically consist of three taboos: the menstruant not seeing light and spending her menstruation in a hut or cave-like dark shelter; her feet must not touch the solid ground for fear of the power of her blood contaminating the earth; and she must not touch water as she will contaminate it.[13] Although blood has been demonized and misconstrued as destructive, the underlying acknowledgement of its potency is evident. Grahn writes,

> I began to see how menstrual rites might have "created the world" for ancient peoples, and to wonder whether the sleepers who awoke and saw landscape, who animated the elements, who separated the above from the below, and darkness from light, were informed by rites of seclusion that specified these very elements, singled them out for my attention through tapua, sacred law of the "woman's friend.[14]

Tapua, the root of taboo, is a Polynesian word for sacred or menstruation,[15] and the kava ceremony was perhaps a time when women gathered together away from the rest of the village, bled together, and tapped into the non-ordinary conscious awareness that bleeding and imbibing the kava root 'tea' brings. As Noble points out, menstruation is "explicitly non-ordinary and requires we be set apart from the ordinary tasks at hand."[16] She continues, "During our menstruation we have a wide range of paranormal abilities and experiences available to us."[17] Menstrual seclusion rites developed partly from the recognition of women's powers during their bleeding time and the need for them to be secluded from everyday tasks. The need for seclusion was not meant to ostracize a woman from the group out of fear, but rather it gave the menstruant the time and space to rest, nurture her self, and get in touch with her creativity and intuition. Unfortunately, women's exclusion from the kava ceremony and other aspects of daily life speak more to a shift in power and co-option of the earlier female rites and practices.

Vicki Noble cites in *Shakti Woman* that "the first blood at the altar was menstrual blood, the free flow of the priestess giving back to the Earth Mother."[18] However, human and animal sacrifice came to replace the original woundless offering of menstrual blood menstrual offerings. According to Grahn, this would be a substitution metaform. The fullness of all cycles from birth to fruition to death reminds us of the natural cycles of earth and sky and that equilibrium is only achieved through balance.

For example, in South Asia, the meaning behind animal sacrifice is a means to give back to the Mother who gives and gives.[19] Human sacrifice, which occurred in Fiji in the last fifty years and perhaps still exists in more remote areas today, can be considered a form of placating the spirit realm, of propitiating the Great Goddess of Life and Death behind all existence. By offering Goddess blood sacrifice, indigenous peoples of past and present hope to dispel the natural catastrophic disasters that threaten those living in the natural world: disease, floods, hurricanes, earthquakes, and tornadoes.

The Dragon and the Octopus

Similar to the serpent, the dragon and octopus are metaformic symbols directly related to women's menstrual cycles and wombs. Moreover, each of these creatures has been worshiped as Goddess in different parts of the world since earliest times. The dragon has had a tutelary role in the Pacific Rim and like the serpent, exists between the worlds. As a "compound metaform," Grahn suggests that the dragon metamorphosized from the serpent to the dragon.[20] Grahn describes them as embodied metaforms of menstrual and earth energies as well as natural forces such as hurricanes, tornadoes, and floods.[21] The volcanic islands above and below the waters of the South Pacific have been likened to a dragon in many cultures. Grahn writes, "The flaming mouth of the dragon in all probability marks the uneasy taming of fire and its association with the earth beneath the crusts. Fire boils out in raging volcanoes all over China, Japan, and the Malay Peninsula, where dragons became a primary symbol."[22] The dragon carries wise and ancient, yet temperamental powers.

The octopus is another metaformic creature popular in the Pacific. Archaeomythologist Marija Gimbutas suggests: "Related to the rising Snake Goddess and obviously associated with the cosmic deep is the rather whimsical Octopus Goddess."[23] The octopus' body can be likened to the uterus—and the shedding of blood to the octopus' dispelling of ink. The snaky arms, 'metaphoric of winding curls,' bring to mind the Gorgon Goddess Medusa with Her writhing snakes for hair. In Fiji, there is a popular myth about the invincible power of the Octopus Goddess and her defeat of a threatening Shark God.

Dakuwaqa, the Shark God guarded the reef entrance of the islands. He is described as "headstrong, fearless, and jealous of all of the reef guardians."[24] The beginning of his myth narrates his warlike confrontations and victories over many other guardians, stealing the islands of Lomaiviti, Suva, and others. One day he meets another shark god who tells him about Kadavu Island, the island of the original deities. This Shark God taunts Dakuwaqa, suggesting he is afraid to confront the octopus guardian of Kadavu. Not wanting to lose his terrorizing status and unable to admit his fear, Dakuwaqa heads for Kadavu. He encounters a giant Octopus and although he attempts his usual warlike tactics, he finds himself powerless in the arms of the Mother Goddess. Her tentacles coil around him, squeezing his jaw shut, and preventing his powerful tail from moving. For the first time in his life, Dakuwaqa begs for mercy! The Great Octopus Goddess agrees to let him go only if the Shark God promises to protect her people when they go fishing. Although the fishers of the other islands must constantly look out for sharks, the people of Kadavu remain protected and shark is now an ancestor deity. All throughout the islands, shark flesh has become taboo. In order to tame the destructive terrorizing force, a taboo is set around eating shark meat. Similarly unbridled female powers are 'controlled' by taboos are set around menstruation. Nevertheless, the island of *original* deities is protected by an Octopus goddess, suggesting the presence of Goddess on the islands since earliest times. Let's now turn to another Fijian myth that exemplifies Grahn's metaformic theory in order to better understand the origin of this culture.

Fijian Flood Myth

In Fiji, the story of the great flood speaks not only of menstrual consciousness, but also to the loss of power to another population of peoples. The Fijian Flood myth begins with the killing of Turukawa, a hawk, who was originally a friend of the snake god Degei, by two of Degei's sons. Degei reprimanded them for killing his friend, and the boys retaliated with threats, ridicule, and by building a wall around the village to keep Degei out. In pre-historic cultures both hawk and snake have long been associated with female power—and Goddess. Although male in this myth, it is interesting that snake, a potent menstrual metaform, has been ostracized from the village. This act of pushing the serpent out of the living space is suggestive of menstrual seclusion. However, instead of the serpent or menstrual blood being the cause of chaos, disorder is invoked by the boys' rage, disrespect, and retaliation. The snake god, Degei, then turns to the elements and invokes a powerful storm to wash away the boys' fortress.

At another word from the god the clouds poured down their floods of water. Every stream became a raging torrent, waterfalls sprang from the steep hillsides, avalanches of mud and stones spread over the valley, blocking the lower reaches, and muddy water welled slowly up the long slope . . . [25]

The waters rose till they covered the mountaintops and killed all but six people. Degei's sons begged for mercy and apologized for killing Turukawa and being disrespectful. Degei launched felled trees on the waters and the six survivors climbed on and were carried to the mountaintop as they witnessed the floodwaters receding. The myth ends stating that two tribes were lost—one of women and another of women and men—and that a new world had begun.

When we consider the floodwaters in the above myth, we recognize that they are analogous to menstrual blood as they are in many other myths.[26] Throughout the Paleolithic and Neolithic eras in Old Europe, Africa, the Aegean, and North America, bird was the Creatrix of All Existence. It is noteworthy that this myth begins with the killing of hawk, an ancient symbol of Goddess. This alone suggests that the old ways of worship were annihilated by aggressive and war-faring peoples, especially when we consider the conclusion of the myth that states that two tribes were lost. Moreover, this myth describes the loss of a tribe of women—perhaps reporting the loss of female power that occurred through the confrontation of different ethnic peoples. We know that the original inhabitants, the Lapita people who most likely came from islands of South-East Asia, settled on the islands around 2000 BCE bringing their pots, hooks, wares, and obsidian cutting tools.[27] Ethnically, the Lapita were of Polynesian blood. They were excellent seafarers and craftspeople and share cultural characteristics similar to other matrifocal cultures. Pottery is characteristic of female-centered agricultural-based communities, in contrast to nomadic ones. In the pre-historic world, the agricultural communities based their planting and harvest times by observing the cycles of the moon. Through the language of symbols on the pottery, we can see that ancient people recognized the interconnected nature between everyday life and natural cosmic cycles.

At some point Melanesian peoples came to the islands and legends speak of an indigenous people (the Lapita) who already inhabited the islands. Waves of migrating Oceanic peoples occurred over millennia.[28] In the 1800s European missionaries came to the island and established feudal/slave societies. Colonization and Christianization makes it difficult to find accurate information on what traditional culture and religion was like. Still, certain qualities emerge through mythologies, cosmologies, and ceremonies. The original Melanesian/Polynesian inhabitants of the island seem to have been matristic and peaceful cultures in contrast to the oppressive feudal systems established by the Europeans. Although most Fijians have converted to Christianity, animism and ancestor worship still are part of everyday life.

Goddesses of the Threshold

Lewalevu and Le-Hev-Hev are threshold goddesses of the South Pacific, goddesses who guard the gates of consciousness:

Before a departing soul could pass to the afterlife, the Melanesians said, it had to confront this goddess, who tried to trick the soul with games. Drawing on the sand in front of her, she challenged the soul to complete the diagram. Should the dead one be unable to do so—or did so incorrectly—Le-Hev-Hev had the soul for dinner. The Malekulans who honored Le-Hev-Hev considered her a goddess, not a monster, offering her boars so she would not eat human corpses. Her earthly forms were the spider, the crab, and the rat; she was also embodied in the female genitalia. Her name has been roughly translated as "she who smiles so that we draw near and she can eat us."[29]

The devouring Mother has a place in mythologies and rites of people around the world; however, this is not Her only function. Lev-Hev-Hev is the Goddess of the Netherworld, but as we see from Her emblem as 'female genitalia', She is also the Goddess of Life and Sexual Power. The labia of the cosmic vagina of the Great Goddess serve as the gates of life and death. She "eats" us at the end of our life cycle, taking our disintegrating bodies back into the limitless void of Her womb, and transmuting our form so that our souls can be reborn. As womb and tomb, She is the sacred continuum of life and death. As threshold guardian, Her fierce face, with boar's tusk fangs and lolling tongue, serves as a warning of the death mysteries that "are too potent to be directly seen."[30]

The Goddess' empowered life-giving position seems to have been disregarded and forgotten as local people, out of fear of her wrath, primarily propitiate her. In her article, *An Archaeomythological Investigation of the Gorgon*, Joan Marler attributes the demonization of Goddess to the rise of heroic consciousness that sought to conquer death (and) could not tolerate reminders of natural mortality and ties to the earth, that . . . took horrific female forms." [31] Instead of worshipping Le-Hev-Hev as a Death Goddess who presides over regenerative processes, nowadays She is most commonly relegated to the underworld and described as having an insatiable hunger. Another source describes Le-Hev-Hev as a "negative female power, a type of devouring ogress," [32] and Her Cook Island sister of the netherworld, Miru, is said to devour the souls of men after stupefying them with kava.[33]

Other female deities who have been deemed 'ogresses,' the South Asian Kali or Greek Medusa, are also depicted with boars' tusks and/or fangs. As sexually empowered goddesses, Le-Hev-Hev and Lewlevu's Indian and Greek sisters also have a reputation for devouring men or turning them to stone. The fearsome fanged face of these liminal goddesses calls to mind the *vagina dentata*, a well-known image that is indicative of male fear of women's sexual power and energy. As death through violent rather than natural means became endemic to the islands, and blood through violent acts of killing humans and animals replaced the original menstrual offerings, we see a shift in the description and worship of female goddesses. The denigration of Goddess reflects the disempowerment of women and the culturally-enforced shame surrounding menstruation.

Boar's Tusks and the Sow Goddess

The curving tusks of wild boar represent the crescent waxing and waning moon and are wilderness metaforms: "the entrainment of menstruation to the moon drew special attention to the crescent-shaped horns of certain animals, which in Africa, Asia, and Europe, became metaphors for the new moon."[34] Boars are extremely significant to agricultural communities throughout the Pacific islands, the Aegean and Mediterranean cultures, Asia, and Africa. They represent fecundity, wealth, power and abundance[35] and are venerated as Mother Goddess in many cultures. In *Lady of the Beasts*, Buffie Johnson writes,

the pig was worshipped whenever women were entirely in charge of agriculture, that is until the invention of the plow. The pig's habit of rooting around in the soil with its snout made the identification with sowing and reaping natural and led to its worship. Its sanctity also rises from its fast-growing body and multiplicity of off-spring. [36]

Great feasts in the Pacific, for example the Hawaiian luau, are centered on roasting pork. The boar gives its flesh, so that others may live. The boar also acts as an intercessor between the living and the dead, and is perceived as a Death Goddess like Le-Hev-Hev, who is used to re-enacting the mysteries of dying to be reborn. [37] In some parts of the South Pacific, it is believed that the souls of the dead transmigrate into wild pigs. [38] In their affiliation with agricultural cycles as well as their role in death, wild boars are the totems or sacred animal companions of the Death Goddess and essentially, if we take the animist view of interconnectedness and the sacrality inherent in all life, boars *are* the Death Goddess. Joseph Campbell suggests,

> the boars, then, are the moon at the moment of its death, consumed by the goddess guardian of the underworld. Their tusks point to the continuance of life, however, waxing and waning over the ground of death. Thus, in their own way they represent the mystery . . . .[39]

The Kumari: Virgin Goddess

While today's ceremonies are conducted by and for men, this was not always the case. Up until the European influence in the 1800s, the kava root was cut into small pieces and originally chewed by a *virgin girl* in the village then strained through *hibiscus* fibre. [40] The role of the virgin girl reinforces the taboo around menstruating women and her chewing is said to bring purity to the drink. Yet, she holds the position of Goddess in this rite through the act of chewing and breaking down the root into smaller bits. In a sense the girl becomes the Death Goddess as scavenger and corpse eater, whose "incessant chewing breaks down matter for recycling into new life." [41] It is interesting to consider the relationship between chewing, which produces human saliva, and fermentation. In his book, *Sacred and Herbal Beers*, Stephen Buhner describes the process from which fermented grains become beer or other intoxicating drinks. He explains that when a seed begins to sprout, an enzyme is released that converts the starch in the seed into sugar, beginning the fermentation process.[42] He points out that a similar enzyme is present in mammal saliva and has also been used in preparing sacred brews: "Since early times, many cultures have masticated grains or starchy roots in order to mix them with human saliva—thus beginning the same starch conversion." [43] This explanation of mixing the virgin girl's saliva with the kava root is more likely than it originating from her bringing "purity." Buhner also contends that the origin of fermentation is connected to early humans facing their mortality. He writes of many legends around the world that acknowledge the intoxicating gifts from plants as having a divine origin and being connected to "an easing of human pain in the face of mortality." [44] It is also significant that kava is a *root* and grows underground, recalling once again the Goddess of Death and the Underworld. [45] The associations with the death aspect of the cycle hold importance in this ritual. The effects of kava take one into a liminal realm, reminding us of the Goddesses' role as intermediary between the living and the dead.

To prepare the drink, the kava powder is strained through hibiscus fiber. Flowers, particularly *red* flowers are clearly metaforms. [46] Often the flower itself resembles the vulva and the red of the hibiscus is obviously related to blood. Le-Hev-Hev is often depicted as a vulva, ancient symbol of the life giving powers of the Goddess. [47] And hibiscus is the preferred floral offering of Hawaiian Pele and the South Asian Kali.

Cowry Shells and the Sacred Cord

Attached to the serpent face on the *tanoa* bowl is a rope cord at the end of which is a cowry shell. It is used to point to who is next to drink. Perhaps the symbolic significance of the cowry as female genitalia indicates who will next be birthed into another realm of consciousness through ingesting the drink. The cowry shell is *the* quintessential symbol of female sexual power and is an obvious metaform. On one side it looks very similar to the lips of our vulva and on the other it is rounded like a pregnant belly. Grahn points out that "Many people speak of a pregnant woman having a snake in her belly, or of giving birth to a snake." [48] The vulvar shaped shell attached to the (umbilical cord) leading up to the womb or tanoa bowl clearly speaks to women's mysteries around birth and menstruation.

Another Polynesian culture, Hawaii, has a myth of umbilical cords that are more obviously suggestive of this association between snakes and bleeding. "The prominent Hawaiian Goddess Haumea sometimes takes the form of a traveling vagina; she is also sometimes known as Red Eel Woman. A related Maori word, haumia, refers both to an ogress and to ceremonial uncleanliness associated with menstruation." [49] Haumea's two brothers are gods who appear in the form of a rope and an octopus—as though metaforms for the umbilical cord, "born" of Haumea, the externalized vagina. Familiar metaformic themes emerge in the Hawaiian myth—the purity taboos around menstruation, the blood red eel or snake, the cord or rope, and once again the octopus. Moreover, we read how the Dark Goddess is demonized and described as an ogress.

Liminal Realms

The kava ceremony begins when the community joins together in chant and clapping. Chanting alone alters consciousness, and accompanied by the kava root participants are opened to the oneness of the natural world. Chanting in a circle imitates the shape of the moon and "whose beats make use of rhythmic timings—all reinforced the (lunar) image."[50] The participants chant to their ancestors who sat in ceremonial circles before them, to the deities, and for the well-being of the community.

The first bowl is always offered to the earth. As the bowl is passed, each participant must clap three times, once for each of the three worlds: for the underworld, middleworld, and upperworld, and to scare away malefic spirits. Clapping is metaformic: "Noisemaking . . . . was a feature of menarchal festivities and processions, intended to frighten away "evil spirits" of the wilderness. Stated another way, the noise reminded the people to stay alert and conscious of their surroundings."[51] Kava helps one become more in tune with nature, it helps us to see things we do not ordinarily see, and that clapping provides protection. Indeed, drinking kava loosens the ego . . . rooted connection to the earth. The muddy liquid numbs the mouths, especially the teeth, and makes one feel uninhibited in spontaneously bursting forth with insights and ideas. Drinking kava in a circle ceremony creates communal consciousness, where each person is respected and acknowledged as part of the whole. As two authors observed, "Kava can facilitate the shift from the old model of conflict and domination (which is fear-based) to one of partnership and cooperation (based on trust and respect)."[52]

The acknowledgment of the interrelationship between all beings is expressed in the way the drinking begins. Each participant must greet the spirit of the kava plant by saying *Bula!* (Greetings!) before imbibing the muddy liquid. One must drink in one gulp, as it is believed to be offensive to the spirit to only sip at it. When one has finished, they cry out "MACA!" Empty! Perhaps crying *maca* refers to the process of preparing ourselves to be channels for the divinities.[53.] In most cultures, emptying oneself psychically is necessary before any sort of divinatory or healing work. Kava is a ritual that opens one's spiritual channels and allows one to communicate with other realms. Yet, it is not always a beneficent force that comes through. Kava rituals are also directed toward malignant spirits who are believed to cause sickness, insanity, and infertility of women and land! Trance possession by participants is a common occurrence in these ceremonies.

A menstruating woman has easier access to the shifts between realms, and her participation in a kava ceremony opens her in deep, powerful ways that eventually became too threatening to men—for women were uncontrollable. "Women used drugs for thousands of years to heighten the psychic effects of menstruation, and mind-altering substances were everywhere associated with menstrual rites, being given to girls at menarche and even more often to boys at puberty, in order to enhance their ability to have visions."[54]

Concluding Thoughts

Despite the benefits men receive from this sacred root, the kava ceremony is no longer open to women and girls. I wonder what the impact females drinking kava in ceremony around their moon cycles would have on female consciousness and status today. Regardless of the male cooptation of the ritual, metaformic elements of ancient Fijian life are evident in the myths, kava ritual, and islands' history. I contend the kava ceremony was originally an initiation ritual for pre-pubescent girls on the cusp of their menarches as well as a sacred rite for women while they were bleeding.

Notes

[1] Judy Grahn, *Blood, Bread, and Roses: How Menstruation Created the World* (Boston: Beacon Press. 1993) 20.

[2] Hyla Cass, M.D. and Terrence McNally. *Kava: Nature's Answer to Stress, Anxiety, and Insomnia* (Rocklin, California: Prima Publishing, 1998), 71, and Jan Knappert, *Pacific Mythology: An Encyclopedia of Myth and Legend* (London: Aquarian Press, 1992), 150.

[3] Cass and McNally, 76.

[4] See Grahn 111-112.

[5] Grahn, 162.

[6] Vicki Noble, *Shakti Woman: Feeling Our Fire, Healing Our World. The New Female Shamanism* (San Francisco: HarperCollins, 1991), 68.

[7] A.W. Reed & Inez Hames. *Myths and Legends of Fiji* (Wellington: Literary Productions, 1967), 18.

[8] Ibid., 10.

[9] Ibid., 11.

[10] Ibid., 19.

[11] Ibid., 26.

[12] Grahn, 20.

[13] Ibid., 11.

[14] Ibid.

[15] Ibid., 5.

[16] Noble, 14.

[17] Ibid., 56.

[18] Lawrence Durdin-Robertson in Noble 1991, 14.

[19] David Kinsley, *Hindu Goddesses: Visions of the Divine Feminine in the Hindu Religious Tradition* (Berkeley: University of California, 1997), 113.

[20] Ibid., 63.

[21] Grahn, 64.

[22] Ibid.

[23] Marija Gimbutas, *The Language of the Goddess* (San Francisco: Harper Collins, 1991), 227.

[24] Hames and Ines, 83.

[25] Ibid., 16-17.

[26] See Grahn, chapter 2.

[27] Patrick Vinton Kirch, *The Evolution of the Polynesian Chiefdoms* (Cambridge: Cambridge University Press, 1984), 41-53.

[28] Ibid., 41.

[29] Patricia Monaghan, *The Book of Goddesses and Heroines* (St. Paul, Minnesota: Llewellyn Publications, 1993), 193.

[30] Joan Marler, "An Archaeomythological Investigation of the Gorgon." *Revision* Vol.25, No.1, Summer 2002), 17.

[31] Ibid., 16.

32 Buffie Johnson, *Lady of the Beasts: Ancient Images of the Goddess through Her Sacred Animals.* (San Francisco: Harper & Row, 1988), 213.

33 Knappert, 189.

34 Grahn, 51.

35 Knappert, 228.

36 Johnson, 262.

37 Johnson, 262.

38. Knappert, 228.

39 Joseph Campbell, *Primitive Mythology: The Masks of God* (London: Viking Penguin, 1959), 446.

40 Knappert,150.

41 Marler citing E. Sikie, 18.

42 Stephen Harrod Buhner, *Sacred and Herbal Healing Beers: The Secrets of Ancient Fermentation* (Boulder, Colorado: Siris Books, 1998), 146.

43 Ibid.

44 Ibid., 138-139.

45 Susan Carter, pers. com. May 2003.

46 Grahn, 231.

47 Monaghan, 193.

48 Grahn, 60.

49 Beckwith in Grahn, 60.

[50] Grahn, 163.

[51] Ibid., 203.

[52] Cass and McNally, 9.

[53] Vicki Noble, pers. com., May 2003.

[54] Grahn, 113.

Bibliography

Allen, Michael. *The Cult of the Kumari: Virgin Worship in Nepal.* Kathmandu: Mandala Book Point, 1996.

Barber, Elizabeth Wayland. *Women's Work: The First 20,000 Years.* New York: W.W. Norton & Company, 1994.

Beckwith, Martha. *Hawaiian Mythology.* Honolulu: University of Hawaii Press, 1982.

Buhner, Stephen Harrod. *Sacred and Herbal Healing Beers: The Secrets of Ancient Fermentation.* Boulder, Colorado: Siris Books, 1998.

Campbell, Joseph. *Primitive Mythology: The Masks of God.* London: Viking Penguin, 1959.

Cass, Hyla, M.D. and Terrence McNally. *Kava: Nature's Answer to Stress, Anxiety, and Insomnia.* Rocklin, California: Prima Publishing, 1998.

Durdin-Robertson, Lawrence. *The Cult of the Goddess.* Enniscorthy, Ireland: Cesara Publications, 1974.

Gimbutas, Marija. *The Language of the Goddess.* San Francisco: Harper Collins, 1991.

_____. *The Civilization of the Goddess: The World of Old Europe.* New York: Harper Collins, 1991.

Grahn, Judy. *Blood, Bread, and Roses: How Menstruation Created the World.* Boston: Beacon Press, 1993.

Johnson, Buffie. *Lady of the Beasts: Ancient Images of the Goddess through Her Sacred Animals.* San Francisco: Harper & Row, 1988.

Kinsley, David. *Hindu Goddesses: Visions of the Divine Feminine in the Hindu Religious Tradition.* Berkeley: University of California, 1997.

Kirch, Patrick Vinton. *The Evolution of the Polynesian Chiefdoms.* Cambridge: Cambridge University Press, 1984.

Knappert, Jan. *Pacific Mythology: An Encyclopedia of Myth and Legend.* London: Aquarian Press, 1992.

Knight, Chris. *Blood Relations: Menstruation and the Origins of Culture.* New Haven and London: Yale University Press, 1991.

Marler, Joan. "An Archaeomythological Investigation of the Gorgon." *Revision* Vol.25, No.1, Summer 2002, 15-23.

Monaghan, Patricia. *The Book of Goddesses and Heroines.* St. Paul, Minnesota: Llewellyn Publications, 1993.

Noble, Vicki. *Shakti Woman: Feeling Our Fire, Healing Our World. The New Female Shamanism.* San Francisco: HarperCollins, 1991.

_____. *The Double Goddess: Women Sharing Power.* Rochester, Vermont: Bear & Company, 2003.

Northrup, Christiane. *Woman's Bodies, Women's Wisdom.* New York: Bantam Books, 1994.

Reed, A.W. & Inez Hames. *Myths and Legends of Fiji.* Wellington: Literary Productions, 1967.

Shuttle, Penelope and Peter Redgrove. *The Wise Wound.* New York: Grove Press, 1988.

Sjoo, Monica and Barbara Mor. *The Great Cosmic Mother: Rediscovering the Religion of the Earth.* San Francisco: HarperSanFrancisco, 1987.

Trompf, G.W. *Melanesian Religion.* Cambridge: Cambridge University Press, 1991.

Sardegnan Nuraghe

Sandy Miranda Robinett

The mysterious nuraghi of Sardegna remind us of the transformational, eternal healing light of the divine feminine. The feeling of standing inside one of these ancient stone structures is that of being inside the sacred birth canal of the Great Mother; Photo © 2004 Sandy Miranda Robinettt

The Motherline:
Laundry, *Lunedi,* and Women's Lineage

Mary Beth Moser

The blackberries are fermenting on the vine, fallen leaves blanket the picnic table, and the slice of sun on my clothesline arrives later each day. With the arrival of fall, the days of being able to hang my laundry outside are growing fewer. Lately I have been pondering my passion for this ritual of outdoor clothes drying. Is it only the sensual pleasure I crave, or something more?

One of my early childhood memories is of being outside with my mother as she hung long rows of clothes with wooden clothespins. Sheets created a labyrinth of imagination. Half of the backyard in our Denver home at various times over the years was claimed by hanging laundry on those days. Numerous cloth diapers testified to the presence of a baby in the house. They hung beside the parochial school uniforms of my sisters and me, my father's work clothes, my mother's aprons, the envied "regular" clothes of my older sisters, my brothers' play clothes, each item revealing something of our lives.

One year, for my birthday party, my mother organized a game in our backyard near the clothesline. The goal was to successfully drop clothespins into the small round opening of a glass milk bottle on the ground. One at a time each child knelt on a wooden chair, facing backward, their arm resting on the back of the chair. The person with the most clothespins in the bottle won. Now when my mother recalls this game she laughs with embarrassment of not having provided a more sophisticated activity. But we kids loved it. It stands out for me as a testament to my mother's inventiveness of transforming everyday items into something special and marks with some nostalgia a certain time of growing up in the 1950s and 60s.

At the turn of the millennium, my younger sister took up the practice of line-drying the clothes when she and her family were living in Rome. Laundry hung in long rows outside the back door of their home while the neighborhood *bambini* played nearby. Will her two daughters remember this ritual with any fondness? The oldest daughter, now age seventeen and living back in the United States, prefers soft, machine-dried clothes, not the stiff sentinels that the clothesline offers up at the end of the day.

In Italy, rows of laundry hang publicly and "shamelessly" high above the streets of some cities and outside the windows of village homes. When I first visited my maternal grandmother's village in 1980, some women still gathered at a public basin to wash their clothes. What stories were told as women did laundry together? My Italian cousin, Daria, deftly hung and strung laundry outside her centuries-old apartment window with a circulating line—reeling it in and out. It was the same line that her mother likely used to hang the laundry when she was alive and lived in that home. Cycles of time passed through the circulating line.

To honor my passion and pleasure of hanging laundry outside, I commissioned a local artist, Theresa Henson, to sculpt a pair of clothesline "poles," each in the shape of the Goddess Tanit. I had first seen the symbol for this Goddess in Sicily in a mosaic of a Roman villa and, then again, a few years later on the island of Sardegna. Several women and I were on a study tour with Lucia Chiavola Birnbaum, a cultural historian and professor who informed us that Tanit's veneration had arrived from North Africa, carried by the Phoenicians around the Mediterranean. Lucia's research on primordial African migration routes opened my eyes to a much older lineage for sacred female imagery and for my European ancestry—that of a dark African mother.[1]

In Sardegna, Tanit's presence in the lives of the ancients is evident in the form of a 3000 year-old "holy well," a remarkable structure of basalt blocks expertly crafted and fitted together to create the triangular shape of her body. Twenty-five smooth stone stairs descend into subterranean space to reach the spring water held below. Twice a year, at the end of the winter and at the beginning of autumn, the sun's beams align with the angle of the steps to penetrate the waters of the well. Precious bronze *ex-voto*, gifts of gratitude and devotion, have been found at the well, now known as the well of Santa Cristina, further marking it as an ancient sacred site.

Descending the steps like so many pilgrims before me, "entering Tanit's body," and blessing myself with the holy water marked a meaningful event in my life. Now, as then, water heals, sanctifies, and washes away.

The bearers of my backyard clothesline, carved of reclaimed Redwood, are no less remarkable or substantial. Their color evokes the red ochre of the oldest sacred artistic pigment, as well as the life-giving blood of the mother. Enduring geometrical forms define their shapes: a downward-opening triangle for the body and a round circle for the head, which together mark the distinctive symbol for Tanit. Their features were selected from twenty reproductions of Tanit illustrated by Italian architect Franco Laner, who refers to the well of Santa Cristina as a temple.[2] One of the clothesline Tanits has her "arms" raised in an *orans*, or praying pose, an ancient sign in sacred iconography for worship or epiphany. The other Tanit has a simple horizontal bar for arms and a crescent moon for her headdress. The lunar adornment links her with menstruation, since the length of both the moon's cycle and the menstrual cycle is 29 ½ days. A further lunar connection has been made by archeo-astronomists in Sardegna, who, after studying the sacred well of Santa Cristina, have discovered that the circular stone opening above Tanit's body aligns with the full moon. Every 18 ½ years, in the middle of the night at the darkest time of the year, the milky moonlight enters the round hole at the surface and shines directly down the bottle-shaped stone column into the water. This holy well is an exquisite vessel of cosmic and Earthly communion, as moon and sun come together in the waters held within the earth and stone, all sanctified inside the female body of the Goddess.

In sharing news and photos of my clothesline, I heard from friends across the country with their own fond memories of outdoor laundry, often beginning with "I remember when . . ." Sicilian American poet Maria Fama sent me her tribute to laundry in a poem, "In Love with the Laundry." I learned of Roberta Cantow's documentary film "Clotheslines" in which she pays homage to women, their work, and their stories.[3] I discovered Holly Smith Pedlosky's photographs of a Venetian mural in Giudecca of Our Lady of the *Biancheria*,[4] who blesses the laundry below and affirms her presence in everyday spirituality. Spinning fibers and weaving them into cloth falls under divine female protection. Women have sat together spinning and weaving for millennia, according to Elizabeth Wayland Barber who has researched the making of cloth and clothing over the last 20,000 years.[5] In the village tradition of the Italian Alps, peasant families gathered together in the stables during the evenings of the winter months for the *filò*, a dialect word from the verb *filare*, meaning to spin. [6] Women spun wool, flax, or hemp and men worked on their tools while the storytellers spun tales in a communal setting, a practice still in existence in the 20th century.[7]

The two Tanits, with silvery clothesline strung between them, stand outside my office window like guardian oracles of ancestral winds. Inside, at my computer, I am working to retrieve my ancestral heritage as part of my dissertation research. Over the months, I have been interviewing my elder female relatives in Colorado and in Italy asking about their lives. From them, I am learning about the life of my maternal grandmother, Edvige Albasini, who died three years before I was born. A century ago, she and my other grandparents emigrated from alpine villages in Trentino, the mountainous region of the Dolomites in what is now northern Italy. Edvige's destination was Russell Gulch, Colorado, a rustic gold-mining town. Like many wives of miners, she was soon widowed, in her case at a young age with a family of three small children. "Taking in laundry" of wealthy people enabled Edvige to manage.

After Edvige remarried and the expanding family moved to Denver, doing the family laundry by hand was a sizable task, which, as daughters, my mother and her sisters were assigned to do. Clothes were placed in a boiler by my grandmother and then carried to a tub where the girls wrung them out and then hung them outside on lines—all of this before going to school. If wintry weather arrived during the day, frozen clothes were relocated inside on long lines strung across the dining room. At age 94, my mother's oldest sister, Aunt Annie, relayed the details of this chore without a trace of fondness. She noted as a memorable event the time when a neighbor gave my grandmother a wringer washer, an upgrade from her washer board. After decades of line-drying the laundry, both Mother and Aunt Louise remembered clearly when they each finally were able to purchase an electric clothes dryer for their growing families.[8]

My mother, Lena, does the wash on Monday, as her mother did, and as they did growing up. In Italian, the word for Monday is *lunedi*, after *luna*, the moon. Lunar cycles permeate my peasant heritage. The phase of the moon governs plant growth, whether fermentation and distillation will be successful, and how quickly hair and nails grow. The *luna crescente*, the waxing moon, invigorates; the *luna calante*, the waning moon, mediates.[9] Lunar rays of the full moon could impregnate, according to the lore of one village in the old country, perhaps recognizing the entrainment of women's menstrual cycle with that of the moon. Menstrual practices, along with lunar practices, survived into the last century in Trentino—including rules about not touching living flowers or metal, and not washing one's hair during the menstrual period. Honoring times of menstruation (or "*le regole*," as it was once called, which translates as "the rules"), links these women to a long line of female ancestors who respected the awesome power of women's life-giving blood.[10] Our oldest foremothers practiced menstrual seclusion rites and maintained strict taboos that kept the blood sacred or separate, according to the cross-cultural research of Judy Grahn, who theorizes that these primordial rites are the origins of all ritual, which allowed the formation of culture.[11]

In a popular Trentino legend known as *I Monti Pallidi*, The Pale Mountains, the *Salvans*—little men who dwell in the wilds of the caverns and forests—spin the moonlight into a silvery cloth which they drape over the rugged Dolomites, giving them their white alpenglow.[12] They perform this task so that a Moon Princess, with whom a Prince on Earth has fallen in love, can come down to live with him and feel at home. In return for their gift, the *Salvans* are granted permanent residence in the caverns of the mountains. Moonlight, women, and wilderness are woven together and remembered in this tale.

In my childhood dream, I am standing alone at night in the backyard between the clothesline and the apple tree. The white beam of the full moon shines from high above and bathes over me. Slowly it begins to lift me up off the ground back to its source. My heart is racing.

Was I remembering my lunar lineage? Were my female ancestors beckoning for me to someday remember their traditions?

Hanging clothes outside for me, in the 21st century, enfolds simple pleasures and deeply held values: the smell of clothes that have been dried by the wind and sun, spending time outside, conserving electric energy, and doing one small thing to reduce my legacy of consumption. In my visits to the folk museums of Trentino, I have witnessed all the stuff of everyday life made by hand. It is impressive—and humbling—to realize that these people of the mountains knew how to make *everything*: a variety of containers, every type of clothing, all food and drink, utensils, tools, and shelter. Older women were valued for their extensive knowledge of childbirth and healing remedies learned from a lifetime of careful observation and care-giving. The elders knew (and some still know) where the likely places for wild *brise* mushrooms are, which herbs to use for medicine, and the specific healing properties of the various mineral springs.

Practical knowledge gained through the responsibilities of work began at a young age for Onorina Bortolamedi, one of the women I interviewed in 2009 in Trentino. Although her formal education was interrupted by the falling bombs of World War II, she said with pride that by the time she got married, "I could do everything!"[13] She exudes the caring confidence of a *bisnonna*, a great-grandmother who birthed her first child at home and has tended to several generations. I look back to my ancestor's wisdom as I look forward to creating a more sustainable life, less dependent on machines and distant others that give me "free time" but take away wellness and health-imparting activity that I must then create in other ways.

From my vantage point of mid-life, the laundry line feels like a connection to my female lineage, my motherline.[14] Not in drudgery, although this task of keeping clothes washed and dried has been formidable over the ages; but in the ritual act itself of hanging clothes, and in the stories that settle around women's lives in the creation and care of clothes. As we retrieve our mother's stories and those of other female relatives we reclaim the value of women's lives in history and restore our inner connection with the timelessness of the cycle of life.

Notes

1   Lucia Chiavola Birnbaum, *dark mother: African origins and godmothers*, (Lincoln: Authors Choice Press, 2001).

2   Franco Laner, *Il Tempio a Pozzo di Santa Cristina: Storia, Tecnologia, Architettura e Astronomia*, (Mestre, Sardinia: Guida 2 Edizioni Adrastea, 2004), 36.

3   See more on the film *Clotheslines* in Filmakers Library, http://www.filmakers.com/index.php?a=filmDetail&filmID=173

4   Photo of *La Madonna Della Biancheria* by Holly Smith Pedlosky: http://www.pedlosky.org/artlinks.html

5   Elizabeth Wayland Berber, *Women's Work: The First 20,000 Years*, (New York: W.W. Norton & Company, 1994), 29.

6   Elizabeth Mathias and Richard Raspa in *Italian Folktales in America: The Verbal Art of an Immigrant Woman*, (Detroit: Wayne State University Press, 1985), 3.

7   The *filò* is portrayed visually in the film *L'Albero degli Zoccoli*, The Tree of Wooden Clogs (1978), directed by Ermanno Olmi.

8   From interviews with Ann Ress, Louise Kulp, Emma Fortarel, and Lena Moser conducted in May, 2009.

9   Doing laundry during the waning cycle of the moon, with its dissolving energy, helps make *biancherie*—linens and cottons—whiter, according to Johanna Paungger, who documents numerous lunar-related traditions of her Tyrolean childhood which she still practices. Johanna Paungger and Thomas Poppe, *Servirsi della Luna: il suo influsso positivo su natura, salute, e vita quotidiana*, (Milano: TEA, 2004), 152.

10   Details regarding recent menstrual practices were kindly provided to me by Giuseppina Trentini of Rovereto in Trentino, Italy via personal correspondence in November, 2010.

[11]   Judy Grahn, *Blood Bread and Roses: How Menstruation Created the World*, (Boston: Beacon Press, 1993).

[12]   Carl Felix Wolff, *The Pale Mountains*, English translation by Francesca La Monte, (New York: Minton, Balch & Company, 1927).

[13]   From interviews with Onorina Bortolamedi conducted in September 2009.

[14]   See Naomi Ruth Lowinsky, *The Motherline: Every Woman's Journey to Find Her Female Roots*, (New York: Jeremy P. Tarcher/Perigee Books, 1992), for more information on the concept of the motherline and on the importance of researching the stories of female family members.

Bibliography

Berber, Elizabeth Wayland. *Women's Work: The First 20,000 Years*. New York: W.W. Norton & Company, 1994.

Birnbaum, Lucia Chiavola. *dark mother: African origins and godmothers*. Lincoln: Authors Choice Press, 2001.

Grahn, Judith Rae. *Blood Bread and Roses: How Menstruation Created the World*. Boston: Beacon Press, 1993.

Laner, Franco. *Il Tempio a Pozzo di Santa Cristina: Storia, Technologia, Architettura e Astronomia*. Mestre, Sardinia: Guida 2 Edizioni Adrastea, 2004.

Lowinsky, Naomi Ruth. *The Motherline: Every Woman's Journey to Find Her Female Roots*. New York: Jeremy P. Tarcher/Perigee Books, 1992.

Mathias, Elizabeth and Richard Raspa. *Italian Folktales in America: The Verbal Art of an Immigrant Woman*. Detroit: Wayne State University Press, 1985.

Paungger, Johanna and Thomas Poppe, *Servirsi della Luna: il suo influsso positivo su natura, salute, e vita quotidiana*. Milano: TEA, 2004.

Wolff, Carl Felix. *The Pale Mountains*, English translation by Francesca La Monte. New York: Minton, Balch & Company, 1927.

Tanit Clothesline;
Photo © 2006 Mary Beth Moser

Sacred Well at Santa Cristina, Sardegna, Italy;
Photo © 2004 Mary Beth Moser

A Poetics of the Placenta:
Placental Cosmology as Gift and
Sacred Economy

Nané Ariadne Jordan

Prelude

I am sitting upstairs in my grandmother's modest bungalow home in East
Toronto as I finish writing this essay. Far from a world of e-mails and
business, there is no Internet connection here. I am sitting in the second
of two bedrooms, which was my grandparent's room many years ago.
Across from this is the room I slept in on frequent nights of my childhood.
The two single beds are still there, just the same as over 30 years ago. My
grandma, my father's mother, was 47 years old when I was born. As I have
been writing and thinking of mothering and the gift economy (Vaughan,
2007, 2004), I think of my grandma in particular, the way she has always
been in my life, a pure giving presence. She taught me a way of going forth
in the world with this presence, with curiosity, interest and love, even as
she herself remained rooted to this very home, husband, place. Hers is
a pre-feminist life in analysis, yet I admire now her rootedness, steadfast,
this home of so many years, this focus she keeps on those around her. She
keeps little in the way of things. Her house is in careful order. She knits
and reads most days, and has a schedule of visits with others. I like to think
of her here as a peaceful, deliberate contemplative. What she does keep
are family pictures, images of all of us, and even now my own children,
her great-grandchildren at such a distance in Vancouver, BC, so far away
from her and her love. She holds us close at heart. The family albums
are carefully piled in the room where I sleep and I love to leaf through

them here before bed, seeing the narratives of our lives and others, those gone before us from my grandma's childhood, her parents, brothers and sisters—I see the gift of all this, how I just am because of her.

The Dalai Lama is frequently quoted as saying that he first learned the quality of compassion from his mother. Compassion, that potential for boundless sense of love and attention for others, given without expectation of return or reward, was given him by his mother. He explains that is how he first knew it, its transmission in his life and now within larger world-stage circles. He circulates this gift of compassion. His point is simple, clear—the work and being of mothers as a central teaching principle of Buddhism. Mothers, and what they do, predate Buddhism.

As I leave my grandma's home in a taxi, she stands just inside the screen door and waves at me, her small, aging frame outlined, she clutches her cane for balance, her pure white hair a halo around her head—I wave back at her, and keep waving as the cab takes me from her view. It is our old habit since I was a small girl, to not stop waving till we can't see each other anymore from her spot in the doorway. We are smiling and beaming at each other, and the cab driver says with great enthusiasm, "You are lucky!!" and I say, "I know I am, I know I am . . . ."

A poetics of the placenta

A recent birth comes immediately to mind. I have been acting as a glorified doula, glorified in the sense of my past midwifery experience coming to bear in my current life as a Ph.D. student. I have the honour of serving and supporting a few sister doctoral scholars at the University of British Columbia as they give birth. These are women having their first babies as they work through Ph.D.s.

At the last birth, I am charging around Women's Hospital, having just learned that my friend's placenta has not been set aside. In fact we suspect that it has been already thrown out and is now un-retrievable. It has not been labeled in the requisite plastic tub and placed in the fridge of the upper floor post-partum maternity ward so that she can bring it home when she leaves the hospital. It is day-one after her birth—she is recovering from the cesarean section of her baby girl. This little girl had been in a breech position during the end of the pregnancy. Despite working to shift her position with moxabustion and physiotherapies, she stayed that way. We had secured a trial of labour for my friend at the hospital, a home birth no longer an option for her within the system.

She began her birth process, and was very close to delivering her breech baby vaginally with a supportive obstetrician and midwifery team, before a c-section was decided upon by the attending obstetrician.

During my friend's hours-long birth process, we discussed the placenta with the assisting maternity nurse. Between contractions, the nurse asked us about this, interested herself in uses of the placenta; she asked my friend and her husband what they intended to do with it. My friend responded that she was thinking of burying it in the earth, to honour the birth, her baby and their new family. This idea had only come to her in the last two weeks, after my own suggestion. In the flurry of decision-making required for the breech birth, I had not talked with her sooner about my knowledge of placentas. I realized almost too late that without my small commentaries and inquiries, she would have had no idea that such things were possible or even thinkable.

My years of work with birth and lay midwifery in a modern North American context have taught me many things, one of which is a common, and near absolute lack of, connection between birthing women and their placentas. That is to say, a disinterest in the placenta, and most often disgust at its blood-filled, mysterious mass. It is treated as disposable, a by-product only of birth, much like menstrual blood. Poet and women's spirituality scholar Judy Grahn names this as women's *blood taboo*. Grahn, who identifies the world-originating significance of women's blood through metaformic theory, points to the modern loss of female origin stories through this hidden blood (Grahn, 1993; Grahn in Jordan, 2007). This is not to say that women, within what was the lay midwifery movement growing from the 1970s onwards (Gaskin, 1990; Koehler, 1985), weren't interested in their placentas, but that in general the placenta—as a very real physical, ritual, and meaningful aspect of the pregnancy and birth process—is under-valued and misunderstood in a modern North American context. This is emblematic of a larger disconnect in modern society between embodied and embedded life processes and our daily lives, especially in what have been identified by many thinkers as *pathologized* female processes such as menstruation and birth giving (Arms, 1996; Chesterfield, 1998; Spretnak, 1982; van Teijlingen et al., 2004). Within birth practices, this kind of disconnect is largely sanctioned and ritualized (Davis-Floyd, 1992) by patriarchal biomedicine within medical and hospital procedures—to borrow a page from Mary Daly's 1978 book, *Gyn/ecology*.

In this context, the placenta has become one of my teachers of birth, of life, of birth/life/death in its deep mystery of human and Earth consciousness itself. I had not set out knowing this. I was not looking for the placenta. But I was an avid and early student of the lay midwifery movement (Gaskin, 1990; Shroff, 1997) since the home birth of my little brother in the mid-1980s when I was 15 years old. Placentas did not figure significantly into my early understanding of birth, beyond the fact that placentas come out after the baby does, and that they need to be watched to emerge in a timely way after birth for the health of the mother/baby diad. Once the baby is born, I learned that the cord should NOT be cut until it stops pulsing. Blood flow between the placenta/mother and baby should subside on its own, ensuring full oxygenation of the baby for her/his first breath. I knew that placentas should not be 'retained' within the mother's uterus after her baby's birth, and they are very bloody and lumpy-looking once born. During pregnancy, the placenta is the key developmental link between mother and child. The umbilical cord can do nothing without the transport of blood, nutrients and oxygen between mother and baby through the placenta. The placenta is singular in its mission; it grows, is born and dies with only one function in mind: to support and sustain the life of the new human, within the body of the mother herself.

It was not until years later, after attending many home births and working intimately with placentas and mothers post-birth that I began to really glean the morphological and spiritual wonders of this kind of being. Also due to my thesis writing and scholarly study within women's spirituality (Jordan, 2002), I began to discern the importance of the knowledge I had been privy to, to use my writing and research as a practice of naming and transmitting what I knew from birth towards larger circles of study (see Jordan, 2009—*What is goddess?*). I want to theorize birth itself, and the significance of what are actually deeply female-based practices and body parables.

I remember seeing my first placenta up close. The midwife I studied with for many years brought a placenta from a recent birth to our midwifery study group. I remember the red, red blood, and wondering how to make sense of this organ, and then under her careful guidance, *I began to see*, to discern its shape. There are two sides, a mother side, and a baby side. The mother's side has lobular, intersecting lobes, almost brain-like, and attaches to the inside wall of the uterine muscle, connecting to the mother's nourishment and lifeblood. The baby side is where you see the roots of veins, interconnecting lace-like, fanning outwards, circular, from where the umbilical cord centres into the placenta. This side is smooth, cosseted by the amniotic sack, which surrounds the baby in-utero.

My favorite placenta metaphor, first taught to me by this same midwife, is that of a *tree*, where the placenta forms the roots, the chord is the trunk, and the baby is the fruits and flowers. In the years since, spending time in coastal rain forests of the West coast of Canada where I live, and observing huge upturned trees over the years, their roots splayed out from the earth, I have written on this deeply symmetrical relationship between placentas and trees. Pushing beyond the metaphor of tree, I now see that in growing babies, women embody the actual morphology of trees through the placenta (see Jordan, 2009—*Roots of Life*). I understand this gift morphology[2] as a physical and spiritual articulation of our deep interconnection to trees and all other living systems. We ritualize, through our bodies, gratitude and interrelation with trees, those living beings that provide the oxygen we breathe. The placenta's tree form itself feeds nutrients and oxygen to our babies through a continual dialogue of blood.

Studying midwifery within home birth practices, I learned that mothers often chose to bury their placentas. This could be done under a tree, or in a yard or park close to where the baby was born, giving thanks for the gift of life of the placenta and thanks to the Earth for the health and birth of the new baby. Some home birth midwives were famous, I think, for the numbers of placentas buried in their yards—rich soil and experience, to be sure. The other use that I learned, which is hard for more mainstream cultural thinking to understand, is to prepare and feed the placenta to the mother, post-birth. Placentas are nutrient and hormone rich—rich with nutrients that balance and mediate mother and baby needs, especially replenishing the mother's physical and emotional well-being post-birth. These many years later, I have also learned, and I'm not surprised, that the cellular structure of placentas is restorative, in the same sense as stem cells from cord blood, promoting speedy healing of all tissues. Cooking the placenta is done by washing off excess blood, trimming bits from the mother side, and carefully cooking on a low heat, so as to not lose nutrients, and adding whatever pleases the mom to eat: carrots, peppers, onions, some oregano or spice. It is a post-birth meal, just as many mammals consume raw placenta post-birth. Small bits of placenta can be eaten fresh, placed under the mother's tongue uncooked within the first couple of days after the baby's birth.

On the desire of one new mother, a friend of mine, she and I taught ourselves the technique of drying placentas in the oven in order to make capsules of placenta powder in a Chinese medicine preparation (Enning, 2007). These could be stored for months, and taken by the mother during times of post partum depression or when she needs restorative support in the long challenges of early mothering and beyond. Thus, I learned of placenta as mother's friend and helpmate, a meta-mother-being herself, an ancient grandmother, who is capable of gifting healing beyond the womb.

In this context of placenta power and medicine, you can appreciate my running around the hospital looking for my friend's lost placenta, dismayed at this now further lack of connection for her in relation to her birth. There are, it seems, so many lost placentas. Even though the couple had specified the desire to keep the mother's placenta to midwives and nurses, some communication link was missed in the shift from a vaginal birth to a cesarean. I don't know what link was missed during the surgical removal of my friend's baby—the placenta is itself removed at this time. After inspection for its health and wellbeing, the placenta is put aside for its usual disposal, use by medical labs, or to be taken by the parents in the rare circumstance that they actually ask for it. At that point, as a friend and doula at this birth, I was consigned to the waiting bench outside my friend's cesarean surgery. Come what may, her placenta did not end up in the post-partum maternity ward fridge.

We might have had a ceremony with the placenta. Being with the placenta itself, honouring and placing it within the Earth can bring healing, deep satisfaction and creative ritual affirmation to women and their families. It may be especially important to re-connect the placenta with the Earth in the case of a woman who has experienced cesarean section, or other such interventions upon the flow of her baby's birth. Until this particular hospital birth, I had not really thought that through. Attending to placentas was an outgrowth of the kinds of holistic, spiritualized midwifery care extended within the home birth practices I learned midwifery within, following the mothers' wishes and needs, and re-claiming women's medicine traditions and healing. Within this collective and individual movement, a large dose of intuition, trust, love and attunement has been at work, a willingness to allow birth itself to teach us all, while gleaning wisdom from intact traditional and indigenous birthing knowledge, and what modern medicine has quantified within its diagnostic practices.

Thus, when I say "placental cosmology"[3] what I am talking about is a way of knowing the world, a consciousness, that arises directly from the sensed perception of birthing wisdom, the ways that birth-body-Earth wisdom is deeply embedded within gestating and birthing mothers. The matriculation of this arises from a mother-matrix of ancient planetary processes in which we are embedded and in ever-evolving, co-creating, relation to.

By sense perception, I include what might be known as the sixth sense. I have never quite understood the distinction between physical and non-physical senses that Western philosophers relate to as distinct. My teachings from the placenta *come from placentas*, from being with multiple forms of this amazing being over time, attuning to its wisdom ways. This is real time and space contiguity. Placentas call to me from the domain of the "real," what feminist philosopher Charlene Spretnak argues for as the resurgence of the real from within modern ideologies of its denial (1999). Spretnak argues that this denial has given rise to the crises of modernity, those of war, environmental devastation, over-industrialization, alienation and loss of 'meaning' within people's lives. The real IS the Earth and all of our relationships within it, an enlarged sense of ecology that is not just environmentalism but Earth of cosmological significance. Birth transcends ordinary sensation and sense of time, yet is firmly rooted in our flesh and blood, an in-body, out-of-body experience.

A placental cosmology extends consciousness as female body parable rooted within life, where life is rooted in birth and from 'gift' itself. Every time a mother or family reclaims their placenta, acknowledges through ceremony, preparations and women's medicine practices, its role in gifting the life of their child, a larger connection is made to the cosmos, to the Earth community. And you can see, literally, the role that men play within this way of knowing, where fathers back-up the experience of the mother at birth, extending such care for life themselves. The gift of mother is made known—we just cannot deny her ultimate reality within the form of placenta. There is no other way to deal with the blood of women and placentas in an exchange economy besides literally 'throwing it out.' The notion of garbage itself is 'refuse,' what is re-fused.

In the exchange economy, value only becomes apparent when the market assigns it to the placenta, which now comes in the form of stem cell research, as well as the cosmetics industry uses of placentas (Enning, 2007). Luce Irigaray speaks of the unpaid work of women (and women's regenerative bodies) as a repression, a "censorship of the desire to trade"

(1993 / 1987, p. 81), and links maternal labour to the 'charity work' of intellectuals; as in work done for women's liberation. Thus, infrastructure functions for free (p. 86), and there is no recognition of this. Society is played out upon this free 'labour' of the intellectual and women, what Irigaray calls a sacrificial understanding of women's labour.

Genevieve Vaughan's work on mothering as gift economy realizes the value of the free infrastructure (2007, 2004). Unlike the exchange economy, the gift is understood as a one-way process. The giver gives value to the receiver, not expecting 'reward.' As in the flow of life from mother to child, and the flow of talking / language communication from mother to child, the gift does not approximate the exchange economy of "I'll do something for you if you do something for me." In maternal thinking (a la Ruddick, 1989), one simply gives because it is given to give. The child is there and requires one's immediate and constant giving or s/he will perish. The gift is present in the Earth's resources as a continual 'free' stream of goods from which we draw our exchange economy in unmitigated taking. The original gift of the Earth, or the mother, is rendered invisible, though it forms the basis of exchange, production, or capital. Reciprocity of the gift lies in acknowledgement or ritualization of return to the Earth and to the mother herself, a sense of gratitude for what we take and keeping the 'balance.' We are given the gift as the gift passes from us to others.

I think of the gift, its female and Earthly origins. Irigaray states that "sexual difference is one of the major philosophical issues, if not the philosophical issue, of our age" (1993/1984, p. 5), though she is critiqued for not attending to the liberatory discourses of race, class and sexuality (Canters & Jantzen, 2005). In my own identification with birth as rooted within female embodiment, yet being a 'pan-human' experience, I am interested in Irigaray's attention to sexual difference. She does not reduce women to fecundity, but sees the fecundity of "birth and regeneration . . . in the production of a new age of thought, art, poetry, and language: the creation of a new poetics." (1993/1984, p. 5). This age will come when women have fully articulated the needs of their difference from men from within their own subjectivity. She cites how political overtures have been made towards women—but no new values have been established (p. 6). "Transition to a new age requires a change in our perception and conception of space-time, the inhabiting of places, and of containers, or envelopes of identity" (p. 7).

In the sense of "gift" and women's spirituality, we already have those 'new' values; they only require our recognition, waiting to be named again, re-named, re-storied, re-turned to consciousness. Midwife turned philosopher Mary O'Brien, deftly analyses the fault of thinking birth is a 'pure' biological process that is "all body and without mind, irrational or at least pre-rational" (1981, p. 21). According to O'Brien, human reproductive consciousness is inseparable from human consciousness, and birth must be philosophized from a female perspective. "We cannot analyze reproduction from the standpoint of any existing theory . . . . what this means is that we must not only develop a theory, but a feminist perspective and a method of inquiry from which such a theory can emerge" (p. 23-24). She discusses the dialectical nature of production and reproduction from male and female standpoints, an ongoing operation of two processes, or capacities that determine human consciousness. Womanist midwife and women's spirituality scholar Arisika Razak proposes that birth act "as the nucleus around which to build a paradigm for positive human interaction" (1990, p. 166). Understanding birth as a "universal and central aspect of human existence" (p. 166), Razak describes the emotional significance of birth for all humans. Significant to this act is that, regardless of what sex we are born, we all pass through female bodies to arrive Earth-side.

Irigaray also catches placentas in her thinking. She discusses the placental relation as an opening away from social determinism, an opening that stems from "female corporeal identity." This relationship is misidentified within the patriarchal imagination as a fusion of mother and baby, from which the baby must valiantly struggle to get away from, when, in reality, it is organized as "respectful of the life of both" (1993/1990, p. 32). Irigaray calls on the almost "ethical character" of this fetal relation to its mother, where one and the other live as distinct entities, citing ignorance of this "placental economy" as a factor within "male cultural imaginary" (p. 36). Irigaray cites returning to a *maternal* order as diverting two imposing structures: that of living as adversaries at the level of life, and that of educating and training ourselves towards repetition in the desire to be 'alike' each other at the level of culture.

Thus, re-turning to human cosmological origins through acknowledgement of such placental relations re-stores and re-stories the mother, from which all diversity of forms continually arise. I honour this sacred gift of life from so many birth-ings. When I finished reading a version of this paper at the Gift Economy conference, at the Association for Research on Mothering in Toronto, Canada (October, 2009), another speaker, from the Seneca nation of the U.S. Northeast, gifted me with her story of the sacred care and honouring of babies' placentas and umbilical cords in the Seneca tradition. It is such a joy to hear of the many sacred honourings of birth, mothers, babies and placentas that continue worldwide. These women and life-centred paths can be traced, re-claimed and followed for their sustenance and life affirmation within women's spirituality and all of our be-ings and know-ings.

Notes

1   "Pathologize" refers to the characterization of female processes such as menstruation, pregnancy and birth into disease, or illnesses, rather than significant features of women's and human lives. This characterization is linked to a long history of gender hierarchies and distortions (male privileged over female—male as 'normal', female as distortion of norm), including the European witch hunts and Scientific Revolution as pointed to by feminist scholars such as Carolyn Merchant, 1980.

2   Morphology is the study of the shapes and forms of things. In biology it is the study of how living things grow and are structured, in linguistics it is the study of the form and structure of words. Attending to form and structure of world, cosmos and its beings is a key aspect of my practice of "poetics". Poetics extends such attention into the craft of writing, art and scholarship in relationship to other beings/world/cosmos—in this case honouring the placenta.

3   Cosmology refers to study of the universe, its scientific, astronomic study. My use of this term refers to philosophical and metaphysical understandings of cosmology. Cosmologies undergird world views, and make or tell stories that make intuitive conclusions about the nature of beings, things, happenings and the storied relationships between them all. A placental cosmology is meant as a transformative framework to the current, still dominant patriarchal system and its world view.

Bibliography

Arms, S. (1996). *Immaculate deception II: Myth, magic & birth.* Berkeley, CA: Celestial Arts.

Canters, H. & Jantzen, G. (2005). *Forever fluid: A reading of Luce Irigaray's elemental passions.* Manchester: Manchester University Press.

Chesterfield, P. (1998). *Sisters on a journey: Portraits of American midwives.* New Jersey: Rutgers University Press.

Daly, M. (1984). *Pure lust: Elemental feminist philosophy.* Boston: Beacon Press.

Daly, M. (1978) *Gyn/ecology: The metaethics of radical feminism.* Boston: Beacon press.

Davis-Floyd, R. (1992). *Birth as an American rite of passage.* Berkeley, CA: University of California Press.

Enning, C. (2007). *Placenta: Gift of life. The role of the placenta in different cultures and how to prepare and use it as medicine.* Eugene, OR: Motherbaby Press.

Gaskin, I. M. (1990). *Spiritual midwifery, 3rd edition.* Summertown, TN: The Book Publishing Company.

Grahn, J. (1993). *Blood, bread, and roses: How menstruation created the world.* Boston: Beacon Press.

Koehler, N. (1985). *Artemis speaks: V.B.A.C. stories and natural childbirth information.* Sebastopol, CA: Na Ulrike Keohler, Haddon Craftsman.

Irigaray, L. (2007 / 1990). *Je, tu, nous: Towards a culture of difference.* A. Martin. (transl.). New York: Routledge Classics.

Irigaray, L. (1993 / 1984). *An ethics of sexual difference.* Carolyn Burke & Gillian C. Gill (trans.). Ithaca, NY: Cornell University.

Irigaray, L. (1993 / 1987). *Sexes and genealogies*. Gillian C. Gill (trans.) New York: Columbia University Press.

Jordan, N. (2009). Roots of Life. *Matrifocus: Cross-Quarterly for the Goddess Woman*. Imbolc. Vol. 8-2. http://www.matrifocus.com/IMB09/connections.htm

Jordan, N. (2009). What is goddess? Towards an ontology of women giving birth. In special issue: *Thinking about Goddesses. Trivia: Voices of feminism*. Spring equinox, March, Issue 9. http://www.triviavoices.net/current/jordan.html

Jordan, N. (2007). The swallowed mother: C-sections, metaforms and male cuts. *Metaformia: The Journal of Menstruation and Culture*. http://www.metaformia.org/article_08.cfm

Jordan, N. (2002). *Birthdance, earthdance: The power and passion of women giving birth, a pilgrim's path to birth*. Unpublished Master of Arts thesis. San Francisco: New College of California.

Jordan, N. (2007). If my body were the text. *Metaformia: The Journal of Menstruation and Culture*. www.metaformia.com.

Merchant, C. (1980). *The death of nature: Women, ecology and the scientific revolution*. San Francisco: HarperSanFrancisco.

O'Brien, M. (1981). *Politics of reproduction*. London: Routledge & Kegan Paul.

Razak, A. (1990). Toward a womanist analysis of birth. In I. Diamond & G. F. Orenstein. (Eds.). *Reweaving the world: The emergence of ecofeminism* (pp.165-172). San Francisco: Sierra Club Books.

Ruddick, S. (1989). *Maternal thinking: Towards a politics of peace*. Boston: Beacon Press.

Shroff. F. (Ed.). (1997). *The new midwifery: Reflections on renaissance and regulation*. Toronto: Women's Press.

Spretnak, C. (1999). *The resurrgence of the real: Body, nature, place in a hypermodern world*. New York: Routledge.

Spretnak, C. (Ed.). (1982). *The politics of women's spirituality: Essays on the rise of spiritual power within the feminist movement*. New York: Anchor Press / Doubleday.

van Teijlingen, E., Lowis, G, McCaffery, P. & Porter, M. (Eds.). (2004). *Midwifery and the medicalization of childbirth: Comparative perspectives*. New York: Nova Science Publishers.

Vaughan, G. (Ed.). (2007). *Women and the gift economy: A radically different worldview is possible*. Toronto: Innana Publications.

Vaughan, G. (Ed.). (2004). Il dono/The gift. *Athanor: Semiotica, Filosofia, Atre, Letteratura*. XV (8). Roma: Meltemi editore.

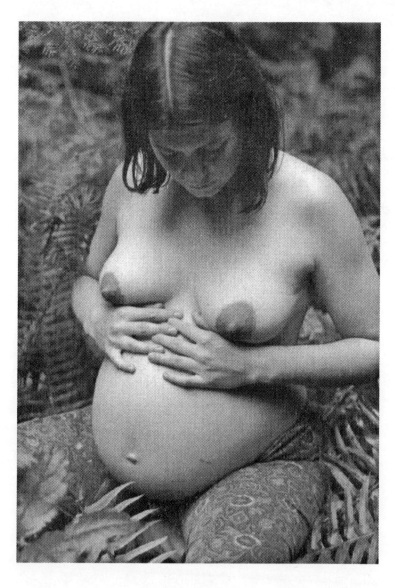

Full of Life;
Photo © 1997 Chris Cordoni

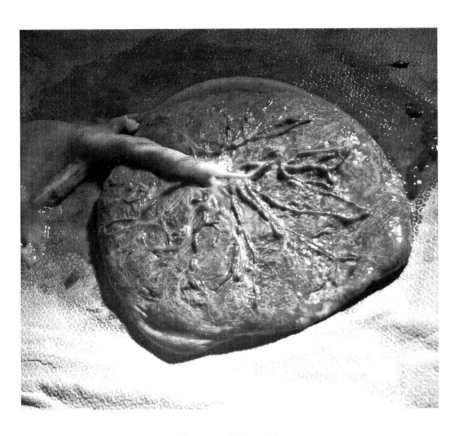

Placenta: Baby side;
Photo © 2004 Nané Ariadne Jordan

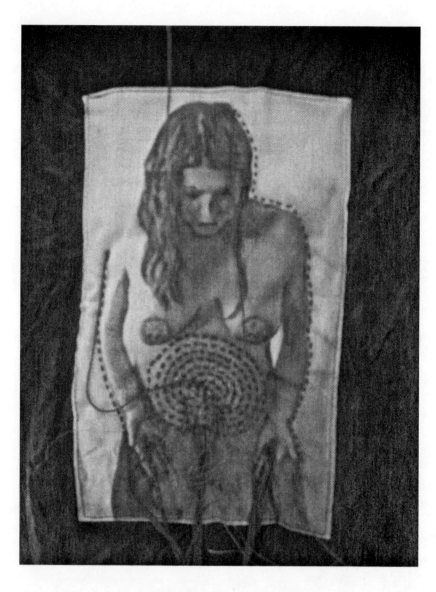

Womb Labyrinth: Birthing the Story Within, transfer to
cloth, with red thread and copper wire stitching;
Artwork © 2003 Nané Ariadne Jordan;
Photo by Nané Ariadne Jordan

Garden Okra

Etoyle McKee

The source of strength found in the spirit of womanhood is veined through generations and woven in the fabric of relationships. It is offered generously. For me, whether it was a surrogate great grandmother, Ma Malone, a silent grandmother, Jesse Mae, or Mother herself, I received all the blessings of the spirit extended in reverent gratitude.

Mother planted victory gardens, made sundresses from flour sacks, learned to use a pressure cooker for quick meals and saved her green stamps to acquire a treat for the house. Mom waited until it went on sale and was comfortable with saying out loud "We can't afford that—it will have to wait." Her voice, like those before her, whispers to us at every "stop" sign to just "yield" for a moment and "light a candle rather than curse the darkness," to "waste not and we'll want not." Her voice can be heard everywhere, but it is strongest when we're seeking direction. If we're silent—after we've stopped crying, feeling guilty, blaming everyone and everything around us—we realize that the life lessons she lived out are now ours. While we can be guided with a wisdom that is centuries old, each generation must find their way and strength of purpose. I listen carefully and I can feel and hear her inner strength spoken and demonstrated in a tone and posture of perseverance. Ma Malone. Jesse Mae. Mother. The legacy of their journeys has traveled through generations. The gifts of stamina they bring forth, if we but recognize them, will allow us to create a better tomorrow—a more appreciative, aware, sensitive and spirit driven tomorrow.

Now in the midst of debts, despair and dishevelment, a generation is blessed with the opportunity to rediscover their inherent resources. Faced with all avenues closed off we can proceed forward with their strength of spirit on a road less traveled in the last four to five decades. They are our mentors—our guides. We recall mottoes: *Time is money, A stitch in time*

293

saves nine, When in doubt do it yourself, Can't never accomplished anything, You are your own best friend, Anything worth doing is worth doing right. And while Mother might have first heard these messages from her fraternal side—she made them hers by living them out and demonstrating an unshakable belief in herself. After all, when all is said and done—what else did she have? So now, *their voices* can awaken our clouded and crowded minds.

Even though the predictions are glum and we are being presented with local and national chilling reports on the climate of our days, months and even years ahead, this isn't the dead of winter—not yet. It is fall. This is our season of harvest, which will lead us, if we so allow it into a season of celebration. We have before us the months of winter to focus, plan and redirect our efforts for making better choices for the next generation and ourselves. Whether it is a season of life or a celestial season the aroma, sounds and colors renew us and prepare us in spirit for the bounty that stimulates that laden part of our consciousness.

My spirit longed to have a replenishing of the lessons taught by my mother. All the efforts of the summer were now coming full circle as the last of September marked the end of the first month of preschool. The morning hours are the busiest greeting children, answering questions for parents and comforting teachers who are trying to console preschoolers dealing with separation anxieties. In reality I could truly identify with the youngest characters in the scenario because I myself felt increasingly anxious and separated from all the things that grounded me, stabilized my thoughts and renewed a sense of security. At age 69+, with my husband in an Alzheimer unit at an out-of-town VA Hospital, having all our retirement resources devoted to dealing with a massive stroke he suffered in 2007, and starting to really feel my age physically, I too was wondering who would pick me up at the close of the days. As the morning settled at school, I retreated to my office to get a cup of coffee.

On my desk was a bulging plastic grocery bag. *I sure hope that isn't a birthday snack like ice cream cups that missed the freezer.* Believe me that does happen. Nope, it was filled with freshly harvested garden okra. *Yum, oh yum.* My senses took flight. *Okra gumbo.* I could already taste and smell it. The memory of that aroma filled my mind. Standing right there I could feel myself inhale, capturing an era thought to be lost. I could feel the sense of wholeness that a meal from a backyard victory garden provided. I realized that rather than traveling back to my childhood, I was actually experiencing time in a circular motion.

Returning home that evening I greeted my family of four-legged members and set about to give myself a concrete (a term over-used with preschool educators) experience. Rather than turning on Rachael Ray and watching her in her retro, state-of-the-art kitchen create a meal in thirty minutes, including commercials, I quickly went about setting a familiar scene from my childhood. I diced the scrubby textured pods and prepared to seal them. (This is a process that reduces, if you'll pardon the expression, the slime from okra.) The seasoned cast iron skillet—that was never washed with soap, just rinsed—is placed on the burner, replaced by Al-clad. I truly missed the smell of the gas burners, but the glass top stove gets the job done. The recipe ingredients still remain basic:

- A colander of garden okra (the smaller pods are better)
- 2 small onions diced
- 2 or 3 over-ripe tomatoes that had out-lived their use in a salad
- A tablespoon of chili powder (you can measure that in the cup of a hand)
- Bacon drippings collected in a small tin placed on the back of the stove

Certain attention to details such as canned organic tomatoes and vegetable oil may have to replace yesteryear's choice. As I move the pieces of okra around in the hot oil the aroma fills up my senses and brings up soulful memories. My mother was actually there almost in a ghostly presence moving the wooden spoon back and forth, allowing each portion an opportunity to seal. I recalled her saying, *"Sometimes you just have to trust that the okra is clean enough by brushing it off. If you wash it, it'll never seal and the gumbo will not have a pleasant texture. The measure portion of chili powder is the final ingredient. Everything seems to need a little pick me up once in awhile."*

The whole experience reminded me of how Mother would *"keep on keeping on"—"putting one foot in front of another,"* knowing that if *"we learn to waste not we'll later want not."* I embrace, and almost celebrate, the opportunity to retrace her steps. In a time wherein every means of media spreads fear over that which is gone—that which we'll not have again—I have her at my side in my kitchen fixing okra gumbo on my glass top stove. Just as she did, I too have the kitchen window open and sounds from the outside travel through my memories. While the lawn mower that I hear humming from next door is gas driven, I hear her mowing the grass and the hum becomes a clack, clack from the steel mower blades. She had carefully sharpened them before beginning her weekly task. There's no point in waiting for Daddy to do it because he is missing from the picture. She doesn't dwell on being a single parent. She doesn't even know the term. What she does know is that if you want something done—do it yourself. Then you come from a sense of empowerment. Now as I face life alone she beckons me to find for myself the meaning of *"When you have a choice you have a problem. When you haven't a choice you have no problem."* And while I'll not mow the yard myself, I can have it done. So I reflect on how that makes me feel. Do I feel limited or limitless?

If you need something to cry about it can be provided *"or you can put on a smile and keep on truckin'."* Never did I feel as lost as the day she finally had to go to work in the mid-50s. No one else's mom was at work. Who would be there? I was coming home to what once was filled with her physical presence and a house full of projects that now seemed lonely and deserted. It was void. *You're not my child or your Dad's child; you're your Creator's child. You can stand on your own two feet.* While she never worried about tomorrow, she never regretted yesterday.

As I stand alone I'm bewildered by questions from my peers like; "I *don't know how you do it."* I do it because she did it. As I broaden my frame of reference from self to the next generation I see her clearly. Mother's two daughters stood on her shoulders, acquired Masters Degrees and bore her five grandchildren, all of whom obtained terminal degrees. They all live by the inner senses of her. They travel through their days, some with children of their own, some without, but each patterning their steps by remembering that whether it is in a household task of sewing or anything else in life, the hardest and most important steps are the beginning and ending. What lies in-between is really the easiest part. Her experiences, like mine, held a soulful grace, a blessing. Even Mother's grandmother, Ma Malone, managed a house, herded cattle and, with a pistol on her belt sat tall in the saddle, was self-empowered. My mother never saw a cup half-full but felt grateful for whatever portion it held. If at any time it was empty, she could fill it from an inner well spring.

Now as I watch my peers reaching the ending of their journeys, I wonder: do they listen to the lessons of yesteryear? As the petals of the flowers wither and fall away, they leave behind their seeds to proliferate at a later time. Sometimes the seeds are blown away or carried to another place but wherever they fall another victory garden can spring forth to nurture the next generation. If I listen, I'll realize that I am the sum total of all creation. Their gift of grace is carried forth in the forbearance of Ma Malone, the fragile spirit of Jesse Mae, and the strength of Mother. She was, I am, my daughter is because we are all Her. *She* is everywhere.

A *Midrash* of Rosary Prayers

Michele Arista

The Apostles' Creed
We believe in God, the Mother and Father almighty,
makers of heaven, earth and cosmos;
and in Jesus Christ, their Son, Our Divine Example.
Who was conceived in union with the Holy Spirit,
born of the sacred womb of Mary;
suffered under Pontius Pilate;
and like Inanna, he was crucified, died, and was buried;
on the third day he rose in Spirit from the dead.
He ascended into heaven,
and is seated at the right hand of the Mother and Father.
He will come again each spring to honor the living and the dead
And his kingdom will have no end.
We believe in the Holy Spirit
the Holy Catholic Apostolic Church,
the Communion of Saints,
peace in the world;
we look for the Resurrection of the body,
and the Life everlasting. Amen.
Hail Mary, full of grace,
the Lord and Lady Sophia are with thee
blessed art thou amongst women,
and blessed is the fruit of thy womb and mine.
Holy Mary, Mother and Creatrix of the Universe,
pray for us,
Remind us to be grateful,
now and at the hour of our death. Amen.

The Lord's Prayer

Our Father, who art in heaven,
hallowed be thy name; thy kingdom come;
thy will be done on Earth which is one with Heaven.
Give us this day our daily bread,
and forgive us our trespasses,
as we forgive those who trespass against us;
and lead us not into temptation,
but deliver us from evil. Amen

Hail Mary*

Hail Mary, full of grace,
the Lord and Lady Sophia are with thee
blessed art thou amongst women,
and blessed is the fruit of thy womb and mine.
Holy Mary, Mother and Creatrix of the Universe,
pray for us,
Remind us to be grateful,
now and at the hour of our death. Amen.

* Used with permission; First published in *The Journal of Feminist Studies in Religion*, Vol. 23, No 2, (Fall, 2007): 87.

Holy Yoni

Mama Donna Henes, Urban Shaman

The Earth, like a woman, in Her lushness, in Her fullness, in Her soft and rugged contours, carries in Her body, in Her spirit, in Her sex, in Her all-embracing nature, the power and potential of creation, procreation. The association is obvious. The correlation, clear. Woman, like the Earth, in her beauty, in her patience, in the cycles of her system, in the passion of her changes, in her constant transformation, in her wild and untamed fury, embodies and embraces the same essential energy. Her electric lust is the force that fashions all life. And her love is the fuel that maintains it.

Like the Earth, which sustains us, which supports us and surrounds us; like the Earth Who is our Mother, our comfort, our cradle and our grave; women in early Earth-identified societies were held in highest honor. Cherished and respected as the mortal sorority sisters of bounteous Mother Earth. Their sexuality was imbued with spiritual significance. Their power: their own inner vision and access to ecstasy. Their self—knowledge led them to understand the universal cycles. They were wise in the ways of the world.

From the very beginning, women have been identified and exalted as the image, as the echo, as the counterpart companion of the Goddess, the Great One, Who is the Earth, Who is our Mother. Archeological evidence suggests that from the Ice Age until only about five thousand years ago, women were the prime technicians of the sacred. They served as shamans, healers, creators of culture. As priestesses they attended the altars, the rituals, the temples of worship. They tended the fires of the Goddess. Her generative heat, Her sex, the seat of Her power.

The vulva, representing as it does the passageway through which we enter life, and metaphorically, through which we leave it, was probably the first religious symbol of humankind. The Sanskrit, *Jagad Yoni*, translates as "womb of the world," though its shape clearly characterizes woman's external genitalia and not her uterus. The yoni has survived as a central sacred image in several cultures and can be observed in Druid temples, domed synagogues and basilicas, and the soaring arches which grace Hindu and Arabic places of prayer. Even the familiar horseshoe which is still hung as protection over the thresholds of houses and barns, owes its power to its shape—a stylized vulva.

Cowry shells, perfect, miniature holy yonis that they are, have long been universally prized for use as ritual paraphernalia. Twenty-thousand-year-old skeletons have been discovered that were decked out in elaborately designed cowrie shell decorations. Their name comes from Kauri, another appellation of the goddess, Kali-Cunti. The Greek word for cowry, *kteis*, also means vulva. Moslem women wear cowrie shells on their body during pregnancy to help prepare their own parts for their impending delivery. For Gypsies, they are the supreme protective amulet. Japanese keep cowrie shells in their wardrobes for good luck. When cowries are unavailable, an acceptable substitute, in a pinch, is a porno picture of you-know-what.

Paleolithic carvings and figures found in caverns and caves are filled with life-affirming female imagery which bear reference to woman as matrix, as Creatrix, to moon cycles and to menstrual magic, and which relay profound reverence in their rendering. Of the more than sixty known Stone Age sculptures collected at sites scattered from Spain to the Ukraine, only five are thought to be male. This is especially interesting given that skeletal remains from the same locations indicate that men outnumbered women by three to two.

This earliest art depicts grandly voluptuous female forms whose sturdy stature suggests commanding confidence, stunning strength and authority. Although they are small enough to snuggle in the palm of one's hand, these goddess totems project a powerful, primordial potency. The Venus of Willendorf, the Venus of Meton, the Venus of Lespugue, with their big breasts and belly, huge hips and ass, stand frank and fecund, self contained, central. Formidable and efficacious. Faceless, their limbs are abbreviated. Their entire focus is centered on their own nubile torso which tapers to a point, a fertile triangle. The tip of the vortex of their sex.

The Venus of Laussel is thought to be the oldest relief sculpture in the world. At least thirty thousand years ago, she presided over the entrance of a cave in southern France which was used as a ritual sanctuary. Glorious, she stands with one hand caressing her own swollen, pregnant belly. With the other arm raised high she salutes the sky with a crescent moon, which is marked with the cycle of her thirteen annual periods. She was originally painted with the earthy red ochre of her holy blood. Inside the cave are pictured scenes of pleasure and purpose; coitus and conception, copulation and birth. What ceremonies might have been celebrated in this sacred sheltered chamber? This recessed cleft womb-room deep inside the body of Mother Earth?

In these ancient sacred images we can recognize the holiness implicit in the female sexual experience. Freely exchanged, unabashed and bold, sex was seen as authentic religious expression. Although this erotic attitude toward worship was all but annihilated by the puritanical and judgmental Judeo-Christian culture, this primal, carnal knowledge of the universal order surfaces in our language today. Sex and prayer are inextricably linked etymologically. "Venerate" and "venereal" both stem from the same root—the Latin name of the licentious Roman Goddess of Love, Venus. And the word, "lust," in the old Germanic language meant "religious joy."

Sex is not now, nor has it ever been, solely for the purpose of procreation. The same fire, the same hot love, which ignites to spark the beginning of babies, also kindles the creation of culture. Once babies are born, they need to be cared for and that necessity was the original mother of invention. The sedentary farming communities, which first began to develop around the circumference of the Mediterranean Sea about nine thousand years ago, venerated a goddess supreme in her creative powers of seduction and fruition. The powerful intensity of her sheer desire, her boundless energy, was potent enough to produce generations, poetry, agriculture, craft. She was the generous mother of creation, Queen of Heaven and Earth. She guided all growth, and especially loved lovers and art. Beauty and Heart. She was later called Ishtar, Isis, Cybele, Inanna, Aphrodite, Yemaya. She was not shy.

My vulva, the horn.
The Boat of Heaven
Is full of eagerness like the moon
My untilled land lies fallow

As for me, Inanna,
Who will plow my vulva?
Who will plow my high field?
Who will plow my wet ground?

As for me, the young woman,
Who will plow my vulva?
Who will station the ox there?
Who will plow my vulva?
  —Text inscribed on a clay tablet, Sumeria 2000 B.C.

Sex, especially as experienced by women, has been all but universally invoked in myth and ritual as symbolic of the primary force of life. Sex as energy. Sex as creation. Sex as abundance. Sex as unification. Sex as divine spirit. Sex as celebration. Sex as sympathetic magic.

The Iroquois used to celebrate a Naked Dance during which a woman and a man would couple in the fields in order to encourage good growth of the crops. This same "heathen" practice of spilling the seed was still observed at festivals of tilling, sowing and harvest in peasant Europe until the end of the nineteenth century. Pagan Norsemen sang songs and danced dances for fertility which the Christians denigrated as "female gyrations." Sexual licentiousness was central to the harvest celebrations of the Bantu and Badago of Africa. One missionary wrote, "It is impossible to witness them without being ashamed. Men and women, who in ordinary circumstances are modest in behavior and speech then abandon themselves."

Symbolic sex is performed by kachina dancers in Hopi ceremonials as a sacred gesture to urge abundance from the Earth. Like bumble bees buzzing around the honey pot which sweetens and nourishes life, the dancers approach each of the women spectators, one by one, until they had mimicked cosmic copulation with them all. The first whites to witness these dances were exceedingly shocked and so the People learned to be discreet. One Hopi man who served as an informant for anthropologists, ultimately, laughingly confessed that he "knew whites can see more sin than pleasure in sex so I edited the old Hopi stories."

Hunting and gathering societies also celebrated a sexual union with nature. The married women of the Cheyenne and Mandan of the Great Plains practiced a rite called "Intercourse with the Buffalo." The elder men of the tribe, wearing buffalo robes, impersonated the Great Bison and shared sexual relations with the young wives of all of the hunters. In this way, power was trance-ferred from the Great Spirit, through the old men to the women who would then offer it to their husbands, upon whom the people depended for food. The hunters, the chief providers, would then pass the energy back to the people with the kill.

> I am as Red, as beautiful as the Rainbow.
> Your heart has just been taken by me.
> Your blood has been taken by me.
> Your flesh has been taken by me.
> Your eyes have been taken by me.
> Your saliva has been taken by me.
> Your saliva and mine are one forever.
> You are a Wizard!
> —Cherokee Song to Fix the Affections

The peoples of old Ireland and India, too, re-enacted mythical intercourse between a mortal and the animal spirit which represents the divine. In India, the Queen engaged in simulated sex with a dead stallion, lying on the ground with him, entwining her legs with his. In this way she was able to transmit energy to her husband. Writings from the turn of the Thirteenth Century attest to the practice of the Celtic kings copulating with a mare, who was then killed, butchered and cooked in a soup. This, the king consumed in order to partake of the power, the energizing principle of Epona, the Equine Goddess.

Sex has been an integral part of Indian religious life since the earliest of times. Hindus maintain that sex with any woman is the same as having sex with the Goddess Herself, since every woman embodies the principle of Shakti. In both Tantric Hinduism and Buddhism, sexual union is practiced as a means of obtaining spiritual ascendancy. Tantra employs methods of meditation, yogic (yonic) exercises, and breathing through which the human couple can ritually become the divine couple, Siva and His consort, Shakti, the source of the female energy of being without which even the god is powerless.

Men are exhausted by orgasm. Each one prostrating them to the point that the male orgasm is frequently referred to cross-culturally as "a small death," *Un petit mort*. Women are, however, capable of achieving multiple orgasms which serve to strengthen them. In Tantra as well as Taoism, man is cautioned to hold back his climax, to recycle, as it were, his sperm. To direct its flow not out of his body, which is debilitating, but rather, back up his spine to the top of his head where it can serve to elevate his spirit. Like a space capsule which hooks up to the mother ship for refueling while in orbit, the feeble male fuses with the female to tap into her indefatigably endless energy.

Sufis and other Middle Eastern mystics follow a similar system in which it is understood that in order for a man to reach enlightenment it is essential that he consort with a *fravashi*, a mystical lady-love. In Greece, similar Tantric techniques were taught in the temples of Venus by Her harlot-priestesses, the *venerii*, sacred prostitutes who also offered spiritual sexual healing. When soldiers returned from war ill of heart from all that they had just seen and done, they were sent to the temple's chambers of recuperative, life-affirming sensuality. Ovid, a devout initiate, wanted to die while making love. "Let me go in the act of coming to Venus, in more senses than one let my last dying be done."

An Orthodox Jewish man who aspires to study the holy *Kabbalah* must first be married with intimate knowledge and experience of woman before he is permitted access to these mystical secrets. The Hebrew word, *hor,* referring to Astarte's Yoni or Sacred Vulva, meant the "hole," "cave" or "pit" filled with water which was found in the inner sanctum of Her temple. Men dived into this pool as if in symbolic intercourse with the goddess, Herself, in order to achieve a spiritual cleansing and enlightenment. The Roman, Alma Mater, "Soul Mother," was a teacher-priestess who instructed matriculating students in the philosophy, the art of love; the love of learning, of philosophy. Her symbol was the cowry shell, *matriculus.*

Sex is also seen as a salve against the solitary confinement of the soul, the painful sense of separation we humans tend to suffer. Through sexual exchange we can, for a moment, experience the ultimate unity. Australian aborigines and certain tribes in Borneo celebrate collective sexual rituals in order to insure a positive communal connection with the primordial universal perfection.

The Romans celebrated the sacred sexual frenzy (*febris,* in Latin) of the Goddess of amorous love, Juno Februa, on February 14, coinciding with the time when the birds in Italy were thought to mate. These orgiastic rites of the Patroness of Passionate Love merged with Lupercalia, the festivities in honor of the pagan god, Pan which were observed on the following day, February 15. On Lupercalia, (named incidentally in honor of the she-wolf who suckled Romulus and Remus), men and women inscribed their names on love notes or billets and then drew lots to determine who their sex partner would be during this festival of erotic games.

At last love has come. I would be more
ashamed to hide it in cloth than leave it
naked. I prayed to the Muse and won. Venus
dropped him in my arms, doing for me what
she had promised. Let my joy be told, let
those who have none tell it in a story.
Personally, I would never send off words
in sealed tablets for none to read.
I delight in sinning and hate to compose a
mask for gossip. We met. We are both worthy.
   —Sulpicia

Lupercalia, which combined elements of worship of Juno Februa and Her Northern equivalent, the Norse goddess Sjofn, was the original Valentine's Day. Naturally, the fathers of the early Christian Church outlawed its observance as lewd and heathenish. However, they were quite unable to halt the practice. Eventually it was necessary to create a sainted martyr whose feast day would be observed on February 14th. In this way, the Church could sanction a celebration that it simply could not suppress. There are, depending on the source, anywhere from three to eight Saint Valentines. Each has a conflicting biography concocted by a different author. But in every version he emerges as the patron of lovers, bowing to the original intention of the occasion.

The symbols of Lupercalia come down to us intact, but thoroughly cleansed, completely abstracted from their original flesh and blood intensity. The cute little chubby Valentine angel, so familiar to us, is an insipid and impoverished characterization of Cupid, the Roman equivalent of the Greek god Eros, the Hindu Kama. He was the son of the Roman Venus and Mercury, or their Greek counterparts Aphrodite and Hermes. S/he was, thus, a Herm-Aphrodite, an embodiment of the duality and opposition of the sexual union. The arrows that Cupid shoots are the phallus, the lingham. These projectiles of passion are often depicted as piercing the heart. The heart, the center of the soul. A bittersweet image which intimates that love hurts. A graphic image of penetration which is reminiscent of the arrows that Hopi's shoot into rounded bundles of corn as a ceremonial gesture of fertility.

But why shoot a phallus into a heart? Doesn't it fit better somewhere else? Somewhere a bit lower? And just what is this heart-shaped symbol supposed to signify, anyway? Certainly it bears no resemblance whatsoever to an anatomically correct actual heart. The zoologist, Desmond Morris speculates that the heart symbol represents a bending over buttocks. A form that is reminiscent of the sexual habits of our ancestor kissing cousins, the apes, who do it from behind. *Please!* Spare me.

The horizontal-double-dip-cone-of-a-shape that we call a heart *has* to be two round breasts riding proudly above the magical fertile triangle of love. A full-figured female torso just like that of the Venus of Willendorf. The tits, hips and lips of the late Great Mother Earth, Herself. The venerated love of our lives

Let Her never be out of our hearts.
My heart, my mother;
My heart, my mother!
My heart of transformations.
    —The Egyptian Book of the Dead

Terra Mater

Mama Donna Henes, Urban Shaman

In the beginning, there was woman. And she was versatile. She breathed, she stretched, she strode, she sat, she foraged, she trapped, she planted, she cooked, she ate, she bled, she danced, she laughed, she slept, she dreamed, she played, she prayed. She made art, she made ceremonies, she made love, she made babies. Our modern minds automatically make a connection between these last two activities. But this is only a relatively recent conception, if you'll pardon my pun.

Woman, like the female of every species, produces young. And she appears to do so without any particular help. Parthenogenic. Of course, we now know that this feat is accomplished with a certain modest participation by the male, but the outcome of copulation was not always apparent. What *was* perfectly clear and obvious, was that she was somehow able to fashion from herself the stuff of life. To bear from her own blood and body a new generation. And, as if that wasn't wondrous enough, she could also manufacture the substance of sustenance so that she could continue to nurture her consummate creations.

She was prolific, capable of repeating the entire miraculous process again and again. In fact it was—and still is in large parts of the world today—quite common for a woman to wean one child only to immediately conceive the next. Our own grandparents commonly came from families with eight, ten, twelve children. Mme. Vassilet, a nineteenth century Russian peasant is the undefeated record holder in the World Fertility Cup. It is well documented that her twenty-seven full-term pregnancies produced sixty-nine children, most of who grew to adulthood. She gave birth to sixteen pairs of twins, seven sets of triplets and four sets of quadruplets. Mother Vassilet was well known in her time and was honored at the imperial court of Czar Alexander II.

Who includes diversity and is nature,
Who is the amplitude of the earth, and
the coarseness and sexuality of
the earth, and the great charity
of the earth, and the equilibrium also . . .
　　—Walt Whitman

Is this not the way of Nature Herself? Does She not constantly produce and provide? Reproduce and recycle? Engender and embrace? The Earth is alive with the fruit of Her fecundity. Inconceivable multitudes of animals, vegetables and minerals. There are more than a million species of animals, 4,000 species of mammals alone. There are more than 350,000 species of plants, 100,000 species of fungi, 100,000 species of protista (algae and the like) and 10,000 species of monera, including bacteria. Each species made up of how many families, how many individuals?

Nature, then, *must* be female. Mother Nature, Mother Earth. Father Earth was a nearly nonexistent concept and has forever remained so. The only exception that I have ever discovered is the ancient Egyptian concept of a male Earth named Geb. Herodotus wrote that all of the known names for the Earth were female. "Nature is our mother," the Latin proverb proclaims. The Gypsies say, "The Earth is our mother . . . the secret of life comes from the ground." Asase Ya is the Earth Mother of the African Ashanti. They tell, "We got everything from Asase Ya, food, water: we rest upon Her when we die."

I stand on the earth
and my body like a plant
absorbs wind, sun, and water
to stay alive.
　　—Forough Farrokhzad

Earth and woman share a correspondence of function, a facility for creativity and abundance, a worldly wisdom. Each is primary and potent. Even in appearance, they are the same. Just as the roundness of the Earth and Her cyclical seasons resonate in every woman, the surface shapes and internal configurations of the Earth are defined by the physical attributes of the female physique.

The soil, smoothly moist and rich, arid, cracked and parched, is Her skin; and the lush foliage, the fuzzy moss, the spindled grasses, are Her many splendid tresses. The trees are arms, legs, limbs, which reach out and dance in all directions. The roots, feet firm on the ground. Gems and crystalline minerals make Her strong skeletal system; and the rivers, creeks and streams are the blood which flows through Her veins. The air is Her hot breath, Her holy exhalation. The seeds of plants are Her sacred monthly flow. Her pregnant belly is indicated in the rounded hills and Her mountainous breasts swell all the way to the sky. The valleys reflect the soft shapes of Her cradling elbows and comforting lap. The ocean is Her womb, the saline-rich source of all life. Rock clefts, like labia, and vulvic caves are passageways into Her cavernous interior; the power of Her hallowed deep places, palpable.

Mother Earth, Mother Nature, has Her moods as well as any woman might. Her emotions, like the weather, are mutable and span the full spectrum. She rainbow-glows, radiant in health and beauty. She twinkles like the stars; sparkles with good humor. She grows overcast, gets dark, oblique, breezy and cool. She weeps with dew. She simmers and hisses on slow burn. She vents her steam. She quakes in anger. She rumbles and grumbles and tears the house down. She sparks, bursts, erupts, explodes, implodes in passion. She can be gentle, generous, humorous, dependable, destructive and very, very scary. Hell, indeed, hath no fury like an Earthy woman scorned.

Humankind in its infancy clung to the primal comprehension of a maternal Earth, in the same way that any completely dependent child hangs onto her mother's hip. The reality of our utter reliance incontrovertible, we held on for dear life. Until only five, six thousand years ago, the archetypal Great Mother, Creatrix of all existence, matriarch of the races of god/ desses, reigned supreme everywhere. Homer sang her praises, "I shall sing of Gaia, Universal Mother, firmly founded, Oldest of all the Holy Ones." Foremost in all early religions, She was personified and identified in many ways, but She was universally regarded with reverence and deference as a living mother.

Newborn on the naked sand
Nakedly lay it.
Next to the earth mother,
That it may know her;

Having good thoughts of her, the food giver.
—Grande Pueblo chant to be sung by the one who first takes
a baby from its mother.

Many creation myths describe how the Earth was made from Her sacred body. According to the Apaches, all creatures came from the Earth, "just like a child being born from its mother. The place of emergence is the womb of the Earth." Asintmah, the first woman of the Athapascan peoples of Western Canada and Alaska, was midwife to Mother Earth. She wove Her a Great Blanket of Earth to use during Her confinement and laid it carefully across Her body. She then reached under this birthing blanket and pulled out a mouse, and then a rabbit, and then, one by one, She brought forth each of the Earth's vast multitude from the loins of the Great Mother.

Earth is often seen as an island floating in the vast sea, very much as an embryo is suspended in the womb. Falling Woman, the ancestress of the Iroquoian tribes of the northeastern portion of North America, was said to have tumbled out of the watery sky into the waters below. Otter, beaver, muskrat and sea bird pulled soil up from under the water to create a mound to soften Her fall and to serve as a solid, dry place between the liquid sky and the wet depths for Her to stand upon. The body of the Sumerian-Babylonian Earth Mother, Tiamat, also defined the division between the watery realms above and below, like a horizon differentiates the heaven from the deep blue sea. Her title, Dia Mater, "Goddess Mother," gives us the word, "diameter," the dividing line which stretches across the center of a circle.

Other myths relate how clay, the flesh of the fertile Earth, is shaped by The Goddess into living beings of skin and bone and breath, blood and brain and flesh. Another version of the Iroquois creation story is that in which the Great Turtle tosses the mud off of Her back to create the Earth and all that lives on Her. As She shimmies, shakes, and shrugs, each clod creates a different species of creature. The Shake Dance is still danced by women in ceremony and at pow-wow gatherings. It is a deliciously, sinuous rendering of the subterranean rhythms of that great grandmother terrapin and a sensuous celebration of the great landmass which She created, Turtle Island.

The Shilluk people of the Sudan tell of the divine Juok who fashioned people from earth. The white people were made from white loam and the Arabs were made of brownish soil. The black people were made of the finest and best earth, which is the fertile black clay from the banks of the Nile. The Ewe of Togo say that good people are created from good clay and bad people are made out of stinking mud. The Efe of the Zaire forest relate that God formed Baatsi, the first man, out of loam, which He kneaded into shape, covered in skin and filled with blood. The creator of the Dogon of Mali is Amma who created the sun and moon out of clay pots decorated with copper and brass, and then created the Earth from clay in the shape of a reclining female figure. Her head faces north, Her feet, south. Her mons veneris is an anthill and Her clitoris is a termite hill.

> . . . His earth, one handful
> His earth, the size of an egg.
> He shaped it like the figure of an ancestor,
> He shaped it in the form of a child,
> His earth, one handful,
> His earth, the size of an egg . . .
> —Traditional Indonesian Nias Creation Song

The Mesopotamian Goddess, Aramaiti was known as, "Mother of the People Made of Clay." Aruru was the Potter who not only fashioned figures from clay, but also breathed into them the animating energy of the universe. The Assyrian Goddess, Mami, "Mother," formed the first seven pairs of people, the original male and female fashioned from clay. The Sumerian, Ninhursay, created the human race from a mixture of clay from Her own body and Her menstrual blood. This clay-converted-into-flesh myth cycle eventually culminated in the ass-backward biblical tale of God creating Adam from clay and then creating Eve from out of Adam's body.

The biblical name, Eve, means "Mother of All Living." Her name is derived from those of much older Earth Mothers. In India, she was known as Jiva or Ieva, "The Creatress of all Manifested Forms." A Tantric appellation was Adita Eva, the "Very Beginning." The Hittites knew her as Hawwah, "Life," the Persians called her Hvov, the "Earth," and the Anatolians named her Hebat, "Virgin Mother Earth." Adamah, the original feminine form of Adam, means "bloody clay," although male scholars usually refer to this generative element as "red earth." Hmmmm. Eve means something like, "Mother Earth the Creator" and Adam means,

"Made from Earth." So I ask you, *who* gave birth to *whom?* And *who*—if you please, Doctor Freud—is envious of *what?*

Clay was also used by human women to fashion figures, facsimiles of themselves, which they blessed with their own life's blood. These were sympathetic magical totems used when petitioning for fertility, for safe child bearing and birthing, for much milk. These feminine effigies were made and employed by European women well into the Middle Ages when the Church began to interpret them as unholy charms assumed to be used in witchcraft for the casting of spells and worship of the devil. During the Inquisition, it was, needless to say, not cool to be caught with one.

> (clay) that stuff of the earth, which
> we work with, talk with, identify with
> and create with. It is so much a part of
> us that the same Tewa word, *nung,* is
> used for both earth (clay) and us (people).
> I have a daughter who is a clay person out
> of whom other clay people emerge.
> —Rina Swentzell, Santa Clara Pueblo

Women, who were the gatherers, the agriculturists, the inventors, the homemakers, learned to shape clay vessels in which to collect, carry, store, mix, dye, cook and serve the offerings of the all-nourishing Great Nature Mother. These, too, they created in their own images. The first bowl, according to Greek tradition, was modeled from Aphrodite's abundant breast. Zuni women have always made pitchers in the shape of female breasts. The nipple is left open until the pot is complete. And then, with great ceremony it is sealed, thus ensuring that the maker, human woman's womb-vessels be richly filled as well. The archetype of the nourishing mother shows up in the form of repeated breast motifs on Peruvian and Old European jars.

A patriarchal twist on the theme of the uterine vessel is the tale of Pandora by Hesiod, an anti-feminist fable, which blames women for all the evils of the world. Pandora, who was made of clay, was originally an aspect of the Earth Goddess Rhea, called, "All Giver." She carried a *pithos,* an earthen honey pot, a womb-like symbol of plenty similar to the cornucopia, from which she poured Her abundant sweet blessings. But according to Hesiod, Zeus sent Her to Earth to punish men who displeased Him by allowing all sorts of doom and devastation to spill from Her jar. In the sixteenth century, Erasmus mis-translated *pithos* as *pyxis*, which changed its meaning from "vase" to "box." Pandora's box, like Eve's apple, is the feminine source of all sorrows. "Box," of course, has come to refer, rather crudely, to the female center of pleasure and power—her syrupy honey pot!

> The women say, truly is this not magnificent?
> The vessels are upright, the vessels have acquired
> legs. The sacred vessels are on the move.
> —Monique Wittig

Clay, adobe, sand, soil, loam, loess, mud, peat, dirt, dust, the multi-paletted, richly-hued flesh of Mother Earth Herself, was considered to be a sacred substance, a sacrament to be used in blessings and prayers. The ancient Greeks used to place a lump of dirt on their head to seal an oath, rather like placing their hand on a bible and swearing to tell the truth, the whole truth and nothing but the truth, so help me God. Russian farmers continued this practice into the twentieth century, making any promise in the honored name of Mati-Syra-Zemlya, "Moist Mother Earth."

The clean, strong spirit of Mother Earth infuses the players of capoeira Angola, an African martial art popular in Brazil, with a pure and righteous energy, which would make any mother proud. They fight with just their feet and heads, as their hands are traditionally reserved for constructive use only. Throughout the match, they reach down to the Earth repeatedly and touch soil to their foreheads and chests in a gesture of self-blessing. In this game, as the practitioners call it, getting thrown to the ground is not a sign of weakness and defeat. Unlike wrestling or boxing, being down is not the same as being out. It is, rather, a chance to check in with the Earth Mother and draw from Her the power of all the ancestors and spirit animals who are buried in Her body.

People seem always to have used mineral pigment as make up to decorate their bodies and those of their prized animals as well, in preparation for ritual and celebration. Wet clay was also commonly applied to the hair of both in order to create ornately coifed headdresses suitable for ceremony, pomp, and spectacle. There is a universally placed importance on being painted, powdered, primped and purified for any personal encounter with the divine presence. It seems fitting, since Mother Earth surrounds us with such great beauty, that we return the favor in kind—offer nature a pretty face to peer upon. Mud baths and clay facials are still widely employed in pursuit of beauty and well-being.

Dirt is sometimes ingested for its health-giving properties; craved, consumed like mother's milk for what ails you. Chimayo, New Mexico is the site of a healing well which is filled not with water, but earth. Known to possess curative powers, the sanctified soil has long been held holy, first by the Pueblo peoples of the desert and then, centuries later by the Spanish Catholic conquistadors. Today it is a popular pilgrimage destination for Latinos, Native Americans and Anglos alike, who travel from far, often on foot, sometimes on knee, to take dirt from the miraculously ever-full hole in the ground. The diminutive sanctuary is overflowing with evidence of its efficacy—crutches and canes, walkers and eye glasses, pill bottles and trusses have been left behind in relieved gratitude by those who have been healed. And, always remembering to say, "Thank you," the faithful offer gifts of flowers, candles, amulets, charms, *milagros*, letters, and hand-painted tin *retablos* to sainted Mother Earth in Her guise as Our Lady of Guadalupe.

Mother Earth, universally worshipped as the fertile, female provider, protector and parent, was always treated with great dignity and care. Cultivated fields were left to rest one year in seven lest they become worn out with the never ending work of producing food, and wars were routinely put on hold during the planting season. Woman was cherished as the incarnate daughter of the Great Cosmic Queen, because she embodied the same supreme capability of life. Her natural understanding was held in esteem, and her body, its terrestrial contours reminiscent of those of Mother Earth, was respected. Once upon a time, that is.

A rather bizarre form of pornography, known as pornotopia, was produced during the Victorian period in England. Mother Earth was personified as a voluptuous female landscape laid bare to the voyeuristic viewing pleasure of man who surveys the scene before him from the perspective of a fly promenading upon Her full-figured splendor. Her hills and caves, rises and recesses, were described in somewhat smarmy terms, which were meant to elicit the fascinating, fearsome, forbidden Oedipal fantasy of a man mounting his own mother in lust. Where in the past, the Earth had once been revered, She was here reviled, defiled, desecrated. Stripped bare of Her powers, She was reduced to a passive sexual object, sacked and soiled.

So, how in the world did "The Good Earth"—the very material (from the Latin, *mater*, meaning, "mother") of life itself—get to be a dirty word? Or "Mutha," for that matter? In English, "dirt" means "grime," "stain," "smut." "Dirty" is "lewd," "defiled," "contaminated," "dingy," "unsanitary," "filthy," "polluted," "foul." How did it come to pass that the Earth Mother whose grace we depend upon for absolutely everything has become so thoroughly sullied?

The body of the Earth, our first mother, is routinely bruised and abused. Raped and burned; dug and dammed; dynamited and nuked. As many as one hundred distinct species of plants and animals are disappearing from existence each day, directly or indirectly due to human domination. And the bodies of women everywhere fare no better.

Have we no shame? Like bad seed, humankind seems hell-bent on matricide.

Unless we *do* something about it. And, do something *now*.

Mother and Daughter/The Forest

Lindy Lyman

First finding these ceremonial dancers at my feet, I was moved by their inviolable wholeness, deep beauty, and royal grace under pressure. Original artwork, branch, paperclay, acrylic; 58" x 22" © 2005 Lindy Lyman; Photo by Marcia Ward, The Image Maker, Denver, CO.

Lotions, Potions and Solutions

Joanna Clapps-Herman

My mother, Rose, the most obedient person who ever lived, was brought up in a culture that controlled through shame. An Italian daughter learns the rules early. At 89 she still washed out her underwear every night by hand. Most nights of her adult life she sat at the kitchen table with files, papers and ledgers. She had notes and letters to write to friends and for business. "I don't know what I am going to do," she'd say. "I have so much work to get done." "Poor lost soul," my father would say and shake his head. She makes work for herself. No one else has all these papers. She had files with all her sales receipts, records of every financial transaction in her ledgers and a copy of every tax form she'd ever filed.

On the farm where she was born and raised her family spoke only the *Tolvese* dialect. It was only when her oldest sister Arcangela started school that she started to teach her brothers and sisters a few words of English. First born in Tolve, Arcangela was her mother's right hand, my mother, first born in America, was her father's. By seven Rosa was his business secretary.

"At night, after all our farm chores were done, milking the cows, collecting the eggs, gathering kindling, making dinner and cleaning up after, sweeping the kitchen floor, he would sit me down at the kitchen table and dictate letters to me in Italian and I would have to put them into English. But I had only been in school a couple of years when I started to help him with his letters and books . . . in this childish handwriting. Who knows what I wrote? What did I know? Can you imagine what those people must have thought getting those letters?" From then on she kept his books, kept track of his banking, paid his bills, kept receipts, account books, and wrote his business correspondence. So she knew how to keep records. All accounts were in order. Caught between the inchoate, pride-and-shame-driven ancient world of the pig farm and being their official face to America, my mother became lettered in every possible kind of accounting: records, rules, regulations, codes, customs and judgments. Until she went blind in her nineties she read all the fine print on every bill, letter or advertisement that came in the mail. She knew what they said, what her obligations, duties and responsibilities were. What the obligations of others were.

She had a greater investment in keeping the law than Moses. And she made herself responsible for all them. Herself and us. Especially every breach, break, violation, betrayal, rupture, every transgression. She kept track. Counted all the wrongs.

"Can you imagine? I was going round the neighborhood to collect for the church. And she comes to the door and says, 'Oh, hi, Rose.' And we stand there talking. And she doesn't ask me in. She gave me a dollar, which was very nice of her, but really. She didn't even ask me in and ask me to sit down for a minute. Offer me a glass of water, nothing. What a pill." Our word for almost anything for which we have contempt is *'merican*. Because this is what *'mericans* were like. They're *scustamade*, rude, without custom, without manners. They don't know the proper way of doing things. My mother did. She was a clear and definite judge of things.

My mother and I were walking down the street one day in downtown, the center of Waterbury's business and social world. It has the charm of citizens conducting their public lives naturally and with pleasure in their home country. As we were walking, my mother noticed someone she knew coming toward us. "She's looking away, pretending she doesn't know me. Don't ever do that. If you know someone, always say hello. People get odd sometimes, they turn their heads away. I don't know why. But you don't do that. You don't have to stop, just say hello."

"Hello, Marie," she called to the woman passing us on the street. The woman feigned having just noticed my mother, who flashed this woman her dazzling certain smile; the woman's face lit up when she saw my mother's smile and she smiled back just as brightly. The simplicity and rightness of that advice pleased. A deeply rule-bound woman, sometimes she was just right.

Just as when she made up this aphorism when someone chastised her for breaking a dish while she was washing up after dinner at their house. "Hey, I wanted to say to them," she told me later, "the one who washes the dishes is the one who breaks them." Right again.

My mother wasn't brought up in the Church—her *anarchico Papa* hated the Church for calling in loans against seed money. When crops failed in Basilicata, they'd confiscate the peasant's land. But his loathing was sealed here in America.

My mother told me: "In those days they didn't have the babies baptized right away. You waited a while and maybe they'd take a couple of the children at once. Then when that terrible accident happened and the baby died, when Papa went to make arrangements for the Mass, Father Scoglio said that he couldn't bring the baby into the church for Mass because he wasn't baptized. My brother was only two years old. That was an awful slap in the face. You have all this pain that you're going through and then Father Scoglio says that to you. After that we were not allowed to go near a church."

But, as my mother and her sisters grew up they were embarrassed, ashamed really, not to have been brought up in the Church. After family, it was an important location of right and wrong, sins and blessings, goodness and badness. When my mother fell in love with my father, she snuck off to take catechism classes to be baptized and confirmed. She didn't know my father was "no churchgoer."

Joining the Church was inevitable, since in every way my mother was a religious zealot—every rule-mandating system was for her. Only loosely at first, then more and more over the course of her lifetime, being Catholic became important to my mother. It was always a part of my sister's and my life.

But, the Church was no match for her. She drew on all systems of rules, regimes, and beliefs. Her deepest beliefs went far beyond the Church or even religion. Her sense of how things should go was far wider and deeper than a system like the Church or even the absolutes of our Italian culture.

She believed there was a prayer for every occasion. If not a prayer, there was a saying. If not a prayer or a saying, then a remedy. If not a prayer, saying or remedy, then a vitamin. "If you have a cold you drink a cup of hot water, two teaspoons of apple cider vinegar and honey, every few hours and before bed. Your cold will go away immediately and it makes you lose weight too. Apply vinegar to your varicose veins to shrink them. Warts, rub with castor oil—twenty times or so. Rub with vitamin A too. For asthma apply one tablespoon of corn oil to eyelids at bedtime.

"For high blood pressure, paprika and honey at every meal. If you get ridges in your finger nails you should eat more Jello or mix Knox Gelatin everyday in a glass of juice. It's good for your nails and hair.

"Vaseline is good for everything. My mother used it for everything that hurt her. I use it on my face at night sometimes. I rotate.

"If you have a water ring on a table from a glass, rub it with mayonnaise and ashes from a cigarette."

If not a prayer, a saying, a vitamin or a remedy, then *the truth*. "All babies know everything when they're born. They just forget it as they grow up. What a shame. They know everything. Look into their eyes and you can see it. You just keep an eye on them." Then a big sigh, "It's such a shame we have to lose all that.

"All children choose their parents. They decide who they want to be born to. So I want to say thank you for choosing me to be your mother," a solemn, even formal look on her good girl face.

Rosa Rosette, her mother called her when she was annoyed with her. My father called her Sugar Lump the night they met, then Rosy, Rosy Baby, Rambling Rose, Gram Baby, Che Billettz, Billetz, finally Billy. Sometimes I think the world would have been better off with her in charge. Rose by whatever name, my mother knew how things should go.

Kiss the bed, *baci' u letz*, before you leave the house, so you'll be sure you'll come back. When I protested her insistence that I should put paprika in everything I cook: "All right, don't! Get sick! See if I care." Most of her friends saw her as generous, beneficent. She would have made a terrific goddess. They also thought she was modern. I found her ways absolute and exhausting. She could have been a queen, she was so comfortable with an edict: "Take that off. You can't wear that to a wedding. You have to call Mrs. M. and make a time to visit her. Did you write to Mrs. Perugini yet?" Maybe a judge.

By middle age my mother went to church regularly, with us and without us. My mother's involvement with psychics and Edgar Cayce increased, too. Her vitamin regime and all of her systems of potions and solutions were on the rise. She never went anywhere without her copper bracelet for her arthritis. When she wanted to affect the outcome of the future she went on a complete regime of fasting and prayers. She might have made a decent Wise Woman with her potions and solutions.

"I'm not eating any sweets for six months," she'd announce airily at the daily coffee klatch she had with her sisters every afternoon before their husbands came home from work. "It worked that time I prayed for Gilda and her heart. I didn't eat any chocolate for a year that time. And I did a novena every night too."

She knew her own power, too. "You know, the other day I really concentrated and I made the clouds go away. I just kept looking at them and really worked at it. And they finally just drifted away."

But her limits, too. More and more, she spent much of her day praying for her children, her nieces, nephews, eventually for grandchildren and her sons-in-laws. "Even when he's sleeping, I can't get through to him."

"What do you mean, Mom?" I was on the phone with her. We were discussing a particularly difficult case for my mother: my sister's husband, John. "Well, you know I pray for all of you at night, when you're asleep. And I think that if you're asleep you hear me better; my prayers can get to you. I've been praying for John Mudd. Even when he's sleeping, I can't get through to him. Maybe because he is Protestant. What are you going to do?"

Once she visited my husband, son, and me while we were living in Paris and she spent most of the time writing postcards to her family and friends. This went on for days and days, buying postcards, going to the post office, getting more stamps. She was driven to fulfill this duty—to each person, she owed a postcard. Finally, one day she said, "All I really want to say is, 'Ha ha, I'm in Paris and you're not.'"

When she died, my sister and I went through all of her files and boxes of papers. An epic archive:

All tax files. Bank books. Nine address books.

All the photograph albums of all the pictures she ever took.

Her grammar school autograph book from 1926-27, where the school yell is recorded as "rah, rah," and with sayings like the following: "When you're in the kitchen drinking tea, burn your lips and think of me." And, "I wish you luck, I wish you joy, I wish you first a baby boy, and when his hair begins to curl I wish you then a baby girl. Yours till the moon shines green." A daring one: "Here's to us, I wish us well and all the rest can go to ____."

My father's pension benefit book going back to 1937 when he was an apprentice ironworker.

A receipt from The Aluminum Cooking Utensil Company dated 9\10\40 for $53.48 for all the pots and pans she bought just before she got married. Also the payment book from Metropolitan Furniture for a houseful of furniture, lamps, and rugs she bought to furnish their first "rent" at 334 Oak Street. In addition, this includes one carpet sweeper and one percolator. The "free" rocking chair she later nursed us in was "thrown in" as a gift from the salesman. The payment book is marked paid off, January 15, 1942.

Many notebooks: On the front page of one of her notebooks in her handwriting is written:

"You shall give an account of every word that is spoken."

Tiny travel notebooks which mentioned time of arrival at each hotel, every meal they ate, every sight they saw, every outfit she wore every day of any trip, including which shoes, jewelry, gloves and pocketbook. The jokes they told on the bus.

A recipe-like file box full of home remedies filed both alphabetically and by organ:

Under *cold sore*: rub with burnt toast. *Infection*: brown soap and sugar. *Mumps*: hemp cut up, egg white, wrap in cloth, apply to affected parts. *Bee or wasp bite*: sliced raw onion, apply.

Under *heart*: carry currants and raisins in pocket and chew slowly while working. Chew tops of rosemary first thing in the morning after breakfast.

A draft of a letter to Wayne Newton complaining because he cancelled a performance on a trip they had booked to Missouri: "You are our favorite performer." The brochure doesn't state in the fine print that this could happen. She signs it, "Two disappointed fans. Anyway we can enjoy your tapes."

She was a dutiful daughter, she was passionately in love with my father, but she was born to be a grandmother—she loved her grandchildren with a joy that made her love pure and complete. She had every single card, drawing, letter she ever got from them. She wrote down every cute thing they ever said. One notebook for each of them. She had their sizes documented through their growing up so that she could buy them the right presents.

She could have worked for the Catholic Review Board: what's acceptable for movies and television. She was watching her soaps one day when she complained to me, "These women, you put them on TV and they all become sluts," she throws up her hands in disgust watching *All My Children*.

"Just leave," she squealed at the TV, "Go! *Chiesta ca*, this one here is taking off all her clothes and drinking tequila and she's trying to seduce him, and he's saying, 'No, no, no,' but he's not leaving the room." She sighs and rests her tired head on her fingertips. She doesn't know what to do. "What's wrong with people?"

As she got older and she started to become legally blind, her hand writing deteriorated, the letters becoming large, rough and crude. Since she couldn't read anymore and it became harder and harder for her to watch television, she began to keep a new notebook, this one of homonyms, "To keep my mind busy." Ate, eight, ail, ale, all, awl, be, bee, buy, bye, berry, bury.

She sent in her weekly contributions to St. Leo's parish until she died at 94, even though by 86 she couldn't drive and eventually was afraid to even leave her apartment. She watched Mass on television, prayed for all of us and sent in her money. And made the sign of the cross over every plate of the food she re-heated in the microwave. Hers was a clear and moral world. And a dangerous one. If you didn't say the right prayer, if you didn't take your vitamins or bring the right present when your hairdresser's daughter had a baby, if you didn't obey your parents' dictates even when they'd been dead for 30 years, who knew what might happen?

Toward the end of her life things, even taking her vitamins, began to wear her out. "I'm just fixing my vitamins," she sighed deeply. "I'd like to dump them all down the drain. Sometimes you're better off being a normal person." Things were changing a little.

Late in my mother's life, Lucia, a woman with a permanent light in her eyes, longing for a piece of our old world, returned to the church and sang in her choir. This was a couple of years before the pedophile scandals broke in Boston. Lucia and John live in Cambridge. When the scandal broke, her spiritual home changed. This was a devastating betrayal to the Catholic world. So it became a part of Lucia and her husband, John's life to stand in protest every Sunday outside the Cathedral of the Holy Cross in Boston on Sunday, with survivors bearing witness instead of going inside to attend Mass. The survivors were men and women who had once been among the most faithful Catholics, who had been raped and molested by priests when they were children and adolescents. One Sunday, when our mother was staying with them, they took her with them. She was going to wait in the van for them and say her prayers for her grandchildren.

Lucia and John were getting out of the van, when, as my mother told it, "Then it dawned on me. 'Hey, I'm sitting here. I want to tell the Cardinal *too*. *I* have something to say. Who do they think they are anyway?

To children!'" Her voice rose each time she told this to a high indignant plane. "These were children! Little children! Their lives are ruined."

So that day my somewhat bent, but clear-minded 89-year-old, Italian-American, Catholic mother descended from my sister's van with her walker: "I call it my chariot," she said and laughed when she told this story, and with John and Lucia at either side, she struggled over the mounds of snow, to stand in protest for the first time in her life. To disobey for the first time in her life.

"We should turn away from the Church and toward the Lord," she said to those she stood with wearing her STTOP button ("Speak Truth to Power"). She toddled along when they moved to the back of the church to man each of the corners of the intersection where Cardinal Law would have to pass in his sleek black car. "He said it was a sin, but it's a crime," said one protester. "It *is* a sin. And *it is* a crime," answered another. "It is a sin and it is a crime and it is heartbreaking," the chant went further. "It's shameful." Shame is something my mother knew something about.

Transformed into truth teller, lawgiver, my mother lifted her hands from her walker and rubbed one pointer finger along the other, first one, then the other, over and over, pointing toward Cardinal Law, showing her fellow protesters how to make sure someone knows, "that they should be ashamed." She said, "Shame, shame, shame. Shame on you!" In our family there is no greater humiliation you can visit on someone.

Cardinal Law ducked his head as he drove past the protesters. It felt good to be against Law. And he should be filled with dread—especially about arriving at the judgment table in heaven, because my mother will definitely be there, right next to God. She might be elbowing God out of the way. She's always been at ease with a judgment. She knows how things should go and she's kept a record. Law's on her list.

Psychic Arrangements

Joanna Clapps-Herman

My parents came in wonder upon each other on July 5th. They promised as long as they both shall live on July 5th. Death parted them on July 5th.

The first was chance, the second was planned and the last was a hospital screw-up, but repetition made it seem like destiny.

Both were born in the difficult, chaotic world of the southern Italian immigrants where everything depended on what had come before and was tied to that ancient rocky past. All of my family's blood was mixed and remixed there. If there was new blood it was brought by the newcomers like the Normans, the Angevins, Argonese. It wasn't a place from which anyone moved or changed.

Characterized by the abrupt mountains rising upward, these people brought with them to America their intense sense of the circumscribed, the insular, the isolated; they were rooted in the craggy mountainous towns where almost nothing has changed or is changeable. Therefore, everything is destiny.

My parents had the good fortune of falling in love at first sight with a romantic sweep on a summer night in 1935 in the Lakewood Park near my grandparent's farm in Waterbury, Connecticut. From that wild early love they made a good life, a solid devoted marriage, always the only person for each other. This good marriage included dancing in the kitchen after dinner when the radio was on, dirty dishes still on the table; necking on the couch in the evening while they read the newspaper, and furious battles, over money; over all the ordinary: "You're driving me crazy! Do you always have to take everything to the extreme?" Doors slamming, fury over ordinary things. But fighting and anger was an ordinary part of our lives; not quite what it means today. It was just the way we were. Not special, not a real indication of wrongness. It was part of the way we lived.

Both romantics by nature and inclination, their love story—meeting each other—falling in love, "keeping company," was the passionate heart of their otherwise decent, hardworking prosaic lives—it was the story that sustained them, the one that gave their adult lives an enhancing largeness, a mythic framing which put them in the movie of life, giving their lives glamour and meaning. It embedded them with a sense that the fates had bestowed blessings, when they had been raised to expect yelling and beatings.

They also had the luck of coming from very similar Italian-immigrant families; though they didn't know it when they met, their fathers had known each other for a long time. Both families had real tragedies at the center of their lives. Those tragedies and their fathers' despotic ways had led them as children to assume misery was what their futures held. Instead, the fates turned and delivered these two, young, gorgeous people wild love *and* their families' good wishes. They stayed in love all of the 60 years they had together and beyond that. Since for each of them the most important thing that ever happened in their lives was meeting and falling in love, an endless ritualistic recounting of "Don't worry about falling in love," they both said on many occasions to my sister, Lucia, and me as we came into adolescence. "When you're young you think love is not anything that will happen to you. It's just stuff that happens in the movies. Then one day you meet that other person and you're in love and that's it. There's no more discussion about it." They'd look at each other across the kitchen table, with a shrug of their shoulders, one hand lifted upward, the same way they might say, "We'll have to drive down to Jersey for the funeral." It just was.

Along with the terrible miseries and *miseria* of their family's lives, the fates gave my parents certain gifts. They lived in the circumscribed world of white ethnic working people where they knew everyone and everyone knew them. They carried themselves with the ease of belonging; both were talented at the small everyday interaction. Their glamorous looks also gave them a confident vitality and they were stars in their own world. Long after their generation had aged, a man came up to my mother and told her that when they all had been young, he would wait for them to come out of the Palace Theater, "You two were the best looking people in town. I'd wait to see you."

"Rose, Rosie Baby," my father would exclaim with pleasure, looking up from the newspaper, still surprised at his good luck all throughout their years.

"You were the prettiest girl at the dance, Rose, tonight," he repeated proudly, over and over. "Did you see that everyone wanted to dance with you? You know Johnny's always been in love with you. He never got over you."

"Oh, Peter," she'd say, embarrassed and delighted, and she'd shake her head laughing.

"That's true, you know, girls. He's still in love with your mother. Well everyone loves your mother. I mean you girls are pretty, but your mother, she was something so special. You can't believe how beautiful she was when I met her." He included us in his pride in her. How lucky he was to have found her.

When my parents were first married they lived in what was called a third floor rent. The top floor was always the cheapest rent in a wood frame house. Our rent had slanted ceilings, large airy rooms, nooks and a large walk-in pantry, as well as a front and back porch.

My mother had been trained all of her life for the job of making a home. But her parents' farm had been rude and rough, and she, who her mother said should have spent her life in a shop window, had been longing to make everything pretty—that was her true art. Now she had her own canvas. She made curtains out of bleached flour sacks, sewing ruffles on the bottom, rickrack on the ruffles. She turned a small barrel upside down and fitted a cushion in the top and made a skirt (with ruffle at the bottom) for the barrel and there was an extra seat in the house. She fussed and sewed and bleached and stitched with the joy of it being her own. There was a shelf in the kitchen with blue plaid oil cloth tacked carefully to the bottom with a set of blue plaid dishes on the shelf.

"Your mother loves to play house," my father said. "She's always playing." It was exactly this lovely ability to make a real and cozy cottage in the sky that finally made him feel he had found a harbor in the storm.

Which is why it was a perfect place for my father to bring his friends over to shoot craps. "Well," my mother would explain with the same certainty with which she told me not to pass by people I recognized on the street, "Your father never had a real home where he could bring his friends. I mean Grampa Clapps was always there with his cronies drinking and carrying on. Even though Mamanonna was there, it was more like the home of a bachelor. No place for a young man to bring his friends home. So, now this was his first home and I wanted him to have a place where his buddies could always come. You know all those years when he was young

328

he and his friends they shot craps on the streets, even when it got dark they shot craps under the street lamp, so when he had a home of his own I wanted him to make use of it."

My mother made sure there was a platter of cold cuts, lots of soda and coffee and a cake; then she'd leave so that they could have the house to themselves and she'd go to meet her sisters downtown to go to the movies. Sometimes they went shopping and, afterward, always they went out for "coffee and . . ."

Through all the years, probably preceding us and certainly all the years of our growing up, after dinner my parents always read the *Waterbury Republican* first at the kitchen table, sometimes on the front porch, and sometimes on the couch in the living room. If they were on the couch this often lead to one of them laying their head on the other one's lap or to their necking. They kissed and cuddled, say my father's hands to my mother's cheek.

Swirled into their destiny and the romantic quotidian were my mother's views of the supernatural. From her mother she inherited typical Southern Italian beliefs: dreams foretold the future, it is essential never to tempt the gods by talking about good fortune and that it was better to be rich in blood than money. *Meglio ricco di sanque e no di ore.*

My mother swept her mother's beliefs into the belief system of Hollywood—the best looking people are the virtuous ones, hard work always pays off—mixed those with Catholicism, psychic beliefs, both ancient and modern, and combined them with her personal system of prayer, vitamins, aphorisms, soap opera wisdom and certainty. She consulted many psychics, read many of Edgar Cayce's books, watched many television shows about psychics, clairvoyants, read stories in *Reader's Digest* about people with extrasensory perception. She found every word to be true: hers and theirs. At the core of her religious life was the god of her good fortune—that she and my father found each other, fell madly in love, married, and lived normally every after. My father found this ridiculous, hilarious and charming. "Isn't she wonderful?" he'd ask the room at large and laugh his fool head off, "Isn't she priceless?" whenever my mother declared her psychic beliefs.

"Put it in the air," she'd say. "If you want something, just put it in the air." There was never any question that if you put it in the air properly you would get what you wanted. She had.

If my father didn't agree with her about this, it never interfered with his love for her. "Rose, come and do tucky-tuck," he'd say after he retired, "I have to go and inspect the ceiling." That meant it was time for a nap. "Tell me I'm no bum," he'd say day after day, thrilled that he had her to play out each of these rituals with.

"You *are* a bum," she'd say, and they would both be delighted with these daily games.

When he got sick and was told he had six months to live—in fact, he had ten weeks—he didn't want to be away from her even for a few minutes. Once, when I insisted on going into a test with him because I was sure my mother wouldn't understand what the doctors were talking about and our decisions depended on what they said, he said over and over, "Go and get your mother. I'd like her to be here." Stupidly, I stuck with the practical and insisted that I stay that time with him.

As those last weeks passed, he'd say, "I'm just worried about your mother. How will she handle this?" That was the closest acknowledgment I ever heard from him about his diagnosis. For the rest, we weren't allowed to talk about it. Silence was so essential that I didn't dare say, "We'll take care of her." The rules were that he'd talk if he was allowed to put his thoughts into the air and we didn't address what he had put there.

July 5th made one more fateful appearance in their life together. He had esophageal cancer. His esophagus was so crowded with cancer that no food could pass through. So they put in a feeding tube in order to start treatment. My mother was sitting by my father's bed, shaving him, the morning after the feeding tube was implanted. Then his nurse came in and said in contempt, "He can shave himself." Shamed by this nurse, my father took the razor from my mother's hand and sang as he shaved himself, "They tried to tell us we're too young, too young to truly be in love." He sang through his last shave as he had sung through every shave of his adult life. He was in such pain that day he asked my sister if she could get him some heroin. "I mean it. I can't take this." He was septic from the feeding tube they had put in the day before. He was toxic in the post-op because his esophageal cancer had spread much further than anyone had figured out. He was strong from all the heavy work he had done as an iron worker, from all the biking he had done since he had retired. He was hours from dying.

But his nurse knew better. "You can shave yourself," she repeated her admonition for emphasis. It was July 5th.

As soon as my father died, it was very clear to my mother that he was keeping in close touch with her. One regular and frequent sign of my father's presence was that he turned lights on and off or set them blinking.

After my mother died, my sister and I found a notebook where she wrote about my father's contact with her from beyond. The first page states: I'm going to write about all the ways my Beloved Peter has kept in touch with us.

Death is the continuation of life—my mother wrote on page two of the notebook.

A typical note goes: *When we were at the wake, Peter I'm sure, put out the lights in the funeral parlor, the rest of the building was lit. Everyone felt that Peter was saying goodbye.*

Another note: *When we came home from Cambridge without our Beloved Peter the lights in the hallway were out. We were still together.*

These occurrences were added to the daily liturgical recitation. *Peter puts the light in the bathroom on and off. I thought I had to change the bulb but it went on fine. I was reading Talking to Heaven by Van Praugh, a book John bought me. Van Praugh says if you want to see a sign from a beloved ask for what you want. So when I said my prayers I asked Peter would he put the lights out in the bathroom when I got up during the night and sure enough they went on and off. I ran to where the light was and kissed the air and thanked Peter.*

I was talking to Vicki on the phone when the bulb in the chandelier went off and I said "I guess I have to change the bulb that just went out." Just as I was saying that it started to go off and on. I told her what happened to the light in the bathroom and it went on and off.

She said, "No Rose, that's Peter trying to get in touch with you. Don't change the bulb." I was so glad she said that. Again, thank you Peter.

Darn it, the next day didn't Terry (her cleaning woman, companion and friend) came along and tightened the bulb in its socket. I said, "Don't do that Terry. That's Peter talking to me." She went ahead anyway. Who asked her? Who does she think she is? What if he's trying to be in touch with me?"

One psychic book advised her: "Give yourself suggestions that you will have contact in the right time."

A few months after my father died, she consulted a new psychic who told her she had many relationships with my father in past lives.

This psychic could see that they had been soul mates for many centuries previously. They had lived many different lives together. My mother told me, "I was his husband in Persia, you know.

"I was his Navaho brother.

"I was one of seven women in his harem in Egypt. (I don't like that one so much).

"We had some hassles, but once we found each other, we were soul mates for eternity. Peter came along to restore my faith in love. I hadn't been appreciated before."

She mourned my father with the same intensity that she loved him in life. She looked for all the signs that he was still with her. That he still loved her.

But as time went on, she began to be afraid that she was holding him back from a higher plane where he belonged. Again in her note book: *I don't want to stop your growth. I don't want to stop your growth but I would like to have contact with you. That is going to help my healing process,* she wrote in the book.

She slept with one of his undershirts close to her face as she said her prayers for all of us each night. She told me that she said this prayer: *May I have contact in the right way at the right time with my beloved Peter.* All of these rituals helped her keep my father near her for ten years until her memory began to fade from dementia.

At the end of her life, my sister and I spent long hours with her in her apartment at an assisted living facility. She had become afraid to walk down the hall to the dining room or even to leave her apartment at all. She'd open her door and say, "What's out there? Those streets out there (the hallway outside her door) scare me. You never know who's going to come along. I don't want to go out there." She took the route that dementia takes—"Do you know where my bedroom is? Are you sure? Can you help me find it when the time is right? I'll just stay here on the bench (her couch)." Our hours were as they are at this stage of life, filled with repetitions and a need to fill the air with connection and talk. If she lay down on her couch for a while and closed her eyes, she quickly became aware of the silence around her and would sit up abruptly. "Where is everyone? Where did everyone go?" She had grown up in a noisy, chaotic, but always peopled world. Quiet wasn't a normal environment to her.

When she met my father she found a man she loved, who loved her. In him she also found the possibility of making the world more like the one she had longed for when she was a frightened Italian girl trying to please her parents and wishing she lived "in a shop window," as her mother said about her.

One day, hoping to revive a favorite piece of her life for her, I asked, "What was the most important thing that you remember happening in your life?"

"Well, falling in love with whoever it was I fell in love with. When I fell in love.

You know, I was young, and a lot of young men wanted to marry me. But I didn't feel anything for them at all. And I thought I'm never going to find anyone. But then this handsome young man came along; he was the only thing I cared about.

"And I was so glad to be in love with him. I wonder, did I ever turn out to marry him? I felt as if I had been waiting my whole life for this person to come along and that now that I had found him it changed my life forever. I finally fell in love."

"What do you remember about meeting him?" I asked her, waiting for the Lakewood Park, July 4th weekend recitation.

"I remember . . . ," she started to say, but the story she had told over and over all her life as if to reassure herself that it had actually happened to her—that she had been that pretty young woman the handsome stranger followed out of the park, that she had been that fortunate, that she had won the love of that handsome stranger who turned out to be a *paesan'*, that their love had sustained them both for all those years, even beyond his death—had disappeared now.

"It must have been my husband, I guess," she said. "I suppose it must have been my husband."

"It was Dad, Mom. It was Peter Clapps."

"Peter Clapps. Who is that? Well, that's a strange name. I don't remember anyone like that."

"Peter Clapps was your husband. The man you were married to."

"Well, then I guess he was the one. The most important thing that ever happened to me was whoever it was that I fell in love with."

Journey to the Center

Giana Cicchelli

Stopping short of infinity, We look to the garden
holding all those lemon trees, geraniums and roses
sniff in the surroundings, pick a lemon
then We are off, to the ending or the beginning
I can't remember which, or if it matters.

I sing a song that came into my head
"everything is how it's always been,
we are going the way we always go"
a new melody, the chorus vibrated
as if singing along would bring me the answers.

(Wondering if they can be found), pick up a mossy walking stick
twice as tall as me, lead the way
Mud on my hands, on my face,
I call myself a traveler.
Tread the trail, which was made by the garden
people, through and to
the curvy street that will bring the hidden forest,
drivers passing too fast to notice.

Humming into my lips, I turn to say
"these are just things,
these are just things, just things,
as they have always been"
take my stick to lead the way into, away from.
We looked for answers in the rocks,

in the mud,
beyond the sky, or hanging off the trees.
We didn't realize they were there, brought the answers along,
not to be found, but
perched on our shoulders
leading the way with whispers.

In the Name of Jesus

Giana Cicchelli

The lady wearing a black bathrobe, a purple scarf
on her head, bares the Bible to all those she passes.
Lipstick disheveled, and slippers grimed
from the length of her pilgrimage,
she crosses the witchcraft shop.
She goes a block down, after smiling and wishing me
a good day, turns her face back
and mumbles something in the name
of Jesus, damning me to hell
as if she had the power.
A week previous, a man
toting his smiling dog on the back
of a bicycle, his clothes also tousled,
carried the Book to convert
us heathens, though we no longer
dwell in the heath, and bared his teeth, proving
how he could devour my demon possessions.
I couldn't help but notice how small
his chompers really were,
those yellowed transports,
lugging curses and prayers
to scream in my face, the drops of spittle
spraying like holy water.

Resounding Response

Giana Cicchelli

I don't want your body-sacrifice
on my sacred altar;
that arrogant offering.
I want nervous
twitching fluidity
shifting with vulnerability,
hips gyrating involuntarily,
as subtle hinting
becomes heavy whispering
thump thump chanting
ankles rattling, stomping
guttural moans of a mystical mantra
arms thrown flailing,
fat beat-ly swinging
praying at the darkness,
splintered with flames,
through the secret forest
with luminous flair,
giving up a ritual, giving in.

I Love You Mom: Do Me A Favor . . . Don't Tell Nobody

Chickie Farella

Now what is wrong with that statement besides a double negative? What makes it one of my mother's favorite stories during family gatherings? Why does it seem to be one of her greatest joys?

Confused?

You're not alone.

But first, here is my favorite bruschetta. The foundation begins with a one-half inch, angle sliced rustic bread that I grill after the slap of a paint brush loaded with fresh garlic and crushed red pepper infused extra virgin olive oil, topped with milky white buffalo mozzarella fresca, which then receives a nearly transparent slice of nutty Prosciutto di Parma. Then I plop a dollop of my end-of-summer basil, just a hint of sage leaves, garlic and almond pesto. For the finale, I crown these four tiers of texture with two small wedges of mini Mexican cherry tomatoes, surrounding half of a pitted Kalamata olive. Someone once told me "It's the little things that count" and this is one recipe that brings me the most joy in the melding of the flavors. However, there is no testing the pesto, or "C'mon Chick, just a small piece of cheese." This is one dish that deems "No tasters allowed" until after the dish is complete and has at least one hour to relax. Trust me. That's the secret!

Now I'm sure you're wondering what bruschetta has to do with the fact that my mother violates a trusted secret with my brother? Allow me to illustrate.

In August 1998, I hopped a plane from the Southern California desert, my home for 13 years, to spend 10 days in Chicago with my birthday-brother Neal. He's the baby boy of the clan and is also one who gives me the most major belly laughs.

He had just moved into a new home in Chi-town and it was my first time visiting, so I really didn't know my way around. On the night of his birthday party, I was picking up some plates and just trying to help my sister-in-law keep up with the clean up. She had put out a wonderful spread from appetizers to dessert that I'm sure she prepped for a week and I knew she was dead on her feet at that point. I tied up a couple of bags of trash and asked my brother where he kept the trash bins. He grabbed the bags and said, "No problem. I'll dump them." I grabbed them back and said, "No Neal, it's your birthday. I can do it myself. Go enjoy your company." He grabbed them back. "Chick, just let me have these bags. I've got it covered, okay?" Well we went back and forth a few more times until I got my way, got the bags, flew out the door, and so did my feet. They flew right out from under me. There I was, lying on the garage floor between their two cars with two bags of trash on top of me!

That fall shattered one ankle, loading it with heavy metal; the other ankle was sprained and also casted. Ultimately a 10-day vacation evolved into a couple of months living with my parents, scooting around in crutches, eventually graduating to a shiny silver cane and a portable cast. Though I was anxious to return to the desert, I was also anxious to have a family gathering and cooking extravaganza for all of us to prepare something special.

So my last day in Chi-town all the womenfolk gathered in the kitchen putting final touches on their respective dishes. My sister made an earthy stuffed mushroom appetizer, my sister-in-law mixed her bountiful salad, my oldest brother plopped down a dish of his mouthwatering shrimp in a magnificently poached garlic oil brew, my mother manned the sugo and, of course, I assembled my sacred bruschetta.

Into the kitchen walks my youngest brother-taster, Neal, doing his usual sashay through the kitchen with an icy tall King of Beer in his hand and a smile from ear-to-ear initiating his tasting ritual. He makes his first stop at my sister's station, and attempts to get a taste. He gets one, tries for two, she gives him the boot. He doesn't give up and moves on to his wife's salad and barely manages a small wedge of avocado 'til she slapped him down. Next comes a little dance over to my bruschetta, tells me how much he's gonna miss me (yeah right) and says, "Hey babe, whadya got there? Think I can snatch up a piece of that prosciutto?" There isn't anything more aggravating to me than when someone tears off a piece of my elegant parma ham! So I gave him the look: "Get lost, you're interrupting my aura." He gives me a "pffff," and makes his last dipping stop at Queen Mother's station, where of course, she begins to pop a couple meatballs in his mouth, grabs a small plate to place a tender spare rib soaking in sugo and orders me to cut him a piece of my bruschetta bread so the spoiled brat can be a two-fisted taster.

We girls just looked at each other and rolled our eyes and told him to hit the patio and mind his designated duty of "barbecue man." Before he exits he puts his arm around my mom and says, "Ma, I love ya." He pauses to look around, then says, "Do me a favor. Don't tell nobody."

My four-foot-eight-inch mother looks up at him like he's Dean Martin or something, and says, "Don't worry, Nelu, I won't say a word."

Then my brother breaks into one of his contagious laughing jags.

So does everyone else, except me. I just about choked!

I looked at Mom and asked, 'What's so freaking funny? He loves you and he doesn't want anyone to know? How does he get away with this crap?"

"Haven't you ever heard this before?" she giggles away.

"I don't think so, Ma and I can't believe you and the rest of you girls are laughing at that idiot!"

Then she says, "Oh it's a standing joke for a couple years now. Your problem is that you never visit us enough and you need to catch up!"

That was in 1998. Since then I have been to many reunions and at every gathering, my mother drags out, "Neal do you remember when you told me you loved me but not to tell anyone?" Then my brother covers his face in embarrassment because she always breaks her promise to keep the secret of his love for her, and the story manifests a good ten minute laugh, in which I also participate and still don't know why.

And by the way, what would happen if we changed genders? What if he was a she—a daughter—or worse . . . . ME?! Now picture my mother the meatball queen, (aren't they all?) feeding me her wonderful meatballs as I wrap my arm around her, looking down into her eyes saying, "I love ya, Ma . . . . but do me a favor, don't tell anyone!"

Now hold onto your pantalone and watch me go to hell!

"Well exCUSE ME!" Ma would surely snap back. "I didn't realize I've been such an albatross in your life! I forgot that I'M the one that just gives, gives, gives, gives, gives GIVES! I didn't realize what an embarrassment I am to everyone in this family!"

As a dancer, sometimes I'm inspired to jump into some Janet Jackson moves because after a while all those "gives" tend to get very rhythmic and will drag me into a "groove move" if you know what I mean.

So what is it? Are the women in charge of all the love? How did it become our job? But before you answer that lets talk about trust. If you saw my mother, say at the Taste of Chicago, the most crowded event of the season, you would pick her out of the crowd and know that she is the one you could trust with your life no matter what, no matter what. When it comes to keeping secrets, let me tell you my mother is the Templar of the Sicilian Code of Silence: Except when it comes to my brother's secret! She breaks it every time!

So when I ask myself, "What is it about that incident that betrays the trust between my mother and her son?" I think it quite possibly has to do with my persnickety preparation of the bruschetta and the rule of "no tasters allowed," being so sacred that it cannot be separated from their original repartee.

Every time our family gets together, and Mom tells her mother/son tale that she promised *never to tell* she always beams at him tenderly when she gets to her favorite part: "Don't worry, Nelu, I won't say a word."

Or perhaps the deeper issue I've yet to confess is that the *Bruschetta Rule* is really my way of taking a stance against patriarchy. How could it be that a daughter is only as powerful as her bruschetta recipe? How could it be that the withholding of the taste of this Earthly delight makes her more visible, more real? More worthy of motherly respect or love?

Maybe that's the secret.

Or, maybe sons get to love their mothers in "their own way." Oh, how I get so sick and tired of hearing that one!

Is this the only way my grown-up brother is allowed to profess his love for his mother? Maybe that's the ultimate taboo—to openly honor, perhaps even adore, the woman who gave birth to him, even though it might not be machismo to admit it.

The ultimate omerta: "Ma, I love ya. But, do me a favor. Don't tell nobody." And maybe, just maybe I need to back off and allow my brother to let his "guido" emerge. He knows better. And he *knows* how he will make her and the rest of us laugh so we will always *remember* his love for her by writing a line that would be "worth repeating."

Is veiled love better than no love at all? My mother cherishes that incident with my brother. It's reminiscent of the first sacred moment she had with him the day he reluctantly crawled out of her womb. Being the oldest of her children, I remember all her pregnancies. Though I wasn't present at the actual deliveries, I sat next to her on the sofa, crawled in bed with her and watched her bond with all her infants when she returned from the hospital.

So you see, I can easily imagine my mother securing the small of Neal's little back with one hand and the other cupping his tiny head. She'd raise him up to her face. There they were, nose to nose, eyeball to eyeball swapping butterfly kisses, so close they shared the same breath! There were NO secrets! Trust me!

But, I'd still like to know how he gets away with this crap and I don't!

Momolina Marconi: An Italian Passionate Scholar of the Goddess

Luciana Percovich

When I was a student in my teens, I attended the Liceo Classico, which in Italy is still considered the pillar of education: a five year high school where the basic subjects are Latin and Greek, Philosophy, and History. Usually, the Greek and Latin teachers, both female and male, seem to preserve some of the ancient inspiration hidden in the texts they treat, and, for me, one of the most vivid recollections of those years is the inspired way they would speak, declaiming the words of authors, flowing through their mouths like streams of forgotten and hidden wisdom.

Similarly, I remember I was struck by the Greek verbal system of tenses, of one tense in particular, called "aorist." "Aorist" refers to a past which we had to translate as a present, as our teachers repeatedly invited us to do, which would cause in us not a small embarrassment, for we didn't grasp the reason of its uncommon use. Only many years later, while studying some of the Native American tongues, did I suddenly get that meaning. In fact, I learned that in the Hopi language, for example, the expected division of time in three great indicators—past, present and future, which is based on the linear vision of time dominating in all the Indo-European languages—doesn't exit. The Hopi have just two great categories to allocate an action in time: a past which is contained in the present action, which gives name to a tense called objective or manifested, and a present (subjective or not yet manifested), which contains as a premise what is going to happen next.[1] The ancient Greek still displayed, also in its sentence structure, a way of organizing thought and language more linked to a circular and cyclic conception on life.

Momolina Marconi (1912-2006), who was a University teacher all her life, writes in similarly inspired prose. The syntax of her writing brings me back to my earlier classroom experiences. This is what also makes her writing challenging to read nowadays, when the majority of us have lost the taste for a wondrous lexicon and an articulated sentence structure. From the 1940s to the 1970s, Marconi was in charge of History of Religion (Università degli Studi di Milano) and was deep inside mythology, literature, linguistic and visual arts, covering an area which extends from the Mediterranean Sea to the river Hindus. Her major work, *Riflessi Mediterranei nella più antica Religione Laziale (Mediterranean Reflections of the Oldest Latial Religion)*, was published in 1939. Searching for the most ancient layers of the Mediterranean religious beliefs, her main point stands on "the study of the linguistic survivals of the Mediterranean Italy in the Indo-European Italy, and on the study of religious survivals . . . . particularly of some female goddesses," so deeply rooted throughout all regions of Italy that they can be still found in the Latin and Roman pantheon, if you are able and patient enough to "follow and dig more deeply the tracks traced in these fields by preceding scholars."[2]

Marconi's work relies on her vast knowledge of the classical sources, of the roots of names of places, often very far from one another, and of the attributes of each divinity. She has a strong memory for cataloguing place-names and epithets and a brilliant ability to create new connections and discover unexpected analogies which, enlarging the frame of her sight, reveal the common features of a civilization she calls "Mediterranean" or "Pelasgian."

It would be impossible in this essay to give full evidence to the richness of her way of proceeding. I will address one example, which concerns the tracing of the area of the presence of Kirke, the famous magician encountered by Ulysses in the *Odyssey*.[3] Marconi discusses this topic in two essays, "Da Circe a Morgana" (From Kirke to Morgana, 1941) and "Kirke" (1942), where she is able to uncover the *Kerketai* in the Caucasic zone (the old way to indicate the local population later called Circassian), the *Gergithes* in Anatolian Troade, and the *Gergesaias* in Palestina, all names indicating "the people of Kirke." Additionally, she points out that the root *kirk-, kerk*—can be frequently found in a vast area spreading from the island of *Kerkyra* in the Adriatic Sea to the city of *Kirkesion* in Mesopotamia, from Egypt to Thracia and Illyricum, and much farther eastward, among the Indian populations, where peoples known as

Kerkitai (*ethnos Indikòn*) and *Kolkoi Indicoi* used to live. Marconi also notes that *Kolkoi* (Korkai, Kolkai) was the name of an important commercial and maritime city in the northeastern part of Cape Comorin in the south of India; it was the ancient capital of the reign of Pandjas, the cradle of the southern Indian civilization and home of three mythical brothers who were said to be the founders of the reigns of Pandja, Khera, and Khola.

The main figure that emerges from Marconi's research, and who is also the key to reaching these deeper layers of history, is a powerful female figure, more ancient than her own names. In the beginning lines of this most renowned essay, Marconi depicts her with loving accuracy, stating:

> Everlasting is the fascination proceeding from divine feminine beings, wonderfully skilled in magic and medicine arts, who alone know the virtues of certain herbs, of certain flowers they arrange in filters and beverages, giving death and life, disease and health in the vast reign of Nature.[4]

The subtitle of "Da Circe a Morgana" states: "How Kirke and Morgana can be interpreted pointing out the features linking them to the great goddess of the Mediterranean religion." Marconi writes:

> If we go back in time with our survey, we always find a goddess, Kirke, Pasiphae, Medea, Hecate, Agamede or Mestra, who well knows the secret properties of the plants . . . This is true because speaking of *pharmaka* (remedies) we enter the field of the great Mediterranean *potnia,* who 'feeds all the beings on the earth, those who live on the divine earth, in the sea, in the air.' She rules the vegetable world made up of an endless range of colours and smells, stalks and corollas, buds and blooms, thousands of infinitesimal lives forming the secret treasure of the great goddess, who knows as many medicines as the wide earth can produce.

Classical poets used to depict absolutely beautiful pictures of these divine experts in magical and healthy arts just as the Mediterranean people had seen and adored them in their worshipping, initially performed in the open air on the green top of a hill, in the shining clearings of a wood, in the murky shores of a lake, in the calm bend of a river where the water flows more quietly . . . . The most famous of them is perhaps Kirke, the magician with beautiful braids, who lives alone in a shining palace rising up like an architectural miracle in the middle of the luxuriant green area of Aeaea.[5]

The topic of the 'open-air cult' is also found in another of Marconi's essays, "Gli asfodeli alle soglie dell'Ade" (The Asphodels at the Threshold of Hades). Published in 1985, it is one of Marconi's last essays:

> Trees then in the backstage. But somewhere else trees strengthened by sacredness: like the poplar forest surrounded by a meadow with a spring dedicated to Athena near the palace of Alcinous where Ulysses stops to pray; it is a beautiful example of open-air cult of the goddess as *phytia*, 'creator', an attribute she maintained even when the olive tree was considered one of her gifts to mankind . . .
> Similarly Demeter, the goddess of grain, cared about a holy wood, which according to Callimachus was also an orchard, where once, in order to protect one of her poplars, the goddess did not hesitate to punish Erysichton's obstinate violence . . . . It is not surprising that, even at the threshold of Hades, a wood and a meadow of asphodels were dedicated to Persephone, as this goddess experienced her great metamorphosis on a blooming meadow: 'whereon they reached the meadow of Asphodel, where dwell the souls and shadows of them that can labour no more.'[6]

When the temple of Hera was rediscovered at the mouth of the river Sele (in southern Italy), Momolina Marconi wrote in "Il santuario di Hera alla foce del Sele" (The shrine of Hera at the mouth of the Sele, 1939):

> Let's stop for a while to observe the worship place: it is located at the mouth of the Sele which flows between two black hedges of trees as old as time. It is the last dying memory of the large forests which once used to cover its banks and where flocks of birds still come and stop in spring and in fall while migrating towards the north or the hot regions of Africa. The forest and the waters are considered two typical elements of a very ancient Mediterranean cult of Hera and many other similar divine figures, first and foremost Leto/Latona, a goddess of Aegean-Anatolian origin. Being in the Lycean and Ephesian land, she is pleased to be in the forests and near the waters, two essential and inseparable elements to her life of *potnia phyton* (lady of the plants) and at the same time *potnia orniton* (lady of the birds).[7]

Marconi notes, as in the cult of Leto, in the cult of Hera, too, the forest:

> rises up in the air as a huge cathedral; and we can easily imagine it as populated by the huge and varied zoomorphic family as replete with a wide and varied collection of herbs and flowers. They form the secret garden of the goddess from which she alone can extract magic and healthy potions . . . In the cult of Hera, there is a calm mirror of water on the banks of which she appears . . . Hence, we are talking about an original identity, which cannot be neglected; an identity enabling me to find in the western Mediterranean area the same forms of cult dominating the Aegean-Anatolian world . . . [8]

> (The whole Italian peninsular) area, where small groups of Mediterranean people used to land, one after the other over a short period of time and bringing with them their tutelary deity, who was nothing but one form of the only great Mediterranean goddess, so, as I was saying, this whole area was full of wild and healthy cults, each one referring to a divine personality, the lady of a *hortus conclusus* (an enclosed garden), an unlimited source of any kind of spells. [9]

The fact that in the most ancient religions in human history, the cult could only occur in the open air—or more precisely in a space not built by human hands, as the Celts still maintained—is a motif that the pre-patriarchal civilizations all over the world have in common. I will mention just one example, which still exists in the Japanese archipelago of Okinawa. [10]

In what is considered the most ancient form of Japanese religion, the Ryu-Kyu Shinto, where priestly duties are performed exclusively by women, there is no difference between the worshipped divinity and the place of the cult (*utakis*). Because the sacredness of these places is full of divine essence, the divinities themselves are simply called by the name of that place.

In this form of ancient Shinto, where no central authority rules the beliefs, every priestess (*noros* and *tsukasas*) enjoys a full independence as regards to the mythology and the form of the cult of which she is the mediator and warrant. Kinamon, the main divine character in this system of beliefs, who is also called Nirai-Kanai (actually a dual creature, being at the same time male and female, which is very common in the most ancient creation myths all over the world), is not worshipped in a temple but in the trees and in the rocks, where she came down at the beginning of creation.

As a result, these places are so holy that they cannot be acceded by anybody but the priestesses and only on some occasions. The access is strictly limited or even forbidden: on the whole island of Kudaka, where the first human creature was created by Nirai-Kanai's daughter, no one is allowed to live, as in the western beach of Okinawa where, up to the beginning of the Second World War, only the *kami-tsukasas* were admitted.

Even when and where a human intervention was carried out to underline the attention and care paid to a sacred place—a practice that finally led in Europe to the erection of the first temples imitating the natural environment through columns of stone where air was still left free to breathe among the marble trunks—the cult, be it for a holy mountain (like Fujiyama for the whole of Japan), a hole, a clearing of grass or sand, a hidden spring in a forest, a cave, a cavern, a wall of rock, a grove, a single tree or simple thick stones "from which the sun rises," had to be in the open air.

As Marconi's work demonstrates, we must not be surprised that, many centuries after Kirke, Morgana, the heiress of an uninterrupted tradition of wisdom and worship, "lives alone in Avalon, a western island, because this is what her superhuman nature commands." But, according to Marconi, Morgana:

> despises loneliness, and so attracts the bravest knights to her island or she moves from here in search of adventures. Avalon looks like Aeaea (the original land of Circe situated in Colchis overlooking the Eastern Black Sea). The magician needs a far-off land away from humans to which people can have access only if assisted by divine help, where the goddess can perform the most varied metamorphoses, be surrounded by faithful animals, cultivate particularly useful herbs and plants for her activity, prepare strange potions and balsams, in short, be free to perform her secret art. Even when the goddess is not on a real island, she lives . . . in remote and inaccessible places where a man cannot enter safely without her will or without being called by her voice.[11]

It is relevant to note Marconi's use of the term *potnia* is clearly distinct and should not be confused with the term *goddess*, which is proper only for the Indo-European layer. In fact, the concept—and the word—god/ goddess enters history only after the disruption of the Mother Civilization and was introduced by the patriarchal peoples who rejected the balanced and peaceful civilization of the mothers, who venerated She who 'feeds all the beings on the earth, those who live on the divine earth, in the sea, in the air'; She who gives life and form; She who is the Divine in Nature, who is Everywhere in the cosmos. This She is the primal source of life, conscience and harmony. Goddesses are the "diasporized" female figures—the matrilineal clans scattered, a woman given to each man, her functions and abilities a resource for the patriarchal family—in the masculine pantheons of Gods.[12]

This all-containing *potnia* (a Greek noun that shares the same root as the Italian "potere, potenza" and the English "power," and which probably translated a lost pre-Indo-European term for the Mother of All, the Creatrix, the Giver of Birth, Growth, Death and Regeneration[13]), often has a male figure at her side, which is her son/lover, her mate and her fruit, her *paredros* (one who is sitting beside), the first God of Vegetation, the Horned God, the male devoted to the mother (such as the many figurines of Hercules and agricultural Mars widely found throughout the Italian peninsula and clearly preceding the myth developed around him in Greek Mythology), the Hero sacred to Hera, the Medieval champion devoted to his Lady, who survived up to his final transformation into the Devil of the Witches in the Burning Times.

Furthermore, Momolina Marconi argues, She can be a *potnia phytòn* (lady of the plants) and a *potnia theròn* (lady of the wild animals). Here I note that the term *potnia phytòn* is mainly found in the west Mediterranean area, while on the Greek-Anatolic side Her image prevailed as *potnia theròn*. In either case, She is the untamed Lady of the Wild, of the beasts, of the flowers, of herbs and trees, from which developed all the "Italian goddesses" (Marica, Feronia, Angizia, Kirke, Mestra, Agamede, Bona Dea, Hygieia, Diana, Flora, and many others), whose major traits, already present in Kirke, witness a progressive differentiation from Her primary Kolkidian form, spread over the southwestern coasts of Europe. In Italy, we have an abundance of "Ladies of the Vegetable World," of "Magicians" who bore the traits that later turned them into fairies and later on into witches.

The boundaries of the Mediterranean civilization traced by Momolina Marconi cannot be confined within traditional geographical borders. They stretch from the British Isles to the Hindus Valley down to Cape Comorin on the south end of India. In the Introduction to *Riflessi Mediterranei nella più antica Religione Laziale,* while delineating a general frame of the oldest populations who inhabited the Italian peninsula before the arrival of the eastern migrants, Marconi writes:

> Special religious analogies and a substantial religious community between the eastern and western Mediterranean coasts outline a cultural unity in the primeval layers of all the Mediterranean countries belonging to the Neolithic and Eneolithic era.[14]

Marconi, a historic foremother, intuited what has later been confirmed by findings in genetics regarding African origins and by Lucia Chiavola Birnbaum's work in feminist cultural history.[15] Although using the scholarly vernacular of her time, (i.e. "primitive" and "negroid") that was considered acceptable in an academia dominated by white male elites before the sweeping changes of the 1960s, Marconi upholds that the great Mediterranean civilization, which hinges on a female goddess, passes through the Black Sea, the Tigris and Euphrates river valleys and reaches the Hindus Valley (finding support in the archaeological discoveries of G. Childe, 1935, and of E. Mackay, 1936):

> The findings in Mohenjo Daro and Harappa reveal previously undiscovered links between the Anatolic-Aegean religious world and the pre-Arian India, and make us think of the Dravidians as a western origin population which, mixing with the primitive negroid population, was the vehicle of the Mediterranean civilization that reached the Ganges's river mouth and Ceylon . . . They were the Pelasgians, a dolicomorphus Mediterranean Pre-Indo-European people, who attested their presence, from the time of the Upper-Paleolithic, westward and eastward into the Aegeo-Anatolian area . . . .

In Italy, we can find traces of these early populations basically in the North with the Ligures and in the central-southern part (including Sardinia) with the Sicules. Probably they came from Africa, spreading eastward and westward . . . . Only in the final part of the Bronze Age, and during the beginning of the archaic part of the Iron Age, it is possible to find traces of a newly arriving people . . . These are the Proto-Villanovians who, pressed by ethnic upheavals in the Balkan area, arrived as migrants, some walking up to Veneto, others sailing the sea and the rivers up to the zone surrounding Mantova, others founding two colonies nearby Ancona and Matera. But the main stream, in subsequent waves, landed in the area of Rimini. From there, through the Apennines mountains, they penetrated the upper Tiber valley, running along the Tuscan and Latial coasts; however they never landed on the Adriatic regions of Central Italy (today Abruzzi), where the descendants of the Neolithic peoples remained untouched . . . .

They weren't sailors or conquerors, but small groups of people practising agriculture, forced to abandon their lands on the eastern side of the Adriatic Sea, and looking for new land to plough . . . . Along the slopes of the Alban hills they built round hut villages . . . From the name of the region in which they established, they were later called Latins, not having a definite name before. Different from the indigenous Mediterraneans, living there since the Neo-Eneolithic times—already Indo-European in language—who used to, since uncountable time, bury their dead, these new Villanovian immigrated peoples practised cremation as funeral rites.[16]

This demonstrates why the early Roman pantheon did not belong to the Greek-Indo-European religion. In this way, Marconi underlines the continuity between what Italy had been before the foundation and the rising of Rome, just as Jane Ellen Harrison had done for Greece,[17] reconstructing the more ancient layers before the invention of the Olympians. Neither Athens nor Rome rose from nothing, nor can they be considered the miracle of a sudden civilization without roots in the land and in the previous local traditions. In addition, the map that Marconi reconstructs lines up with the map Marija Gimbutas identified for the Balkans, in the northeastern area of the Adriatic and north of the Aegean Sea, where the civilizations of the Danube flourished. There is no evidence left that Marconi had knowledge of either Harrison's (1850-1928) work or Gimbutas' (1921-1994) work, just a surprising synchronicity of the same flow of re-emerging memories.

In closing, let's look at what Marconi writes about the substance of myths and rituals. She affords this fascinating topic in her 1969-70 academic course. She defines myth as "sacred history" and as "pronounced word which is repeated again and again because it owns decisive power in that it is referred to as divinity." Then she classifies myths and rituals, gradating them according to their strength and the consequences they determine. We have *idle myths* (myths for their own sake), *existential myths* (or cosmogonies, which explain the origins and through their secret force bring forth life), *technological myths* (a subcategory of the latter, for example the myth of the invention of fire), and *providential myths* (more than cosmogonies, they guarantee the salvation of future life). But, she underlines, the function of a myth is practical: "it begins to signify something from the moment in which it is danced or told; only in this way the primordial fact goes into action: the primitive man . . . doesn't create but reproduces, doesn't improvise but acts following the sacred tradition . . . . every myth is charged with past, and pregnant of future."

It follows that we can also distinguish two more categories for myths: *acted myths* and *recited myths*. The former are played in dancing, where dancing is not for the divinity but "dancing the divinity," expressing her/him, manifesting and pulling her/him down from his/her time. As for the place, it can be recreated only through the re-enacting of the mythic time and not vice versa. The latter are scrupulously told by heart, because "the mythic page is not written, but fixed in the memory of the holders of the religious tradition, who don't modify even a comma, for the text is sacred and nothing can modify it until it is believed, until we trust in it." All this enactment is the ritual itself, which "witnesses the strict link between the components of each religion: sacred history and sacred action; myth and ritual."[18]

These were the thoughts while we students were marching in the streets, during the boiling years of the rebellion of the Movimento Studentesco, and on one occasion she was personally invested in the protest, during an occupation of the University. She continued on in her research in complete isolation; at that time, the philosophical belief systems that informed the rising feminist groups arose from a vastly different perspective and place than Marconi's work.

And still today, strangled between Catholicism and market rules, her books are out of print, with the exception of a recently published collection of her essays, edited by Anna De Nardis, which has borrowed its title from the above-quoted essay *Da Circe a Morgana* (*From Kirke to Morgana*). This notwithstanding, for women on the path of rediscovering their spiritual and historical roots, Marconi is becoming one of the beloved Mother Ancestors, from whose research we can draw a passionate and forgotten knowledge to enrich and deepen our process of re-membering.

Notes

1 The main reference text is B. Lee Whorf, *Language, Thought and Reality*, The M.I.T. Press, Cambridge, Massachusetts, 1956.

2 Introduction to *Riflessi Mediterranei nella più antica Religione Laziale*, G. Principato, Milano, 1939, p. 11.

3 The genealogy of Kirke, as always happens when a matrilinear genealogy is forced into a patriarchal one, is multiple: daughter of Hecate (Hes. *Theogonia*) and Helios, or of Perseide and Helios, or, following another source (Hes. *Argon.Orph.*) of Asterope—another Oceanine Nymph—and Hyperion. If daughter of Helios, she is not only Medea's sister but also of Pasiphae's and Aietes'. In both cases, she has been generated by the ocean and by the sky.

4 "Da Circe a Morgana", reprint in Anna De Nardis ed., *Da Circe a Morgana. Scritti di Momolina Marconi*, Venexia, Roma, 2009, p. 69.

5 Ibidem, p.70.

6 "Gli asfodeli alle soglie dell'Ade", reprint in Anna De Nardis ed., *Da Circe a Morgana. Scritti di Momolina Marconi*, p. 121.

7 "Il santuario di Hera alla foce del Sele", reprint in Anna De Nardis ed., *Da Circe a Morgana. Scritti di Momolina Marconi*, p. 130.

8 Ibidem.

9 "Da Circe a Morgana", reprint in Anna De Nardis ed., *Da Circe a Morgana. Scritti di Momolina Marconi*, Venexia, Roma, 2009, p. 74.

10 Jean Herbert, *La Religion d'Okinawa*, Collection Mystiques et Religions, Dervy-Livres, Paris, 1980.

11 "Da Circe a Morgana", reprint in Anna De Nardis ed., *Da Circe a Morgana. Scritti di Momolina Marconi*, pp. 69-96.

[12] I borrow the term "diasporized" from Mary Daly in *Quintessence. Realizing the Archaic Future*, Beacon Press, Boston, 1998.

[13] In the words of Marija Gimbutas, in the Introduction to *The Language of the Goddess*, HarperSanFrancisco, 1989.

[14] Introduction to *Riflessi Mediterranei nella più antica Religione Laziale*, G. Principato, Milano, 1939, p. 10.

[15] Lucia Chiavola Birnbaum has widely researched this African origin of the Dark Mediterranean Mother, who survived and still survives in the much diffused veneration of the Black Madonnas. See Lucia Chiavola Birnbaum, *Dark mother: African origins and godmothers* (New York, Chicago, Lincoln and Shanghai, iUniverse, 2001).

[16] Introduction to *Riflessi Mediterranei nella più antica Religione Laziale*, p. 10-12.

[17] Jane Ellen Harrison, *Themis. A study of the social origins of Greek Religion*, Cambridge University Press, 1912.

[18] All the quotes in this paragraph are from "Le spose di Zeus nella Teogonia di Esiodo", reprint in Anna De Nardis ed., *Da Circe a Morgana. Scritti di Momolina Marconi*, pp. 22-56.

Bibliography of Works by Momolina Marconi

Marconi, Momolina, *Riflessi mediterranei nella più antica religione*, G. Principato, Milano, 1939.

Marconi, Momolina, "Melissa dea cretese", in *Atheneum*, 1940, pp, 164-178.

Marconi, Momolina. "Da Circe a Morgana", in *Rendiconti del R. Istituto Lombardo di scienze e lettere* (1940-41): 533-73.

Marconi, Momolina, *Kirke*, Studi e Materiali di Storia delle Religioni, XVIII, Milano, 1942.

Marconi, Momolina, *Ch. Picard: Les religions prehellenique*, Paris, 1948.

Marconi, Momolina, "Mito e Paesaggio", in *Archivio Glottologico Italiano 39*, 1954, pp. 37-43.

Marconi, Momolina, "Maternità divina e androginismo nella religione mediterranea", in *Atti dell'VIII Congresso Internazionale di Storia delle religioni (Roma 17-23 aprile1955)*, Sansoni, Firenze, 1956.

Marconi, Momolina, "Can the Cosmogony of the Greek be reconstructed?", in *History of Religions 1, 2* (1962), pp. 274-280.

Marconi, Momolina, *Lezioni di storia delle religioni, anno accademico 1969-70*, La Goliardica, 1970.

Marconi, Momolina, *Lezioni di storia delle religioni tenute da Momolina Marconi, anno accademico 1971-72*, La Goliardica, Milano, 1972.

Marconi, Momolina, "Tratti di remota preistoria nella mitologia dei Greci", in *Studi in onore di Ferrante Vonwiller*, Como, 1980, pp. 223-228.

Marconi, Momolina,"Divinità greche fra suoni e danze," in *Numismatica e Antichità Classiche: quaderni ticinesi*, Arti Grafiche Gaggini, Lugano, 1972.

Marconi, Momolina, "Goddess Worship in the Hellenistic World", in *Encyclopedia of Religion*, Mircea Eliade ed., Mac Millan, London-New York, 1987, vol. 6, pp. 49-52.

Marconi, Momolina *Preludio alla storia delle religioni*, Jaca Book, Milano, 2004.

Pestalozza, Uberto, *Religione mediterranea: vecchi e nuovi studi*/ordinati a cura di Mario Untersteiner e Momolina Marconi, Fratelli Bocca, Milano, 1952.

Underworld

Nancy Caronia

Legend has it you were picking wildflowers that morning, but
The eucalyptus trees surrounding Lake Pergusa were your desired
destination.

> Your mother Demeter needed the oily medicine
> —You would not deny her.

If you had arrived at the hillside forest, you might have crawled
Into the knot of a tree, plucked a pink flower from a blossoming
branch,

You could have outrun your uncle, hidden in the deep green of the woods,
but
The smell of the salt called you to the naval—

> The lake, the center of time:
> Where swans sang all season—

> Lake Pergusa
> > Where your uncle grabbed you—
> > Was about to bleed

Underworld

Its yearly cleansing

The smell of a salty lake red at its time, the distant eucalyptus, the lemon
trees
Your heart beats the memory—

What is it you wanted?

Little did you know that once snatched
It is difficult to be found.

The clock tick tock

Even your mother's searching comes to grief.
Demeter's lament fiercer than Orpheus' songs.

Who said it is good to be Queen?

The girl waits

The mother weeps for six months out of the year
Then another six when the girl does not notice the sun.

Desire is nothing compared to the subjects keening at the gate.
There is no garden here—

Your uncle couldn't stand the reminder—

Your creamy skin, eyes bright with hope,
A body lithe with expectation.

All that remains is the mouth set at an odd angle:
There is no voice—

I'll be home before dinner your goodbye hymn.

Lilith

Sheila Marie Hennessy

Original sculpture ©2007 Sheila Marie Hennessy

Shaman's Dream/Shanti

Sheila Marie Hennessy

Original sculpture ©2008 Sheila Marie Hennessy

Vagina Dentata

Andrea Nicki

There was a time when women
actually had these teeth
an evolutionary adaptation of female warriors
not just a morbid fantasy, a myth

Somehow the teeth started to fall out
stopped growing in newborn girgoyles
but people feared they might return

and then what was spread to stop their re-emergence
keep women flaccid and slow to revolt?
a story about a woman deeply interested in teeth
but not for herself, not for her own needs and safety—

The Tooth Fairy—
giving children money for useless teeth
disposing of them discretely
out of the kindness of her heart
performing a thankless and exhausting task
of visits to thousands of children every night
all the time gentle and benign
her arms never tugging forcefully at a pillow
and knocking a child in the head
wanting no return or reward
not even a child's dozy smile, an iron bust in her honor

Vagina Dentata

I tell you now, children and adults
there is no such thing as the Tooth Fairy
but there is the Tooth Witch
Wherever you may have disposed of teeth
she will find them and use them in a potent brew
with motherwort leaves, deer antler, watermelon seeds
in a spiritual invocation to make the warrior teeth
come back, back to the ancient sheath

* "Sheath" has the meanings of both case for a sword and a vagina. This poem was inspired by the movie *Teeth* written and directed by Mitchell Lichtenstein.

From The Lust Poemz ov Persephone

Elisabeth P. Sikie

Author's Note: "Descent" is from "The Lust Poemz ov Persephone," a series of eight poems that marks Persephone's myth until she becomes the resurrected or renewed Kore.

Descent

The maiden walks thru grasses swollen with rain
Dark green earth pushes up her feet
Storm clouds descend merge with the grasses
Mom sez don't go too far but she's pulled
Toward a waving tease red blur of flowers
Tossed by wind she's got to touch the red narcissus
Pluck it from the earth wear it home wet in her wet hair
Far from home she tugs the red flower so open to the rain
Get the root pull up the stem and the ground opens
A jaw jagged hole down and in the maiden falls till
She hits rock under earth skin calls for her mother
So dark Persephone cries the loss
Of her life picks herself up wanders thru the rock corridors
She knows this place from some dream
Touches the sand stone walls, fingers the etched symbols
Persephone walks down thru the dark alone with herself
And no light, spiraling down with her hunger
And her memories and her mourning
Orange light seeps from earth cracks
Reflects from iridescent dragonfly wings
Moves thru the translucent passing dead
Persephone's face cracked with weeping

Eyes swollen from loss curls around
The wounding in her gut and a throbbing
Shifting womb disoriented she wants
To die or anything just
Stop my life
The tunnel spews foul wind
She no longer needs her eyes
Instinct pushes her forward
The only sound her panting
Finally the tunnel opens to a circle
Of dark walls, a shadow waits still
On a stone in the center waits
For her she knows he's waiting
For her feels him knowing
No thought she runs to him driven
Mad like a salmon for his smell

Tantra With Beloved Hades

I sit on beloved legs split mouth open
Mind split heart open
And he holds me like a father
And he holds me like a mother
And he holds me like a lover
I squeeze him with serpent tension
Each breath I take each kiss forces
Deeper each stroke peels
More revealing his hunger
We devour thee other eat dark parts
Chew heart fascinate our selves as one
Commingle as two take turns
Pushing each others' head down
Into core self hard darker deep
We tease till we remember
We remember and make
A new dream

Song to Demeter

Mother did you know it could be this good
Mother did you feel yr lover wrap yr body like seaweed
Gentle but tightening as you move just enough
To tease you to fight to open licking you back down
Containing you till you'd burst the sensation of tension
Mother have you lived like two as one swaying down
Here with the ocean smells and the creatures who live off debris
Who turn flakes of skin into iridescent scales and bones
Into soft ocean floor
Mother my hair is always wet and my skin preserved
Mother I am so happy in the dark places
under the cover of earth
Where the whispers of ghosts teach me songs lost
On the world of light
Whistling songs of love lost and mourning
It is always dusk here, mother, full of purple
I only miss the moon
Mother did you ever quake at the merging before
The corn ripened
Mother I cannot come home.

Browned Beauty

Nancy Cosgriff

I see you tiny snake, hiding behind your stillness.
I see largeness of meaning lying
in your early autumn browned body.
My ancestors called you Goddess, transformer of death into life,
Unifier of worlds—above and below, time and eternity.
Those diamonds patterning your back—
all meanders and labyrinths—
And the coiled curves of your body
resting on the old bluestone by my house,
They speak to me your message, your ancient wisdom ever-new.
You herald hope for good fortune returning from winter's darkness.
You promise a stirring in the belly, a birthing of new blessing.
You signify our awakening and welcoming of the Great Mother.
You tell us she will come again in beauty.

Hecate Speaks

Nancy Cosgriff

I sit at the crossroads with the dark moon above and black dog below.
I sit here at that place of choice for each of you.
Eight directions.
You stand at the center.
Which path you decide to walk I do not know.
But once you choose I see what lies along your way—
Possibilities and potentialities—
And how and where they will transform.
I am truth and consequences.
I see the wind and howling storm slashing at your body,
I hear the gentle breeze and hummingbird sing softly to your heart.
I can feel the sun warming your weathered face,
Caressing your eyes as you rest.
I envision strangers asking for your help,
Dear ones tugging at your sleeve, requesting merriment or mercy.
There in my intuition's eye appear the accidents, the wrecks,
The deliberate and unintended maimings you occasion along the way.
I hear the cries, the laughter—feel the loves and infidelities.
I do not spare you. There is no escape.
All is inevitable. All is choice.
Each of you must enter the world above and the world below,
The world behind and the world before.
Light and dark, death and life,
All goes round in endless cycle.
Here at the center is your fear.
Here at the center is your unknowing.
Here, at the heart of the matter, is your surrender.

You don't know which way to go.
None of us knows for sure.
We do the best we can.
We choose again.
We begin the next journey.

Sojourn: Stories of the Spiral to My Self

Kirsten Schilling

Puberty

I don't remember the first time that I got my period. But I remember Lily who, unlike my other friends that year, still liked to climb trees and play on the tire swing with me. We often got very dirty when we played together, skinning our knees, tearing our clothes and having fun in a manner that was still childlike. At the same time, we were both aware (she had two beautiful older sisters with breasts and periods to prove it!) that adulthood was soon coming to claim us.

Once, we fell off a horse we were riding bareback.

We had just been out to where the parents were, sitting in the back yard with their iced teas, enjoying the sun and each other's company, when our horse walked under a clothesline. I remember how easily we were swept to the ground, landing in two small heaps of skinny-girl arms and legs, our matching strings of Mardi Gras beads colorfully askew.

The breath had been knocked completely out of me and, as my lungs struggled to catch my first, next breath, I just laid there and looked at the sky, feeling defeated. Defeated because we had just announced to our parents and siblings, shirtless, on the back of the horse (and me with the slightest, tiniest beginnings of breasts, already) that we wanted to rebel. We wanted to be like boys, like her younger brother Eddie, who didn't have to wear a shirt on hot summer days.

The China Line

Note: From a journal entry, March 27, 2004

I think it was the best thing my husband did for me when he broke my grandmother's china teacup. I've used it continuously, unthinkingly, since I first went away to college at age seventeen. It was delicate and bone-colored, with two hairline cracks and a chip in the place where you'd most want to put your lips if you were to drink from it.

Hastily packing my boxes and bags, I snatched it from the stark disarray of my mother's china cupboard when I first left home. I chose it, simply, because it was beautiful. But I realized today that I was drinking my tea from a china line of women who I didn't really know. What was it I was sharing with them? Carrying on for them?

He apologized profusely to me as he tried to glue it back together. But it was too badly broken and it wouldn't hold. He felt horrible. But I said, as I contemplated the pieces, that perhaps it is best left unglued, unused?

So it still sits, like a broken egg, on the top shelf of our cupboard.

I must decide what to do with the pieces.

Secret Hair: A Postmodern Self-portrait in Words

Mischa Geracoulis

What had begun as an ordinary play day veered the instant my mother called me inside to change my clothes. Already? I was only just getting warmed up on my swing. She was speaking in clipped sentences, and her body language was stiff. Unmistakable signs that blurted "danger ahead." Was I in trouble?

My mom had well-earned herself the description "high strung." She was frequently edgy or upset, and more often than not, the reasons for her frayed nerves were a mystery to those around her. All business, she hurried me into one of my Sunday dresses. Are we going to church? There'd be no time for questions from me. Within moments, I was whisked into the car and riding off into the unknown. I remember wishing so much to know where we were going.

When we walked into the doctor's office, I assumed my mother had an appointment. Yes, of course. That would explain her nervousness. Neither of us was keen on doctor visits. But, when we were called into the examining room, and she picked me up to lay me on the doctor's table, I started to cry. I was nearly four years old, and Mom rarely picked me up. She always said that I was too heavy. This appointment would not be for her.

Turns out, I was not only in trouble, but I was abnormal too. Turns out, it was my body hair that was causing all the commotion. When I developed pubic hair at age three, unbeknownst to me, my parents fretted horribly. Looking for advice, my young mother talked to family about my problem. Dad, apparently embarrassed, got mad at my mom for divulging such secrets. This stigma would become the first of many secrets that I'd learn to keep; thusly, I was firstborn to the next generation of secret-keepers.

Shivering and whimpering, I was like a new puppy at its first trip to vet's when the endocrinologist's gloved hand intruded on me. Evidently, the doctor was suspicious of tumors. These invasive and humiliating exams that I despised went on for several years. Like those alleged alien abductions reported in *The Enquirer*[1], I too was captured, held and probed against my will. Even at that tender age, I was a quick study, and learned to be acutely aware of the wrongness of my body. I lost my innocence at the hands of that endocrinologist, and took up the burden of cyclic shame.

The hair on my head is dense, coarse, and grows profusely. As a child, it tangled easily. This hair was also a source of upset for my mother—and for me whenever she decided to shampoo it. She had a way of going at my scalp and hair much in the same way she scrubbed the pots after dinner. The comb-out was equally exhausting, a wild tug-of-war between my mother and the comb. On more than one occasion, the comb broke off in my hair.

One day—without advance notice to my dad or me—Mom took me to a barber shop. I was overwhelmed by the barber's massive chair. It was made for adult men, not little girls. So he stacked up editions of the *Yellow Pages* for me to sit on. Within minutes, my long dark hair lay lifeless on the barber shop floor. In several fell strokes, he'd buzzed it off, and I cried when I saw myself in the mirror. Now I was definitely abnormal. I looked like a boy. This was all wrong. Too much hair down below and not enough on top. I was upside down! When my dad came home from work that day and saw my nearly scalped head, he got angry with my mom. I was angry too. And embarrassed.

Eventually, the endocrinologist concluded my case by telling my mother that sometimes babies born to people of the Levant and the Mediterranean, or descendants thereof, develop androgenic hair early. She in turn explained this to my dad and me. Now maybe I'd get another shot at being normal! But there was that word again. Levant. In my parents' era, the label *Levantine* held disparaging implications. It was a thin disguise for "odd" and "different." My father preferred the more benign *Mediterranean*.

Levantine, Mediterranean—I was confused. My grandparents spoke of the Old Country and Asia Minor, of exile and the American dream. At this mythical place where worlds collide, where would be my jump-off point? I'd spend a lifetime trying to sort this out. Growing up in a postmodern melting pot culture, I was all the more confused about personal identity. According to federal demographic collections agencies, I am Caucasian. The curious thing is that no one in my family has ever considered themselves to be white. Nowadays, in a private victory over bureaucracy, I check the "Other" box.

When I was born, my father, maternal grandfather and uncle came to visit my mom and me in the hospital. So the story goes, my mother's brother complimented God on creating a perfect "Armenian baby." Fighting words. Upon hearing these words, my dad retorted that the baby is not Armenian, but Italian. Right there in my mother's hospital room, on the day that I entered the world, my father, grandfather and uncle argued over my ethnicity. Livid, Mom threw them all out. How early, and seemingly innocuously, the branding begins.

One summer as an adult, I traveled to the Middle East. While in the Armenian Quarter of Old Jerusalem, I'd met a Diasporan Armenian gentleman who offered to show my then-boyfriend and me around. This man insisted on speaking Armenian to me even though I'd assured him I was not fluent. To him it was unthinkable that I could not speak this language. Eventually—thinking to get myself off the hook—I told him that I'm not one-hundred percent Armenian, that I am Italian too. He startled me when he responded by telling me how preposterous that is—to be two things, and furthermore, he persisted, I must choose one. My three-fourths Armenian boyfriend laughed loudly, as I fell paralyzed by a too-familiar feeling of confused self-identity. How could I possibly choose one and reject the other? And why must I pick one over another anyway? Is one superior, or by choosing one, would that make me more whole, more normal?

As a small child, I had three babysitters whom I utterly adored. Three sisters from Lebanon, three Arabian princesses, as far as I could tell. Sometimes Mom and Dad went out on Fridays, our night to watch *Sonny and Cher.*[2] While sitting mesmerized by Cher on the TV screen, the unassumingly beautiful babysitters let me take turns at brushing their dark tresses. They would imitate Cher by bowing and flipping their hair upside-down. I never tired of watching Cher perform her songs, "Half Breed" and "Gypsies, Tramps and Thieves." Having no conscious understanding of the lyrics, something about them, nevertheless, resonated deeply within.

During a trip to visit family in Italy, my cousins there warned me of the perils of shaving the armpit and bikini areas. *Non è sano.* "It's not healthy." Years later when researching for an article on the safety of deodorant and its role in breast cancer, I learned how microscopic shaving nicks in those delicate, lymph-laced areas become open pathways for toxic chemicals to enter the body. One outing to any Italian seaside confirms the feminine anti-shave societal agreement. *Vai naturale.* "Go natural," my cousins advised, and so I did. In my mind I was transformed into Modigliani's *Red Nude*[3], a painting from which to this day I take inspiration.

Going natural was a first step in my personal liberation as a woman and symbolized the beginnings of my return to self. My husband at the time was turned off by my unrestrained hairiness. He'd said that my bushy armpits made him feel as though he was making love to a man. On the brink of divorce as we were, his opinion paled in comparison to this glimmer of emancipation. After that trip to Italy, to remove my body hair or not would thereafter be my choice. With equal parts lamentation and catharsis, allowing myself a choice is one way that I make reparations for the years of delusions and dilutions.

When I was eleven, I'd begged my mother to let me shave my armpits and legs. It was my first year in public school, and my wooliness served to be yet another thing that stood me out as weird among the other kids. Previously, we'd lived in ethnic neighborhoods, and most of the kids at my former school were from the Levant and Mediterranean. Moving away to a different, predominantly Anglo-Saxon populated town, we stood out. It was a strange and telling phenomenon because there were almost as many African-Americans living in the town too. The atmosphere in this new place, however, was literally black and white with negligible room for middle shades. People there frequently asked if we were Spanish or mulatto.

As Mom extolled the virtues of my youthful furriness, I could not be swayed from an obsession to shave. Ultimately, she conceded. Fervent to become as smooth as the other prepubescent girls at school, I'd shorn myself into bloody disarray. Later, sporting legs criss-crossed by Band-aids, I was deflated, and admonished by my mother for not waiting until I was older. Seems as though I'd jumped off some sort of cliff. There's no turning back, she warned. For the rest of my days I'd enslaved myself to an endless pursuit of the clean shave.

One Sunday at church, Joey diPalma's[4] mom and my mom arranged our first prom date. Joey and I strode into the prom—head-to-toe coordinated powder-blue polyester with carnation corsage and boutonnière. Standing awkwardly side-by-side for our formal photograph, our "waspy" peers called us "wops," and teased us for our big noses and for looking like twins. A fine match we made: two sets of prominent noses eclipsing faint shadowy-black mustaches, unibrows, and coarse hair shellacked into his-and-her "wings." Feature for feature, we were mirror images of each other—mirrors that, at that moment, neither of us could bear looking into; mirrors that would only reflect an abiding and mutual embarrassment. In all our freakish, twin-like glory, the photographer's cruel camera seized our moment of shared mortification. Despite the fact that Joey and I had both gotten extensions on our curfews that night, we went home early with stomachaches and never spoke again.

I spent years in and out of the electrolysis's office. Electrolysis—the process of injecting a tiny, electrified needle into a hair follicle to kill its growth tissue—is touted to be permanent. So for a dollar a hair, I sentenced the hair on my face, chest and breasts to death by electrocution. In retrospect, I also sentenced myself to an expensive and needless agony.

The first guy I lived with was of a non-ethnic persuasion. He repeatedly told me that I might be beautiful if only I'd get a nose job and have my belly electrolysised too. I moved out instead.

Throughout my 20s and 30s, I had a recurrent dream—a nightmare really—in which I was forcibly held so that someone could cut off my long hair. The haircutter always appeared faceless and sterile, mildly evocative of the endocrinologist or barber from long ago. In my dream, I was panic-stricken, struggling and crying. I'd jolt awake and instinctively grasp for my hair. Finding it all there, relief and gratitude would flood through me. When I was 37 and had the dream analyzed, it stopped. According to the analyst, the dream symbolized an internal fight, one of repression and revolt.

As Dr. Finch from the film *Running with Scissors* rhetorically asked, "Where would we be without our painful childhoods?"[5] Indeed.

My primary and permeable years were marred by a fractured, incomplete, and irregular sense of self. I used to believe that it was my body's fault, that it had betrayed me. Really it was the other way around, and my body bears the scapegoat's scars to prove it. I'd tweezed, plucked, depilatorized, electrolysised, waxed, shaved, sugared, honeyed, and bleached myself clean. I'd whitewashed my ethnicity into short-term remission.

Discovering the likes of Ronald Suny and Edward Said in my college days, I related to the dilemma of Occident versus Orient, the complexities of dominant and subservient hemispheres, of other peoples' truisms, shattered paradigms, and the consequences of labeling *the other*. The psychoses of the world started to make strange sense. Now in my fourth decade on the planet, I find an inner sanctum of reconciliation. I can be hybridized, as well as a natural element unto myself. It's a matter of choice.

On a recent visit to my mother's, she told me that I needed to shave my armpits. (I don't even know how she could've seen in there!) For a fleeting moment, I felt spied on. And for another moment, I felt a rebellion that I thought I'd put to rest. The wiser part of me, nonetheless, realizes Mom's innate immigrant's mentality, the one that indentures itself to the prevailing culture, the one that assumes it mandatory to water itself down and homogenize, the one that's been indoctrinated to believe that blander is better. This realization turns to profound self-appreciation for having chosen the way of counter-culture, not in reactionary habit, but in favor of sovereignty. I decided to shave my armpits while I was there with Mom. It wasn't an act of submission, more like one of respect and acceptance for who she is and from where she's come. These days I don't always feel so compelled to make statements and prove points.

Historically, I've had more success with the ethnic boys. There's generally less pressure to squeeze into the confines of conventional, Anglo-Saxon beauty. On one of my first dates with the man to whom I'm now married, he asked if he could run his fingers through my long hair. (Yes!) He's quite a smolderingly dark-handsome, ethnic, hirsute one himself. In fact, our little nephews like to call him "Mr. Frodo" (from *The Hobbit*) because of his hairy feet. Talk about less pressure!

Notes

1   Perel, David, Ed. *The National Enquirer.* Boca Raton, 1926-present.

2   Bono, Sonny, Cher. *The Sonny & Cher Comedy Hour.* Fisher, Art, Dir. CBS. Hollywood, 1971-1974.

3   Modigliani, Amedeo. *Red Nude*, 1917.

4   Not his real name.

5   *Running with Scissors.* Murphy, Ryan, Dir. TriStar Pictures, 2006. Burroughs, Augusten. *Running with Scissors.* Picador. New York, 2002.

6   Tolkien, J.R.R. *The Hobbit.* London, 1937.

Orphic Mysteries and Goddess(es) of Nature: Greek Hymns Honoring the Divine Feminine

Harita Meenee

"Nature, mother goddess of all . . . almighty one . . . primordial . . . law-giver of the gods . . . Leader, ruler bringing life . . . Destiny and fate, fiery breath . . ." These phrases belong to the Orphic Hymn to Nature (*Physis* in Greek, from which the words *physics* and *physical* are derived). It's hard to find a more telling description of the Divine Feminine's immense powers in all of the Hellenic literature!

The Orphic Hymns form a collection of 87 poems, each one dedicated to a specific deity. They were used in the rituals of a group practicing a mystery religion, most probably in Asia Minor. Those initiated in the Orphic Mysteries claimed Orpheus as their founder—he was the most famous legendary musician of Greece, son of the Muse Kalliope, and husband of Eurydike. His existence (real or imagined) is shrouded in the mists of a mythical past, but his followers were active from the 6th century BCE on.

The dating of the hymns is a controversial subject. Some scholars think they were composed in the late Hellenistic era (3rd–2nd century BCE), while others place them in Roman times, in the 1st–3rd century CE. However, it seems quite likely that the content of these verses is based on much older material.

The powerful presence of goddesses in the Orphic collection is unquestionable—out of 87 poems, 41 are dedicated to female deities, many of whom are also mentioned in the hymns to gods. Olympian figures, like Demeter and Aphrodite, are highly praised, often in unexpected ways:

Everything from you derives; you yoked
the world and rule over three realms,
giving birth to all that is in heaven,
on the fruitful earth, in the ocean depths . . .
(Orphic Hymn to Aphrodite, 4-7)

Moreover, some of the poems honor primordial goddesses of nature, such as Gaia, Nyx (Night), Selene (the personification of the moon) and Tethys, an old and venerable sea deity. They also praise Rhea-Cybele, the orgiastic "Mother of Gods and human beings" (14, 9; cf. 27, 1, 7). The goddess of justice in her diverse forms, as Dike, Dikaiosyne and Nemesis, also figures prominently in the collection.

Could this highly important role of female divinities reflect the significance of women in the group using the Orphic Hymns? We certainly know that women participated enthusiastically in most of the mystery religions of the ancient world; it seems that the Orphic one was no exception, in spite of certain misogynist elements present in it. We might wonder then if some of these verses, whose poets remain anonymous, could have been written by female authors. Why not, after all? Hellenistic women, like Anyte, Nossis and Moiro, are often delighted to mention and praise goddesses in their poems.

One way or another, it is exciting to see female deities honored in such a whole-hearted and fascinating way as revealed in the Orphic texts. Above all, the Hymn to Nature brings to light the age-old Mother Goddess of many names, the supreme Creatress, "dancing with whirling noiseless feet" her eternal dance of life and growth . . .

Orphic Hymn to Nature

Nature, mother goddess of all,
ingenious mother, crone!
Creatress of many, sovereign
ruler, all-taming, always untamed.
Celestial, all-shining, almighty one,
+ * honored and supreme in every way,
imperishable, primordial, first-born.

Praised by people, seasoned and wild,
nocturnal, light-bringer, dancing
with whirling noiseless feet.
Pure, law-giver of the gods,
unending and the end,
shared by all, yet
alone untouched.

Self-fathered, fatherless,
desired and sublime
full of lovely flowers, delightful one.
Friendly and knowing,
weaving, mixed with many things.
Leader, ruler bringing life,
maiden who nurtures all.

Self-sufficient, lady of justice!
You of many names
the Kharites obey.
Protectress of the air,
of land and sea,
bitter to the wicked,
to the obedient sweet.

All-wise, all-giving, care-taker, queen of all,
growth-bringer, fertile, ripener of fruit.
Father and mother of all,
nurturer and nurse,
giver of swift births.
Force of the seasons,
fruitful one and blessed!

Giver of all arts, creator, many things
you shape, setting all in motion,
eternal, + goddess of the sea.
Prudent and skilled,
in everlasting swirl whirling the swift

flow, ever-flowing, moving
in cycles, shape shifting.

Seated on a fine throne,
honored, you alone
decide, being far above those
who scepters hold.
Loud thundering,
fearless and strong,
force that tames all.

Destiny and fate, fiery breath,
eternal life, immortal providence;
all + is in you, + since
you alone create.
Goddess, to you I pray:
bring + in rich + seasons, peace,
growth to all and health.

Author's Note: *The symbol + indicates that the manuscript is worn out at this point, hence the words cannot be read clearly and their interpretation is uncertain.

Bibliography and Further Reading

Athanassakis, Apostolos N. *The Orphic Hymns: Text, Translation and Notes.* Atlanta, GA: Society of Biblical Literature, 1988.

Guthrie, W.K.C. *Orpheus and Greek Religion.* 2nd ed. Princeton, NJ: Princeton University, 1993.

Long, Asphodel P. *In a Chariot Drawn by Lions: The Search of the Female in Deity.* Freedom, CA: The Crossing Press, 1993.
_____."Orphic Hymns." *Arachne* 9. 1989. Available online, http://www. asphodel-long.com/html/orphic_hymns.html.

Mystical Hymns of Orpheus. 2nd ed. Translated by Thomas Taylor. Chiswick: 1824. Reprinted by Kessinger. Available online, http://www.theoi.com/ Text/OrphicHymns1.html.

"Orphic Hymn to Demeter." Translated by Harita Meenee; http://hmeenee. com/1773/index.html.
Orphic Hymns. 3rd ed. Translated by D. P. Papaditsas and Helen Ladia. Athens: "Hestia" Bookstore, 1997.

Snyder, Jane McIntosh. *The Woman and the Lyre: Women Writers in Classical Greece and Rome.* Carbondale, IL: Southern Illinois University, 1989.

Neolithic marble figurine from Sparta, Southern Greece. The *polos* on her head indicates that she was probably a goddess, 6th millennium BCE; National Archaeological Museum of Athens, Greece; Photo © 2008 Harita Meenee

Spelling and Re-Creating Her

Glenys Livingstone

"Goddess"

"Goddess," as I understand the term, is the Female Metaphor for the Great Creative Principle of the Universe. As such, She is both the Matrix and a wholistic template of Being: that is, She is whole and complete within Herself. To my mind this implies that there is no need to masculinize certain of Her qualities, though She includes qualities that have been termed "masculine." As I understand Her, She is a complete illustration of the process of living and dying. Her three aspects as we may term them and know them today—Virgin/Maiden, Mother/Creator, Crone/Old One—may be based on chronological phases of a woman's life, but are not in any way limited to those phases, and may not have been so limited in the earliest of times when this triple aspect dynamic was first perceived. The three aspects are phases of the whole process of living and dying that the ancients in many cultures observed and celebrated. I contend that these three aspects were understood as a dynamic of Creativity—that was perhaps first related to by humans in the vision of Moon's cyclical pattern. One witness to the perception of the three aspects as Creative Dynamic is the triple spiral engraved in central position at Newgrange—Bru-na-Boinne—in Ireland. The significance of the Bru-na-Boinne[1] monument may yet to be fully understood, as our ethnocentric minds only now begin to remember the "Goddess"-centred minds that built it. This is true also of other monuments and art in Old Europe that have puzzled our patriarchal earth-alienated minds.[2] I propose that the Triple Spiral encoded at Bru-na-Boinne specifically celebrates the Triplicity[3] as Cosmic Dynamic of Creativity, given that it is lit up at the moment of Winter Solstice, the Seasonal Moment[4] that celebrates Origins and Earth-Sun creativity.

384

I understand "Creativity" as another name for the Mystery of Being, and it is what I understand as the *essence* of Being: *essentially* the point of it All. "Creativity" is also a term used by process philosopher Alfred North Whitehead for "the Category of the Ultimate" (1929:28). He refers to it as a "threefold creative act" (Cousins: 1971:91)[5] just as I understand *Goddess*—the dynamic, triple-faced Metaphor. She may enable the identification of Life itself, with the manifestation of the ultimate Mystery at the Origin of All. To further this identification I have associated the three faces of the Female Metaphor—Goddess—with Thomas Berry's three characteristics of what is scientifically known as Cosmogenesis, the omnipresent creative dynamic essential to all structure and form in the Universe (Swimme and Berry 1992:71-79). Cosmogenesis is referred to by Brian Swimme and Thomas Berry, in their story of the Universe, as having three central tendencies which are "the cosmological orderings of the creative display of energy everywhere and at any time throughout the history of the universe" (ibid:72); and those aspects are termed "differentiation," "communion," and "autopoiesis" (ibid).[6]

The three chronological phases of a woman's life in which the sacred Three of Goddess are mirrored are: pre-menarchal young one; menstrual mother; and post-menopausal elder. Thus, they have been known as Virgin/Maiden, Mother/Creator, Old One/Crone. Women these days may not wish to be confined to these three phases, feeling they are not sufficient to express the multivalency of themselves and their lives, but I feel that this is in large part an outcome of limited patriarchal narrative for millennia, wherein the full picture of these aspects has been diminished and distorted, even demonized. "Queen"/sovereign[7] or "Hera"[8] for example are qualities of all three at all times. The three are never separate and are part of each other at all times. I have found it necessary to re-story the articulation of the ancient Creative Three, since women and men in our times no longer understand them in their full integrity. Whereas, in the earliest of times of consciousness, and even later, these phases seem to have been sensed as aspects of the Great Creative Process whereby Life continued, they had in recent patriarchal times lost their sacred essence. Indeed the Great Creative Process itself, expressed in the female as sacred, had become background. As Miriam Robbins Dexter describes (1990:161-183): the mother became mere vessel and useful in this mode, the young virgin became a prize to be taken—and the older virgin became a harsh deviant to be avoided, and the old one became *used up* and troublesome. Adam McLean advises that:

> To find the Triple Goddess . . . we must go back to an early stratum of myth. Long before the ascendancy of the Christ myth, the primal myths of the Goddess had been overlaid with generations of masculine Gods usurping her place in the scheme of things, taking over her sacred centres and grasping for themselves some facet of her attributes. If we go back to the earliest myths of humankind we will find the goddess in her purest, usually triune, form (1979:12-13).

The re-storying of women—the Being of the female, is a preface to being able to speak sensibly of how Virgin-Mother-Crone could be a Metaphor for the Mystery of Being. It is then possible to relate these three aspects to the evolutionary cosmic dynamics—Cosmogenesis—as a way of deepening awareness of them in the present moment and as a way of entering into the Female Metaphor—into Her—more fully, as a way of comprehending or sensing *Goddess*. Celebration of the Seasonal Moments, then, expressive of Her Creativity, may become a way of accessing the Metaphor, the Poetry that She is; the ritual celebration of the Seasonal transitions become doorways to Her centre, each and every time . . . more deeply, developing personal and cultural relationship to Cosmos, as one joins Earth, our Place, in Her annual journey of descent and return.

The Body—Essential or Not?

All knowledge is an experience of body—what else can it be? Mind is body, body is mind. Humans know enough these days—including empirically—to end the dualistic notions of body/mind, to enter or perhaps re-enter in a new way, an integral comprehension of the bodymind we each are. In his recent book *The Spell of the Sensuous* David Abram affirms that:

> Without this body . . . (could there be) . . . anything to speak about, or even to reflect on, or to think, since without any contact, any encounter, without any glimmer of sensory experience, there could be nothing to question or to know (1997:45).

I ask then: what difference if this body menstruates, lactates—if these body processes were considered and sensed as the norm? The modern woman—she of recent centuries—was held down by this difference, by the fact of her organic processes. The postmodern woman, convinced that the body can be "erased" (Spretnak 1993:122), that its substantive presence can be dismissed, may expect herself (and be expected) to deny that it matters, that it affects her experience in any way.

The organic processes of the female body, her "elemental capabilities" (ibid), are not cultural inventions, though much cultural invention about woman's physicality has occurred (for example, the cultural idea that she was unsuited for education). And cultural invention continues to occur—across the full spectrum of thinking (for example, the persistent cultural notion that menstruation is a disability, or that physically strong women are "masculine"). And whilst it is true "that everything in human experience, including nature and human physicality . . . (is already an) . . . entity shaped into cultural perceptions" (ibid),[9] it is an error to deny any foundational experience. We, like our primal forebears, breathe, drink water, excrete, feel. We do have a genetic code within each cell, that is a physical memory of origins . . . we are seeded with memory. This is especially true of the female body, whose ovum transmits the cytoplasm from one generation to the next.[10] The inability or unwillingness of a philosophical position to deal with a reciprocity between the being and environment—that the being itself has some innate foundational integrity, is a trait of the patriarchal mind that does not allow the *materia* any agency, sentience or autopoiesis. As an example typical of such a mind is that of Nobel award winning scientist Francis Crick[11] who claimed that human emotions, memories and ambitions, sense of personality and free will "are in fact no more than the behavior of a vast assembly of nerve cells and their associated molecules" (cited by Forbes 2001) as if to assert that this "vast assembly" has no sentience (ibid).

I am suspicious of texts that would erase the body—deny physical sentience or difference—since it is the female particularly that is associated with physical reality. Whose body is it that is primarily being erased, that has been erased since the emergence of the patriarchal mind? (Yet artists have been obsessed with her body, as if trying to paint her back into the picture perhaps—for She will always carry on[12]—or at times to frame her there as object?) The early Greeks denied her inclusion in the "kosmos" (Guthrie 1960:34-40) because of her messy body. In other cultures where her body had been the lap upon which rulers sat and thus gained their right to rule (Neumann 1974:98-100) her body was gradually stylized into furniture—a throne, and then forgotten; her body became *part of the furniture*, utilitarian. As Melissa Raphael describes (1996:21), "female sacrality"—the sacrality of the female body—has been "unnamed non-data in secular culture;

peripheral sub-data in the phenomenology of religions," and considered essentially "pagan" or unclean "in Western religious culture" (ibid). All bodies exchange substances with the environment—the land—whether or not it is obvious to an etherealised and sanitised culture. Aboriginal cosmologies have never forgotten this exchange. The body of these cosmologies is:

> an organic body which is consubstantial with, and permeable to, the living environment. It is composed of flesh and blood, bones and spirit, and is subject to the organic processes of fecundity, growth and decay (McDonald 2001:20).

And the exchange of bodily fluids with land in such cultures is valued and significant—a participation in the very flow of life, and relationship with "the ancestors" (ibid: 21). David Tacey points out that the spirituality that arises from the land in Australia, carried in the themes of its poets, and known by its indigenous inhabitants, is one that is profoundly continuous with the body (2004:9-10).

It is likely that when humans really remember the body, all bodies—this relational dynamic, this *materia*, in which we are—we will remember the female body, and once again will have to deal with a foundational cyclical experience of life: regeneration—which includes birth and death. How we story that experience is really very open, but it will be a recognition of the web of life into which we are woven, as well as being weavers.

Life—birth and death—may not seem like much of a foundational cyclical experience to many: seeming more like a one way trip—linear, birth to death. But that depends on one's perspective . . . if taken from within each particular small life, it may appear that way. An analogy may be drawn to Euclid's parallel lines.[13] While his postulate that parallel straight lines will never meet holds true within a limited space (or in a perfectly flat featureless space), it does not hold true in the actual world that we inhabit—a spherical Earth (Abram 1997:198). Within the context of Earth, the lines will meet. So with each individual lifeline viewed from a larger perspective, there is regeneration, a cycle in which we participate: a much larger entity—Earthbody/Gaia—where things come around. We live in a Universe where planets are spheres, they spin and orbit. All *materia* is recycled.

I am aware of the possible critique of the work of re-creating Her, by gender-skeptical feminist theory as essentialist, as a perceived collapse of *female* into *nature*.[14] But, I am actually identifying *all* being—not just female and male, or just human, but flora and fauna and stars and rocks as well, and even human culture—with nature. I am *collapsing* them all! I then metaphorize the *dynamics* of all being as female, which again could be construed as essentialist. It *does* invoke "female sacrality" (Raphael 1996:8-10), which for some indicates an essentializing of sacredness as female. I acknowledge that it *may* be so, but assert that it need not be. In the case of my work, there is a recognition or naming of "female-*referring* transformatory powers" (Raphael op.cit:8)[15] that are identified as cosmic dynamics essential to all being—not *exclusive* to the female. For example, *conception* is a female-*referring* transformatory power (Raphael op.cit:8-9),[16] that is, it happens in a female body; yet it is a multivalent cosmic dynamic, that happens in all being in a variety of forms. It is not bound to the female body, yet it occurs there in a particular and obvious way. In past ideologies, philosophies and theologies—many of which still make their presence felt—the occurrence of *conception* in *that place* (the female body) has been devalued; *conception* has only been valued in the *place* of the mind—usually the male mind—as *concept*. Then in some circles of women's spirituality particularly, there has been reversal of this so that the female body—and sometimes her bodymind—was the *only* place for significant *conception*. I am not saying that. I affirm *conception* as a female-referring transformatory power, which manifests multivalently in all being, thus affirming female sacrality as part of *all* sacrality. I thus affirm the female as *a* place, as well as a *place*.

My Search for Her, which was able to include academic form,[17] was an inquiry into the affects of such recognition on the hearts and minds and actions of participants—female and male, and including myself.

The Moon Goddess Heritage

The triple-aspected Female Metaphor that has long captured my attention and imagination and lured me into the Search has in other times been known as "The Moon Goddess." That "aspect of Creativity of the Cosmos that manifests in the Moon" could be the long modern title for Her perhaps.[18] The phases of the Moon have described a pattern that, at some point, was noticed to resonate with the human female cyclical pattern, and indeed, that of all human body cycles.

Moreover, the Moon's cyclical pattern—of waxing and waning through lightness and darkness—was noticed to be reiterated in flora and fauna everywhere. In some cultures Moon is male, noting how the phases manifest phallic magic, and perhaps other qualities that the male may aspire to. A Scots Gaelic prayer describes the Moon as "lovely leader of the way" (Matthews 200:302), and so She has been for many humans, who have noticed Her cyclical pattern imbued in All, including in the seasons created by the annual Earth-Sun relational transitions or "movements." Moon was perceived as a teacher, **the** Teacher for many.

The Moon Herself is a Presence often taken as secondary, extraneous, romantic. Yet without Her gravitational pull on Earth, creating the tides—the ebb and flow—the biosphere may have never evolved.[19] The Moon's central role in our manifestation, in Earth's Creativity as we know it, largely goes without recognition. The same is true of the role that the female human cycle most likely played in the early development of human consciousness: its role may well have been central yet this body of conjecture is missing from much of what passes for the story of human beginnings. Rarely is it thought, as for example researcher Alexander Marshack thought, that the lunar notations found on bone, stone, antler and goddess figures may "have laid the foundations for the discovery of agriculture, the calendar, astronomy, mathematics and writing" (Baring and Cashford 1993:20).

As Judy Grahn points out, "human perception began, many creation stories say, when we could distinguish between light and dark"; that:

> Disciplined separation is clearly a major factor of human culture, and the most complex and fundamental separation practice is that of the first menstruation, or . . . menarche (1993:11).

Yet a recently produced documentary about the earliest of humans[20] that put forth all kinds of detailed descriptions of their lifestyles and projections about their emotions and actions, did not postulate such a thought: the female body processes so rarely considered as significant to the evolution of consciousness and culture, the possibility that the female cycle and its replication of the Moon cycle exactly in timing, may have impacted on the human psyche in a primordial, foundational way. Perhaps, as Grahn suggests, it was the "menstrual mind" that first connected to an external frame of reference—the Moon—and began to acquire external measurement and non-instinctual knowledge (op. cit:12-14). When humans first performed ritual burials, one hundred thousand years ago, what was their referent for thinking about death? What did they observe around them every day about death and renewal? Could it have possibly been that "the Female Metaphor"—*She*, in its/*Her* lunar cycle and its/*Her* human female cycle, may have played a central role in the earliest developments of the human mind—our sense of time, and existential wonderings and celebrations of life and death—just as Her resonant Cosmic Moon cycle played/plays a central role in the evolution of life on Earth? Could contemplation of the pattern that the Female Metaphor suggests, in Her mandala-like rhythm, have been the source of earliest human insight? Shuttle and Redgrove define a mandala as:

> a pattern which is effective in connecting one part of experience with another, and the contemplation of which leads to insight. A mandala has a centre, a boundary or circumference, and cardinal points. It often depicts a rhythm, which one can see at a glance in a single image (1986:263).

They describe the Moon cycle as forming a mandala, and that "the menstrual cycle can take a similar shape" (ibid). Could the cosmic ubiquity of this metaphorical pattern have been the basis for knowledge/wisdom that served humans and their growing conscious relationship to Cosmos? Could the primordial experience of witnessing this trustworthy rhythm have been the beginnings of "the inexhaustible creativity of humanity," as other Goddess researchers suggest (Baring and Cashford 1993:19)?

For a culture to have abstained from asking these questions, to have, for millennia been unable to form these questions in the mind, reveals an alienated mind—a mind that is out of touch with the Earth and Cosmic cycles, as well as that of the human female. An alienated mind is one that does not know participation, that "unconsciously participates" as Barfield describes (Kremer 1992:172-173)—a mind that has severed its connections, wherein phenomena exist separately, a mind that has dissociated. Most humans today live in cultures that are alienated in this way, though it is expressed diversely. I speak mainly from within my own white Western Christianized culture, but it is by no means unique in regard to alienation from the Context/Earth/Universe—in which humans find themselves/ourselves. If humans regard themselves as alive and sentient, then so is our Context/Matrix. We, and our consciousness, are "not some tiny bit of the world stuck onto the rest of it" (Kremer op.cit:169 quoting Barfield 1979:18). We are inside Her—our Matrix. Our Context appears to be alive and sentient, as Creativity spills up from within Her at local and universal levels, but it appears from the ecological crisis that we find ourselves in that we humans have on a large scale shut ourselves off from this knowledge. Speaking for my own cultural context, we humans today find ourselves living *on* a planet. For some time, we have mostly not participated *in* it. We have understood ourselves as apart from it, as an addendum or superior; and, now, we often understand ourselves as inferior. Some humans who are still closely linked to their indigenous heritage have not lost the knowledge that She and they are alive in each other. These humans have remained intimate with our[21] Context, and the understanding of the local not being separate from the Cosmic, and that this Context is the Matrix of all humans and beings.

I have been re-linking with my own indigenous heritage, one that lives in my very bodymind. It has an actual tradition—of female-based metaphor—that has been nearly obliterated in relatively recent human history, that is, the last few millennia. It would be simplistic and short-sighted to single out the Inquisition of the last millennia of this Common Era as the only gynocidal event of the West, though it was certainly a horrific one. Though my indigenous heritage has its most recent roots in Old Western Europe—in the Earth-based tradition that goes back to pre-Celtic times—it also has roots in the bodyminds of other ancients of my line, who observed and knew a resonance of being with Earth and Cosmos. This heritage ran into difficulties long before the Inquisition, as Starhawk outlines in her overview of culture, politics and mythic cycles (1990:37-40) and as many others including Merlin Stone (1978) and Gerda Lerner (1993) document. Lerner says, "in the period when written History was being created, women already lived under conditions of patriarchy" (op.cit:249); our roles, public behavior and sexual and reproductive lives were already so defined—our bodyminds had already been locked up, the Goddess temples had long been emptied, the integrity of the priestesses had long been trivialized. It had long been anathema to receive and speak Her Wisdom[22]—a Wisdom I call "Gaian" (Spretnak 1991), and of which in our time, we may come to know in a new way.

More Context—Personal/Cultural/Cosmic Stories

My personal context, which cannot be separated from the cultural and cosmic context of my organism and which has fired my passion, is that I have written as *a daughter born into the patriarchy;* as a daughter hungry for the Mother, I understand what Monique Wittig means when she says: "The language you speak is made up of words that are killing you" (1973:114). Personally, I have been so hungry for the Female Metaphor, for the Mother—for words for Her, for knowledge of Her, that I could perform terrible and radical acts to find Her. I went away from my young children for a long period of time for this—to find the Mother for myself, and for them. I did not want to give my children the world I had grown up in—the world they needed had to be integral with Matter, or there would not be a world at all.

I have been told that to look at history, theology, philosophy from the female perspective is myopic. It is commonly assumed that these disciplines have been regarded from the "human" perspective, that the male has incorporated both female and male perspectives, that he has been fair in all these matters, and indeed, capable. A casual perusal of most history, and "pre-history," from a "fair" perspective would leave one wondering how the human species reproduced itself, let alone that the female had any further creative input to the human enterprise.[23]

Even a recent text on the world's religions, which could be regarded as more "fair-minded," fails significantly in its balance. This text, *The World's Religions* (Smart 1998) notes the increasing role of women "in religions where in the past a patriarchal perspective has prevailed" (ibid: 586). Smart is aware of the gender issues in the language and organization of religions, yet in his own text while he gives extensive treatment to the Holocaust, Marxism, and various Chinese cults, nowhere does he reference Mariology, nor is there any reference to the Inquisition. Witchcraft is mentioned once, and negatively, in the context of Polynesian religions (ibid: 169). The Great Isis is referred to as "Osiris' wife" (ibid: 203), the main focus being Osiris. Goddess Inanna is described as "a harlot" without qualification of the term, and as "supposed even to have become queen of heaven, as consort of An" (ibid: 200). The *Enuma Elish*,[24] which describes the murder of Goddess Tiamat, is told by Smart completely unsympathetically to the indigenous tradition (ibid: 200-201). The epic is praised as celebrating (the incoming god's) victory; and the god, Marduk, is praised nonchalantly by Smart as "great" (ibid: 200). There is an apparent acceptance of the slaughter of the female at the base of creation. Philosopher Paul Ricoeur writes, in regard to this epic:

> Thus the creative act which distinguishes, separates, measures and puts in order, is inseparable from the criminal act that puts an end to the life of the oldest gods, inseparable from a deicide inherent in the divine (1969:180 quoted in Catherine Keller 1986:76).

This "criminal act" then, this shedding of blood by the blade, may be seen as a replacement of the "menstrual mind" that separated and distinguished, which Judy Grahn speaks of (op.cit). Ricoeur goes on to describe creation as "a victory over an Enemy older than the creator" (1969:182 quoted in Keller ibid)—thus tracing the historical outcome of a "theology of war" (Keller ibid) and the enemy behind all enemies; but it is Catherine Keller who notes that Tiamat's sex is a salient fact (op.cit:77). To state Her sex is to state/*status* Her—this "Goddess-Mother" as Her name means (Walker 1983:998) as the Enemy within all enemies. It is to understand war as the act of a Cosmically and Maternally alienated mind. Tiamat's slaughter is described graphically in the epic, as it is also by Smart in his text: her corpse is used "to create the present universe, slitting her in two like a fish, one part being heaven and the other earth" (op.cit:201).[25] As Joseph Campbell points out, this:

> great creative deed of Marduk was a supererogatory act. There was no need for him to cut her up and make the universe out of her, because she was already the universe (1988:170).

My Body/Earthbody as Object

A strong part of the cultural milieu in which I grew, was that I felt identified as sex object . . . with no subjectivity, no space to Be—much as Earth Herself has been object. Pornographic magazines of the days of my childhood depicted women being constantly pursued by salivating men—either there was an assumption that she desired this, or they did not care to ask her. And Christian cosmology appeared to condone the imposition of a dominant will upon another—at the very heart of it is "the sacrifice of the lamb." Women have been especially vulnerable, with their submission openly advocated.[26]

As a child, I was very conscious of being looked at. I felt transparent and vacuous. I was told the male Deity knew all about me. The male humans imitated the Deity with constant Gazing, in magazines, movies, wall calendars. I could only hope to be chosen to be worthy of his desire, yet at the same time it was known that he could be dangerous. I felt acutely the identification of myself with the "inanimate" world, as it was understood to be—dead and inert. I had no words for it of course. Ursula Le Guin says,

> We are told in words, and not in words, we are told by their deafness . . .
> (that) . . . the life experience of women is not valuable . . . to humanity.

We are valued by (the patriarchal viewpoint) only as an element of their experience, as things experienced . . . only if said or done in their service (1989:155 brackets my paraphrase).

The male in this worldview was also "inanimate," albeit the machine that was expected to perform.

I began to find words and consciousness of my assigned cultural destiny. I wrote in my journal:

What did it take to move from that . . . to pull the shades on the imposing mostly male Gaze, to allow a fertile darkness within my being, where "I" could begin? What did it take to create this kind of darkness, a safe place to Be, to shut out the world and scream "I"? . . . A sex object has to completely fall apart before she can rebuild herself in her own image. She has to fall into the mud, begin again, perform her own acts of Creation, mold herself of this solid material. It is out of the mud that the lotus blossoms. It does not grow on some pedestal, under the light of the eternal Gaze. How ironic that our paternal mythmakers made Medusa's gaze the deadly one!

Falling Apart—Re-Creating Her

I was fortunate, my life did fall apart; I was lost. The journey into Her story, means a participation in Her descent and return, it means a shattering of what went before. How does a woman, how does a world, stop being object, and become subject? How does she/She—my body, Earthbody—become the body in her/our own mind? It requires more than rhetoric; it requires the descent of Inanna, a falling apart. What does it take to move from alienated narrative, to allow a fertile darkness within, from which the Self may begin? The regaining of integrity, and an understanding of why we lost it, or did not have it, can require a great darkness: an immersion in the Darkness of She, Her autopoietic aspect, Her sentience. *Goddess* may be the naming of a Wisdom that has had no name, may be the recognizing of the Power within each being, and making the Hera's journey for ourselves—female and male, all beings. In Goddess cosmology, we may participate consciously, intentionally and "directly in the cosmos-creating endeavour" (Swimme 1992:75).[27] I am not, we are not, passive recipients or bystanders.

We may celebrate Her Creativity, participate in Her process, with *religious* practice: that is, with practices that reconnect us. We are Her daughter-selves—female and male alike. The Mother hands us *all* the wheat, the sacred knowledge of Life, as in Eleusis of Old. We all may be Her *Daughters*, entitled just so, to the seamless Original Heritage in Her core, our Core.

Notes

1.   Bru-na-Boinne is the indigenous name of the place, and refers to being the Place of Goddess Boann: so I will use it henceforth.

2.   See Michael Dames *The Silbury Treasure*, Paul Devereaux *Earth Memory* p.34 and 120-124, and Claire French *The Celtic Goddess* p.22 for specific references. Also the comprehensive work of Marija Gimbutas, and that of an increasing number of scholars such as Joan Marler and Max Dashu.

3.   I capitalize this word and some others because I am referring to Ultimate Cosmic Creativity—*Deity* as it has been understood.

4.   This term for a *Sabbat*, as such seasonal transitions are often named, is capitalized, because it refers to a holy day.

5.   And there are some congruencies of this threefold composition as he describes them with my perceptions of the Female Metaphor, as well as some points of departure: see Glenys Livingstone, *PaGaian Cosmology*, p.123-125.

6.   See Glenys Livingstone, *PaGaian Cosmolgy* p.112-123 for how these three may be associated with the three dynamic aspects of Goddess.

7.   I am conscious particularly of the work of Donna Henes, in her book *The Queen of My Self*, and the many women who are nurtured by her work.

8.   A term suggested by Charlene Spretnak for all courageous individuals, in *The Politics of Women's Spirituality*, p.87.

9.   Referring to the philosopher Derrida.

10.   See Irene Coates, *The Seed Bearers*, for more on this.

11.   Francis Crick was credited with the co-discovery of the double-helical structure of DNA along with James Watson. Rosalind Franklin whose work appears to have been crucial to the discovery remains uncredited and even discredited—see Ethlie Anne Vare & Greg Ptacek, *Mothers of Invention*, p.214.

12 As The Pretenders sing in their song *Hymn to Her*.

13 David Abram refers to Euclid's postulate in a slightly different context: *The Spell of the Sensuous*, p.198.

14 See for example Plumwood 1993 and 1991.

15 emphasis mine

16 emphasis mine

17 The academic outcome was a doctoral thesis: Glenys Livingstone, *The Female Metaphor—Virgin, Mother, Crone—of the Dynamic Cosmological Unfolding: Her Embodiment in Seasonal Ritual as a Catalyst for Personal and Cultural Change* (University of Western Sydney, Australia 2002).

18 Just as "Bear Goddess" could be expressed as "that aspect of Creativity of the Cosmos which manifests as Bear", and so with other zoomorphic and descriptive Goddess titles. She—the Creative Principle—is as diverse as Being is.

19 See Lynn Margulis' research into the beginnings of the biosphere, as referenced in Connie Barlow, *Green Space, Green Time*, p.186-188, and Connie Barlow (ed.), *From Gaia to Selfish Genes: Selected Writings in the Life Sciences*, p.48-66.

20 *Neanderthal's World* shown on SBS Australia in mid 2001

21 It is "our" Context, not "theirs" as some of my cultural context might describe it: all of us do live in Earth and in the Universe. Although it can be argued that in most cases, the indigenous person's mountain for instance, is not the mountain of the Westernized mind—"their world is not ours!" (Kremer 1992:173), it can also be argued that at a deeper place, we may find "among the silent spaces, realities where cultures and their peoples touch in ways that are yet to be fully explored" (Kremer op.cit:174). Also I think it is time to move into the assumption that some previously Westernised minds have made steps towards their own indigenous mind; there is a growing

"we" of "future participation"—a term Kremer uses (ibid:172-173) to speak of regained, intentional participation in our habitat.

22   I mean "Wisdom" here to be understood as a name for a religious tradition—that has had no name—much as "Buddhism" or "Taoism" are understood to be names.

23   As an example, one such weighty tome called *The Last Two Million Years* (Reader's Digest 1974*)* as in all its four hundred and eighty-eight pages of text and plates, remarkably little evidence of female presence to the human enterprise. She rates a mention every now and then in relation to "problems of reproduction" (ibid: 22) greater sexual receptivity than female apes (ibid: 17), and men insisting that "their sisters married outside the family" (ibid: 19). The very occasional Goddess or woman of note is most often a mistress, consort or wife. Queen Elizabeth I stands alone as a woman of power in the last two million years.

24   The *Enuma Elish* is generally accepted as the Babylonian creation epic, but it is actually the creation of patriarchy in that culture describing as it does the murder of the indigenous deity Tiamat.

25   The use of the metaphor of "fish" in the tale is perhaps a conscious reference to the Goddess' yoni (See Walker 1983:313)—this is where She was cut, and where women in cultures of this creation myth, continue to be mutilated today.

26   See Rita Brock, "Can These Bones Live? Feminist Critiques of the Atonement."

27   This may be what Jurgen Kremer describes as "future participation" (1992:173).

Bibliography

Abram, David. *The Spell of the Sensuous*. NY: Vintage Books, 1997.

Barfield. Owen. *History, Guilt and Habitat*. Middletown, Conn.: Wesleyan University Press, 1979.

Barlow, Connie. *Green Space, Green Time*. NY: Springer-Verlag, 1997.

Barlow, Connie (ed). *From Gaia to Selfish Genes: selected writings in the Life Sciences*. Massachusetts: MIT Press, 1994.

Brock, Rita. "Can These Bones Live? Feminist Critiques of the Atonement" in *What's God Got to Do With It? Challenges facing feminism, theology, and conceptions of women and the divine in the new millennium. CONFERENCE PROCEEDINGS*, Kathleen McPhillips (ed). University of Western Sydney Hawkesbury Publications, December 2000, pp. 17-30.

Coates, Irene. *The Seed Bearers—the Role of the Female in Biology and Genetics*. Durham: Pentland Press, 1993.

Cousins, Ewert H. (ed). *Process Theology*. NY: Newman Press, 1971.

Dames, Michael. *The Silbury Treasure: The Great Goddess Rediscovered*. London: Thames and Hudson, 1976.

Devereux, Paul. *Earth Memory: The Holistic Earth Mysteries Approach to Decoding Ancient Sacred Sites*. London: Quantum, 1991.

Forbes, Cameron. "Thirst for Thought," *The Weekend Australian* February 3-4 2001, p.4.

French, Claire. *The Celtic Goddess*. Edinburgh: Floris Books, 2001.

Grahn, Judy. *Blood, Bread and Roses: How Menstruation Created the World*. Boston: Beacon Press 1993.

Guthrie, W. K. C. *The Greek Philosophers*. NY: Harper Torch Books, 1960.

Henes, Donna. *The Queen of My Self: Stepping into Sovereignty in Midlife*. NY: Monarch Press, 2005.

Keller, Catherine. *From a Broken Web: Separation, Sexism and Self*. Boston: Beacon Press, 1986.

Kremer, Jurgen W. "The Dark Night of the Scholar: Reflections on Culture and Ways of Knowing." ReVision, Vol.14, No.4, Spring 1992, pp.169-178.

Livingstone, Glenys. *PaGaian Cosmology: Re-inventing Earth-based Goddess Religion*. Lincoln NE: iUniverse, 2005.

Lerner, Gerda. *The Creation of Feminist Consciousness*. NY: Oxford University Press, 1993.

Matthews, Caitlin. *The Celtic Spirit*. London: Hodder and Stoughton, 2000.

McDonald, Heather. *Blood, Bones and Spirit: Aboriginal Christianity in an East Kimberley Town*. Melbourne: Melbourne University Press, 2001.

McLean, Adam. *The Triple Goddess*. Grand Rapids MI: Phanes Press, 1989.

Neumann, Erich. *The Great Mother*. Princeton: Princeton University Press, 1974.

Plumwood, Val. *Feminism and the Mastery of Nature*. NY: Routledge, 1993.
_____ "Gaia, Good for Women?" Refactory Girl. No.41, Summer 1991.

Raphael, Melissa. *Thealogy and Embodiment: the Post-Patriarchal Reconstruction of Female Sexuality*. Sheffield: Sheffield Press, 1996.

Ricoeur, Paul. *The Symbolism of Evil*. (trans. E Buchanan). Boston: Beacon Press, 1969.

Robbins Dexter, Miriam. *Whence the Goddesses: A Source Book*. NY: Teacher's College Press, 1990.

Shuttle, Penelope and Redgrove, Peter. *The Wise Wound: Menstruation and Everywoman.* London: Paladin Books, 1986.

Smart, Ninian. *The World's Religions.* Cambridge University Press, 1998.

Spretnak, Charlene. *States of Grace: The Recovery of Meaning in the Postmodern Age.* SF: HarperCollins, 1993.
_____ "Gaian Spirituality". Woman of Power Issue 20, Spring 1991, pp. 10-17.
_____ (ed). *The Politics of Women's Spirituality.* NY: Doubleday, 1982

Starhawk. *Truth or Dare.* SF: Harper and Row, 1990.

Stone, Merlin. *When God Was a Woman.* London: Harvest/HBJ, 1978.

Swimme, Brian and Berry, Thomas. *The Universe Story: From the Primordial Flaring Forth to the Ecozoic Era.* NY: HarperCollins, 1992.

Tacey, David. "Spirit and Place", EarthSong Journal, issue 1, Spring 2004, pp.7-10 and pp.32-35.

Vare, Ethlie Ann and Ptacek, Greg. *Mothers of Invention.* NY: Quill, 1987.

Walker, Barbara. *The Woman's Encyclopaedia of Myths and Secrets.* San Francisco: Harper and Row, 1983.

Whitehead, Alfred North. *Process and Reality.* NY: Macmillan, 1929.

Wittig, Monique. *Les Guerilleres.* NY: Avon Books, 1973.

It Is My Heart Who Reminds Me

MamaCoAtl

That I shall weep over the grave of my desires
That I shall mourn over my failures
My long lost hope, *mi copalera ardiendo*[1] and my ideas about Love
Love? is a little frozen man spinning on the palm of my right hand,
And I am the fool blowing kisses in the air.
It is my heart who reminds me
That I must weep over the loss of my illusion
That I shall mourn over my pride, my resistance turned poison
Of the blood stream like liquor, like shame
The piercing pain of violent raids
The broken will, the heavy load . . .

It is my heart who reminds me that I've been lost
On this river of oblivion, my face swollen with lies
My blood at war with itself; *el Indigena Vs. el alienigena*[2]
Eternally killing and dying in the theaters of my flesh.

It is my heart who reminds me that I will cry
Blinded and bound by the laws of the empire,
By the gods of fear
FEAR
Is a broken feather on the palm of my left hand
And I? am the same fool . . .

But the crows are laughing you see and great winds are finally here
It has been written in stone that we got to remember the song
Totlazotlanazin Anuahuak cantame la cancion del jaguar[3]
Corazon del monte[4], *Tezkatlipoka*[5]

I am calling you back with all my essence
Calling you back with all my Soul
Calling you back from the cathedrals of genocide
Back from the realm of the white man
Back from the grid, the collapse of the dollar
From the federal reserve, from the memory of rape
Way back
Back with all my Soul,
Back, back, my jaguar is back!
And it is my heart who remembers that before I was called Woman
My name was keeper of wisdom, my name was sister, mother, precious child,
She who listens, owner of the fire of the house,
She who investigates deep down under the secrets of the cosmic mind,
The music of the inner god, the scent of precipitation-thunderous rapture
of knowing, act of illumination.
It is my heart who remembers *a mis abuelas cantando*[6]
Sitting around the fire making food for hard times,
Food made with *palabras de trueno*[7], seeds to keep inside until the day comes,
Bitter roots for protection and the careful instruction
To hold hands
Open the eye on your chest
Stay strong
Be together for the first rays of dawn.

Notes

1 *mi copalera ardiendo:* ardent copal burner

2 *el Indigena Vs. el alienigena:* indigenous versus alien

3 *Totlazotlanazin Anuahuak cantame la cancion del jaguar:* Beloved and respectable Mother Earth Anahuak (the true name of these lands we call the U.S.A.) sing for me the song of the jaguar

4 *Corazon del monte:* Heart of the mountain ranges

5 *Tezkatlipoka:* metaphor for conscience

6 *a mis abuelas cantando:* my grandmother's singing

7 *palabras de trueno:* words of thunder

Contributor Biographies

Laura Amazzone is an author, teacher, jewelry artist, and Yoginī. She completed her master's degree in philosophy and religion, with an emphasis in women's spirituality, at the California Institute of Integral Studies in 2001. Her book, *Goddess Durga and Sacred Female Power* (Baltimore: Hamilton (an imprint of Rowman & Littlefield Press), 2010), explores the millennia-old rituals and manifestations of the Goddess in South Asia and honors female creative and sexual power as a divine force. Laura teaches classes and workshops on Goddess spirituality and Eastern religious traditions and is adjunct faculty in the Yoga and Philosophy program at Loyola Marymount University in Los Angeles. She has published numerous articles discussing myth, ritual, adornment, and the significance of South Asian Goddesses as divine models of female empowerment. She blogs for the Religion section of the *Huffington Post* and has a column at OurInnerLives.com, a special project of Feminist.com. She lives in Venice, California. www.lauraamazzone.com.

Michele Arista, M.A. is a mother, health physicist, a Ph.D. student at the California Institute of Integral Studies and the owner of Dance of the Dark Mother Studio in Manchester, New Hampshire where she teaches belly dance. She is an artist of world Goddess icons, a photographer and poet. Her *midrash* of the Hail Mary prayer was printed by the *Journal of Feminist Studies in Religion*, edited by Harvard Divinity School.

Gael Belden is teacher, author, and editor. She has an M.A. in Depth Psychology and Mythology, and was lay-ordained by Thich Nhat Hanh. She leads Zen groups with a mythological flair, and is busy with her project, *100 Clay Buddhas*, which places figures near waterways in order to help re-enchant the earth. She lives in Ojai, California.

Lucia Chiavola Birnbaum, Ph.D. is a feminist cultural historian and the author of numerous books and articles including *Liberazione della donna: Feminism in Italy* (Wesleyan University Press, 1986, Award, Before Columbus Foundation, 1987); *Black Madonnas: Feminism, religion and politics in Italy* (Northeastern University Press, 1993); italian edition, (Palomar Editrice, 1997); Premio Internazionale di Saggistica (Salerno, Italy, 1998), iUniverse reprint 2000; *Dark mother: African origins and godmothers* (iUniverse, 2001), Enheduanna Award, Serpentina, 2002, the California Institute of Integral Studies—WSE "Founding Mother Award, 2003; *La Madre o-scura* (Cosenza, Mediterranee, 2004); *La mere noire* (Paris, Editions Menaibuc, 2007); Award: "Gran Protectrice des Nations Negres" 2008; Founder, *She is Everywhere! Writings in womanist/feminist spirituality*, gatherer, volume one (iUniverse, 2004); co-gatherer with Annette Williams and Karen Villanueva, volume two (iUniverse, 2008). Volume one of *the future has an ancient heart. african legacy of caring, sharing, and healing on world migration paths. case of the mediterranean* is scheduled for publication in Alberobello, Italy by Laboratorio Poiesis and by Editions Menaibuc in Paris, 2011.

Nancy Caronia is a Ph.D. candidate in English at the University of Rhode Island. Her essay, "Meeting at Bruce's Place: Springsteen's Italian American Heritage and Global Notions of Family," is forthcoming in the anthology *Essays on Italian American Literature and Culture* (Bordighera Press, CUNY). Additionally, she is co-editing a critical anthology with Edvige Giunta entitled, *Personal Effects: Essays on Memory, Culture, and Women in the Work of Louise DeSalvo*.

Giana Cicchelli, M.A., High Priestess & Shaman, is an artist, teacher, healer, and eccentric! She is constantly looking to learn new modalities of spiritual practice and to weave them all into her mystical 'understanding' of the Universe. She finds that it is very easy to bring them all together; Spirit works through all. When she is not out tomfooler-ing she is hard at work on paintings, poetry, and magick! She has attended Women's Circles with many of the 1970s feminist reclaimer Goddess Worshipers, met and worked with the new resurgence of spiritual practitioners, attended Native American sweat lodges (Lakota and non-Lakota), and traveled to both the sacred valley and the jungles of Peru to participate in healing ceremonies and work with the local Shaman. She feels blessed to be doing this work at this time! Blessed Be! www.gianacicchelli.com.

Lori Coon is the Executive Director of The Mandala Center in New Mexico. Previously, she worked for over 25 years as a social worker in child welfare and in various healthcare settings. Lori is an artist (sculptor), and a teaching artist, promoting the use of visual arts and writing as a pathway for healing mind, body, and spirit and an advocate of arts in education. The Divine Feminine has been part of her adult life and she attended the California Institute of Integral Studies for Women's Spirituality for some graduate work. Many of her early sculptures were inspired by Goddess images around the world along with inspiration from nature. Lori has been a workshop facilitator in the areas of wellness, stress management, creativity, and personal growth for over 20 years.

Randy P. Conner, M.A., Ph.D. currently teaches as adjunct faculty in Women's Spirituality at the California Institute of Integral Studies in San Francisco. He has taught at Florida Atlantic University, U. C. Berkeley, the University of Texas at Austin, and elsewhere. His publications include *Blossom of Bone: Reclaiming the Connections Between Homoeroticism and the Sacred*; *The Encyclopedia of Queer Myth, Symbol, and Spirit*; *Queering Creole Spiritual Traditions*; and essays in *Parabola*; *This Bridge We Call Home*; *Sexuality and the World's Religions*; and *Fragments of Bone: Neo-African Religions in a New World*. He studies Vodou with Mama Lola. He is currently completing *The Pagan Heart of the West*.

Nancy Cosgriff, M.A., D.Min. facilitates spiritual development and Goddess-centered workshops for women in Minnesota, Tuscany, and France. She teaches in the Spiritual Guidance and Leadership program through WomanWell and offers workshops through Wisdom Ways Center, both in St. Paul, MN. In her women's circles Nancy honors feminine wisdom and integrates the creation-centered evolutionary universe story throughout.

Elizabeth Cunningham is the author of *The Maeve Chronicles* as well as three previous novels and two collections of poetry. The direct descendant of nine Episcopal priests, Cunningham is herself an ordained interfaith minister and a counselor in private practice. She lives in New York State's Hudson Valley. www.passionofmarymagdalen.com; www.highvalley.org.

Max Dashu founded the Suppressed Histories Archives in 1970 to research global women's history, priestesses, goddesses, mother-right and the origins of domination. She has photographed some 15,000 slides, created 100 visual presentations, and written numerous articles (www. suppressedhistories.net). A founding mother of the Goddess resurgence, Max practices and teaches Goddess traditions and shamanic arts. Recently, she created a DVD, *Women's Power in Global Perspective*, and the Female Icons poster showing the global range of ancient female figurines. See her paintings at www.maxdashu.net and her online courses at www. sourcememory.net.

Leslene della-Madre is a mother, priestess, shamanic voyager, "shemama" (shamanic spiritual midwife) author, TV host, and holder of sacred female shamanic wisdom. She has taught the feminist shamanic healing arts for 30 years and has traveled the shamanic path for over 40 years. Grandmother Agnes, chairwoman of the *Thirteen Indigenous Grandmothers*, says about Leslene "she has an important message and many people need to hear it." www.midwifingdeath.com; www.femunity. blogspot.com.

Chickie Farella is a multimedia artist/writer in Women's Spirituality, native of Chicago, Illinois who has been transplanted to the southern California desert. She is the recipient of the 1981 Chicago International Film Festival Video Music award and the 1982 Athens Film Festival Video Music Award and a contributing writer to several Italian American anthologies. www.Godthemother.com.

Catlyn Fendler is an educator, speaker, and writer on topics in Women's Spirituality, with emphasis on the Black Madonna, the Sacred Feminine, and the labyrinth. She holds an M.F.A in Poetry from The University of Iowa Writer's Workshop and an M.A. in Interdisciplinary Consciousness Studies from John F. Kennedy University. She is an advanced certified labyrinth facilitator, trained by Veriditas, The World-Wide Labyrinth Project. She teaches in a wide variety of workshops, study groups, and university settings and currently is working on writing projects in both poetry and on her journeys with the Black Madonna, the Sacred Feminine, and the labyrinth.

Jean Feraca is the host and originator of *Here on Earth: Radio Without Borders*, Wisconsin Public Radio's international news and global cultural affairs talk show (www.hereonearth.org); the author of three books of poetry and the memoir *I Hear Voices: A Memoir of Love, Death, and the Radio* (University of Wisconsin Press, 2007), winner of the Kingery/Derleth Nonfiction Award from the Council of Wisconsin Writers.

Annie Finch's books of poetry include *Eve, Calendars, and Among the Goddesses: An Epic Libretto in Seven Dreams*. Other works include a CD of calendars, anthologies, poetics, and collaborations merging poetry with music, art, and theater. She is Director of Stonecoast M.F.A. program at the University of Southern Maine.

Mischa Geracoulis is on a mission to share information that is empowering to the grassroots as well as to the global community. With a background in art history, political science, sociology, and holistic health, her body of work reflects the multifaceted human condition. Her repertoire includes profiles of remarkable people, reviews, and academic and journalistic publications. Sharing a corner of Los Angeles with her husband, she is an essayist, researcher, and editor.

Tricia Grame, **Ph.D**. is an artist and educator who continues to explore, from an historical and personal perspective, how the language of the female symbol is revealed and released through the creative process, becoming tangible in the work of art. She considers her art to be a dialogue, a spiritual expression in which the female form symbolizes an everlasting archetypal presence. Her passion for the sculpted symbol took her to Italy and the islands of Malta where she did her research. She has curated over 40 exhibitions and lectures nationally and internationally and is an adjunct in the Women's Spirituality program at CIIS and the MFA, Writing Consciousness and Creative Inquiry program at CIIS. She serves as the Art Commissioner for the city of Danville, CA and is a board member of the International Caucus for Women. http://tgrame.com/.

Donna Henes is an internationally renowned urban shaman, eco-ceremonialist, spiritual counselor, award-winning author, popular speaker, and workshop leader. Mama Donna, as she is affectionately known, is the author of four books and a CD. She is a columnist for *The Huffington Post, Beliefnet* and UPI Religion and Spirituality Forum. In addition to teaching and lecturing worldwide, she maintains a ceremonial center, spirit shop, ritual practice, and consultancy where she works with individuals and groups to create personally relevant rituals for all of life's transitions. www.DonnaHenes.net.

Sheila Marie Hennessy has many iterations as a wife, mother, ceramic artist, and student of Ayurvedics. For decades, her ceramic sculptures have honored the feminine form. Her latest body of work takes an integral approach, building images of the divine feminine taken from world myths, spiritual symbols, Jungian conversations, and images from ancient archeological sites around the world. Art-making is a way to leave a mark on the outside world, something akin to a message in a bottle. Visual images can sometimes emote and say more than words can express or honor.

Theresa Gale Henson is an artist and writer. Her sculptures are featured in both public and private collections—and she has had the great honor of carving the Black Madonna in the presence of many visiting animals: osprey, bats, deer, and eagle to name a few. Other projects have included the White Tara and the Hand of Fatima. She recently published her first novel, *Shift* (Sharon Press, 2011) and is the Communications Manager at the Monastery of St. Gertrude in Cottonwood, Idaho. www.theresahenson.net.

Joanna Clapps-Herman's latest publication is *The Anarchist Bastard: Growing Up Italian in America* (SUNY Press). She co-edited two anthologies *Wild Dreams* and *Our Roots Are Deep with Passion*. She has essays in *The Milk of Almonds, Don't Tell Mama, Oral History, Oral Culture, and Italian Americans, Lavandaria*. She has published extensively fiction, poems, and creative non-fiction. She has won the Bruno Arcudi Prize and the Henry Paoloucci Prize. The *Litchfield Review* awarded her their medal for Literary Excellence. She teaches at The City College (CUNY) Center for Worker Education and is on the Graduate Writing Faculty of Manhattanville College. www.joannaclappsherman.com.

Helen Hye-Sook Hwang, Ph.D., resides in Ontario, CA and teaches online for Religious Studies and Women's and Gender Studies at the University of Central Missouri, Warrensburg, MO, while working towards her second M.A. degree in East Asian Studies at UCLA. She earned an M.A. and a Ph.D. in Religion, completing the Women's Studies in Religion program at Claremont Graduate University, CA. Her ongoing research concerns Mago, the Great Goddess of East Asia, and Her tradition Magoism, a pan-East Asian gynocentric cultural matrix that venerates Mago as the supreme divine. Hwang views Magoism as a lynchpin that reconstructs not only East Asian ancient histories and cultures but also cross-cultural transactions between ancient cultures of the world. Previously, she worked as a member of the Maryknoll Sisters in Korea, New York, and the Philippines. Encountering Mary Daly's Radical Feminism led Hwang to translate Daly's two books into Korean and to pursue graduate studies.

Nané Ariadne Jordan is a Ph.D. candidate in Education at the University of British Columbia. She holds a B.F.A. in photography (University of Ottawa) and an M.A. in Women's Spirituality (New College of California). Profoundly nourished by her M.A. studies, her doctoral dissertation co-explores faculty and student experiences of Women's Spirituality graduate education through narrative, arts-based, and ritual inquiry. Her working background in pre-regulation Canadian midwifery informs her research into women's birth experiences, midwifery, and women's spirituality. Her research and writing is published in a variety of journals. She continues a mixed-media art and performance practice, often exploring Earth-based themes, and the body as a site of knowledge and elemental interconnection. She lives in Vancouver, B.C. with her husband and two daughters.

Anne Key, Ph.D. is adjunct faculty in Women's Studies and Religious Studies at the College of Southern Nevada. A graduate of the Women's Spirituality Program of the California Institute of Integral Studies, her investigations centered on Mesoamerica. Dr. Key was Priestess of the Temple of Goddess Spirituality Dedicated to Sekhmet, located in Nevada, from 2004-2007. *Desert Priestess: a memoir* (Goddess Ink, 2011) is her first full-length book. She is co-editor of *The Heart of the Sun: An Anthology in Exaltation of Sekhmet* (Goddess Ink, 2011). See more of her publications at www.annekey.net and www.goddess-ink.com. She currently resides in Albuquerque, New Mexico with her husband, his five cats, and her snake, Asherah.

Lê Phạm Lê, a Buddhist poet and singer born in Viet Nam, has worked for many years as the lab coordinator for the English Department of Los Medanos College in northern California. Her poems have appeared in journals including *World Literature Today*, *Nimrod International Literary Journal*, *Arabesques International Review*, *The Fence* (Japan), *Drumvoices Revue*, *Rattle*, *Beacons*, and *Zoland Poetry*. Her first publication, *From Where the Wind Blows*, a bilingual collection of Vietnamese poems, was translated into English by Nancy Arbuthnot and Lê (Vietnamese International Poetry Society, 2003). Her highly individualistic blending of traditional Vietnamese chant and ballads with contemporary art song has been internationally praised.

Glenys Livingstone, Ph.D. (Social Ecology) has been academically and culturally involved in the resurgence of female imagery for the sacred for over three decades. She is the author of *PaGaian Cosmology: Re-inventing Earth-based Goddess Religion*. She lives in Australia—the land of her birth. She has teacher training, and completed post-graduate theological studies in Berkeley, California in 1982. She is a celebrant of the annual seasonal rituals according to her place on the planet—a priestess of Gaia, and in the tradition of her ancestral European roots. Her website is http://pagaian.org, where her book is live.

Yvonne M. Lucia is a community activist, spiritual companion, and self-taught multimedia artist. The common thread that unites the different facets of her work is her passion for inspiring others to create soulful lives with intention, intuition, and imagination. She lives in upstate New York where she offers workshops and women's circles in her Art Barn Studio. Yvonne blogs at http://singingoverthebones.com.

Lindy Lyman believes that artists are "the seers, the shakers, the shamans, and the shapers." She transforms the ordinary into the extraordinary by coaxing together paint, pen, paper, canvas, and clay. She knows that art has the power to captivate, move, and change us. She is inspired by the cycles of day and night, sun and moon, the seasons, the elements, and the wonders of many cultures—dancing together. She is also an educator, singer, dancer, and performer of West African music.

MamaCoAtl holds an M.A. degreee in Women Spirituality with emphasis in Performance Activism and an M.F.A. in Creative Inquiry from New College of California. She is also a Reiki Master and an Absolute Balance Mastery practitioner. Her fusing of art, healing Shamanic practices, and social justice makes her a popular speaker in universities and community colleges when it comes to human rights, femicide, and the reviving of ancestral ways of healing.

Nicole Margiasso-Tran, M.A., is currently working on a book based on her six-month pilgrimage in Ireland. Nicole teaches and lectures on Women's Spirituality in the San Francisco Bay Area. She is also presently organizing pilgrimage journeys for women to experience Brigit's sacred sites in Ireland.

Kathy Martone, Ed.D. is a Jungian psychologist, artist, and published author in private practice in Denver, Colorado. She specializes in dream work (including dream/spirituality retreats for women) and other psycho-spiritual approaches to healing. Inspired by a dream in 2005, Dr. Martone began making velvet tapestries based on her own dream images and embellished with Swarovski crystals, glass beads, ribbons, and pieces of jewelry. Like the magical nets of ancient shamans, these colorful banners ensnare the features of her dream spirits and call out for deeper reflection and connection with the watery world of the feminine spirit. She is currently taking commissions for customized dream tapestries. www.dreamagik.com/.

Judy Millyard-Maselli is a 70-year-old wild woman living in Denver, Colorado with her terrier. She has loved writing since she was child and has been published in a few small magazines. She co-founded a creative writing publication in college and was one of the founding members of The Foothills Poetry Group in Denver. Judy is a student of the Divine Feminine and has been facilitating women's circles for over 20 years.

Etoyle McKee has nurtured the spirits of individuals from the ages of two to seventy. She has an M.A. in Social Gerontology from the University of Incarnate Word and a B.S. in Education from South Texas University. Etoyle had been a teacher and principal in the private school sector for fifteen years. For the past ten years, she has been the administrator at a preschool in New Braunfels, Texas.

Harita Meenee is a Greek independent scholar of classical studies and women's history. She has presented cultural TV programs and has lectured at universities in Greece and the U.S. She is the author of five books, as well as numerous articles published in Greek, British, and American magazines. She has translated W.K.C. Guthrie's *Orpheus and Greek Religion*; her English translations of ancient and modern Greek poetry have been included in various anthologies and journals. www.hmeenee.com.

Mary Beth Moser holds an M.A. in Women's Spirituality and is a Ph.D. candidate in Philosophy and Religion at the California Institute of Integral Studies in San Francisco. Mary Beth is passionate about her ancestral homeland of Trentino, Italy and its folk traditions, which is the focus of her dissertation research. She is the author of *Honoring Darkness: Exploring the Power of Black Madonnas in Italy* (Dea Madre Publishing, 2008) and other publications, including "Blood Relics: Menstrual Roots of Miraculous Black Madonnas in Italy" in *Metaformia: A Journal of Menstruation and Culture*, www.metaformia.com. When she is not exploring the back roads of Italy, Mary Beth lives among the natural beauty and tall trees of the Northwest. http://deamadre.home.comcast.net.

Andrea Nicki has a Ph.D. in Feminist Philosophy from Queen's University and did postdoctoral work at the University of Minnesota, Minneapolis. Her first book of poetry, *Welcoming,* was published in 2009 by Inanna Press at York University. She is completing a second collection called *Beehive Love.* Her poems have been published in anthologies and journals, including *Philosophy Now.* www.andreanicki.com.

Malgorzata Oleszkiewicz-Peralba is associate professor in the department of Modern Languages and Literatures at the University of Texas at San Antonio. She has lived, studied, and travelled widely around the world, and is fluent in seven languages. Her cross-cultural, comparative research on syncretic religions, rituals, and the divine dark feminine took her to conduct fieldwork in Brazil, Mexico, Peru, Uruguay, Cuba, Puerto Rico, Spain, France, Poland, Russia, and Lithuania, among others. She is the author of *The Black Madonna in Latin America and Europe: Tradition and Transformation* (University of New Mexico Press, 2007 & 2009), *Teatro popular peruano: del precolombino al siglo XX* (Warsaw University and the Austrian Institute of Latin America, 1995), as well as of numerous scholarly articles, lectures, and conference presentations.

Luciana Percovich, a member of the Italian Feminist Movement since its beginnings, has lived and worked in Milano, acting as an activist in Lotta Femminista, Gruppo femminista per una Medicina delle donne, Libreria delle donne, and Libera Università delle Donne. She is a teacher, an editor, a translator, and an author: *Posizioni amorali e relazioni etiche,* Melusine, Milano, 1993 (also in *Figuras de la madre,* Madrid, 1996); *La coscienza nel corpo. Donne, salute e medicina negli anni Settanta,* Franco Angeli, Milano, 2005; *Oscure Madri Splendenti. Le origini dl sacro e delle religioni,* Venexia, Roma, 2007; *Colei che dà la vita, Colei che dà la forma. Miti di creazione femminili,* Venexia, Roma, 2009. With others, she has also published: *Verso il luogo delle Origini,* La Tartaruga, 1992; *Donne del Nord/Donne del Sud. Verso una politica della relazione tra diversità, solidarietà e conflitto,* Franco Angeli, 1994; Theodor G. H. Strehlow, *I sentieri dei sogni. La religione degli aborigeni dell'Australia Centrale,* Mimesis, 1997. She now lives in the country, on the hills of Abruzzi.

Shelley R. Reed is a Master of Applied Theology who resides in Oregon. She is an academic researcher, writer, and lecturer on the spiritual traditions of the Pipe and Dreamer religions of the Columbia Plateau and Great Plains. The past five years have been spent photographing a series of endangered pictograph sites in Montana. It is theorized that the indigenous spiritual systems and oral traditions of tribal people can be used to interpret and appreciate pictograph images and symbols. She is a spiritual traditionalist who follows the teachings of White Buffalo Calf Woman.

Sandy Miranda Robinett has been a radio host and producer for twenty-one years on Pacifica Radio's KPFA (Berkeley), KALW (San Francisco), and on the CBC (Toronto). Her specialty is World Music and Culture, and she completed her M.A. in Women's Spirituality at the California Institute of Integral Studies in San Francisco in 2004. She produced a 19-part radio series "Women, Spirit, & Peace" with guests including Marion Woodman, Alice Walker, Anna Halprin, Joan Baez, and many others.

Lydia Ruyle, M.A. is an artist, author, and scholar emeritus on the Visual Arts faculty of the University of Northern Colorado (UNC) in Greeley, Colorado. Her research into sacred images of women has taken her around the globe. Ruyle creates and exhibits her art and does workshops throughout the U.S. and internationally. Her Goddess Icon Spirit Banners have flown in dozens of countries spreading their divine feminine energies. A book about her work, *Goddess Icons Spirit Banners of the Divine Feminine*, was published in 2002. UNC created the *Lydia Ruyle Room for Women's Art* in 2010 as a resource library and eventual home of the Goddess Icon Spirit Banners. She is honored, humbled, and excited about the room in her name, which was dedicated on January 29, 2010. It is one of the few centers for women's art in the U.S.

Bridget Saracino is a native of upstate New York. She graduated from Cornell University in May 2011 with a Bachelor's degree in Theatre Studies and intends to pursue acting as a career. In her free time Bridget enjoys throwing on the potter's wheel, playing her ukulele, and doing Bikram yoga.

Mary Saracino is a novelist, poet, and memoir writer who lives in Lafayette, Colorado. Her most recent novel, *The Singing of Swans* (Pearlsong Press, 2006) was a 2007 Lambda Literary Awards Finalist. Mary's short story, "Vicky's Secret," earned the 2007 Glass Woman Prize. Mary's other book-length work includes the novels *No Matter What* (Spinsters Ink, 1993) and *Finding Grace* (Spinsters Ink, 1999), and the memoir, *Voices of the Soft-bellied Warrior* (Spinsters Ink Books, 2001). Mary's Pushcart Poetry Prize-nominated poetry appears online at www.newversenews.com. Her poetry and stories (creative nonfiction and fiction) have been widely published in a variety of literary and cultural journals and anthologies, both online and in print. Mary is a writing coach and writing teacher. As the founder of MOTHEROOT, Mary leads workshops and embodied art-making and creative writing classes centered on the Dark Mother/Divine Female. marysaracino.com; marysaracino.blogspot.com; pearlsong.com/newsroom/marysaracino/marysaracino.htm; and redroom.com/author/mary-saracino.

Lisa Sarasohn is a writer and teacher who adores showing women how to tap into the ancient knowing, creative power, and intuitive guidance concentrated in our body's center. She's the author of *The Woman's Belly Book: Finding Your True Center for More Energy, Confidence, and Pleasure* (New World Library, 2006). Lisa offers an online course, "Initiation 2012: Awakening Your Sacred Center," through Susun Weed's online Wise Woman University. Her short story "Poetry at Six" was a final selection in National Public Radio's Three-Minute Fiction contest. For book excerpts, essays, poems, and more visit http://lisasarasohn.com.

Kirsten Schilling is studying writing and the publishing arts as an M.F.A. student at Antioch University, Los Angeles. An enthusiast of the personal narrative, Kirsten has kept a journal since the second grade. She has cultivated a love of mythology, symbolism, folklore, and fairy tales through her work as both historian and craftswoman of perfume and period aromatics.

Elisabeth P. Sikie is a joyful and jaded Ph.D. candidate in Women's Spirituality at the California Institute of Integral Studies in San Francisco who is passionate about retrieving suppressed European herstory. She is a yoga instructor, pagan practitioner, and trained medium who stands on her head, drinks beer for the nature gods, and talks to dead people. She lives in Alameda, California and can be reached at esikie@esikie.com or www.esikie.com.

David Hatfield Sparks, M.M., M.L.I.S. is a writer, musician, ethnomusicologist, librarian, educator, gay father, and LGBT activist. His publications include an essay in *First Person Queer*, "Hecklers and Christians," and "Dancing the River: Fluidity of Eros and Gender in Music and Dance of African Diasporic Spiritual Traditions" in *Postscripts: The Journal of Sacred Texts and Contemporary Worlds*. He has also recently finished a chapbook of poems, *Princes and Pumpkins*, as well as *The Wings of Eros*, a book documenting his spiritual journey as a gay man. He has also co-authored a number of texts with his partner Randy P. Conner, including *The Encyclopedia of Queer Myth, Symbol, and Spirit*, "And Revolution is Possible: Re-Membering the Vision of *This Bridge [Called My Back]*," and *Queering Creole Spiritual Traditions*.

Claudia von Werlhof, born 1943 in Berlin, Germany, mother of a son, a Professor of Political Sciences and Women´s Studies, University of Innsbruck, Austria. Masters in Economics, Ph.D. in Sociology, University of Cologne; Habilitation in Political Sciences, University of Frankfurt, Germany. Empirical research in Central America and Venezuela. Co-founder of the international Women´s (Studies) movement. Activist against globalization and neo-liberalism. Theoretical work on a feminist theory of society, patriarchy, matriarchy, and alternatives to western civilization: elaboration of the new paradigm of "Critical Theory of Patriarchy." Foundation of the "Planetary Movement for Mother Earth" in 2010. English book together with V. Bennholdt-Thomsen and N. Faraclas: *There is an Alternative. Subsistence and Worldwide Resistance to Corporate Globalization*, London 2001. Her most recent book is: *The Failure of Modern Civilization and the Struggle for a "Deep" Alternative. On "Critical Theory of Patriarchy" as a New Paradigm* (Peter Lang International Publishers 2011).

Solace Wales bought a ruin of a house in a tiny Tuscan village with her artist husband in 1973. The village had a small, enigmatic Black Madonna statue (Santa Maria del Carmine), which was later stolen. In the 1980s, love of this statue prompted Wales to study Ean Begg and other sources of information on the Black Virgin and to visit Her sites. Wales has written several long journal pieces on her visits to Black Madonnas, but has not as yet attempted to publish them. She is currently looking for a publisher for her just finished nonfiction book: *Braided in Fire: Buffalo Soldiers and Tuscan Villagers in WWII*. (The book does not contain information on Black Madonnas).

About the Co-editors

Mary Beth Moser holds an M.A. in Women's Spirituality and is a Ph.D. candidate in Philosophy and Religion at the California Institute of Integral Studies in San Francisco. When Mary Beth is not exploring the back roads of Italy, she lives among the natural beauty of the Northwest where she is nurtured by the rains, mountains, tall trees, and the night sky.

Mary Saracino is a novelist, poet, and memoir writer who lives in Lafayette, Colorado. Mary loves Earl Grey tea with half & half, nature walks, the roar of the ocean, travelling, and spending time with friends and family. She feels renewed by natural beauty—and is awed by Colorado's vast cerulean-blue sky, abundant sunshine, and majestic mountains.

Our friendship took root on a study trip in Sardegna, Italy in 2004 with Dr. Lucia Chiavola Birnbaum. A few years ago when we participated in a workshop with Vicki Noble, Vicki prepared our astrological charts and pronounced that—having been born only five days apart—we were essentially "astrological twins." It has been a journey of discovery to work on this project together, each in our own supportive environment. May your journey through its pages be rewarding.

With connection and gratitude to all of our contributors and readers,
Mary Beth and Mary